THE MAKING OF THE PENTECOSTAL MELODRAMA

Anthropology of the Media
Series Editors: John Postill and Mark Peterson

The ubiquity of media across the globe has led to an explosion of interest in the ways people around the world use media as part of their everyday lives. This series addresses the need for works that describe and theorize multiple, emerging, and sometimes interconnected media practices in the contemporary world. Interdisciplinary and inclusive, this series offers a forum for ethnographic methodologies, descriptions of non-Western media practices, explorations of transnational connectivity, and studies that link culture and practices across fields of media production and consumption.

Volume 1
Alarming Reports: Communicating Conflict in the Daily News
Andrew Arno

Volume 2
The New Media Nation: Indigenous Peoples and Global Communication
Valerie Alia

Volume 3
News as Culture: Journalistic Practices and the Remaking of Indian Leadership Traditions
Ursula Rao

Volume 4
Theorising Media and Practice
Edited by Birgit Bräuchler and John Postill

Volume 5
Localizing the Internet: An Anthropological Account
John Postill

Volume 6
The Making of the Pentecostal Melodrama: Religion, Media, and Gender in Kinshasa
Katrien Pype

The Making of
the Pentecostal Melodrama

Religion, Media, and Gender in Kinshasa

Katrien Pype

berghahn
NEW YORK · OXFORD
www.berghahnbooks.com

First published in 2012 by

Berghahn Books

www.berghahnbooks.com

©2012, 2015 Katrien Pype
First paperback edition published in 2015

Library of Congress Cataloging-in-Publication Data

Pype, Katrien.
   The making of the Pentecostal melodrama : religion, media, and gender in
Kinshasa / Katrien Pype.
      p. cm. — (Anthropology of the media ; v.6)
   ISBN 978-0-85745-494-2 (hardback : alk. paper) — ISBN 978-1-78238-681-0
(paperback : alk. paper) — ISBN 978-0-85745-495-9 (ebook)
   1. Motion pictures in ethnology—Congo (Democratic Republic)—Kinshasa.
2. Video recording in ethnology—Congo (Democratic Republic)—Kinshasa.
3. Anthropology of religion—Congo (Democratic Republic)—Kinshasa.
4. Pentecostal churches—Congo (Democratic Republic)—Kinshasa. 5. Television
in religion—Congo (Democratic Republic)—Kinshasa. 6. Kinshasa (Congo)—
Religious life and customs. 7. Kinshasa (Congo—Social condtions. 8. Kinshasa
(Congo)—Politics and government. I. Title.
   GN654.P97 2012
   791.45096751'12–dc23

                                                                    2011052126

British Library Cataloguing in Publication Data

A catalogue record for this book is available from the British Library

Printed on acid-free paper.

ISBN: 978-0-85745-494-2 hardback
ISBN: 978-1-78238-681-0 paperback
ISBN: 978-0-85745-495-9 ebook

The use of a study of melodrama must at the last repose

on a conviction that the study of aesthetic form

– modes of expression and representation –

can be useful in situating ourselves.

Aesthetic forms are means for interpreting and making sense of experience.

Any partial rewriting of cultural history must be

a rethinking of how we make sense of our lives,

of the successive episodes in the enterprise of *homo significans,*

of man as the creator of sense-making sign-systems.

—Peter Brooks, *The Melodramatic Imagination*

Contents

List of Illustrations   ix

Acknowledgments   xi

On Language   xvi

1. The First Episode   1

2. Cursing the City: The Ethnographic Field and
the Pentecostal.Imagination   27

3. New Fathers and New Names: Social Dynamics in
an Evangelizing Acting Group   62

4. Variations on Divine Afflatus: Artistic Inspiration,
Special Effects, and Sermons   100

5. Mimesis in Motion: Embodied Experiences of Performers
and Spectators   130

6. The Right Road: Moral Movements, Confessions, and
the Christian Subject   168

7. Opening Up the Country: Christian Popular Culture,
Generation Trouble, and Time   197

8. Marriage Comes from God: Negotiating Matrimony and
Urban Sexuality (Part I)   232

9. The Danger of Sex: Negotiating Matrimony and Urban
Sexuality (Part II)   258

10. Closure, Subplots, and Cliffhanger   291

Bibliography   299

Index   316

Illustrations

Figures

1.1. Cinarc members filming (2006)   4

1.2. The author playing the role of a siren (screen shots from *The Nanas Benz*)   20

3.1. Cinarc actors and fans at the troupe's New Year party (2005)   64

3.2 and 3.3. Cinarc men in discussion while Cinarc actresses wait (2006)   71

3.4. and 3.5. Rivalry between the pastor and the troupe's leader on screen (screen shots from *The Maquis Boys and Girls*)   84

4.1. Wood-carvers at work on Lumumba Boulevard (2004)   104

4.2. Pastor anointing followers (2005)   109

4.3. and 4.4. The witch locks her victim's double in a bottle (screen shots from *Kalaonga*)   120

4.5. The divine fire captured in a photo during a prayer vigil (2006)   125

5.1. Itinerant musicians (2005)   137

5.2. Women dancing in church (2003)   143

5.3. Screen shot of evening prayer (2006)   148

6.1, 6.2, 6.3, and 6.4. Pastor Chapy heals Deborah, who then confesses (screen shots from *The Heritage of Death*)   187

7.1. A "bad girl" (screen shot from *Kalaonga*)   211

7.2. Maman Jeanne visits a diviner (screen shot from *Kalaonga*)   213

7.3. Announcement for a prayer event (2005)   222

8.1, 8.2, 8.3, and 8.4. Theresia dies by lightning (screen shots from *The Open Tomb*)   250

9.1. Detail from a mural in a bar in Lemba (2006)   260

Moving Images*

1. Kalaonga seduces Caleb (*Kalaonga*)

2. Maman Deborah's confession in *Heritage of Death*

3. The young girl is a *Mami Wata* (*Kalaonga*)

4. Maman Jeanne visits a diviner (*Kalaonga*)

*These moving images are available at http://www.berghahnbooks.com/title.php?rowtag= PypeMaking

Acknowledgments

Rather early during my fieldwork, Bienvenu and Raph, two leading men of the Cinarc troupe, compared their acting work with a palm tree. They used the Lingala proverb *Nzete ya mbila bakokata ekokola bakokata ekokola*, translated as follows: "You can cut a palm tree, it will grow again, and if you cut again, it will grow again." Bienvenu and Raph explained the proverb thusly:

> A palm tree continuously offers fruit, which makes it a very prosperous and wealthy tree. It is used to make food, and drink, like palm wine, but also material utensils like brooms, and the soap that can be made of it helps to care for the body. The palm tree thus offers many products, and no one can really explain why this tree is so rich.

The actors were referring to the economic, social, and symbolic capital that working as Christian TV celebrities offered them. Throughout this volume, I will deal with the richness that making teleserials offers to the artists. But its fruits are not reserved only for them. For me as a researcher, my work with them could be compared with a fruitful palm tree. One of the fruits, this book, is now in your hands.

I could not shake that palm tree on my own, nor can I claim to have plucked the fruits by myself. Before, during, and since the fieldwork, I have enjoyed the assistance of so many people that I can honestly say that this book is the outcome of a collective endeavor. Therefore, I would like to acknowledge the assistance of the following people and organizations that have contributed to the completion of this project.

Firstly, I am grateful to the Katholieke Universiteit Leuven, and in particular the Faculties of Psychology and Pedagogy and of Social Sciences, which provided me with the position of a research and teaching assistant and the financial means to pursue the research. Filip De Boeck was the promoter of the dissertation that inspired this book. I am thankful to him for having offered me the chance to start my doctoral research. He invited me to go to Kinshasa, helped me single out a research topic, and did not object when I changed the subject matter. He accompanied me on my first trip to Kinshasa, and our tours around the city and visits to his acquaintances immediately immersed me in the city's ambiance. He furthermore introduced me to local artists, cultural centers, and university institutions. During these initial weeks, he also taught me how to move around the city, advised me on how to approach people, and brought me to the Nlanza family, with whom I lived during a major part of the fieldwork. I greatly value Filip's aid in Kinshasa and in Leuven. His knowledge about Kinshasa and its cultural world is impressive, and his infinite willingness to read drafts and revised versions of chapters and to comment on both content and style has greatly improved the quality of my writing.

In Kinshasa, I enjoyed living with two host families. The first, headed by Mme Hermelinde Nlanza, oriented me in all aspects of Kinshasa's social and cultural worlds. During the final part of fieldwork, I sojourned in the compound of Mme Antoinette Kongo (Lemba). Her house really became like a home, and I cherish the hospitality of Maman Anto, her children Kethi and Benz, and the other compound dwellers.

It is impossible to express the value of the friendship that I developed with the family Florent Mbungu-Six. Mr. Six, his wife, and their children became like a second family to me. The birth of their daughter, Katrien Pype Mbungu-Six, added another dimension to our relationship. My deepest gratitude goes to them.

I cannot name all the drama groups and artists that I worked with in Kinshasa, but I wish to mention especially Canacu-théâtre and Écurie Maloba, whose drama work and hospitality I eagerly embraced. The Cinarc crew, and in particular Cinarc's leader, Bienvenu Toukebana, offered me the opportunity to do extensive participant observation. The two churches with which the group was affiliated also offered me possibilities to do valuable research. Pastor Gervais Tumba and the members of the Église Montagne Sainte, and Pasteur Flavien Mbuyamba and the Église Foi-en-Action accepted my presence during their gatherings. It was with much regret that I learned of the death of Maman Pasteur. Rendering her words here can offer no solace to her husband and children, though it is one way, apart from our memories, in which this young woman of my own age continues to live on.

Since starting my research, I have greatly valued conversations with colleagues in Kinshasa, such as Thierry Nlandu, Victorine Nlandu, Lino

Pungi, Leon Tsambu, Pedro Monaville, Bob White, Peter Lambertz, and Joshua Walker. Professor Shomba and Professor Lapika welcomed me warmly each time I visited the anthropology departments at the University of Kinshasa. I likewise benefited from Mr. Aneeki, an older but very vital man who could best be described as the living history of Kinshasa's performance arts. As a journalist for the national radio channel, since the mid 1970s Aneeki has accumulated enormous knowledge about Kinshasa's dramatic artists, the plays performed in the city, the so-called high culture of the city, and the inhabitants' cultural preferences. One can find this man at all cultural events, carrying a small tape recorder and interviewing artists after their plays. His love of dramatic arts, his encouragement of young and novice performers, and his objective but passionate reporting has not only enabled him to amass a large network of friends among the city's drama artists but has made him, in my view, a crucial source of expertise for any researcher attempting to study the city's cultural history.

Michel Mulumba Molisho played an important role during the fieldwork. In one way or another, his hand is present in most of the gathered data. It would be beyond the bounds of the possible to describe what his actions have meant for the development of my research and for me. He was ever present. He took on the role of research assistant and was at times a driver, a translator, and an informant. During my stay in Kinshasa, he became a good friend and much more. Marius Muhunga was a real support during the revision of the manuscript.

I also thank Renzo Martens for our conversations in Kinshasa and Belgium. Our talks obliged me to distance myself from my informants and the retrieved data and helped me to understand my own biases by forcing me to be aware of the possible connotations of my being Belgian.

Cricri Lammers and Alex VanMeerberghen organized wonderful New Year festivities in Congo, and I enjoyed our dinners in Matadi and Kinshasa. Through them, I met Kim Gjerstadt, who became a good friend. In his apartment in the city center, I was able do interim analysis and occasionally take some time off from research. Baudouin Possemiers, Annick Mertens, and Hans Declercq were other friends whose good cheer I very much appreciated.

Back in Leuven, I enjoyed conversations with colleagues at the two anthropology research units. I mention in particular the members of the Institute of Anthropological Research in Africa: René Devisch, Ann Cassiman, Steven Van Wolputte, Koen Stroeken, Knut Graw, Jeroen Cuvelier, Tom Devriendt, Elias Namkap Lamle, Els Hoorelbeke, Laura Bleckman, Julie Poppe, Dominique Joos, Frederik Lamote, and Kristien

Geenen. Not only were they an attentive audience for my description of my field experiences, but their comments on seminars aided me in exploring my data fully. I have fond memories of sharing an office with Johan Meire, Greet Verbergt, and Julie Poppe. And I wish to thank Jogchum Vrielink, Frank Renders, Iman Lechkar, Hannelore Roos, Ann Trappers, Zana Mathieu Etambala, and Kathleen Geens for being such supportive colleagues. I also value the continuous encouragement of Marie-Claire Foblets and Johan Leman.

I completed the final revision of this book as a Newton International Fellow (British Academy) at the Centre of West African Studies (CWAS), University of Birmingham. I am greatly indebted to the CWAS staff for their hospitality and wish to mention how much I enjoyed and learned from conversations with Karin Barber, Lynne Brydon, Tom McCaskie, Insa Nolte, Kate Skinner, David Kerr, Olukoya Ogen, Paolo Freiras, Toby Green, and Nozomi Sawada.

Peter Crossman deserves special credit. He corrected my English to a great extent. His familiarity with Congo and African religion was also of great help in clarifying concepts and formulating ideas. I also thank Anna Balogh and Arthur Rubinstein, who did major linguistic revisions in earlier drafts of this work.

Several parts of this book have been presented at conferences, workshops, and seminars. I have benefited from comments and encouragement during these formal encounters and also in the informal meetings at the margins of these events. I mention especially Zoe Strother, Faye Ginsburg, Wyatt McGaffey, Ch. Didier Gondola, Michael Barrett, Wendy Willems, Winston Mano, Bob W. White, Jean-Luc Vellut, John Postill, Kelly Askew, Birgit Meyer, Joshua Walker, Patience Kabamba, Herman Wasserman, John Postill, Matthias Krings, Brian Larkin, Ono Okoome, Valentin Mudimbe, Joel Robbins, Richard Werbner, Rosalind I. J. Hackett, Marleen De Witte, and Claudia Boehme for their inspiring conversation. Written exchanges with Honoré Vinck, Keyan Tomasselli, Paul Hockings, and Joost Fontein were also very inspirational.

Finally, I also wish to express my gratitude to the three anonymous reviewers for Berghahn Books who have made very helpful suggestions. Marion Berghahn, John Postill and Mark Allen Peterson, the editors of the series in which this book appears, immediately believed in this project, and their encouragements were extremely motivating. I also thank Melissa Spinelli for her hard work on the manuscript and Jaime Taber for copyediting the text with expert care.

Friendship is a valuable thing. I wish to express my gratitude to Elke Truyens, David Claes, Hannelore Samyn, Barbara Samyn, Miep Lambrecht, Miriam Tessens, Eva Declercq, Odeta Barbelushi, Jennifer Miksov,

Yogi Pardhani, Ana Kolonko, and Taina Taskila for having been around at the time of writing in Leuven, Brussels, and Birmingham.

I would also like to thank my parents, Marcel Pype and Magda Viaene. They offered me the opportunity to study, and although I know that it was hard for them each time I left for Kinshasa, I very much appreciate their continuous encouragement while I was in the field. Finally, Karien, my sister, has been of utmost support during the whole project. As a real "double," she closely followed the research and writing process from its inception to its end.

On Language

Throughout this book, I will translate key concepts and phrases from Lingala and kiKinois, the street language in Kinshasa. If the word is commonly used in French, then I will add the French. At times, a concept might have acquired a particular form or meaning in kiKinois. If this is the case, then the kiKinois term will be mentioned. Lingala and its derivations (kiKinois and Hindoubill) are tonal languages. Because confusion between different meanings is often unlikely, and because indication of tonality might only render the reading more complex for the reader, I have chosen not to give any indication of the tones in my orthography of Lingala and kiKinois.

Biblical verses are a salient feature of both quotidian talk with born-again Christians and the speech in the teleserials. Most of the Bibles I came across in the field were in French, although Lingala translations are also read. For the translation in English of quoted biblical verses, I have opted to use the New International Version (Protestant) because this edition is more in line with the modern English language.

I mainly use the real names of people, places, and narratives. At times, however, when some informants had very discreetly conveyed private information about themselves or others, I decided to use this material without indicating the source.

With regards to the teleserials, I will use the English translation of the serials' titles: *The Cursed Neighborhood* (*Le Quartier Maudit*, TropicanaTV 2002), *The Devouring Fire* (*Le Feu Dévorant*, TropicanaTV, November 2003–January 2004), *The Moziki Women* (*Bamaman Moziki*, TropicanaTV, January 2004–March 2004), *Caroline and Poupette* (*Caroline et Poupette*, TropicanaTV, March 2004–April 2004), *Back to the Homestead* (*Retour au Bercail*, Tropicana TV, April–June 2004,*) The Maquis Boys and Girls* (*Les Macquisards*, RTG@, July 2004–September 2004), *Apostasy* (*Apostasie*,

RTG@, September 2004–November 2004), *The Open Tomb* (*Le Tombeau Ouvert,* RTG@, November 2004–February 2005), *The Heritage of Death* (*L'Héritage de la Mort,* RTG@ in February–April 2005), *The Nanas Benz* (*Les Nanas Benz,* RTG@, April–July 2005), *Dilemma* (*Dilemme,* RTG@, June–September 2005), *Mayimona* (*Mayimona,* RTG@, April 2006–July 2006) and *Kalaonga* (*Kalonga,* produced between March 2004 and November 2005, in first instance for the diaspora). The website contains moving images which are subtitled in English.

CHAPTER I

The First Episode

This book is about the production of Pentecostal[1] television fiction in contemporary Kinshasa. Kinois people (inhabitants of Kinshasa) refer to the TV dramas as *télédramatiques, théâtre populaire,* and *maboke.*[2] The title of the book can be read on two levels. On the one hand, it is an ethnography of the ways in which Pentecostal concepts and practices are presented to the urban audience in the space of television fiction and beyond (in TV talk shows discussing the teleserials, in church settings, in conversations among Christians). I will show how the Pentecostal message is negotiated in the religious and cultural spaces of Kinshasa. A major argument is that "the Pentecostal ideology" does not exist. Rather, Pentecostal concepts and ideas are constantly put into question and spur continuous reflection and debate. The Pentecostal imagination is all the time in the making. Second, this book offers at the same time an ethnography of the generation of TV fiction in Kinshasa. I trace the origins of plotlines and of fictional characters while also paying attention to the various social and spiritual interactions that occur during and beyond the filming, that is, in the interactions between the TV actors and their audiences, sponsors, spiritual counselors, and invisible agents such as demons and the Holy Spirit.

The material was gathered during seventeen months of fieldwork between 2003 and 2006.[3] In the first month of fieldwork, when I was planning to study development-related theater in Kinshasa, the capital city of the Democratic Republic (DR) of the Congo, I attended a meeting of actors who had specialized in folkoric drama (*ballet*). The group, called Afrik'Art, felt disappointed by the directors of the Walloon-Brussels cultural center (CWB), which promotes local arts. Two years before my visit to their rehearsal space, the theater company had requested CWB staff to consider Afrik'Art for financial support. I was shown the official letter that had finally arrived after a year of waiting, in which a CWB official promised to attend one of their rehearsals. Since the arrival of the letter, the Afrik'Art actors had been anticipating the CWB visit at every single rehearsal session. Much to their disappointment, the official never showed up, and the group became aware that they needed to consider other routes if they wished to gain money and eventually make a living out of acting. My first visit was at an emergency meeting the group's leader had organized to discuss the future direction of Afrik'Art. At one point, one of the actors suggested doing TV drama. Nearly every month, new TV stations were being set up, so the actor assumed they would not have any difficulty finding a TV patron who would give them a time slot and provide them with the material to film.

The idea was taken seriously by the others—and by the troupe's leader, who apparently had considered this option as well and did not have to weigh the idea, since there were no other real alternatives. Very quickly he began to issue orders. One actor was to prepare a letter to the heads of the local television channels. This was not such a difficult task, since all of the twenty-six television stations[4] on the air at that time broadcast local television drama (and continue to do so). Someone else had to approach shopkeepers and businesspeople who might have an economic interest in cooperation with the group. Much to my surprise at the time, another troupe member was told to ask the pastors in the neighborhood for spiritual guidance. If a pastor demanded that the troupe be part of the church as well, the leader added, they would not refuse. When summarizing this conversation in my notebook, I added an exclamation mark next to this third order. Little did I know then that I would be sucked into the world of born-again Christians and that pastors would become key informants.

Before I traveled to Kinshasa, development-related theater produced in a society concerned with social and political renewal seemed an original and highly relevant entry into the study of Kinois society, which at the time was coming to terms with the legacy of Mobutu's failed political program and trying to find the right track to a prosperous future. In the initial months of fieldwork, I spent much time following theatrical troupes that produced plays on issues such as citizenship, domestic violence, and HIV transmission. Yet, I noticed, the Kinois themselves were far more fascinated by locally produced TV drama than by NGO-sponsored theater. I suddenly found the teleserials much more relevant than stage plays that people attended only if they were paid. Because of the strong interference of Pentecostal pastors in the promotion and design of local TV drama, this change of research topic meant that religion would become a major research matter, and I could not ignore the social value of the ubiquitous fictionalized visualizations of witchcraft and conversion to Pentecostal Christianity, which are the two main motors of the story lines in Kinshasa's teleserials.

In Kinshasa, a city where ratings are unavailable to prove which are the most viewed shows and the most popular acting groups, it is commonly assumed that the acting companies Muyombe Gauche, Cinarc, the Evangelists, and Esobe produce the "best" serials and draw the most viewers. The ethnography draws on field research with various TV drama groups. Leaving aside the troupes Sans Soucis and Muyombe Gauche, each of which I worked with for a week, the bulk of my material derives from participant-observation with the company Cinarc, whose telenarratives are broadcast on privately owned channels (Tropicana TV: 2001–2005, RTG@: 2005–). TropicanaTV, the channel on which Cinarc's serials were shown at the beginning of my fieldwork, is led by two journalists. In 2005, conflicts with the patron of TropicanaTV led Cinarc's founder and leader Bienvenu Toukebana to search for another TV station to air their work. The politician Pius Mwabilu Mbayu Mukala offered the group the same broadcasting hours on his channel, RTG@, and an advantageous contract. Since the Cinarc serials' inception, and even after moving to another television channel, the episodes have been aired on Thursday evenings (9–10 P.M.) and rerun on Friday afternoon (4–5 P.M.) and Sunday morning (9–10 A.M.).

Cinarc was, at least during my fieldwork, by far the city's most popular TV acting group (fig. 1.1). In 2005, two Cinarc actors were selected by all of Kinshasa's television performers to receive awards for best actress and for best *kizengi* (fool, a stock character in Kinshasa's serials; see Pype 2010). In 2006 and 2007, Cinarc won the annual Child of the Country Award (Mwana Mboka Trophy) for best TV acting group. This prize was awarded to them by audience vote via digital technology (mobile phone text and email). These local evaluations confirm that Cinarc is a significant player in the city's media world. An analysis of Cinarc's serials as well as its actors offers a relevant insight into Kinshasa's popular culture.

Most remarkable for the Cinarc group is its explicit Christian proselytizing mission. Although most of Kinshasa's troupes portray urban life from a Christian perspective, not all of these theater companies designate themselves "evangelizing groups." The young Cinarc members imagine themselves as correctors of Kinshasa's society. As I discuss in Chapter 7, the Cinarc artists intend to transform the city along Christian lines. Some of the actors even hold key positions in Pentecostal churches. It is exactly this explicit juncture between entertainment and religion that renders the Cinarc group the most popular in the city. Cinarc's appeal

Figure 1.1. Cinarc members filming (2006, © Katrien Pype)

reflects the hegemonic role of Pentecostal-charismatic Christianity in Kinshasa, and it accordingly guides the viewers' media preferences.

Religion, Media, and Kinshasa's Public Sphere

Like most of Kinshasa's teleserials, the Cinarc serials primarily deal with domestic and social situations from a Pentecostal angle. One can understand this focus on the private and the "apolitical"[5] as an escape from a harder, more "political" public sphere in a nation without a tradition of freedom of speech. During his long rule, President Mobutu[6] attempted to control political discourse and did not hesitate to put artists in jail for criticizing his regime or mocking him or his collaborators. Laurent D. Kabila, Mobutu's successor, also had a harsh take on media. Given such a legacy, we might gather that Kinshasa's television actors hardly refer to political candidates or refrain from making overt statements about the state.[7]

Yet the religious nature of local TV serials, the existence of various television stations to which the Afrik'Art actors could write, and the fact that Cinarc's proselytizing teleserials are broadcast on private, political TV stations resulted from several drastic changes that DR Congo's society experienced during the 1990s. At that time, Mobutu's power had considerably eroded, which was reflected in a more lenient political stance toward broadcasting technologies. In 1996, the president ordained freedom of press, thus enabling private patterns of media patronage. Joseph Kabila continued this openness of media.[8] Immediately taking advantage of this opening to establish their own TV stations were all kinds of entrepreneurs, among them, in particular, commercial and political TV patrons. Crucially, since then, a significant part of Kinshasa's local TV channels have been set up by Pentecostal-charismatic pastors, who have become increasingly influential in Kinshasa as elsewhere in urban sub-Saharan Africa. The public favor of this charismatic type of Christianity and the zeal of its evangelizers are so invasive that the Pentecostal message even spills over to non-confessional channels. State-run media and TV stations belonging to political and economic entrepreneurs also broadcast religious films and music and invite Pentecostal leaders onto talk shows as well. They do this because, as Pius Mwabilu Mbayu Mukala, a politician[9] and also the director of the television channel RTG@, told me, "this is what the public begs for."

The public role of Pentecostalism in post-Mobutu[10] Kinshasa should be understood as functioning in a society where the state and its officials have difficulties to mobilize the citizens. Churches seem to be more successful in engaging Kinois for public work. This became most striking to me one Saturday morning when I witnessed crowds sweeping the main boulevards in a highly ritualized manner. Brandishing their brooms, chanting Christian songs, and praying out loud, these Christians removed all the rubbish from a particular street or roundabout while simultaneously chasing away the impure spirits identified by their leaders. This activity reminds one of the Salongo work that Mobutu inaugurated during his reign, when people ("citizens") were obliged to clean their compounds, streets, and neighborhoods on Saturday afternoons. Fines were imposed on those who failed to help keep the city clean. Nowadays, rubbish is all around in the streets, and the state cannot discipline Kinois to keep the public space clean. It is a gripping example of the ways in which Christian leaders took over governmental tasks in the early 2000s.

The impact of religion on Kinshasa's public sphere coincides with the new role played by religious media in many other societies (de Vries and Weber 2001; Meyer and Moors 2006). The crisis of the Congolese nation-state that started in the early 1990s created a vacuum, allowing Christian leaders to occupy public arenas like politics and stimulate entertainment, both in physical settings (ranging from church compounds to public spaces like roads and public transport) and mediated through electronic media. Pentecostal-charismatic churches have embraced television in particular as a useful instrument in their evangelizing mission. Although Kimbanguist, Protestant, and Catholic groups too have their own TV and radio stations, prophets and pastors who identify themselves as born-again Christians are much more successful in establishing media ministries. In the first instance, they set up electric churches to attract new converts. Broadcasting recorded prayer events and sermons in church is intended to stir religious enthusiasm among spectators and draw them to the church compound on Sunday mornings. Christian church leaders are eager to use television as an instrument in their proselytizing mission because most households in Kinshasa have a TV set. The participation of Pentecostal groups in Kinshasa's mass media world is so pervasive that radio and television in Kinshasa have become important discussion forums as well as visual arenas of the religious imagination and the construction of an imagined Christian community (Anderson 1991).

Pentecostal churches are characterized by youthful enthusiasm and appeal, personally charismatic leaders, an explicit location in the modern sectors of life, and an overwhelming use of modern means of communication such as video, radio, and magazines (Van Dijk 2000: 11). They represent an utterly modern, cosmopolitan, transnational, and economically oriented type of Christianity (Coleman 2000; Van Dijk 2000; Corten and Marshall-Fratani 2001; Ellis and Ter Haar 2004; Gifford 1998; 2004; Meyer 2004a; Maxwell 2005; de Witte 2008; Marshall 2009). Pentecostal-charismatic pastors are often called "religious entrepreneurs," thus hinting at participation in the local market and their fixation on business. In Kinshasa, and also in Ghana, as Gifford (2004: 33) documents, because of the mainline churches' monopoly of the fields of education and development, Pentecostal churches draw most of their resources from their involvement in local media. Inspired by American televangelists, African

Pentecostal-charismatic leaders videotape their services; publish and sell Christian pamphlets, DVDs, books, and other recordings; and establish their own radio and TV stations. Their commercialization and mediatization co-construct this new type of Christianity.[11] As Gifford (2004: 33) notes for Ghanaian charismatic Christianity, "these media presentations are molding what counts as Christianity."

Although Kinshasa's religious field thrives on other economic, political, social, and cultural dynamics than what we encounter in west Africa, the Pentecostal-charismatic world and the media network overlap to a great extent in both locations. Much airtime is devoted to Christian talk shows; most services in churches are filmed. This footage then appears on the church's television channel, or is simply sold within the congregation, or travels along transnational networks to the Congolese diaspora, where it structures their religious practices. On channels owned by Pentecostal pastors, and also in TV programs on non-confessional channels, narratives of witchcraft and occult events are presented, and pastors perform miracles and deliver people from satanic powers in the TV studio and via the screen. Further, Kinshasa's teleserials are not imaginable without recurrent references to biblical figures, or even without mentioning pastors' names and the programs of church services.

Many researchers are turning to the social, religious, and economic worlds of these new churches. Anthropologists are now also studying the interface of media and Pentecostal-charismatic Christianity. This has led to fascinating ethnographies that document how sub-Saharan African pastors use visual and aural media (Hackett 1998; de Witte 2008; Kirsch 2008; Meyer 2003a; 2003b; 2004b; 2009b). With this book, I aim to contribute to this growing literature on Pentecostal Christianity in Africa.[12]

In Kinshasa, Pentecostal churches have moved into the domain of television fiction also because the leisure segment is nowadays to a high degree free from state control and intervention. This contrasts with the Mobutu era, in which the services of the General Secretariat for Mobilization and Propaganda (MOPAPA, a part of the Ministry of Information) established national troupes that produced a theater of political cheerleading (Botombele 1975; Conteh-Morgan 2004). Political slogans, marching band music, and carefully choreographed performances not merely entertained the Zairians (as the Congolese were named then) and their visitors; they also produced intense emotional identification with the nationalist program (Conteh-Morgan 2004: 112; Kerr 1995: 205). Congolese television serials too originated from Mobutu's propaganda. The first broadcast plays were commissioned by the head of state in order to mobilize Zairians to work for national development. Zaire's first teleserial was called *Salongo*, meaning "work" (see Pype 2009b).

The *Groupe Salongo* still exists today, though it now produces Christian teledramas.

At the beginning of the twenty-first century, under Joseph Kabila's rule, however, the Congolese state did not inspire any cultural performances that ensured national cohesion, nor did it order the production of TV drama. Rather, Congolese state officials worked closely with foreign aid organizations to support the production of stage theater, music, and cultural festivals initiated by UNICEF, Doctors without Borders, and the like. In the realm of Kinshasa's TV drama, state-led intervention was totally absent. As long as no overt political positions were expressed against the rulers, then the troupes, and the churches that supported them, could operate as they wished.[13]

The difference in politics at play in the domain of Congolese TV fiction is best thrown in relief by comparing ethnographic material on TV production in the 1980s and twenty years later. Johannes Fabian's (1990) widely acclaimed ethnography of popular theater in Katanga during the 1980s offers a unique insight into the various debates that construed a performance during Mobutu's time. Incited by his question about the saying *Le pouvoir se mange entire* (power is eaten whole), the Mufwankolo troupe framed a play, set up as part of the festivities of the twenty-fifth anniversary of national independence, around this expression. In the detailed description of how this idiom eventually led to a TV show broadcast on national television, we not only encounter the Mufwankolo actors in an interpretative struggle about the meanings of power (and in particular the apt Luba translation of the French *pouvoir*), but we also read how the program director of Lubumbashi's state channel intervenes in the scripting of the plot. The channel's representative imposes a happy ending (which the actors had not foreseen), and overt critique of Mobutu's regime is to be omitted (Fabian 1990: 76–77). Such interventions by program directors did not occur during my fieldwork. In fact, I hardly noticed any channel leaders taking interest in the production process at all—nor did I meet them easily, except at the occasional celebration. As I explain in Chapter 3, charismatic pastors and spiritual counselors showed up during the filming and commented on the characters and the plots.

The appearance of religious leaders on the set is not a total surprise if we take into account the political and social changes, mentioned earlier, that occurred in Kinshasa and its media world around the mid 1990s. Also of interest is the circular migration to Nigeria, which follows from the Pentecostal wave at the same time elsewhere in Africa and the appeal of Nigerian Pentecostal pastors to Kinois. As a result, Kinois people move to Nigeria not only for economic but also for religious reasons

(Pype forthcoming a). In 1998, Pasteur Kutino, a Pentecostal pastor, returned to Kinshasa with a Nigerian film called *Karichika,* which he showed in his church. Since then, the aesthetics of Nigerian witchcraft films have captivated Kinshasa's TV audiences.[14] More so, Kinois TV actors have adapted their own plots and images to the sensational stylistics of films such as *The Prince of Darkness, Magic Love,* and *Traces of the Past,* which are all ingrained in the collective urban memory.

Christian actors use the medium of television serials instead of film for practical reasons. First, because of the wide range of TV channels—which seems to be a unique situation for all of sub-Saharan Africa—the producers of visual fiction can easily and quickly find spectators. The small video/DVD production that exists creates mostly DVDs for the Congolese diaspora.[15] Second, the mere fact that not all households possess the needed equipment to view VHS tapes or DVDs makes the market an unattractive one. Furthermore, as opposed to Nigerian and Tanzanian cities, video parlors in Kinshasa screen especially pornographic films and action movies and thus reach out to a male public. These spaces are therefore associated with sexuality and masculinity, limiting the audiences that film screenings can reach.[16] TV programs, by contrast, air in the living room (nearly every compound has a TV set, and often more than one), on the street, and in other public places where a TV set is installed. TV productions thus guarantee a larger viewing audience, which, as I will show, is imperative for the social and symbolic capital that Christian TV actors aspire to.

The Christian Key Scenario

The locally produced teleserials are inherently melodramatic (Brooks 1976; Abu-Lughod 2002: 116), in the sense that they visualize a strong division between good and evil, showing a Manichaean universe where Good and Evil are in a constant battle that takes place in the invisible and visible realms of reality. The main characters in this fight are not mythic creatures or epic heroes of folkloric tales, but common citizens who share many similarities with the intended audience.[17] A strong moral justice underlies the plot and the close of the story. The end of the narrative is therefore always the most important event in the whole script, since it accentuates the message. Emotions are important, both in the story and in the reception of the serials. This symbolic structure appears also in sermons, Christian songs, and personal narratives such as confessions.

Since most of Kinshasa's teleserials follow the same plotline and feature the same fictional characters, I am inclined to group them under one generic noun, the Pentecostal melodrama.[18] I agree with Karin Barber (1987; 1997a) who states that the field of cultural creativity on the African continent is difficult to categorize. Yet when I explicitly asked informants to orient me toward troupes who produced "non-Christian" serials, none could think of such a drama group. On comparing several theater groups' story lines, I noticed that all the Kinshasa theater companies producing serials during my fieldwork responded (some more than others) to an ideal type of "good serial." They all used the same stock figures (the witch, the fool, the pastor), the same plot, and most importantly the same closing, spreading a Christian message. The serials produced during fieldwork thus are aptly called "Christian serials"; however, I prefer to define them as "Pentecostal melodramas," as the Pentecostal-charismatic influence and the symbolic structure of the melodrama are significant.

The value of the religious teleserials transcends mere entertainment: both producers and spectators hold them to be instructive, in that they teach the audience what it means to be living in Kinshasa and how "the good life" can be attained.[19] The serials thus obtain a strong symbolic value in the sense that the cultural producers identify good and bad moral behavior, the best strategies for social success, and the dangers of not following socially rewarded routes. In this respect, the teleserials visualize a "key scenario" (Ortner 2002 [1973]) of Kinshasa's society. Sherry Ortner identifies a "key scenario" as one of a culture's key symbols. Key scenarios sort out complex and undifferentiated feelings and ideas and make them comprehensible to the individual, communicable to others, and translatable into orderly action (2002: 161). They are analytic and occupy therefore a central status in their culture. Ortner illustrates this concept with the key scenario of the United States, best known as "the American dream," which she formulates: a boy of low status, but with total faith in the American system, works very hard and ultimately becomes rich and powerful (Ortner 2002: 162). This key scenario offers a clear-cut mode of action appropriate to correct and successful living in America. More abstractly, key scenarios formulate local definitions of good life and social success, as well as key cultural strategies to attain these. The Christian key scenario professed in Kinshasa's teleserials—and beyond, in the churches and in other evangelization practices—could be voiced thusly: "Life in Kinshasa is hazardous because of the workings of the Devil and his demons. They invade the domestic sphere with the help of witches, who threaten collective and individual health (in a physical and social sense). Christians, however, can arm themselves against evil through prayer and by listening closely to the advice of pastors." Conversion to Pentecostal Christianity, confessions, and deliverance rituals are identified as important turning points in the unfolding of the plot. The representation of Christian rituals as effective means to purify society promotes Jesus's path. It offers success and inspires one to be good.[20]

The Christian key scenario is expressed in various genres such as sermons, music video clips and also the Christian teleserials. Because of the combination of image and discourse, the Christian *maboke* offer a privileged entry for an analysis of how Kinois society imagines social success and how it should be represented.

Working with Cultural Producers

This ethnography not only studies media aesthetics but also zooms in on the lives and works of evangelizing TV actors as well as their ambitions, aspirations, and anxieties. As public figures, these actors occupy a central position in Kinshasa's society. In public spaces the actors are called by their fictive names,[21] and fans mention events or cite phrases that pertain to the characters they are performing on screen. The TV celebrities could well be understood as "grassroots intellectuals" because they are important meaning-makers. "They occupy an empty space of creativity where new ideologies and cultural strategies are shaped and deployed", Benetta Jules-Rosette (2002: 604) writes about "grassroots intellectuals" in Africa. Introducing anthropological analysis of documentary and film makers around the world, George Marcus (1997: 8) refutes the notion of "grassroots intellectuals" for various reasons, preferring the analytical category "cultural producers," which he defines as "those who engage in intellectual work in various genres and who are difficult to pin down by any single specialty, craft, art, expertise, or professional role" (1997: 8). Marcus rightfully argues that the concept of "grassroots intellectuals" is too easily associated with Marxist theory and the political struggle of subalterns. A concept such as "cultural producers" liberates the people we are studying from the so-called "proletariat" and allows inclusion of the professional middle classes, shifts the attention to issues of identity and culture, and ties the intellectual work involved in media production to its embodied practices while retaining the connotation of commitment to cultural critique and activism (1997: 9).

In the 1980s and, to a lesser degree, during the 1990s, popular paintings (*tableaux*)[22] and comic strips were widely produced and distributed around Kinshasa. The painters and comic producers were, next to local musicians, Kinshasa's most important social commentators. Nowadays, dramatic artists have taken over their position as transmitters of social knowledge and commentators on their society. Since most of the TV actors produce Christian teleserials, the *maboke* are translations of Kinois' lifeworlds, immediately interpreted through the frame of the Pentecostal ideology. Besides showing Kinois life, the actors portray the city, its inhabitants and urban sociality in such a way that they sustain Pentecostals' interpretations of city life and their views on how to bring about change. The television serials seem to work as "cultural negotiations," created to attempt to reconstruct society and a particular public sphere during and after the social traumas of the postcolonial Mobutu regime.[23]

Another characteristic of the concept of "cultural producers," according to Marcus (1997: 8), is that it "signifies a cross-cutting or blurring of genres of media in their activities". This fits the work of Kinshasa's Christian TV actors, whose activities are not only limited to cultural work, very well. Rather, they and their audience see them first and foremost as religious leaders. Various members of the Cinarc troupe also hold important positions in churches. Chapy, who became an important informant, led a chapter of the church in which the Cinarc group was embedded for a long period during fieldwork, while some actresses led children's groups in the church. Further, the TV troupes not only produce teleserials but also perform stage plays (in schools and in churches), and, in some cases, participate in (religious) orchestral performances. One actress hosted a televised religious music show for several months; another actress moderated religious talk show on the radio.

Because of this multiplicity of roles and activities performed by cultural producers, it is important to approach the media producers as social persons with their own motivations, their own social networks, and their own reflections on the limits and merits of their careers and projects as cultural producers. An anthropological study of cultural producers as social actors allows us to study how meanings come into being and how these meanings and messages are socially and historically rooted. When studying these cultural producers both as *media producers* and as *social actors,* we are also able to deconstruct the communicated content as fixed ideologies. As will become clear throughout this ethnography, even though Kinshasa's proselytizing TV actors transmit a firm message, they all grapple with the Pentecostal ideology themselves. This occurs both at the collective level of the drama group and in the personal lives of the TV actors. Within a troupe, some actors have to be instructed on the Pentecostal message, while even those who appear to be the strongest evangelizers also hesitate, stumble, and sometimes even fall. The Pentecostal imagination is not well-defined or closed. Rather, Pentecostalism is expressed in idiosyncratic ways, leaning on personal experiences, questions, desires, and anxieties. It is a religion that constantly emerges, that is "in the making," often in confrontation with daily lived realities. Therefore, we need to attend to negotiations of theological concepts such as sin, conversion, and salvation, because it is exactly these arbitrations and articulations of doubt that produce various interpretations of Pentecostalism. These come to the fore in particular during rehearsals and when filming, especially when reflecting on the appropriate closing for a serial.

Participant-observation among the producers of Kinshasa's serials also brings out the contested nature of the fabrication of meaning. During my fieldwork, I observed discussions about the "right" representation of characters and events that often obliged the performers to pause and debate, for example, how one should perform the role of a pastor, or what a witch should look like, or what language a *féticheur* (a "traditional healer") uses. These dialogues were interesting material for me, as they prompted one or more actors, in their attempt to influence the storyline, to explain ethnic beliefs or biblical events to their fellow actors. Here, I not only got a privileged view of how the teleserials as cultural documents are the outcome of a collective endeavor, but I also observed competing perspectives among the young born-again Christians. As a result, I learned much about the intra-politics of the drama group (i.e., about whose perspective would prevail, and how), and about the uncertainty, loose ends, and confusion in my informants' understandings of their own lifeworlds.

By moving out of the set where a serial is filmed and following the actors in their daily lives—on their way to church, on visits to relatives, lovers, and sponsors—I was also able to integrate those spaces "beyond the studio" (Ginsburg et al. 2002: 1) in which the serials are produced. Kinshasa's teleserials are very much "alive" in the sense that interactions with fans, sponsors, and spectators constantly feed into the production and development of the plotlines.[24] This is to a large extent the outcome of the production modalities. Kinshasa's serials are not shot in studios but in real houses that relatives, neighbors, and fans offer the drama group for an afternoon. Each week, the troupes film one episode of a serial, which usually consists of between eight and eighteen episodes. The episode is immediately broadcast the same week, often with two repeats. Viewers comment on the storylines, on the behavior of particular characters, and on how they think the narrative should evolve (see Chapter 7). The narratives also emerge from church sermons and the stimulus of the performers' private lives. These off-screen realities both design the tales and transcend the cultural work to reach a collective level. The serials thus become concerted narratives, in which Kinois actors, Pentecostal leaders, and spectators join and communally reflect on what it is to live in Kinshasa, and especially about the rift between "what is" and "what should be."

Mediation and Remediation

The cultural producers do stand not outside of society. Their goals are very much anchored within the social realities of Kinshasa, which they aim at changing. As such, the evangelizing TV actors are mediators: they try to negotiate between lived realities and what they think is the best way to actualize a better society. "Mediation" is a concept that currently receives much attention within anthropology. Following research in political science and conflict studies, mediation relates in the first instance to attempts to find agreement and thus to *end conflict*. In this sense, mediation does not envisage a status quo; a transformation—often toward harmonious conviviality—is rather the ultimate goal. Audiovisual media can play a significant role in the mediation of conflict, as research on the Truth and Reconciliation Commission hearings in post-Apartheid South Africa has shown (McEachern 2002).

Two main themes weave through the serials' content and the discourse of the television actors: morality and gender relations, both of which are core areas in which Kinshasa society needs, according to born-again Christians, change. Born-again Christians identify the Holy Spirit as the major agent in a transformation. Conversion to born-again Christianity is promoted as the most apt way to end a society in chaos and disorder and to produce the good, the orderly, and the healthy. Therefore the Christian teleserials mediate to produce not only material change but significant redress on the spiritual level as well. The evangelizers hold that there are too many "pagans" in Kinshasa. By producing Christian *maboke* that show the power of the pastor and the Holy Spirit and juxtapose these with the destructive effects of demonic activities, the teleserials and their producers also mediate between various religious worlds. Vivid illustrations of miraculous interventions of the Holy Spirit and of pastors' powers are filmed in order to persuade the viewers about the efficacy of born-again Christianity.

If we approach the teleserials as persuasive tools, then we gather that alongside its cognitive dimension, mediation also works on the senses. The Pentecostal melodrama aims to trigger the emotions of awe and amazement that might push viewers to become born-again Christians. It is probably in this appeal to the viewers' emotional lives that the teleserials intend to constitute an "imagined Christian community" (Anderson 1991) in Kinshasa. As Meyer (2009a) recently argued, imagined communities should be understood as "aesthetic formations." Communities, which are constantly in the making, draw primarily on corporeal and stylistic processes that produce ties between subjects. Such an approach invites us to move beyond the mere representations to study the embodied experiences of viewers and producers. In a society like Kinshasa, where spiritual forces are said to produce material reality, the teleserials are also embedded in this interplay of uncanny forces. In their attempts to produce a new, Christian city, the Christian performers also try to bring the power of the Holy Spirit onto the viewers. Here, the medium is used to bridge the distance between the material world and the Otherworld (Robbins n.d.). Mediation means thus also *transmission*: the transfer of messages from the otherworldly via sermons and Christian popular culture, as well as the circulation of spiritual powers via in-between figures such as pastors and TV actors.

In an attempt to understand the various ways of narrowing the distance between the otherworldly and the "thisworldly," Robbins (n.d.) directs attention to the "mediational complexity" present in the field. As will become clear, within the Kinois Pentecostal culture there are various ways to diminish the distance between the divine and the human world; television actors themselves partake in this as well. Moreover, some are both religious artists and pastors, while the materiality of the camera and the television set also constitute tools to connect the here and now with the divine. The "mediational complexity" becomes even more complex when taking into account the potential for undesirable conflation of the otherworldly and the visible reality in the context of demonic possession and witchcraft. While the complete convergence of the divine and the here and now is what Christians (artists and viewers) aspire to, they work zealously to rule out the presence of evil, occult forces. In these Christians' mindset, Kinshasa's society is governed by the Devil and demons, an unwanted situation for which witches, traditional healers, and their clients are responsible. Adding to the complexity is the fact that the technological tools that pastors and proselytizers use— the camera, the radio, the television set—can equally effectively be put to use by their adversaries. This ambiguity toward mediation and mediators, as well as uncertainty as to their desired and unwanted effects, is an outcome of the overall religious insecurity in Kinshasa's society. As I show in Chapter 2, spiritual confusion reigns hegemonic, and Kinois are unsure as to the "real" spiritual identities of their leaders and fellow-citizens. The Pentecostal melodrama illustrates this uncertainty while heightening this *Angst* about the Other.

Moving back to the aesthetics of the teleserials, remediation seems an important strategy to attain the persuasive goals. Remediation, or the insertion of other media in new contexts, is most clearly visible in the use of the Bible. Bible verses are shown in the screen corners and also often read out loud in the fictive conversations. Yet the serials also feature significantly "traditional" songs and dances, as well as the modern, rumba dance forms, in scenes with witches and demons. Remediation thus follows the bifurcated ideology of Pentecostal thought: scenes and characters appear either on the good or on the bad side.

While remediation enables us to embark on an analysis of the circulation of forms and meanings, it also draws our attention to the ruptures, changes, and larger transformations that embedding signs and forms might entail. For instance, when performing rumba dances, which are held to be unchristian and to mediate demonic powers, the Christian actors and their audiences are concerned about their own spiritual safety. A focus on remediation allows us to move beyond the mere transfer and incorporation of forms and styles, and to study how new sensational experiences can come into being as soon as a form is integrated in a new context.

Kinshasa's evangelizing television actors thus mediate not only between various religious groups and between religious worlds, but also between cultural forms. This book will show how the Pentecostal actors balance between these various worlds and forms.

Research Methodologies

So far, no guidebook has been written on an appropriate methodology in media anthropology. In writing about popular culture in general, Fabian (1998: 99) states that "the conventions of ethnography, its habits of collecting information and its forms of description, make popular culture a subject difficult to study and even more so to represent." During the process of outlining an appropriate methodology, I considered it meaningful to decide whether I would do research on the production and/or the reception of the serials.

Acknowledging the partial nature of the knowledge an anthropologist can gather, the plurality of sense-making systems in a society, and the diverging meanings that signs and symbolic worlds can acquire through time and space, I chose to limit my focus to meanings intended by the producers of *maboke*. In no way did the choice to focus on the production of media texts entail the total exclusion of spectators in the research. In light of the writings of renowned specialists in the field of cultural studies such as John Fiske (1989) and Stuart Hall (1997), it is difficult to maintain a rigid distinction between producers and spectators. Reflecting on African popular culture in general, Barber (1997b: 358) understands production and reception as "moments in a cycle" rather than as two poles at opposite ends of a process. This certainly applies to the production of Kinshasa's teleserials in a very literal way. As I already mentioned, the narratives are constructed in a collaborative process that invites spectators to participate in the "writing" of the plotlines. Accordingly, the artists do not monopolize the direction the stories take. Viewers' comments on the teleserials—given during talk television shows, e.g., *Personnes et Personnages* and *Théâtre de Cité* (Theater in the Township)—pastors' comments on the storylines, and actors' engagement with the audience in the street and in religious settings (since the celebrities invite their viewers to their churches) all contribute to the making of the stories. In this way, the evolution and closure of a teleserial's plotline are the result of a collective effort between members of different groups embedded in Kinshasa's media world. These production particularities lead me to argue against the maintenance of a rigid distinction between "producer" and "spectator." More so, these observations add another dimension to the taken-for-granted understanding of the audience as "active producers of meaning" (Askew 2002: 5).

Probably the most important method I used was participating as an actress in a proselytizing acting company. Television drama groups in Kinshasa consist of huge groups of individuals, and people continuously leave the group while others join. Because of this it was impracticable to connect with all of them to a similarly intimate extent. I selected eight Cinarc performers, four actors and four actresses. The actors were the troupe's founding leader (Bienvenu Toukebana); his right-hand man (Clovis Ikala); his maternal cousin, who was in training to become a pastor (Fiston Muzama, better known as Chapy); and a boy who had joined the group a few months before my arrival (Ance Luzolo). As for the female members, I worked closely with Cinarc's most popular actress (Mamy Moke); an actress who had been a Cinarc member since the creation of the troupe (Beti Ikwa); a girl (Nene Nyongoni) who, alongside her activities with Cinarc, also leads a youth group in a befriended church; and a newly arrived actress (Dorcaz Mbombo). I noted their personal biographies, visited them regularly in their homes, and conducted series of formal individual, open-ended interviews with them. I questioned them about their personal lives and observed them during the filming. They were usually very open to answering all my questions. Still, it was rather difficult to receive answers from them when discussing witchcraft, an important topic of the teleserials. Their reluctance was no doubt part of their management of their Christian identity, since displaying too much knowledge about the occult might render them suspicious. Also, the firm belief that evil spirits are all around and may follow conversations led them at times to abruptly end discussion on the topic.

I asked my main informants to summarize the serials they had produced and the ones they were going to create, and to reflect on their fictional alter egos. I thus gained clear and exceptional insight into the stories, into the selection of the major story lines, and the messages they wished to convey. I also watched the episodes I was able to gather, either alone or with one or two of the actors. I then selected a few scenes (*tableaux*) in the serials, which the Cinarc members helped me transcribe.

Because drama groups are affiliated with several revival churches in Kinshasa, participant-observation research on the production of the teleserials required not just observation and active participation as an actress in the rehearsals and shootings of the episodes or attending television programs to which the performers were invited, but also participation in prayer gatherings and teachings about the born-again Christian ideology. The spiritual leaders that supervise the artistic and religious quality of the actors' work thus became main informants too. The artists likewise invited me to other, more personal gatherings such as funeral ceremonies, different stages of marriage ceremonies, anniversaries, and presentations of babies. These events offered me thorough insight into their social environment, in particular their extended families, neighborhoods, and other social networks. In addition, I conducted semi-structured interviews with the bosses of both of the television channels (TropicanaTV and RTG@) that broadcast Cinarc's serials at the time of my fieldwork.

Though I spent most of my time focusing on Cinarc, I also attended rehearsals of other TV drama groups (Groupe de Muyombe Gauche, Théâtre Simba, Groupe de Sans Soucis). I did not confine myself to the TV world and followed several theater companies producing development-related drama (Canacu Théâtre, ATA-Théâtre). Complementary material on cultural performances was gathered during events organized by folkloric associations (Ballet Mesa na Kiti, Afrik'Art, Nyota Théâtre). And I likewise attended the plays of groups such as Ecurie Maloba, Marabout Théâtre, and Théâtre des Intriguants, whose audiences are more select. These groups tend to attract individuals who are interested in keeping folklore alive or keen to see Western-inspired dramatic performances. Discussions with these artists taught me that most acting groups that do not produce TV drama have a deprecating take on their colleagues in teledrama. Several arguments were mentioned in this respect. First, it was commonly held that TV actors were not "real artists," since most of them had not obtained a degree from an official cultural institution such as the National Institute of Arts (INA) or the Academy of Fine Arts (Institut des Beaux Arts). It was frequently stated that the TV performers lacked creative genius, and that they were merely copying the aesthetic conventions of Nigerian films. These arguments voiced a rivalry between practitioners of so-called "high culture" and those of popular culture. Surprisingly, the Cinarc members themselves acknowledged the superiority of actors with degrees from formal cultural training institutions concerning technique and finesse in scripting and performing. However, they did not consider themselves artists of a lesser kind. As I show in Chapter 4, spiritual inspiration imbues the performers with a particular charisma that non-Christian artists do not necessarily possess.

The overt connection with Pentecostal churches was another major point on which other performers rejected the artistry of TV actors. This objection echoes the paradoxical positioning of Pentecostal churches in Kinshasa's society overall. Although everybody recognizes the public significance of these churches and their leaders, not everybody applauds their social power. Yet all of Kinshasa's actors, whether they were working in the field of TV drama, folkloric *ballet,* Western-style theater, or even development-related performances, had to acknowledge that TV drama groups such as the Cinarc troupe were by far more popular than any of the other theater companies in Kinshasa, and that the Cinarc serials best expressed the ways in which most of Kinshasa's residents imagined their lives and futures.

Becoming an Evangelizing TV Actress

Research on popular culture requires "presence, action and interaction," Fabian writes (1998: 87). Commonly valued as an important tool to gain privileged data, the method of participant-observation is not unchallenged. As has been argued, the presence of the researcher, her theoretical approaches and individual characteristics, and the context in which the work is performed shape the gathered data and analysis to a great extent (DeWalt et al. 2000: 261). DeWalt et al. (2000: 291) therefore call for a systematic study of "the effects of biases, predilections, and personal characteristics" on the research enterprise. Any anthropological analysis should articulate the researcher's position, place her within the field in terms of bias, and delineate the particular research contexts, the subjective disposition of the researcher, and the social experiences that have bearing on the data gathering.

Figure 1.2. The author playing the role of a siren (screen shots from *The Nanas Benz,* © Cinarc)

During fieldwork, I was constantly reminded of my female status (fig. 1.2). This also was what led me to cooperation with the Cinarc troupe. As De Boeck (2004: 241) writes, in many ways Kinshasa is a female body that is constantly penetrated by the male gaze. Patriarchy is undisputed, and gossip about suspected sexual relationships circulates quickly. In the period during which I explored Kinshasa's TV drama groups, I tried to work with two different troupes. However, being a young, single, white woman did not facilitate my work in these acting companies. The troupe's leaders would spread rumors of me becoming their mistress, or they would stop me from speaking with male performers of the acting group. An unexpected event changed the unfortunate course that my fieldwork had taken: in the week following my departure from a second acting company with which I had unsuccessfully attempted participant-observation, I was told that two Cinarc actors, whom I had met earlier when making a directory of theatrical activity in the city, had mentioned my name on a television show and invited me to attend their rehearsals. Taking this information as an invitation, I called the Cinarc leader. That same day, I visited the group, which was at that moment on a prayer camp in a church compound. They prayed for me, laid hands on me, and asked God's blessing for a fruitful cooperation. This meeting proved to be very beneficial for my research project. Since these TV stars publicly claim to be part of a Christian group they cannot afford any kind of negative publicity, rumors, or gossip. Their concerns about their reputation offered me a more constructive working environment than the groups with which I had previously tried to cooperate.

In hindsight, I think that the Cinarc members welcomed me not as a young woman but as someone to be evangelized. From day one, the troupe's members invited me to participate in their spiritual life, not just the prayer gatherings that the crew held nightly but also the weekly sermons in church. They accordingly made the same requests of me that any other new members of the crew would hear, which surely facilitated my integration into their group. I was the one asked to read certain passages of the Bible out loud, a practice that would continue throughout the fieldwork. They also urged me to dance with them to the Christian songs. Much to my surprise, at the close of the first nocturnal ritual I attended I heard the Cinarc leader assigning his maternal cousin, Chapy, to give me a crash course in God, praying, and spiritual life.

As a young man already studying to become a pastor, Chapy did a wonderful job. He eventually became my "spiritual father" (*tata ya Nzambe*), meaning that he replied to all my questions on religion and morality and guided me to "the right Christian path." Our talks, which took place almost daily, created a strong bond of friendship between us. It also meant that Chapy had considerable knowledge about my private life, the people I was seeing, and the places I would visit when taking time off from the research. At times, Chapy felt he had to redirect me to God's path, which he did very subtly. Without a doubt, he was much harsher on his Congolese "spiritual children" than on me, because whether I wanted to or not, I still remained an outsider. Chapy also played a meaningful role in my analysis of life on screen and off, and he is therefore one of the most important voices in this book.

At the request of the Cinarc board, I became an actress. This participation offered me a privileged vantage point from which to observe the production of the teleserials and also gave me a public identity. From that moment on, I came to be known as "Caleb's white girl" (*mundele ya Caleb*). Caleb is the fictive name of the Cinarc leader and the name by which he is best known in the city. I was no longer a young, white woman who might have been working for an embassy or a foreign NGO; I became an actress playing the roles of Paco's wife (in the serial *Back to the Homestead*) and a demonic goddess (a siren in *The Nanas Benz*), among others. While I was now something of a group insider in the roles attributed to me, the actors nevertheless exploited my outsider status. Sometimes the troupe's leader would ask me to speak English or even use my native tongue, Dutch. Usually they asked me not to speak Lingala. Although I was a member of the Cinarc troupe, and recognized as a Christian, I was never allowed to play a character that would make me one of them.

Structure of the Text

The text of this volume constantly shifts back and forth between descriptions of what I saw and heard in the field and what is shown on television, and analysis of these data. A website (http://www.berghahnbooks.com/title.php?rowtag=PypeMaking) complements this written text with recorded footage from the important scenes discussed in the chapters. Small CD boxes in the margins of pages guide the reader to the relevant track on the website.

Although each chapter can be read separately, the sequence progresses logically: the first chapters examine the social fields of the media world and the drama group, the following chapters focus on the principles of the Pentecostal churches, and the final chapters delve into the narratives.

Chapter 2, "Cursing the City," portrays the city and aims to be an introduction to the influence of apocalyptic thinking on daily life and mobility in the city. It demarcates the Christian landscape in the city, spells out beliefs about the divine, the occult, and witchcraft, and delineates their impact on the cityscape.

The following chapter, "New Fathers and New Names," takes the evangelizing drama group as its main focus. The theater company is considered as one of many voluntary associations that constitute social life in an African urban society. Social groups outside the lineage foster new networks that create identities and spaces of freedom. However, the rigid internal hierarchies within both leisure groups and church communities immediately limit this freedom. Artistic and spiritual kinship are studied alongside loose connections ("contacts") and relations with fans. These social dynamics, fictive kinship relations, and "contacts" thrive on long-standing matrixes of patronage and clientelism. The final part of this chapter moves beyond the individual need for extra-familial social relations and analyzes ties of friendship and rivalry among drama groups, and between troupes and church groups.

Chapter 4, "Variations on Divine Afflatus," explores the distribution of authority and knowledge. I detect how pastors and Christian artists acquire the power to speak for and to the Christian Kinois. The fact that charisma, spiritual knowledge, revelation, and secrecy are paramount features of the Christian leaders' discourse reveals similarities between strategies that pastors and Christian artists apply to impose their power and meaning on city dwellers, on the one hand, and the efforts made by diviners, priests, and magicians in non-Christian settings to acquire authority, on the other. The chapter concludes by pondering the Christians' discourse on secrecy and revelation as it relates to the serials. Research on African arts has shown that these are two key features of the aesthetics of local artwork. I examine how the Christian serials, and in particular the special effects, are embedded in these aesthetics.

The following chapter, "Mimesis in Motion," continues the previous chapter's concluding discussion about aesthetics, now with a focus on its embodied aspects. Ethnographic data on actors', and their audiences', experience of the acting work give insight into Pentecostals' politics of the body and its impact on the media world. The main argument of this chapter is that technological mediation has not deteriorated the aura of visual arts. The chapter ends with the mediation of aura feeding into the format of the teleserials themselves.

In "The Right Road," Chapter 6, I explore how the unfolding narrative of the proselytizing serials and the moral evolution of the fictional characters represent a Christian subjectivity that sustains and reflects modern Christian subjects. The chapter analyzes Christian notions of evil and its impact on personhood and morality. Based on a discussion of evil agents in three Cinarc serials, *Dilemma, Heritage of Death,* and *The Maquis Boys and Girls,* I approach consciousness and confessions as the main themes in discourse on human's positionality within the global spiritual battle.

Chapter 7, "Opening Up the Country," studies discourse on development in the social space of Kinshasa's post-Mobutu teleserials. The actors proclaim that their work will transform society, counter the social and political crisis, and improve the nation on various levels. The main focus of this chapter is the way the fictive representation of witchcraft relates to a Christian diagnosis of the crisis. I first discuss the role of television serials in the reconstruction of the nation. Then I expand on the representation of elders in the serials and the discordant encounters between young and old in this urban setting. Here, I characterize the serials as witchcraft accusations. The chapter concludes with an exploration of the Pentecostal politics of time as it relates to the endings of the serials.

"Marriage comes from God" (Chapter 8) and "The Danger of Sex" (Chapter 9) investigate the serials as instruments in the production and reflection of Pentecostal gender ideology and youth alliances therein. I relate the representation of marriage preferences, incest, adultery, sexualities, and "strong women" to configurations of power and marriage processes in the city.

The conclusion of the volume emphasizes the historicality of the tele-serials and wraps up an issue that appears in various chapters yet is not addressed as a theme: the role of the living room in the cultural public sphere.

The book has several flaws. Foremost is the way my bias toward the production of the serials limits my understanding of their reception. There is no doubt about the popularity of these visual texts, and the gathered data on the audience's contribution to the unfolding of the plotlines includes the reception. But what Kinois actually do with the images—how these affect their lives, subjectivities, and social relations—is an issue that remains unexplored. Second, I cannot offer an exhaustive view into the lifeworlds of the Christians. The research studies the acting Christians as propagators of an ideology, as evangelizers of the city. Interviews and observations were structured by an interest in the overlap and contrasts between the ideology and their personal lives. Themes that do not appear in the social space of the teleserials are not discussed. Third, the economic aspects of the *maboke* are also unexplored. In particular, the inserted commercials that construct the viewer as a consumer and the ascribed value to the commodities are all-important aspects of these media products, which I could not take into account in this analysis. Finally, the role of Kinshasa's diaspora, not only as avid spectators but even as producers of these telenarratives, opens fascinating terrain for a fuller understanding of the social significance of the serials but is not discussed here either.

Notes

1. By "Pentecostal," I refer to churches that are inspired by the Pentecostal movement but are not inserted in the Pentecostal Church. In the academic literature, these churches can receive various names: sects, fundamentalist churches, millennial movements, and so on. In my view, these denominations are often derogatory, and they express a Western viewpoint that misreads the agency of these church leaders and congregations. In my use of religious appellations, I try to follow the vocabulary of my informants as closely as is feasible. I am cognizant of the general use in religious studies of the term "Neo-Pentecostalism" to indicate more recent forms of Pentecostalism that reoriginated in the United States during the 1960s (Hollenweger 1972). In the following, I prefer the labels "Pentecostal-charismatic Churches" (*églises pentecotistes*), "born-again churches" (because followers also indicate themselves as "newborns," *des nouveau-nés*), and "revival churches" (*églises de réveil*), and will use them interchangeably. In Chapter 2, I situate these revival churches within Kinshasa's religious landscape in terms of origin and theological orientations. Although they are not the same, I use here "Christians" as a shorthand for "born-again Christians"; here, I also follow the vocabulary of my informants.

2. The appellation *théâtre populaire* (French for "popular theater") suggests that the city's TV fiction is rooted in stage theater. As Fabian (1990) describes for the emergence of television drama in Katanga (a province in central Congo), in Kinshasa too, at the end of the colonial era, local stage actors moved from the theater space to the radio and then appeared on Kinshasa's television screens. The word *maboke* derives from Yeya Maboke, who led the group that in 1961 began playing sketches on a radio show in Kinshasa (called Léopoldville at the time). For a diachronic outline of the emergence and transformations of Kinshasa's television serials, see Pype (2009b).

3. Fieldwork was spread over four periods: February–March 2003, October 2003–March 2004, November 2004–April 2005, and April–July 2006.

4. Generally, several troupes are affiliated with a TV channel, which beams weekly episodes of serials that are produced solely for that television station.

5. By "apolitical themes," I refer to those that do not explicitly address national political representation or evaluations of political actors and events.

6. Mobutu was Congo's notorious ruler. His regime lasted over three decades (1965–1997). He was succeeded by the former rebel Laurent D. Kabila, who was killed in 2001, whereupon his son Joseph Kabila took power. Democratic elections in 2006 conferred democratic legitimacy on Joseph Kabila.

7. This contrasted to a high degree with development drama, in which, during the transition period, performers did not shy away from speaking of politics. They openly or more subtly criticized certain political actors and events, sometimes even naming some of the corrupt politicians. Backed by foreign NGOs and the Mission of the UN for the Congo (MONUC), these actors had a safety net that allowed them to speak more openly than television actors, who did not have this backing.

8. Laurent D. Kabila (ruling between 1997 and 2002) initially severed the grip of the state on the media world again. Yet, Joseph Kabila, who came into power early 2002, has an open take on media. But there is still a strong control by the state on media content (see Frère 2007, Pype 2011b).

9. He is a lawyer and Member of Parliament for the ruling political party (PPRD).

10. The qualifier "post-Mobutu" is here used uniquely in its temporal sense, meaning that the teleserials were produced in the era that followed Mobutu's regime. Readers might hope for an interpretation of the past, but these serials are extremely devoted to the "present tense," in which Mobutu hardly plays a significant role. Therefore, this book does not offer insight into how Kinois people have come to terms with the legacy of Mobutu's regime. This is in a sense addressed, but it is not the main orientation of the teleserials or of the public sphere that is constituted by these fictive texts.

11. Maxwell (2005) shows how mass media play an important role in the construction of southern African Pentecostalism.

12. My analysis and gaze are very much indebted to the pioneer work of Birgit Meyer, who is one of the first anthropologists to tackle the interplay between Pentecostalism and visual media in Africa. Although her work centers on Ghana, there are many similarities between her writings and my findings. These convergences will be articulated throughout the text.

13. The case of Pastor Kutino, however, illustrates that the state does keep an eagle eye on the political discourse of church leaders. After Pastor Kutino exclaimed during a Sunday sermon in 2003 that President Joseph Kabila was not a rightful

leader, he received death threats and military men ransacked his church. The pastor fled via Congo-Brazzaville to London, where he resided in exile for three years.

14. The film is also highly popular elsewhere in sub-Saharan Africa, for example Tanzania (Krings 2009).

15. Content and themes hardly differ because the TV serials are copied and sent abroad. Sometimes media entrepreneurs pirate the teleserials themselves and sell them in video shops in African districts of Western towns. Since most of the copyright belongs to the TV channels, the serials' titles are changed. An example is the Cinarc serial *The Devouring Fire (Le feu dévorant)*, which was sold in Brussels and Paris as the DVD *Caroline, Mwana ya nani? (Whose child is Caroline?)*.

16. See Werner (2006: 152), who has observed a similar situation in Dakar.

17. The artists do not wear special costumes (except for the fool, Pype 2010); rather, they perform in daily, urban outfits, usually their own clothes but sometimes borrowed from shops that try to advertise in this way.

18. The categorization of the serials under the genre of "Pentecostal melodrama" is my own. I am aware of the potential power issue inherent in the designation of a genre (Fabian 1998), but the use of the labels "Pentecostal" and "melodrama," a concept from literary theory, enables me to convey the character of the serials as I encountered them during fieldwork.

19. Masquelier (2009), Spronk (2009), and Fair (2009) document that elsewhere in Africa, spectators have similar expectations of TV fictions: apart from being entertained, they want to be instructed when watching films and soap operas.

20. Just as symbols can change over time, so do "key scenarios." Throughout their history, Kinshasa's mass-mediated dramas have promoted different "key scenarios" and concomitant social models, being the *convert*, the *évolué*, and the *citizen*. Importantly, not only were these characters staged as social ideals, but the producers also belonged to these categories (Pype 2009b).

21. Kinshasa's artists usually retain their fictive name when starting a new serial and embodying a new character. In some instances, the fictive name also intrudes in the private sphere, when these individuals are no longer called by their personal name but by their artist name.

22. Kinshasa's popular paintings have been studied by Jewsiewicki (1991; 1995; 1996; 2003; 2004) and Fabian (1996).

23. Cf. Fischer (2001: 468) about visual products in posttraumatic societies.

24. This contrasts with Hobart's (2002) reflection, on the difference between theater performances and TV drama, that the latter are dead performances since there is no interaction with the audience. The production modalities of Kinshasa's teleserials allow spectators to contribute to the developing storylines. I discuss this in Chapter 7.

Cursing the City

The Ethnographic Field and the Pentecostal Imagination

The Cinarc serial *Ekonda, The Cursed Neighborhood,* filmed and broadcast in 2002 and spanning ten episodes, offers a good introduction to how born-again Christians imagine Kinshasa. The plot is set in motion when, somewhere in an unidentified township in the city, an impoverished couple, Fataki and his wife, consult a magician to obtain money. The ritual specialist triggers a set of occult transformations that enables the couple to become wealthy. In exchange for material gain, Fataki and his wife agree to become servants of the Devil, which means they have to sacrifice souls in their surroundings. This mission can only be accomplished through witchcraft (*kindoki*). From that moment on, a "bad wind" (*mopepe mabe*) blows through the neighborhood, causing illnesses, accidents, and death.

Fataki's wife, who sells beignets at the market, can easily bewitch her customers through bewitched food. The enchanted young girls who buy the delicious food each evening join a group of prostitutes, headed by Theresia, a very beautiful young woman who manages to seduce the wealthiest man in the area, Dinghi Zwayou. Through her ruses, he spends all his money on Theresia, which obviously leads to problems with his wife, who needs the money to feed their children. Theresia's malevolent powers are effective as far away as Europe, and she manages to have Paco, Dinghi's son who has left for London, repatriated. It so happens, however, that a very Christian family resides in the neighborhood. Julien, his wife Deborah, and their adolescent son Caleb pray hard and are known in the neighborhood to be ardent Christians. The witches target this family and encounter many difficulties in attempting to infiltrate this household. The King of the Dark World therefore sends Mamy La Chatte, a female demon, to seduce Caleb. She manages to capture his soul and imprison it in a bottle so she can dominate him.

Through Caleb, a door to the household is left ajar, and the problems start: Julien loses his job. Deborah convinces Julien to go to their pastor and request a special prayer session on his behalf. The family goes to the church, but Mamy, the one Caleb wants to marry, refuses to accompany them. Caleb's parents denounce their future daughter-in-law's behavior and try to convince their son to search for a Christian girl to marry. But Mamy La Chatte has Caleb under her spell, and he disregards his parents' wishes and ignores their advice. At the very moment that Julien and Deborah are holding a prayer meeting in their living room, Mamy La Chatte suddenly disappears. Only then do they realize that this beautiful young girl is a spirit (*molimo*). This event encourages the pastor and his assistants to embark on door-to-door evangelization. It slowly emerges that, in apparently every household, there is at least one bewitched person who has been doing the Devil's bidding. The Christian leaders need to purify the neighborhood through multiple exorcism rituals, which they perform in each of the homes. The serial ends with Fataki and his wife confessing that they have been at the root of all the problems their neighbors have endured.

This narrative, explicitly set in Kinshasa, presents a grim image of the city and its residents. It spells out how the uncanny invades, intrudes, and subverts the material world. Buying food on the market, falling in love, starting a sexual relationship, and even becoming a member of a girls' association are, so the serial dictates, actions with potential detrimental spiritual effects. Of course this apocalyptic image of Kinshasa constitutes only one particular, and even highly politicized, way of representing life in DR Congo's capital city. It contrasts strikingly with the ways in which urban dance musicians represent Kinshasa. In urban dance songs and the accompanying music video clips, seductive female bodies, a zest for living, lavish spending, and a joyful atmosphere following the rhythm of rumba tunes constitute the essence of what it means to live in Kinshasa. Proselytizing artists (drama actors and musicians) and ardent Christians attack this image of Kinshasa at its core. Modern dance music, popular meeting places such as markets and bars, and girls and women who appear to be able to enjoy the fruits of capitalism and its concomitant Afromodernity are diabolized. In painting this unpleasant picture of their city and fellow urbanites, Christian evangelizers encourage the Kinois to counter these demonic actions by inviting the divine through prayers and participating in a parallel Christian popular culture.

In order to contextualize the depiction of Kinshasa as a cursed city, I offer here a brief introduction to the cityscape, the religious field, and the main principles of the Pentecostal imagination as I encountered it between 2003 and 2006. I then bring the teleserials back to the center of our attention, situating them within other narrative genres of Kinshasa's charismatic scene. A reflection on the apocalyptic mimesis construction concludes the chapter.

I argue that the religious teleserials are part of a larger, more encompassing proselytizing "moment." It is difficult to identify the master brains behind the anonymous machine that promotes the main principles of Pentecostal Christianity in Kinshasa. It seems more appropriate to speak about a "moment" in which many find much value in the teachings of Pentecostal leaders. These teachings speak to the experience of crisis, the urban culture of *ambiance,* and the diversified religious landscape in the city. By borrowing signs and images from politics, from the city's eroticized and hedonistic cultus, and also from other religious worlds present in Kinshasa; by reinterpreting their codes and practices; and by assigning moral values to everything that makes up the urban environment, Kinshasa's Pentecostal leaders produce a particular sense of place and time that orients the expectations, experiences, and desires of their audiences and also produces new patterns of social exclusion and inclusion. While the formation of social relationships and the qualities attributed to particular connections in the urban social environment will be discussed in the following chapter (Chapter 3), this chapter aims at situating the Pentecostal adherents' principles of moral and spiritual expertise, notions of witchcraft and deliverance, and popular culture within the urbanscape.

The Heat of Kinshasa

Unofficial estimates put Kinshasa's population at eight million inhabitants. This makes Kinshasa the largest urban center in central Africa.[1] Because of a steady, natural growth of the city's inhabitants and constant regional migration, Kinshasa continues to expand. As the capital city of Congo, it occupies a specific place in the Congolese mindset. It is the place where things happen, where political decisions are made, where the most popular music is produced,[2] and where life promises (from an outsider's perspective) to be easy and pleasant. People speak about *Kinshasa moto,* the heat or fever of Kinshasa, to indicate the buzz, the radiant ambiance (*Kinkiesse*) of the city and the promises of city life. This particular mood is expressed in the notions of "*La Kinoiserie*" and "*KinKiesse,*"[3] which are frequently described in terms of an ambiance, a joyful atmosphere. Several districts in the city are identified as zones where this "*joie de vivre*" is most visible. These are the neighborhoods of Matonge (in the community of Kalamu), Beaumarché (in the community of Barumbu), and the community of Bandalungwa. Kinois qualify these places as "hot" (*moto*), using the hot-cold idiom that pervades sub-Saharan African discourse about the rhythm, difficulties, complexities, and simultaneity of flows of people, goods, and information in the city as opposed to the "cool" village (see Stroeken 2001). There is an interesting paradox in this paradigm: usually "heat" is an unsettling and disturbing quality; "coolness" and "cold" (*malili*) are perceived as positive qualities denoting calmness, peace, balance and health. Still, this does not prevent people from being attracted by the city's "heat."

La Kinoiserie

When speaking about their city and *La Kinoiserie*, Kinois display much pride. They tend to minimize the general atmosphere of distrust, preferring to point to the zest for living that is said to unite all Kinois and to attract others. Sony Labou Tansi's text *Le Sexe de Matonge* (1984), recently republished in a special edition of *Politique Africaine* on cosmopolitan African cities (2005–2006), captures the stereotype of *La Kinoiserie:*

> The heart of this city is in Matonge. All its flesh and blood, its sweat, its odours, and especially its sexuality stemming from music and the never-ending rumba dances; ... During the nighttime, I feel this so strongly; Matonge becomes a city in erection, male or female. Who knows? But sex. It sings. It dances. Sometimes it cries. It gives the impression that all houses sell Skol and Regla [two beer brands], in which one can enter, drink and dance a bit, get out, spend ten zaïres, and spend ten more zaïres, and again ten zaïres, again ten zaïres, and again, and again and again.
>
> ... This city is a long song, a continous presence of Tabu Ley and the almighty Lwambo Makiadi [two of the most important singers of Congolese music] ...
>
> She dances to prove me that being a woman is not nothing, and being it in Kin is savory. (Tansi 2005–2006: 118–122, author's translation)[4]

The main protagonist moving about in the spaces of *La Kinoiserie* is the *ambianceur*. In this cliché Kinshasa is filled with men who enjoy rumba music and female eroticism. The ideal of a man with money (*mobali mobali poche*) and a girl with a beautiful figure (*mwasi mwasi nzoto*) is celebrated (see Chapter 9). Cultivating elegance in dress and displaying proficiency in French are two additional features that Kinois identified to me as meaningful when one yearns to stage oneself as a Kinois. From time to time, my informants ridiculed men wearing shorts. "He thinks he is in the village," it was said. The same mockery was also pointed at people who did not know how to express themselves in French, or who did not understand French. "Forget it, he is a villager" ("*Ah, tika, aza villageois*"), people would say then. Upon hearing that, the other person would put extra effort into speaking French.

These characteristics indicate that being "a true Kinois," someone who lives *la Kinoiserie* to the full, does not depend upon one's place of birth or color of skin or on the fact of having lived a long time in the city. It is more a matter of style, in the sense put forward by James Ferguson (1999) when discussing urban culture in Africa. A "Kinois" is described in terms of action: which dances one performs, what music one listens to, how one dresses, or how one speaks. We can easily define *La Kinoiserie* as a cosmopolitan style, in contrast to a localist style that displays an orientation to "the village" (Ferguson 1999: 102–108). The concept of "style" is apt, particularly for Kinshasa, in that it emphasizes the performative nature of the demarcation of the social categories "Kinois" versus "non-Kinois." Kinois identity thus transgresses all ethnic boundaries, but it also thrives upon other patterns of inclusion and exclusion. Especially significant is the distinction between "urbanite" and "villager." Kinshasa's inhabitants are proud to live in the capital city and denote villagers, even the Congolese living in provincial capital cities like Matadi and Mbandaka, as "people from the village" (*mbokatiers*).

Twenty years after Labou Tansi wrote the text cited above, the idea of Kinshasa's ambiance is still present in the city's visual culture: music video clips of modern urban singers, popular paintings, media advertisements for locally produced beer. Yet the experience of the political and economic crisis has somehow transformed the content of *La Kinoiserie*. Bienvenu, the Cinarc leader (age 35), born and raised in Kinshasa, described *La Kinoiserie* in the following way:

> A Kinois is a *talker*. He likes to speak, often using a deformed Lingala [kiKinois]. He is a *yankee*, a *gaillard*, and believes he is above all other Congolese. He likes to dress well, despite his poverty. He will invariably wear nice trousers and shirts that are neat and ironed. Even if he has nothing, he is immaculately groomed. He likes beer and women, and dreams out loud of leaving for Europe. He likes many things at once; and you will notice: a Kinois will always find money, one way or another. This creativity is what expresses the essence of *La Kinoiserie*.

Bienvenu's explanation points out that the genius of survival (finding money and food) in a city in crisis is an additional feature of a "true Kinois." Bienvenu expressed his admiration for Kinois' capacity to survive (*débrouillardise*) and was amused when mentioning kiKinois and Kinois' love of clothes, alcohol, and women. He himself used to be like that before becoming a born-again Christian. But now that he has acquired a new identity, he has abandoned the city's lifestyle. The Bible imposes another body language on him, telling him not to do whatever he wants, but to behave like a Christian. Leading the life of a "real Kinois" is no longer possible after conversion to Christianity. Bienvenu's Christian discourse attacks the city's key symbols: music, beer, elegance, sexuality, and bars. These are demonized and said to be weapons or spaces of the Devil. As a Christian, therefore, one should avoid them.

Nene, also a born-again Christian, described *La Kinoiserie* from a female and Christian point of view. Her examples included young girls who stay in the house during the day, who only bathe late in the afternoon and then dress up to go out in the evening. Strolling around in the streets, these girls seduce men and beg them for money. Or, "take those people who brush their teeth outside the house," Nene contended:

> It is an intimate act to brush your teeth, but many people, with a naked upper body in case of the men, or even women only dressed in a cloth, brush their teeth and spit out the filthy water while passers-by can see them. And of course, *La Kinoiserie* also means the clothes that young girls wear these days: sometimes their underwear is showing because they wear transparent clothes or because their clothes are too small. And did you not notice all the rubbish in the streets? Yes, that is also part of *La Kinoiserie*.

For Nene, as for many others who have a critical attitude toward their city, *La Kinoiserie* depicts a loss of morality and altered sociality that is reflected in how people interact, how they use public space, and how they present themselves. *La Kinoiserie* is a quality that those who regard themselves as "real Christians" oppose and criticize. Therefore, the concept of *La Kinoiserie* cannot be viewed as an expression of how all Kinois perceive life and the identity of their city, since it is a much-contested image.

Competing Christianities

In Kinshasa, nearly everybody claims to be a Christian when asked about religious identity, although other religions are also practiced in Kinshasa. There are several mosques in the city, but most Muslims are of foreign origin (Lebanese or west African). I encountered one young Kinois who had tried Islam in between divergent Christian churches. For him, it was another step in his path toward spiritual growth. The small Indian community meets in one of the two Hindu temples in the city, which are seldom visited by Kinshasa's other inhabitants. The city also includes two synagogues. As non-Christian religious spaces rarely frequented by Kinois, these spaces do not belong to the lifeworlds of Kinois. Other, non-Christian churches, such as Eglise Primitive (the Primitive Church), which stresses animism, ancestrality, and "Africanity"; the Bunda Dia Kongo, a religious-political movement from the Kongo ethnic group; and Teaching of World Messianity,[5] a Japanese syncretic religion, also have adepts in the city, but their numbers remain extremely low.

Christianity is omnipresent in the social imagination and in the social life of Kinois, though it has diverse faces and shelters a wide variety of religious practices. I experienced Kinshasa's Christian landscape as ever-changing, consistently in flux and continuously reinventing itself and adapting itself to the imperatives of a cosmopolitan urbanity that does not exactly know which direction to take. New churches emerge, religious vocabularies are revised and extended, and Christian rituals are thickened with rhythms, props, and images borrowed from televised narratives as much as from the urban modern dance scene and even the capitalist market.

How to make sense of the various Christianities (Cannell 2006) in this prolific religious universe? Without a doubt, my attempt to catalogue the local Christian currents stemmed from a Western desire to control and manage the universe in which I had arrived and about which I would later be expected to speak on with authority. One way was merely to stroll around the city and look at the various names painted on buildings. The Catholic, Protestant, and Kimbanguist churches are most visible due to their long history and the large compounds they occupy, frequently with school compounds in the vicinity. Kinshasa's neighborhoods are also dotted with numerous, smaller *revival churches,* which outnumber the other Christian churches and do not belong to the mainline Christian Churches (Catholicism, Protestantism, and Kimbanguism). Everywhere one notices compound walls displaying names of revival churches, advertisements for their weekly programs, and huge boards announcing upcoming religious gatherings. Not all revival groups have their own church space, though: depending on the seniority of the church group and its financial resources, it may take several months or even years before a revival church can claim to gather in a space of its own. Often, these groups have to congregate in regular compounds, frequently occupied by several households. At set times, these premises become religious spaces where pastors and their followers hold prayer meetings, sermons, and other religious activities. The location of these churches is transportable. A number of reasons might lead the group to search for a new meeting place, but chief among them are inability to pay the rent, conflict arising with the compound dwellers, or simply a steady increase in the group's numbers.

Members of these movements meet both in the day and at night; vigils are enacted weekly, often complemented by special vigils, for example, around Easter, at the end of the year, or in the face of pressing national or communal problems. The leaders of these revival churches, called pastors, and their congregations alike also claim to worship the Christian God (*Nzambe*), and great value is attributed to the Holy Spirit (*Molimo Mosantu*) and the Bible, both in its materiality and concerning the message it spreads. These smaller churches, which are, via the *maboke*, the object of this study, seem to have outranged the Catholic Church in the public sphere. Many leaders of the revival churches have become media stars, and their words are received with much authority. That is not to say that the Catholic, Protestant, and Kimbanguist leaders have lost any credit. Yet the media-savvy charismatic leaders are undeniably much more present in the cityscape, in ways both visible and audible. For example, up until August 2009, near Kinshasa's largest football stadium, a poster of approximately 3 by 1.5 m displayed General Sony Kafuta Rockman in front of an enthusiastic crowd, which was apparently extremely moved by the mere presence of the man. Some were crying, while others were visibly full of admiration for the general, who, facing the passers-by, was inviting the Kinois to attend the Big Crusade (held in 2003) in which he promised to heal, bless, and offer solutions to all kind of problems. Apart from such large posters, without which I cannot even imagine Kinshasa anymore, oft-repeated announcements on the radio and on Kinshasa's television channels draw Kinois to smaller and larger events organized by charismatic groups. Electronically amplified songs and predications, which travel beyond half-open compounds and at times disturb one's sleep, have become the acoustic background of the smaller streets in Kinshasa's townships. These practices firmly anchor the charismatic pastors and their groups within the city in a way that Catholic, Protestant, and Kimbanguist groups are unable to match. Although the three mainline churches also have their own radio and TV stations, the persuasion strategies of the charismatic groups are much more effective because of their omnipresence and multitude.[6]

Revival churches started to mushroom in Kinshasa in the mid 1990s. During Mobutu's time, these church groups operated underground in fairly limited numbers due to political prohibitions. When Mobutu, in a dramatic sense, acknowledged having failed to offer the Congolese economic stability, the churches started to flourish. The appeal and meaning of these churches is fundamentally anchored in the end of Mobutu's power regime (Devisch 1996; De Boeck 2004). Moving from the underground to the center stage, these churches are inherently related to the new political era, the economic crisis, and the search for new meaning.

At the turn of the millennium, many of these charismatic Christian churches grouped themselves in a platform called Eglises de Réveil du Congo (ERC, Revival Churches of Congo).[7] The Combat Spirituel foundation (Church CFMCI) headed by Elisabeth Olangi Wosho, better known as "Maman Olangi," is probably the most notable church to participate in this network. Strictly speaking, Combat Spirituel is a foundation. The difference between "foundation" and "church" is not clear, and for most Kinois, Combat Spirituel is Kinshasa's best-known revival church. This foundation has its own mega-church in Limete, but there are many chapters in Kinshasa as well as elsewhere in Congo and in Europe. The other mega-churches are the Army of Victory (Armée de Victoire), led by Pastor Kutinho; the Amen Church (Eglise Amen), headed by Bishop Mutombo; and the Army of the Eternal (Armée de l'Eternel), a church created and coordinated by Sony Kafuta. These churches also have their own private radio and television channels, often carrying the name of the church so that identification is easy (e.g., AmenTV, or Kafuta's channel RTAE—an abbreviation for RadioTelevisionArmée de l'Eternel). They have well-known orchestras and invent new songs, dance movements, and shouts (see Pype 2006), which are also performed at religious meetings of other, smaller revival groups.

The revival churches display great variety concerning their relation to the political establishment, the necessity of economic action to achieve divine blessing, and their views on the most suitable purification rituals (e.g., in the case of child witches). One can even question whether it is apt to speak of a "revival movement" as such. Paul Gifford (2004), who has studied Pentecostal-charismatic churches in Accra and encountered similar variety, prefers to write about "the charismatic scene" in order to avoid the impression that this religious field constitutes one homogeneous unity.

While it was impossible for me to attend all churches that are part of the ERC or even to visit all churches that designate themselves as revival churches but do not hold to the ERC platform, and acknowledging the fact that Pentecostalism lends itself to idiosyncratic interpretations, some generalities can still be made about the revival churches. Full membership in these churches occurs after having been baptized in the spirit and in water. Participants are promised wealth, health, and prosperity if they obey the pastors' instructions and remain in their vicinity. These churches emphasize Jesus as one's personal savior; they profess the same idea of salvation and forgiveness; and they encourage thorough knowledge of the Bible (in particular the New Testament). Influenced by the charismatic movement within the Catholic Church, the revival churches insist on spiritual gifts (such as the gifts of healing, speaking in tongues, and prophecy) that Christians receive from God. They encourage trances and "falling in the spirit" for the individual to connect with the Holy Spirit, while exorcism and anti-witchcraft rituals reflect the urge within these movements to purify the body and the community.

Another feature is the role of the pastor (*Pasta*). *BaPasta* are perceived to dispose of a preferential relationship with the Holy Spirit, who bestows spiritual powers and knowledge on them, in particular to fight witchcraft. Pastors thus possess charisma (*charisme*), a quality that sets them apart from ordinary people (Weber 1947). These pastors prove their unique status by prophesying, divining, faith healing, and performing miracles. In Chapter 5, I will discuss the charismatic features of the pastors more in detail.

I encountered many difficulties gathering information concerning the scope of these smaller churches in Kinshasa. In an interview with Bishop Albert Kankienza, leader of the ERC platform, and General Sony Kafuta, leader of the ERC's council of wise men, I was informed of a census taken in 2005, which recorded 12,000 member churches in Kinshasa. The accuracy of this number is questionable, in particular because I could not lay hands on the census results. Alexandre Matangila (2006: 78), who conducted a small statistical survey in Kinshasa's communities, gives a more modest impression of the number of revival churches in Kinshasa: he counted over 3,000, of which only 391 were officially members of the ERC platform. Even orienting ourselves to Matangila's more modest number of revival churches, then, it is clear that these churches are numerically significant in the city.

Defining a "Christian"

Hard statistical material about the number of revival churches was not the only information I had difficulty obtaining. The exact definition of these churches and, for that matter, of "a Christian" posed another problem, not least because the churches go by various denominational names such as evangelical, messianic, Pentecostal, charismatic, and so on. An ongoing struggle as to who is "a Christian" and who is not often comes to the fore when the plurality of Christianity in Kinshasa is mentioned. Conversations with born-again Christians compelled me to examine the self-definition of Christians, and I took this opportunity to gain a glimpse into emic categorizations of Kinshasa's Christians. In an article in which William Garriott and Kevin O'Neill (2008: 389) advocate for an "anthropology of Christianity" in its own right, the authors contend that it is methodologically innovative to pay attention to this semantic issue. The way the word "Christian" (Li. *mukristu,* Fr. *chrétien*) is used in Kinshasa does not at all reflect the Western hegemonic understanding of "Christians," and it urges us to acknowledge both the variety within a society that identifies itself as Christian and also to study the conflicts that emerge out of the competition. In Kinshasa, the members of the revival churches designate themselves as "Christians" (*chrétiens*) in contrast to the *Catholiques,* the *Protestants,* and the *Kimbanguistes.* Although from time to time my informants indeed called themselves "*pentecôtistes,*" "*charismatiques,*" "*nouveau-nés*" (newborns, i.e., born-agains), they above all claim to be "*bakristu*" (Fr. *des chrétiens,* Christians). Members of the revival churches accordingly attempt to monopolize the definition of what it is to be "a Christian." Among these "Christians," much debate is ongoing about the right definition of "who is really a Christian and who is not."

Overall, the main competition seems to be one between Catholics and born-again Christians. Kinshasa's revival church leaders and their members imagine themselves primarily in opposition to Catholicism. They call Catholics "children of the mother" (*bana ya maman*) and contend that the Catholic esteem of Mary is nothing less than veneration of a human being.[8] For born-again Christians, this belief conflicts with the acknowledgement of the one and almighty God. Furthermore, unlike in Catholic churches, where babies are baptized a few weeks or months after birth, a "Christian" is expected to choose Jesus as a conscious adult and must receive a calling or an awakening.[9]

From the perspective of those belonging to the mainstream churches (in particular Catholics and Protestants), the Pentecostal-charismatic churches are derogatorily called *binzambe-nzambe,* meaning "churches of the small Gods." This expression points at the weight the revival churches give to spiritual agencies based on beliefs that some of the Pentecostals' adversaries deride as mere superstition. Exactly because their teachings emphasize spiritual actions, some leaders of Kinshasa's charismatic churches have at times been accused of possessing mystical, destructive powers. Although one might expect that such suspicions about pastors' morality may lead Kinois to abandon these churches, this is hardly the case. By contrast, these kinds of stories can even strengthen these pastors' reputation for being liminal, transgressive figures with a privileged entry into the supernatural worlds.

The revival churches distance themselves from independent African churches such as the healing church Mpeve ya nlongo (church of the

Holy Spirit). Born-again Christians denounce these churches as too much in line with ancestrality. Kimbanguism is refuted on the grounds that the born-again Christians do not accept a substitute for Jesus, while Kimbanguists believe Simon Kimbangu to be Jesus's reincarnation. This internal rivalry depicts uncertainty as to the limits of cultural extraversion.

Signs of the Apocalypse

Probably the most important characteristic that all revival churches share is a strong belief in the demonization of quotidian life and an invisible battle (*lituma ya molimo,* "a spiritual fight") between God (*Nzambe*) and the Devil (*Satana*) (see De Boeck 2005a). This fight, which affects human beings, involves demonic entities—witches—and their opponents, Christians. Death is omnipresent, and the world is in the grip of Evil. De Boeck calls this "the apocalyptic interlude," which he describes as follows:

> Life for most in Kinshasa situates itself in this interlude in which Satan fully reigns. For some others, the world has arrived at the end of the thousand year day of judgment and thus at the moment in which Satan is briefly released again. Thus, the popular understanding of the Apocalypse very much centers on the crack of doom and the omnipotent presence of Evil, thereby contributing to the rapid demonization of everyday life in Kinshasa. (De Boeck 2004: 98)

Kinshasa's Christians perceive signs of the Apocalypse everywhere, and they experience reality as being dominated by the Devil. Christians should not fear, because the Bible and their spiritual leaders promise that they will be saved on the final day. Chapy, one of my informants, who finished an undergraduate course in theology during my fieldwork and led a chapter of a revival church, believed, for example, that the European Monetary Union and the growing ecumenism are foretold in the Book of Revelation. He followed international news with a particular eye for the Israeli-Palestinian debate, which, according to him, is the clock of the world and of its crucial spiritual battle. "As soon as fighting between these nations ends, the Apocalypse will enter into its final stage," he told me.

Despite frictions between the different Christian denominations, adepts of all types of Protestant, Catholic, and other Christian churches share this apocalyptic view. The following account of an event that occurred during my fieldwork indicates that Christians do not always agree among themselves as to the content of Christianity (whether more adapted to an African local system or remaining closer to the Western Christian ideology). Nevertheless, the commonly shared background of the spiritual combat between God and the Devil, and the imposition of an apocalyptic time frame structure these disputes. At one point in a later stage of my fieldwork, my host family and I were watching a televised talk show called *Zoom*, which was aired live on CanalKin at around 4 P.M. A major, wearing his military uniform, was the principal guest. Behind him were seated some soldiers, also in uniform. Next to the major lay an open trunk revealing a pile of rather old-looking books. The major held some of them up for the audience to see, and some pages were filmed in close-up. He explained to the show's host and viewers that these books proved that the kind of Christianity that was propagated by the "white men" (*bamindele*) was in fact the Devil's lore. He did not clarify how he had gotten his hands on these books, and this question did not seem to bother those present in the studio, or the viewers who called in to ask questions, or even the people with whom I was watching the TV show.

During the show, many viewers, surprisingly mostly men, called in. The first caller refuted the value of the major's words, saying that the military man himself might be active in the occult world. The following caller lambasted the first one, pointing out that if he did not enjoy the show he simply had to switch channels. This caller congratulated the major for his courage in demonstrating that "Africans need their own religion" and "should resort to their own God." He passionately admonished the audience that the Devil operates on all levels, even the highest level of Christianity. The last caller was a woman who repeatedly yelled "*Au nom de Yésu*" ("In the name of Jesus") through the phone and told the major he needed to be delivered from demonic spirits. She concurred with the first caller on the occult dealings of the military man.

This program was televised several times, and many people talked about the major. People disagreed about his assertions, and debated as to whether he was on God's side or not. From then on, the same man quite regularly appeared on the Kimbanguist television channels (RTK and RATELKI). His discourse about Africans turning away from the "white Jesus" toward African Christian prophets meshed well with the independent Christian ideology of Kimbanguism. This anecdote indicates that Kinshasa's Christians sometimes disagree on the "right" type of Christianity, but the Christian God and the spiritual battle between God and the Devil are never questioned.

The apocalyptic imagination thrives on a whole set of social and spiritual oppositions. Aligned with God are Good and Order, while the Devil is associated with Evil and Chaos. The good-bad paradigm thus coincides with the order-disorder paradigm, which also dominates more long-standing autochthonous beliefs (Bekaert 2000). *Kimia* refers to peace, order, calm, tranquility, and control, while *mubulu* means conflict, chaos, turbulence, rebellion, and violence. *Kimia* constitutes an ideal, both on the level of society at large as well as within an individual's social world, thoughts, and bodily disposition; *mubulu,* however, should be avoided.

On a more material level, filthy environments are said to be spaces where the occult might thrive, whereas cleaning up and removing rubbish are acts that not only create order in the physical world but also discourage demons, it is said. The same dualist scheme also indicates social categorization: women, children, and youths are more easily identified with turbulence and chaos than men. Marriage ends youth, the chaotic stage of life.

Replies to greetings are framed within the paradigm of order and disorder: one either replies with *kimia* ("order," "peace") if everything is fine; *mwa kimia* ("a bit order," "a bit peace") if things are somewhat satisfactory; or *mubulu* ("disorder") if the person is facing difficulties. Children who are too energetic and have difficulty obeying their elders are said to be *mubulu* (disorderly, chaotic) or "children of the Devil" (Lingala Singular, *mwana ya Satana*).[10] Persons who make no effort to reach a consensus when in conflict, or who go their own way without consulting others as to appropriate behavior, are (often jokingly) compared to the Devil, who similarly does not seek to harmonize his interests with those of others. Furthermore, Christians will frequently, even in daily conversation, say "Amen" when they agree with a statement. These are only a few examples of how Christian thinking influences sociality and how the scheme of the spiritual battle is used to inspire thoughts, actions, and discourse.

Two Worlds Colliding

The realm of God (*mokili ya Nzambe*) and the realm of the Devil (*mokili ya Satana*) are thoroughly distinct. For simplicity, and following my informants' terminology, I will frequently refer to these opposed worlds as "divine" (*sacré, divin*) and "occult" (*occulte, ténèbre*). My use of the concept of "the occult" is thus opposed to what Henrietta Moore and Todd Sanders (2001) recommend. Following Peter Geschiere's remark (1997: 13–15) on the difficulty of translating "witchcraft" and "sorcery," Moore and Sanders (2001: 4) discard both because in the Western mind they evoke only negative images and associations. In their opinion, the term "occult forces" is more neutral and "leaves open the question of whether the force is used for evil or for good." Harry West and Todd Sanders's concept of "occult cosmologies" suggests the same impartial approach toward the hidden. They define it as "systems of belief in a world animated by secret, mysterious and/or unseen powers" (West and Sanders 2003: 6). In emic discourse in Kinshasa, however, *le monde occulte* encompasses experiences, actions, people, and thoughts of the negative, the detrimental, the troubled, and the grim moored in a hidden underworld. In that local context, "occult" powers are by definition harmful and bad and therefore often associated with (destructive) witchcraft. Another oft-used concept, "occultism," has a particular meaning in Kinshasa: it denotes Freemasonry, Rosicrucianism, and other secret religions that sprouted in the West and were introduced in Kinshasa via colonialism. Therefore, when dealing with Kinshasa's context, the concept of the "occult" is not neutral at all. In this book, I prefer to use the concept "occult" in the same way as my informants do, that is, to denote demonic, wicked, and spiritual activities, agents, and symptoms.

Apocalyptic ideology, as professed in Kinshasa's Pentecostal churches and reflected in religious performances, is heavily inspired by indigenous beliefs, which are reinterpreted within an apocalyptic Christian grid. De Boeck writes:

> In Congo, as elsewhere in Africa, there has always lurked, in a rather unproblematic way, another reality underneath the surface of visible reality, and the crossing from one world into the other has always been easy to effectuate, even though it could sometimes prove to be dangerous. Today, however, within the specific time-space of the apocalyptic interlude, this, "second world," increasingly seems to push aside and take over the "first world" of daily reality. (De Boeck 2004: 69)

Two tropes emphasizing the interconnectedness between the otherworldly and the material world recur in Pentecostal discourse. First, the Devil works in secret and hides his actions, it is said. Consequently, Christians are called upon to pay utmost attention to certain signs that might reveal the diabolical nature of persons and events. The slightest remarks, abnormal behavior, look in the eyes, or irregularity in one's clothing is warily perceived and interpreted along the lines of the divine or the occult. Second, Satan is considered an imitator who not only has created an exact invisible copy of terrestrial reality but tries to lure human beings by means of copies of things that are vested with demonic power. Accordingly, the trope of secrecy is complemented by the powerful idiom of "the true" and "the false." Kinois people constantly question whether prophets, banknotes, jewelry, or even partners are "false" or "real." The "false" may appear in the form of these characters or items, but it remains the fruit of the Devil, who uses it to destroy the earth and humanity. Here, it is assumed that the copy is not merely a copy but possesses the maleficent power of the copier.

In mid-July 2006, for example, as Kinshasa's inhabitants approached the first organized democratic elections, they witnessed how street children (*bashègue*) looted the compound of one of the city's most popular singers and, about a kilometer southward, the church of one of Kinshasa's notable born-again Christian leaders. Musical instruments were destroyed or stolen, a fire was set, and the children plundered the prophet's private rooms. City dwellers and the media agonized over this sudden outbreak of violence. In particular, they were apprehensive about the loss of authority on the part of the local musician, who was held in social esteem and considered the sole person to have sway over the street children. Most attention, however, was directed at the loot discovered in the church: children were shown on television with condoms and pornographic videotapes they had found there. Unsubstantiated reports told of weapons being found and circulated as well. For some, the emergence of these facts was perplexing: was one of the city's most acclaimed and popular Christian leaders a "false pastor" (*pasta ya Satana,* Fr. *faux pasteur*)? For others, these rumors confirmed exactly what had long been suspected.

Confusion and doubt—not only about the integrity of Pentecostal Christian leaders, but also about the spiritual identity of ordinary citizens—abound in contemporary Kinshasa. People state that it is rather difficult for ordinary human beings to understand who and what is connected to either the divine or the occult. Only "those with four eyes" can see in the physical world. These are people who have privileged vision due to a special connection with the invisible. This type of "sight" does not imply the actual seeing of the invisible; rather, other senses and sensations are involved in receiving knowledge about the otherworldly. Significantly, several pastors and a "traditional" healer (*nganga*), people belonging to two categories known to have a privileged capacity for vision, told me that the invisible origins of persons are revealed through the feelings these persons arouse rather than through visually perceptible signs. A particular intuition informs the astute observer that "this one is with God" or "the other one is with the Devil."

A young man initiated into the occult world explained this with reference to a fashion in clothing during the time of my fieldwork: there was, he pointed out, a noticeable increase of the color red in people's clothes. Fashionable red was inserted into local theories of color. This perpetuates more autochthonous significatory mechanisms, as for most

Kinois the color red refers to blood (Bekaert 2000: 307–330, Devisch 1993: 65–69). In apocalyptic ideology, red is understood as a sign of blood sacrifices. Blood reminds many of the sacrifice of Jesus, who willingly died for the future Christian community. It can also hint at blood sacrifices demanded by the Devil. It is argued that the Devil demands both the physical as well as spiritual shedding of blood. In a physical way this happens, for example, by way of bodily incisions (*nzoloku*), indicating human sacrifice, but also by means of the sacrificial offering of animals, such as chickens. Apocalyptic dichotomization persists in the attribution of meaning to clothes: some people wear red shirts, it is said, as a sign of their belonging to the dark world, referring to sacrifices they have made to the Devil. In such cases, red clothing functions as a device to communicate with those active within these nocturnal activities; others might of course wear the same shirts simply because of the dictates of fashion. The *nganga* told me that he could discern between those who were active in the occult worlds, and those who were not. For those who have only two eyes, such things are imperceptible.

These phenomena manifest an uncertainty as to the boundaries between so-called "occult" on the one hand, and, on the other hand, "divine" phenomena and experiences. "*Mayele esili!*" "There is no knowledge anymore!" Kinois state when discussing this entanglement. The spiritual uncertainty is rampant all over contemporary sub-Saharan Africa (Tonda 2002; Ellis and Ter Haar 2004). Joseph Tonda (2002: 21), writing about this semiotic crisis in central Africa at large, poses the question: "How to discern between the people of God, and those of the Devil or the witch in the imaginaries of faith, beliefs and power?"

Stephen Ellis and Gerrie Ter Haar (2004: 191) understand the current religious renewal in Africa precisely "as an effort to end this spiritual confusion." An emic discourse prevalent in Kinshasa's churches would vouch for this explanation of the mushrooming of Pentecostal-charismatic Christian churches in the city: in order to transcend the perplexity, born-again Christian leaders promote a "spiritual knowledge" (*bwanya ya Nzambe*, Fr. *la sagesse spirituelle*). This is described as a wisdom that derives from a privileged connection with the holy. As a *pasteur* said during a sermon: "If you are a son or daughter of God, then you must know things. He who is a child of God knows, for example, that the way a certain person provokes me is not normal. If you are not a child of God, then you will never know." Remaining in the vicinity of a pastor, seeking his advice on the morality of others, and also limiting oneself to the Christian popular culture are all practices held to transmit this spiritual knowledge. This will be explored in more detail in the following chapters.

There is more firmness concerning the particular spiritual value of certain places. According to the Pentecostals, particular places in the city favor the interaction between the visible and the invisible. In the Pentecostal imagination, Kinshasa's cityscape is dotted with mystical spaces that are inhabited by impure spirits or by the Devil himself. Chiefly, rivers, cemeteries, and the bush are the preferred loci of occult agents. These relate to more autochthonous imaginations of the interplay between the material and the otherworldly. Five other categories of places are also readily identified by Kinshasa's Christians as being mystical: sites of religions that have no Pentecostal-charismatic character; places of *La Kinoiserie;* places that are easily associated with "tradition" and "custom"; places related to politics (like the house of parliament or the president's residence and workplace); and educational institutions (universities and institutions of higher education). Kinois who do not publicly identify themselves as born-again Christians share the beliefs that political and educational institutions are spaces where evil spirits connive, but they deny the occult character of the first three categories. The leaders of Pentecostal-charismatic churches, however, repeatedly mention the occult character of these three spaces in their discourse. This selection reflects the major preoccupations of born-again Christian leaders, inasmuch as they desire to increase their power by devaluing their opponents: other religions, "traditional" practices, and the major attractions of urban life.

Significantly, the mapping out of occult spaces in the city does not necessarily mean that Christians do not frequent the places that are identified as demonic spaces. They do, but the apocalyptic ideology imposes consciousness and expectation of the potentiality of evil when wandering in the city. Most of my Christian informants stated that they pray much harder and are more vigilant when setting foot in suspicious places. Collective prayers may transform the demonic quality of a particular place, as described in the first chapter when people sang Christian songs and ritually cleaned streets and roundabouts where various car accidents had happened. A place like the Rond Point Victoire is impracticable to avoid in driving through the city because it connects the main roads and it is a public transport hub. When moving around at this square, stepping from one bus into another, my informants would invariably walk very quickly to the buses. They did this not only because crowding made finding a seat very difficult, but because they were convinced that people with "bad intentions" dwelled in this place.

Even more important than the notion of Kinshasa as a space crowded with demons and witches is the representation of the domestic world as the ultimate locus of occult invasion. Sermons, witch testimonies, and proselytizing serials emphasize that the house and the compound—the two places where people sleep, wash, and eat—are favored places for the Devil to lurk. As a consequence, sociality in the street and the compound consistently reveals a measure of concern with regard to the assumed spiritual activities of those in the vicinity. When new renters arrive in the compound, they are closely observed for some time in order to interpret their behavior and determine where they should be placed within the categories of "Christian" or its other, "the pagan." This same cautiousness also explains why strangers—anyone who is not known by the family—are rarely invited into the home. Instead, they are made to wait outside, where the reason for their visit may be discussed: "you never know who has sent this person to you," my host in the Lemba household warned me.

Witchcraft, or the Extraction of Life

What exactly witchcraft is, and how it should be defined and recognized, are issues that often escape city dwellers. They understand their own position in a world where visible and invisible realities interact, and the individual disposition within the social and the spiritual is embedded within the interplay of material causality and the action of uncanny forces.

I believe it is in the first instance discursive acts such as confessions, rumors, and diagnostic interpretations made by pastors and other experts of the invisible that make the witchcraft phenomenon "real." That is, it is exactly in the act of interpreting signs, and voicing the interpretation, that witchcraft is constructed. Through a close reading of the Bible and its adaptation to Kinshasa's daily reality, the revival churches offer the Kinois a particular interpretation of the concept of witchcraft (*kindoki*) that, as I show below, is rather far removed from endogenous understandings of witchcraft. This resignification of witchcraft is not a new process. It started during the early years of the Christianizing mission,[11] and probably also even before the Christian missions. The witchcraft concept has recurrently been subject to semantic change. According to Geschiere, the capacity of the witchcraft idiom to be adapted to new contexts is exactly what explains its pervasiveness in urban Africa (1997: 10, also Moore and Sanders 2001: 11–13). A genealogy of the discourse about witchcraft in Kinshasa falls beyond the scope of this book. Meanwhile, the polyvalent and elusive nature of witchcraft renders it difficult, maybe even impossible, to give a complete overview of witchcraft beliefs in the city. Here, I only analyze the current discourse about witchcraft as Pentecostal Christians and their leaders used it during the fieldwork period. We must approach their presentation of witches, fools, and pastors, and thus of witchcraft and the occult, as intended constructions. It is probably in such a particular (re-)presentation of witchcraft that we see how, quoting Bayart (2005: 137), "the imaginaire is first of all an interaction"—not only an interaction between past, present, and future, but also "an interaction between social actors" (ibid.). Born-again Christians do not live in a vacuum and do not invent the metaphors and images of witchcraft. Their (re-)presentations of this material depart from the existing dominant imaginary, which they present in a particular fashion that sustains their own agenda.

For born-again Christians in today's Kinshasa, witchcraft refers to occult forces (*kindoki* or *nguya ya Satani*), opposed to the divine force (*nguya ya Nzambe*), which is embodied in and distributed by Christian objects and persons like pastors. In the logic of these born-again Christians, witchcraft, perceived as the outcome of evil spirits, withdraws life (*bomoyi*) from the body, whereas the Holy Spirit imbues the praying Christian with life. Since Christianity, all witchcraft has become criminal witchcraft.

Before we move on to the definition of witchcraft, the notion of "life" needs some more exploration. According to Pentecostals, the person consists of a material body (*nzoto*) and a soul (*molimo*). The soul, which is closely related to one's shadow, connects the individual with the invisible realms of the world via an invisible force, "life force" (*bomoyi*) or, as born-again Christians explained, the "breath" (*mopepe*) or the "wind of life." The idea of life force, or vital flow, forms an integral part of Congolese ethnographies.[12] Health, emotions, desires, well-being in general, strength, virility, courage, contentment, character, and sentiment are all related to the absence or presence of the life force (Devisch 1985: 126; De Boeck 1991: 197–198; Creten 1996: 413; Stroeken on *moyo* among the Sukuma 2001: 102). This vital force permeates everything—rain, plants, human beings, objects—and "weaves" (Devisch 1993) or "knots" (De Boeck 1991) life and lives. All living entities are set in a strict hierarchal structure, depending on the amount of life force they possess.[13] In addition, it is exactly this life force that links kinship groups to the ancestral spirits. This vital force is explained as being endowed by God, and passed on to individuals through both God and the ancestors (Devisch 1985; De Boeck 1991: 197–199; Bekaert 2000: 194). *Bomoyi* is then transmitted physically, through both paternal semen and maternal blood. As a consequence, it unites father's and mother's matrilineages. In this way ancestors and elder relatives occupy an important place in the individual's vitality. It is believed that through occult work such as cursing and witchcraft practices, these elders can withdraw the "life" of their descendants. Indigenous healing cults then aim to restore the flow of life, often appeasing ancestors and elders who have blocked the smooth transmission of *bomoyi*.

Kinshasa's born-again Christians (and followers of other independent Christian churches in Congo as well) attach great importance to this vital force. In their parlance, it is closely related to the "power of God" (*nguya ya Nzambe*). Both the life force and God's power are transmitted through the Holy Spirit. According to Allan Anderson (1991: 9), it is the ready correlation between the life force and the Holy Spirit that has rendered the diverse spirit-type Christian churches highly popular and influential in African societies. Yet the diverse Christian churches that give the Holy Spirit a central place in their doctrine and practices reflect a variety of interpretations of the concept of the "Holy Spirit." Dealing with Kinshasa's churches of the Holy Spirit, Devisch (1996: 556) postulates that rituals and discourse in these churches clearly indicate that the Holy Spirit has replaced the role of the lineage ancestor. Born-again Christians refute these churches of the Holy Spirit precisely on the grounds of their too overt link between the Holy Spirit and the ancestors. Pentecostal Christianity demonizes tradition and associates ancestrality with witchcraft. They therefore denounce matri-centered healing churches and charismatic churches of the Holy Spirit as being involved in ancestral worship. For Pentecostals, the Holy Spirit is disconnected from ancestors, and in their rituals and discourse they are careful not to show clear links with ancestor-related traditions.

Pentecostals state that God gave and gives physical and spiritual life by blowing "wind-breath" into human bodies. My informants referred to the Bible when explaining this to me, but these thoughts also echo long-standing local beliefs. During prayers, I often heard, one can feel how the Holy Spirit enters the room or even the body. A "strong wind" (*mopepe makasi*) fills the room. One informant told me that this wind is sometimes so powerful that one is struck down.[14] Every day, Pentecostals must breathe in a spiritual way in order to stay alive spiritually. If not, they lose touch with the spiritual life-source and become zombies. "Zombies" (Sg. *elima:* image, shadow, *mobutwa*—literally: someone from the night) are human beings whose souls are monitored by evil spirits. They walk around like "living dead," because their soul has been extracted from their bodies (*molimo na ye etambola na nse*). They are not considered to be "real," for their spirits are located within the occult, where only "the false" dwells. Born-again Christians distinguish, thus, between the physical breath that keeps a body alive (*mopepe*), and a spiritual breath (the wind of God, *mopepe ya Nzambe*), which gives life to the soul. Everybody receives physical breath at birth, but exposure to spiritual wind, which is only possible at the age of consciousness, is achieved through the baptism of the Spirit and the water baptism ritual.

Turning back to the Pentecostals' understandings of witchcraft, I gathered that *kindoki* is an umbrella noun at once indicating both the use of witchcraft power through techniques (*fétichisme*) like poison and charms, and the possession of witchcraft power inherent in one's body. In the latter case, merely having evil intentions or thoughts can set occult forces in action. All witchcraft upsets social and personal bodily orders because it gives the occult the opportunity to intervene. Christian leaders repeat that witches and demons install "antennae" in households to gather private information, which the Devil's accomplices use to bring these families down. This will eventually also destroy humanity as a whole. Their large and devastating project, however, begins with the individual, whose soul they are after. It is said "witchcraft is in the blood" (*kindoki eza na makila*), and witches try to capture the blood because "life" resides in the blood. "They eat life" (*bakoliya bomoyi*). This eating idiom or vampiric act is perceived as a spiritual attack: consuming one's blood in the spiritual world equals stealing one's soul.[15]

Young Christian Kinois refer to the Bible when queried about how *kindoki* (witchcraft) entered into the world. One of my informants (Chapy) spoke in the following way about the origin of witchcraft:

> The Devil lived with God in heaven, where he was the angel of the light. He sang for God's glory and therefore was God's chosen angel. As such, he was very close to God and learned all the secret knowledge. At a given moment, however, he became arrogant and craved for more and more power. God chased him away and threw the Devil down to earth, but the Devil took his secret knowledge with him and started to use it, not to do good but to destroy humanity. The other angels who followed the Devil became demons, and sirens are angels who fell in the water when leaving God's world.

The explanation given by born-again Christians as to where and how witchcraft entered the world differs radically from what has been witnessed by ethnographers of autochthonous societies. Mary Douglas (1999), for example, in writing about the Lele in the Kasai region, noted that for the Lele, God made witchcraft, and thus installed death, at the demand of a Lele chief. This chief was supposed not to tell anyone, but he revealed the secret to his friend, and thus the knowledge of witchcraft spread. Douglas (1999: 181) writes: "As God is one, the world is one, knowledge is one, so it follows that the sorcerer taps into the same channels as the priest and the diviner." In contrast to the Lele world as described by Douglas (or by other ethnographers of Congolese societies before Christianity altered religious and social life), for contemporary Christian Congolese the world is not one but dual, and the origins of their knowledge about the Otherworld—and thus the powers of both sorcerer and priest (or, better for Kinshasa's setting, *pasteur*)—are not the same. Inasmuch as the world is the arena of the battle between God and the Devil, some human beings and events are related to the second world and are life-taking instead of life-giving.

MacGaffey (1986), Devisch (1993), De Boeck (1991), Bekaert (2000) and Van Caeneghem (1955), in their discussions of magic and witchcraft among the baKongo, baYaka, Aluund, baSakata, and baLuba, describe a structure similar to that noted by Douglas: diviners, healers, priests, and even customary chiefs possess and/or use the same divine power for good and bad purposes. In this autochthonous perspective, all four religious categories possess and master the power of witchcraft; however, whereas magicians and priests can apply it to heal and the chief deploys it on behalf of the community, the witch's witchcraft benefits the witch him- or herself or satisfies personal grudges. In this logic, *kindoki* can heal and kill, give life, and sow death.

Experts of the Occult and the Divine

The new boundaries drawn between witchcraft and divine power in the apocalyptic imagination create a partition within the categories of bearers of invisible knowledge: specialists of the occult are opposed to experts working with God's power. The strong distinction between "the good" and "the bad" introduced by Christian missionaries, which erased the ambiguity of spiritual forces, has also led to an absolute split between so-called "Christian" and "occult" experts.

The main human agents of the occult are the witch, the magician, the diviner, and the "traditional" healer. It is said that all these agents "have one father: the Devil" (*Baza bana ya tata moko, tata na bango diable.*). *Ndoki* (witch, Fr. *sorcier*) denotes any person working with occult spirits, consciously or unconsciously. A witch bewitches others: he or she captures the spirit and eats souls. These witches transmit a maleficent power (*kindoki*) through the senses: food, clothes, beverages, and the touch that takes the soul of the one who accepts the food, drinks the beer, inhales the bewitched perfume, and so on.

Féticheur (*nganga*) refers to either a diviner (*ngang'a mbangu*) or a "traditional" healer (*nganga n'kisi*). According to Christians, the knowledge that diviners and "traditional" healers possess is "false" and stems from the world underneath. The latter is known to use *nkisi* (fetish objects), which according to "traditional" thought are said to heal or give power. Born-again Christians, however, contend that these *nkisi* do not heal but rather are demonic substances. Using them establishes a connection with the occult world and inserts the individual into a reciprocal relation with the Devil. The category of the *ngang'a n'kisi* dominates in Kinshasa's popular culture, where they are sought for healing, gaining money, attacking rivals, and attaining other goals. The other category of experts, the diviner, can read horoscopes and predict the future. This particular imagination of the diviner is interesting, since "traditionally" divination was more oriented toward an explication of the past. The insertion of horoscopes, a non-Bantu practice, emphasizes the modernity of witchcraft beliefs.

Magic (*soloka* or *likundu*) is considered to be the highest dimension of all occult practices and knowledge (*la haute sorcellerie*). Magicians (*moloki*) can transform someone into a bird, provoke car accidents, or kill people in another way. It is also believed that magicians can easily travel to the different dimensions of the dark worlds. Each magician allegedly governs over a *nganga* and a *ndoki* (witch). Therefore, as was explained to me, magicians do not hide their work or knowledge: they know their power dominates both the physical and the spiritual world. By contrast, an *ndoki* does not dominate the earth and accordingly must hide his or her identity. A magician can operate at any moment and in any place, but an *ndoki* is limited to the night and confined to filthy places, the preferred locations of evil spirits.

It is argued that diviners, magicians, and *féticheurs* have acquired their occult knowledge and power through special initiation. It is furthermore believed that all witches have an occult power located in the belly (*libumu, likundu*). Although *féticheurs*, diviners, and magicians need to learn incantations, the use of herbs, and other techniques, they are unable to perform anything successfully without this substance in the body to connect the visible to the invisible world. Clovis, a Cinarc actor and a pastor in training, declared: "In Europe, witchcraft can be learned through books. Here, one becomes a witch through eating something. One can know how to sing incantations, but if he has no *likundu*, his acts will fail to work. The substance in the body functions as an antenna between our world and the occult."

Yet there is another idea of magic that, more than any other local definition of witchcraft and magic, refers to the colonial encounter. It was a common thread in discussions with informants that magic (*magie*) as such had originated in the West but was brought by colonists and missionaries to Congo. People often mentioned the secret societies of

Freemasons and Rosicrucians, reputed for their tentacles in academic, military, and political circles. Mobutu has been suspected of partaking in these circles, which are identified as demonic worlds where the occult law exchanges blood sacrifices for material success (wealth, power, authority, beauty). New Age spiritualism and popular culture on witchcraft (such as the Harry Potter films and the American TV series *Buffy the Vampire Slayer* and *Bewitched*) are also very popular in Kinshasa, and one can expect that these media products have enlarged Kinshasa's Christians' imaginings about Western magic.[16]

On the other end of the spectrum we find the "Christian" leaders. And in this domain too, expertise and roles are differentiated. The differentiation follows carefully the biblical order as explained in Ephesians 4:11–12, "So Christ himself gave the apostles, the prophets, the evangelists, the pastors and teachers, to equip his people for works of service, so that the body of Christ may be built up."[17] People working for God, spreading his word, organizing prayer meetings, and performing miracles are generally called "*pasteur.*" Although some pastors call themselves archbishop, bishop, or reverend, or use other denominations, Kinshasa's Christians remain familiar with another typology among Pentecostal-charismatic leaders: important persons are categorized as prophets, evangelists, pastors, teachers, and apostles. These denominations hint at the dominant activities of the spiritual leaders: God's men and women are known cover a wide range of spiritual work.

A prophet[18] (*mosakoli*), who is sent by God to warn people about things to come, is blessed with the gift of prophecy (*bolakeli*). An evangelist (preacher, *mopalanganisi*) speaks about the Bible in public, climbing onto buses and into taxis, speaking into microphones at busy roundabouts, and explaining God's word in churches and during mass-mediated programs. A pastor (Fr. *berger,* or Li. *mobateli bapate*), when used in its strict sense, is a spiritual leader who groups people around him and offers them personal spiritual assistance (*mobateli* stems from *kobatela*, to protect). A teacher (*docteur*) serves as a crisis manager within the Pentecostal community: when conflicts within churches or between churches arise, this spiritual teacher is called upon. The final category, the apostles (Fr. *apôtre* or Li. *apotolo* or *mosangeli*) are perceived as the "builders" of the Christian community. They speak about Jesus in places where Christianity has no stronghold. In Kinshasa's context, this refers to certain neighborhoods reputed for their many "traditional" healers or to spaces where prostitutes work, as well as to Kinshasa's outskirts, where practices such as ancestral cults have a lively following. Having laid the basis of a church, the apostle invites pastors and evangelists to continue the work in that particular area. As most of these spiritual leaders enter the private households of Kinois and have groups of followers, the general word used to indicate all these spiritual leaders is "*pasteur*," which stresses the intimate relationship between the religious authorities and the community.

Both the so-called "occult" and "Christian" categories of experts can be consulted to obtain money, wealth, a good job, a lover, or a child, or to fulfill other material desires. Christian discourse, however, has it that *féticheur*s work with demonic spirits, in contrast to pastors, who work with the Holy Spirit. The impure spirits are said to capture the souls of human beings and give them a double life at night in the immaterial realm of reality, which is a reversal of their lives during daytime. The Christian interpretation of these *féticheur*s as life-takers is unsurprising when reading, for example, MacGaffey's statement regarding the four adult religious roles (chief, priest, witch, and magician): that they "all yield their power from the dead" (MacGaffey 1986: 6–7).

To conclude this exposé of experts of invisible worlds, I want to point to the categorization of "customary chiefs" in the apocalyptic imagination. Among Kinshasa's born-again Christians, these leaders are perceived as possessing occult forces and working together with witches and diviners. Nevertheless, I heard several accounts of "traditional" chiefs who are members of charismatic churches. It would appear paradoxical, within a cultural logic that quickly diabolizes whatever aspires to "traditional" powers, that "traditional" chiefs could be Christians. Many, even close relatives of customary chiefs, assume they leave their occult objects at home when they attend services, so that they will not be unmasked as demonic. My own questions—put to these chiefs about the pairing of their identity as "traditional" chiefs and the discourse of the charismatic churches—were met with silence or radical denial. One "traditional" chief (of Luba origin) told me he visits only Catholic churches without a charismatic signature and of the Christian teachings accepts only the Ten Commandments. He also refuted the belief that the ritualistic objects and his enthronement as a chief had vested him with occult powers, since, in his words, "We all worship the same God."

A Christian Key Scenario

Kinshasa's contemporary teleserials are deeply engrained in this apocalyptic imagination and partake in the resignification of experts, witchcraft, the soul, and urban sociality through the lens of the spiritual battle. The following is a synopsis of one serial, *The Devouring Fire* (*Le Feu Dévorant*), produced by Cinarc and broadcast on TropicanaTV in Kinshasa in late 2003 and early 2004.

The serial deals with the private problems of four "newborn" Christians who occupy important positions in a young, Pentecostal church. Caleb receives the discomforting news that he may not be the real father of his daughter. Paco is crushed between, on the one hand, a custom that obliges him to marry his cross-cousin, who lives in the village and whom he has never met before, and on the other hand, the romantic love he feels for Belinda, a city girl. The third protagonist, Chapy, has violated the taboo of premarital sexual intercourse, seduced by his future spouse, who has become pregnant. For Victor, life becomes difficult when a girl from the church seduces him just as her parents enter the house; they wrongly accuse this young spiritual leader of having seduced the teenage girl, and his reputation declines thereafter. After three episodes, when the audience indicated a preference for Paco's story line, the Cinarc troupe decided to weaken the other three subplots to allow the difficulties of Paco and ethnic marriage preferences to come to the fore. Pentecostalism demonizes such customs, and in the serial the village girl is shown as possessed by evil spirits, as are Paco's parents, who insist upon this practice. To complicate things, the city girl Belinda falls victim to the occult practices of Paco's relatives. She perceives apparitions of witches and eventually is bewitched. Paco nevertheless continues to pray and keeps a "strong spirit."

As the story unfolds, the families of the four Christian leaders and their women begin to deal with personal problems ranging from physical uneasiness to domestic chaos. Both "traditional" healers and Western medical doctors are consulted, but they are unable to solve the problems and illnesses that confront the protagonists and their family members. Time and again Paco, on his way to evangelize people, meets the ill and their desperate family members and friends. Each time, he positions himself next to the body of the unconscious victim and shouts, pointing constantly at the ill person: "*Satana, bima.* I say leave this body. Oh, *alleluiah. Nzambe. Alleluiah.* Jesus, the Holy Spirit, the Almighty. Chase this diabolic spirit." Miracles invariably happen: Demons leave the bodies, and without pills or herbs, the ill get up and walk away.

Paco's colleague, Julien, who has witnessed all the events in the households of the four, preaches in Paco's paternal home about the incestuous nature of certain customs. Through his divine power, Julien heals the blindness of Paco's father (an affliction visited upon him through the evil spirit that possessed him) and converts this old village man to

Christianity. As a newborn Christian, Paco's father can no longer thwart his son's desire to marry Belinda. The final scenes of the serial are devoted to the marriage.

As in the *Devouring Fire* narrative, Pentecostal TV dramas polarize good and evil. This opposition is symbolized in the spiritual battle played out by Christians and demonic agents like witches and demons. The following rather extensive quotation of Brooks is key to an understanding of how close Brooks's definition of the melodrama is to the Kinois apocalyptic experience:

> We find there an intense emotional and ethical drama based on the manichaeistic struggle of good and evil, a world where what one lives for and by is seen in terms of, and as determined by, the most fundamental psychic relations and cosmic ethical forces. The polarization of good and evil works toward revealing the presence of God and the Devil and their operation as real forces in the world. Their conflict suggests the need to recognize and confront evil, to combat and expel it, to purge the social order. Man is seen to be, and must recognize himself to be, playing on a theater that is the point of juncture, and of clash, of imperatives beyond himself that are non-mediated and irreducible. This is what is most real in the universe. The spectacular enactments of melodrama seek constantly to express these forces and imperatives, to bring them to striking revelation, to impose their evidence. (Brooks 1976: 12–13)

According to Brooks, who analyzed the symbolic structure of the melodrama in nineteenth-century France, the representation of a clash between good and evil stems from a desire to understand the real, which itself is hidden and masked. He condenses "the main *raison d'être* of the melodramatic mode as to locali[z]e and to articulate the moral occult" (1976: 5). We could argue that the same holds for Kinshasa's Pentecostal evangelizers, whose melodramas point out that the occult is fostered in the urban interpersonal sphere. Matrimonial conflicts, adultery, the search for a good spouse, rivalry between church members or even between Christian leaders, loss of a job, and unruly offspring are some main themes of Kinshasa's TV serials that reflect the hardship of social and economic survival in a precarious urban African society and thus are interpreted as the outcome of occult workings. The fictional characters are rooted in the urban universe: teenage schoolgirls, Christian pastors, relatives who arrive from the village, colleagues, fellow members of the Christian congregation, diviners, magicians, and "traditional" healers dwell in these fictional worlds. Yet the "real" identities of these fictional characters stem from their connections with the divine or the demonic.

During the narrative evolvement of the Pentecostal melodrama, the protagonists are confused about how to understand the misery that suddenly befalls them. In this they strongly resemble Nigerian witchcraft films, of which Larkin (2008: 190) writes, "Society, as it is depicted, is comprised of people who appear to be one thing and are revealed to be something else." The puzzlement over the "real" intentions of the serials' characters, their hidden agendas, and the spiritual nature of their powers reflects the uncertainty and bewilderment Kinshasa's denizens experience every day. To counter the uncertainty, pastors are staged as the new culture heroes, the only strongholds in society that can counter evil and occult attacks (Pype 2010).

Intergeneric Dialogues

The evangelizing teleserials do not stand alone in Kinshasa's popular culture. Rather, they dialogue immediately with sermons and religious music video clips, and in terms of narrative and visual style they often strongly resemble Pentecostal music video clips. But probably the genre closest to Kinshasa's TV dramas is that of Nigerian witchcraft films. Local television serials copy titles, characters, plots, and even visual effects from popular Nigerian films (Pype forthcoming b).

Pentecostal TV dramas also reference ethnic epics and myths. Although many of the proselytizing TV actors are unfamiliar with ethnic texts, names of some tricksters (e.g., MoniMambu, Pype 2010) appear in the evangelizing *maboke*. The appearance of ethnic tricksters in Kinshasa's television serials is not so surprising, since the Christian *maboke* are not far removed from the essence of Congo's epic tales. Daniel Biebuyck, who analyzed the Mwindo epic of the baNyanga (eastern Congo), wrote that "The interconnection between terrestrial and supernatural events and the interaction between the hero-chief and the divine are essential to the epic" (1978: 61). Transposing the figures of trickster and hero-chief to those of the witch and hero-*pasteur* captures the main significance of the *maboke* as they were produced in Kinshasa around the turn of the millennium. The emphasis remains on the tension between the visible and its counterpart: the Cinarc character Mambweni is a female witch, someone who can look into the invisible world. She initiates her children into the dark secrets of the invisible realm. More importantly, the TV serials offer insight into the manifestations of the invisible world through a skillful use of the new medium's *trucage* techniques (special effects and other ways of manipulating images). Ethnic epics and Christian teleserials thus share the emphasis on social and spiritual transgression (see Pype 2010).

Kinshasa's proselytizing artists downplay the similarities between ethnic tales and their own *maboke*. For them, the Bible is the most important narrative source of inspiration. The Holy Book, now the sole ground on which all born-again Christians judge and interpret reality, inspires Christians during rituals and guides them in their daily life as well. Conversations with young Kinois are permeated with references to the Bible. *"Bible alobi"* ("The Bible says") frequently introduces a reference to a particular biblical passage that may clarify certain statements in a conversation or explain actions. Furthermore, Scriptural references abound in Kinshasa's public space: one reads, for example "2 Corinthians: 10, 5" or "Jeremiah: 29, 11" on the walls of compounds, on taxis, on television (often placed in the left corner of the screen), at the entrances to shops, and so on. Stickers bearing biblical phrases are sold around town, and people paste them to dashboards ("Jesus is the sole protector of this car"), on books, and around their homes. Most often, these biblical words are used as protection against occult attacks. In other instances they are testimonies of God's acts or demonstrate one's Christian identity.

One might even notice that, nowadays, biblical verses are used in the way proverbs used to be (Jewsiewicki 2004). The actors in Kinshasa's melodramas also refer constantly to Scripture. They throw out phrases such as "Leviticus: Chapter 3, verses 4 to 7," both in the fictional narratives and when talking about their serials. Regularly, as certain fictional characters read the Bible, the camera zooms in on the passages read. Pentecostal TV actors furthermore frequently blend customary proverbs and biblical verses in the serials. Examples include *"Nde bible aloba: 'Vérité nionso eza ya koloba te'"* ("The Bible says: 'One should not say always tell the truth'"), or *"Bible alobi: 'Kolya na mwasi, kolya na ndoki'"* ("The Bible says: 'Eating with a woman is equivalent to eating with a witch'"). Although these expressions are strategies to trigger humor, the insertion of proverbs into a biblical frame highlights the dominant authorial voice the Bible occupies in Kinshasa.

The television serials also display spillover from public testimonies (Sg. *botemo*). Former witches and, to a lesser extent, their victims are invited to church compounds and into television studios to talk about how they were introduced to the dark world, what their mission was, how they communicated with the Devil and his demons, and how they managed to abandon the dark world and accept Jesus. Many similarities between public testimonies and the serials are evident in their structure. The internal organization of the testimony narratives resembles the plotlines of the teleserials, and public testimonies are often told in episodes. Former witches usually spread their accounts over several evenings. Furthermore, actors in the locally produced serials state that the material for plotlines is not invented but inspired by witches' public confessions. This correlation between confessions and teleserials is not uncommon in African visual texts; Meyer (1995: 251) has noted a similar approach toward these products of popular culture in Ghana: "Although that visual product is not a direct confession, for the audience it amounts to one."

To Conclude: (Re-)Presenting the Apocalypse

I understand the discourse employed by Pentecostal Christian leaders about the world and its people as nothing less than a fundamental reorganization of mimesis.[19] "Mimesis" is here taken very broadly as the interpretation and representation of all kinds of signs, perceptible both to the eye and via other sensory modes. In Kinshasa after the turn of the millennium, Pentecostal leaders steer the ways in which people should read the world, how human beings are situated within the Real, and how reality can and should be represented. In the cognitive dimension of mimesis, the perceptive mode of "being in the world" and "understanding of the life world" is emphasized (Maran 2003). According to Jean and John Comaroff, this reorganization of mimesis (or, in their terms, "the ongoing re-evaluation of signs," 1993: xxii) has consistently been a feature of African creativity. They understand poets, prophets, and even witch finders "as experimental practitioners: they try to make universal signs speak to particular realities … whose activities produce a particular consciousness: they shape the ambiguity of the postcolonial condition into techniques of empowerment and signs of collective representations" (Ibid.). The Christian spiritual leaders and the proselytizing artists can well be understood as experimental practitioners who produce an apocalyptic consciousness. This apocalyptic frame advances a particular understanding of the world that locates the "real" meanings, events, and entities in the Otherworld. In turn, this understanding enforces the idea that the interpretation of signs—including sensations, dreams, desires, and other modes of being—happens by relating them to the invisible. Here is mimesis constructed: similarities between the tangible and the immaterial are recognized and interpreted accordingly. Here is the city cursed.

Referring back to the serial *The Cursed Neighborhood*, summarized at the opening of this chapter, I would emphasize that the religious *maboke* occupy a paradoxical position within the apocalyptic experience of urban life in present-day Kinshasa. The serials reflect the dominant mood and interpretation schemes offered by pastors and so voraciously accepted by many Kinois. Yet at the same time the serials also add to the apocalyptic experience, since the repetitive act inherent in any genre production reinforces the beliefs in the workings of demons and witches. In other words, in representing (or diagnosing) the urban life-world as a *cursed* space, the evangelizers are precisely *cursing* the city and also its residents.

Still, I want to point out that the Pentecostal ideology at large is something that is still being fashioned: it is a belief system in the making, under construction and certainly not (yet) fine-tuned. An example of the ongoing reorganization of mimesis is the resignification of the concept of the "ancestors" (*bakoko*). Pentecostal leaders demonize all "traditional" knowledge, customs, and rituals, but Kinois are nonetheless puzzled about the spiritual destiny of their deceased family members. Here we encounter the imbalance documented by Douglas (1999: 179) almost half a century after her initial field work among the Lele: "Forty years later, memory of the past culture had gone out of balance: everything that was part of it was reduced to sorcery and judged to be bad; nothing of the old beliefs was good. Even the ancient lore of herbs and symbols was condemned."

Some say that those ancestors who did good deeds and did not cooperate with the Devil during their lives have joined God in His kingdom. This represents a continuation of older beliefs about the dead, for not every deceased person could become an ancestor. Only those who had led morally good lives—those who might be models for the continuation of the group—became ancestors. Others, however, believe that all ancestors reside with the Devil because their power was derived from occult objects (*fetishes*) and supernatural alliances. The latter are sure that these ancestors are in the earth (*mabele*), living with the Devil and his demons. *Pasteurs* and other spiritual leaders provide another explanation: according to them, the ancestors are together with the spirits of the recently deceased, waiting for the Judgment Day. When that time comes, the spirits will learn whether they will be allowed to go to heaven or sent to hell. The hesitation about the location of the ancestors or the customary chiefs (as mentioned above) in the good-bad paradigm shows the extent to which the "Pentecostal imagination" is unstable. Most Pentecostals agree on the main principles of diabolic work, pastors' efficacy in countering demonic witchcraft, the miraculous, and the primacy of the almighty Christian God, but other topics, such as ancestrality and the distinction between the soul and the spirit, are not clear to many. This ambiguity produces space for creativity and improvisation and consequently leads to variety within the Pentecostal scene.

The uncertainty is both symptomatic of a larger spiritual confusion that Christian experts seek to solve, and self-perpetuating via the production of revelatory genres such as the Pentecostal melodrama and sermons. Evangelizing teleserials themselves sometimes present this uncertainty over the "right" representation and interpretation of things and phenomena. After all, even for the proselytizers themselves, apart from the Bible there is no complete handbook they can fall back on when teaching about the Apocalypse. An erroneous statement or impression may slip in. Furthermore, while much of the production itself—the filming, sound, light, and text—may be in the purview of the Christian drama group, the final editing is done in the studio by the TV channel's personnel. The Cinarc leader attempted to control the editorial work, but at times other obligations prevented him from directing the cutting and pasting of the footage.

A compelling example in this regard is the interpretation of a special effect that symbolized the soul. In the Cinarc serial *The Maquis Boys and Girls,* trucage was used to show how the witch Monica attacks a young Christian girl during the night. By means of a special effect, a glittering star appears to emanate from the besieged girl's forehead. When I watched this episode with Ance, one of the youngest Cinarc actors, he told me the image editor had made a mistake. "The soul does not reside in the head, but within the heart," he explained. Furthermore, one's soul is usually represented as a copy of one's physical appearance. I learned that Bienvenu had not assisted in the editing of this episode and did not seem to care much about this minor mistake. I, by contrast, did not take it lightheartedly because here I had come across a crack in the apocalyptic message. I looked in vain for the image editor and later found out that he had moved to South Africa. He had not been fired, and his mistake had gone unnoticed by many, though fortunately not to Ance.

I take the editor's mistake as meaningful. Inspired by MacGaffey's ethnography of the baKongo (1986), I conjecture that the image editor might have been influenced by "traditional" Kongo thought, which locates the soul in the forehead; furthermore, Kongo statues represent the soul as a circular or a rectangular metopic spot. "Such shapes are sometimes also called stars, and the soul is said to be like a shining star" (MacGaffey 1986: 124). This "mistake" reminds us of the fact that both the *maboke* and the Pentecostal imagination are "emergent" narratives. A general frame inspires pastors and Christian actors to represent the Apocalypse discursively and visually. Filling in the details means allowing individual preferences for certain themes and personal interpretations, but it also brings along the risk of minor mistakes, such as insertion of the symbols of other worlds. In the end, though, this "filling" up the gaps does not seem to be very prickly: as long as the Christian God finally wins the battle and the Christian protagonist is rescued, then "unchristian" traces are excused.[20]

Notes

1. In 1984, official statistics counted 2.5 million inhabitants (Institut National de la Statistique 1991). Between December 2004 and February 2005 the population was counted, but the results had not yet been published by the end of fieldwork (July 2006).
2. Although this music is often recorded in music studios abroad.
3. White (1998: 496) speaks in this respect about *la Kinicité*.
4. Original: "Cette ville a son coeur à Matonge. Toute sa chair et tout son sang, sa sueur, ses odeurs, et surtout son sexe fait de musique et d'interminables rumbas ; ... La nuit, je le ressens fortement comme tel, Matonge devient un sexe en érection, sexe d'homme ou de femme. Qui saurait ? mais sexe. Qui chante. Qui danse. Qui hurle parfois. Qui donne l'impression que toutes les maisons vendent la Skol et la Régla [two brands of beer], qu'on peut entrer, boire ou danser un coup, ressortir, lâcher dix zaïres, en lâcher dix autres, puis dix autres, puis dix autres, encore, et encore, et encore.

   ... Cette ville est une longue chanson, une longue présence de Tabu Ley et du tout-puissant Lwambo Makiadi [two of the city's most important singers]....

   Elle danse pour me prouver qu'être femelle n'est pas rien, et que l'être à Kin est savoureux. » (Tansi 2005–2006: 118–122)
5. Lambertz (2011) mentions the Church of World Messianity in Kinshasa as having 2,000 members.
6. Kamate (2009) offers biographies of Catholic and Protestant Christians in Kinshasa who also participate in meetings organized in revival churches and listen to and watch revival programs on religious radio and TV stations. One's first entrance into a charismatic group often follows a personal invitation by a friend or relative and also the witnessing of miracles performed by certain pastors on TV stations.
7. See Ndaya Tshiteku (2008) for an examination of the *Combat Spirituel* both in Kinshasa and in its chapters in the Low Countries (The Netherlands and Belgium).
8. Saints are neither revered nor prayed to in the revival churches.
9. This contrasts with the Christian rivalry in the neighboring Congo. Elisabeth Dorier-Apprill (2001: 298) observed a rejection of the name "Pentecostal" among the revival churches in Congo-Brazzaville. In Kinshasa, the historical link with the Pentecostal and established Protestant churches is never discarded.
10. Usually this gesture remains within the sphere of threats issued to children to get them to obey their elders. In a few instances, however, such intentions go deeper and may lead to submitting the children to exorcism rituals.
11. See Meyer (1999) for a diachronic discussion of how, in the context of Ghana, Christian beliefs were mingled with local Ewe principles.
12. The baYaka call this force *m-mooyi;* the Aluund speak about *mooy;* the baSakata denote it with *(k)énima.*

13. See the hierarchical scheme of the baKongo: MacGaffey (1986: 75).
14. Pentecostals nevertheless stress that the sensations of the Holy Spirit are individual and may vary in time and from one person to the next. One informant, for example, said he feels cold and starts shivering when the divine wind enters his body.
15. Witchcraft can also work in more cunning ways. Kinois believe that God has already counted the days he gives to humans in the world. It is believed that witches can steal a few of these years. There is no exact noun for this practice, but it is said that witches make their own calculations and know how many years they need to collect. By contrast, some *pasteurs* claim that they can prolong one's life on earth by a decade or even more.
16. Research on this topic remains to be undertaken.
17. I thank Allan Anderson for drawing my attention to this.
18. The category of the prophet has a long history in Congo's religious society and is thus not a product of the apocalyptic imagination (see MacGaffey 1983).
19. De Boeck (2004: 56–60) uses similar terms to discuss the penetration of the invisible in the visible, yet he describes it as "mimetic excess." From a semiotic-structuralist perspective, he explains the transformation of earlier belief systems into the apocalyptic ideology as a rupture in the links between signifier and signified. This is a semiotic crisis characterized by an increasing importance of death, the invisible, the double, the shadow, the image, or the symbol in daily reality (2004: 59).
20. With this discussion of a "wrong special effect," we have moved into the fascinating field of the meanings and the aesthetics of the invisible. These are the subject of Chapters 4 and 5.

CHAPTER 3

New Fathers
and New Names

*Social Dynamics in
an Evangelizing Acting Group*

Bob's Story

Bob Kabesa (age twenty-two), of Luba ethnic origin but born and raised in Kinshasa, told me how he first met Clovis Ikala and Bienvenu Touke-bana, the two leading men of the Cinarc troupe. Bob was staying with his eldest brother because their father had remarried and his stepmother refused to feed and shelter children of her husband's first marriage. Bob's sister-in-law happened to be Bienvenu's maternal aunt. Bienvenu paid a visit to this house, and the Cinarc leader impressed Bob. At the time, Bob felt unwelcome in his brother's house; he was also having difficulty paying his tuition and experiencing problems with his girl-friends. Bienvenu, apparently sensing Bob's turmoil, explained to Bob that several years before, he had lived through a difficult time, but now that he had God in his life he felt calm, and success was coming his way. Bob told me how Bienvenu's words had consoled him. He accepted an invitation to join the two men at their church, and rather quickly Bob became a member of the Church of the Holy Mountain, to which the Cinarc group was attached at the time; eventually he was baptized.

Bob had noticed the privileges that Bienvenu enjoyed thanks to his appearance on television: people offered him free rides, cheered him in the streets, called him, and sent their greetings. Observing this, Bob longed to join the Cinarc company and become a television star too. A year and a half later, Bob was known throughout town as "Johnny," his fictional alter ego. In our conversation, this young man mentioned several times how this meeting with Bienvenu, whom he considered a "big" man (*moto makasi, moto ya kilo,* "heavyweight person"), had changed his life. Since joining the revival church, Bob had moderated his love life, thus diminishing many worries. Furthermore, now that he had become a born-again Christian, his sister-in-law seemed less hostile toward him. More importantly, Bob's star status had attracted several people who gave him money from time to time, which he saved toward tuition for a university degree. By the end of my fieldwork, Bob had left his brother's house. He was renting a small house and had started his first year in economics at the Protestant University (UPC).

Bob's story reminds us that not all Christian TV stars enter a Christian acting company for religious reasons alone: it was more the privileges of celebrity status that appealed to him. As is true elsewhere in postcolonial Africa, the TV star is only one of the various new figures of success in post-Mobutu Kinshasa. The intellectual (*évolué*), which used to be the social ideal during colonial times and early independence, has been displaced by a whole range of new social heroes: athletes, musicians, politicians, people in the diaspora, religious leaders, and *Yankees* (people who become wealthy through cunning and illegal practices without facing punishment).[1] Television celebrities too occupy a central position in popular imaginaries of success in urban Africa (see Banégas and Warnier 2001; Behrend 2002). Appearing on television is perceived as a major route to success and personal achievement. As Nancy Munn has brilliantly described in her study of fame among the Massim society in Papua New Guinea (1986), fame extends a person's name apart from his physical presence; it "frees names from their particularities and offers a virtual identity to individuals in other times and places" (1986: 117).

For many young Kinois, the desire to become famous (*connu*) is fed by aspirations to social mobility—a longing to transcend their own life worlds, in which they experience a strong sense of limitation. They hope that, by becoming known throughout the city and beyond, they will gain access to a whole range of technologies that will allow them to make a better living. Bibiche, one of the Cinarc actresses, once told me that through the teleserials "I have made my name" (*nasali nkombo na ngai*).[2] Making a name (*nkombo*) primarily means extending one's social identity into the life worlds of people one does not know. Being known by others is an important strategy of self-realization. It is exactly the movement or the circulation of a name that constitutes fame (Munn 1986: 105–118), which then promises social success. In Kinshasa, it is commonly held that the more people speak about a person, the more chances that individual has to acquire money, a lover, and social prestige. Other benefits of being known include easier access to medical treatment, fewer difficulties with police officers, nicer seats on public transport, or even finding sponsors who will help pay for one's studies. Those aspiring to fame count on the fact that the broadcast images and narratives feed into "pavement radio" (*radio trottoir*) and can even accelerate the spread of gossip (*basonghi-songhi*), accordingly extending an individual's social radius and network. The "magic of the screen" (used in its Western sense) is so attractive that people speak about the *star-ization* of Kinshasa's inhabitants (fig. 3.1).

Kinshasa's young people make no distinction between genders when scrutinizing the appeal of a media celebrity. Although the public sphere is still masculine to a high degree, *vedettariat* (being a celebrity) also appeals to female youth. As early as 1974, Jean La Fontaine noted that the *vedette* was one of the new models of femininity that reigned in the young postcolonial city. While attaining the status of a media *vedette* was rather difficult at the time because of the limited number of local television channels, the situation is totally different thirty years later. Mass mediated talk shows and other programs in which people can participate are quite numerous, so achieving temporary or more permanent television fame is not that difficult. Many youth who join a music group or TV acting company also do this chiefly because it may offer an entry to the media.[3]

The goal of this chapter is to give more detail on the social networks of the young evangelizing TV stars and the identity dynamics, in particular the hierarchies, in an acting group. To do this, I will briefly interrupt the religious dimension of the drama work and shift attention to the intersubjective relations among performers, between TV stars and their

Figure 3.1. Cinarc actors and fans at the troupe's New Year party (2005, © Katrien Pype)

fans, and between television celebrities and religious leaders, which have much in common with the micropolitics of musical groups so well analyzed by White (2008). After all, both troupes and orchestras in Kinshasa are structured by the same social codes and strategies of authority and leadership that thrive in the city as a whole.

I have chosen to present the material through life narratives spoken by some of my key informants. This allows me to introduce the main protagonists of the research and the origins of the drama group. I will scrutinize the personal stories about their publicness, their motivations to join the evangelizing TV drama group, and the value of new relationships they have established as Christian TV celebrities. Interspersed with the narratives are broader analytic discussions of context and of the theoretical implications of the troupe's social radius. This will further our understanding of the diverse range of forms celebrity management takes, and it will also display the heterogeneity in Christian worlds. Attention will be drawn to the various kinds of authority (*bokonzi*) and social and cultural capital (Bourdieu 1980) that membership in a religious acting group imparts.

Another important theme is "belonging." Jeannette Edwards and Marilyn Strathern (2000) demonstrate that the sense of belonging and relatedness is vested in diverging modalities that range from "natural images" of "ownership" to loose contact-enabling chains. In the making of social worlds in Kinshasa, "natural" (based on blood relations) and "social" ("fictive") kinship are the basic units of belonging, but broader and less permanent networks and connections likewise construct and mediate a sense of belonging. These temporary relations do not always lead to clearly profiled social groups with a public identity or a genealogy. Yet Kinois persistently attempt to connect with others in a temporary manner, without necessarily obtaining a firm social position in the lives of these "contacts." Actors' contacts fall into two main categories: fans and sponsors (or patrons). It is therefore meaningful to differentiate between so-called families (Sg. *libota*) or communities (Sg. *lisanga*), and contacts (Sg. *bokanga, bosimbi*) as two distinct modes of belonging in Kinshasa. The notion of "family" (whether consanguinal or fictive) depicts a particular social group, whereas the term "contact" denotes a less firm attachment between individuals.

Bienvenu Toukebana: Setting Up and Managing a Drama Group

In 1999 Bienvenu Toukebana (then twenty-eight) founded a theater company called Cinarne (Cinéma-Arche-de-Noe), of which Cinarc

(Cinéma-Arc-en-Ciel) would later become an offshoot. At the time of founding Cinarne, this young man had just returned from a long stay in Lagos, where his mother had sent him abroad for five years. During that time Bienvenu engaged in petty trade, buying mattresses, clothes, soap, radios, and other goods to export to Kinshasa, where his mother sold these items on the market. While in Lagos, Bienvenu became intrigued by Nigerian film and quickly joined a group of actors whose skills, techniques, and themes he learned. Back in Kinshasa he tried to set up an acting company of his own, initially without much success. Things changed only after he had a dream in which God asked him for his help. Bienvenu would frequently repeat this dream narrative during television shows and at times when he sensed that his leadership in the troupe was threatened:

> God asked me to work for Him. He knows that I love television, and He asked me to work as an actor for Him. Through the serials, we can show people the goodness and the love of God. We also have to let people know that the Devil is among us. God loves us, but we may not cooperate with His enemy. The morning after my dream, I started to pray, and there God revealed to me the strategies to find good performers.

To recruit actors, Bienvenu spread the word in his community (Lemba), his church (at that time Arche de Noe, led by the Prophet Dennis Lessie), and on several television channels. He also invited his cousin Chapy, with whom he had been raised, and Jef Kabangu, his older half brother. Jef was born out of a relationship predating that between their mother and Bienvenu's father. The relationship had not lasted long, and after the breakup Jef's father took his son with him. During their childhood, Bienvenu and Jef knew of each other's existence, but they never met. Only when Bienvenu began Cinarc did he search for and find his brother, who immediately joined the project. Though Bienvenu is the troupe's head, Jef has much authority because of his blood relationship with Bienvenu.

According to the foundation narrative, Bienvenu's leadership is based on a call from the Christian God. His authority in the artistic association is therefore founded on this divine gift, and his leadership can be defined as "charismatic leadership" (Weber 1947: 328–349). Yet Bienvenu's account of Cinarc's history is contested by other actors. Cinarne, the original drama group, still exists today and produces *télédramatiques* for NzondoTV, the channel of the Prophet Dennis Lessie, with whom most of the Cinarc actors were initially affiliated. It is an important characteristic of *écuries* in Kinshasa to split when the popularity of the leader is contested by the popularity of another member. Unsurprisingly, the relationship between Cinarne and Cinarc is one of rivalry.

For those who consider Bienvenu the Cinarc leader, the way he has arranged his life is a sign of his rightful leadership. He is perceived as a courageous man (*un courageux*) who managed to create a group of followers—the members of his troupe and his fans. Although Bienvenu very successfully upheld the public image of a courageous man, he doubted about it himself. On one of the rare occasions that Bienvenu and I spoke alone together, he once asked me, "Katrien, do you think that I am courageous?" His question surprised me, and I could only answer in a positive way. I knew how much this question mattered to him, since in previous discussions Bienvenu had explained that the biblical Caleb was inspiring him. He wanted to identify with the courage and stubbornness of the biblical protagonist, seeing himself as a lonely proselytizer in a city full of sinners, much as in the world of the Old Testament.

But Bienvenu also played the role of a "patron" (*mokonzi* or *mopao*). And I certainly regarded him as "*un grand*" (a big person) because, along with all the Kinois, I noticed that Bienvenu was accumulating wealth. Only a few months before, Bienvenu had included me in negotiations to buy a Mercedes Benz from the painter Bodo Fils. This meant that he no longer had to rely on public transport to move between different filming locations or travel to the city center with the taped scenes. His dwelling had improved as well. At the beginning of the fieldwork, he and four younger relatives were sharing a two-room house at the back end of a tiny compound in Lemba Terminus, one of the community's most densely populated areas because of its low-rent housing. Bienvenu shared his bed with his younger brother and maternal cousin, while his two younger sisters slept on a mattress on the concrete floor in the adjacent, windowless room. The actors, who gathered nearly daily in the leader's dwelling space, could not all enter the tiny house; they always had to wait, either in the small open space of the compound or on the street. In 2006, when I traveled to Kinshasa for a final stint of fieldwork, I found him and a larger group of relatives in Lemba Salongo, a more prestigious neighborhood in the Lemba community. The new house, with three bedrooms and a private cooking area outside, was more befitting the leader's social status. It was also more practical, since the good-sized living room offered ample space for the core actors (usually eight to ten people) to eat or watch television while waiting for the shooting to begin.

Bienvenu was also a big man because of the group of followers (other actors and fans) he gathered around him. In Kinshasa, "big people" are *big* because of the "small people" (*petits*) that dwell in their social environment. Participation in *grands-petits* relations increasese the social power and esteem of both sides, patrons and clients alike, and networks of benefactors form through the forging of ties of patronage and dependency, often with lucrative consequences. In the time I had known him, Bienvenu had indeed become a big man, sheltering, feeding, and clothing his siblings and even members of his drama group.

When it comes to the running of the troupe, six other male actors with artistic seniority participate with Bienvenu in the *comité du directeur.* These are invariably unmarried young men in their early thirties, and they take the most important decisions with regard to the distribution of roles, internal disputes, and the choice of who is to represent the company on any particular social occasion or mass-mediated activity. Additionally, the other actors must request their permission for absences from prayer gathering or rehearsals, or to leave a shoot early. Other issues such as lack of money, health issues and spiritual difficulties should also be addressed to them, and here the elders decide what action the artistic association should take.

A larger committee, the so-called "*comité directeur élargie,*" is comprised of the "*comité du directeur*" as well as the most important actresses in the theater company. In practice, this group is never convened, and the impact of the actresses is therefore minimal. The remaining members of the troupe are subdivided into groups such as *les bules* (Hindoubill for *les bleus,* the new ones), also called *les balikili* (a military name for new recruits), and the "elder siblings" (*bayaya*). *Bules* are not paid for their work for the troupe. *Bayaya* are those who have been active in the company for some time; they may be younger than newly arrived members, but they have artistic seniority.

Social rules concerning deference (*bonkonde*), respect (*botosi*), and taboo (*ekila*), which structure social encounters in Kinshasa, also fashion intra-group relations. The troupe's leader requests total respect from the actors and actresses, and he is the only one who may punish and reprimand them. Troupe members usually address him with the title *président* instead of by his first or screen name. If someone shows him a lack of respect, he responds by withdrawing him or her from the screen for a few weeks, regardless of the importance of his or her role in the serial being filmed at the time. Both girls and the younger boys in the group must approach the older boys in respectful ways. Furthermore, with the principle of artistic seniority, those who arrived later in the group must be respectful toward those with longer membership in the troupe. Petty conflicts constantly arise when one of the actors gains more popularity by, say, playing a specific role that resonates at the moment, or creating a shout.[4] The most popular performers tend to neglect social rules of authority and respect, which threatens the harmony (*kimia*) and stability (*bobongi*) within the company. Bienvenu is therefore frequently obliged to take steps to reinforce his authority over these young people, whose sudden stardom can influence their behavior. Sometimes these decisions affect the *maboke:* due to intra-group strife, a fictional character can be written out of the script for several episodes or even the whole serial.

Bienvenu often repeats the Cinarc slogan during TV talk shows: "To win souls, educate them and send them out" (*gagner, former et éduquer*). A main step in this mission is to convert people to Pentecostal ideology. The Cinarc members seek to achieve this goal both through their serials (attempting to persuade and convince their audience) and by other means, such as conversing with those who attend their rehearsals, explaining the message of their serials on television talk shows, or inviting their audiences to attend their religious services. On an intragroup level, the Cinarc company welcomes all newcomers, even those who wish to join the artistic association primarily because of the promise of stardom. As Bienvenu told me, he cannot refuse anyone, since "all people should have the opportunity to be informed about the Word of God."

Because of the troupe's evangelizing project, novices first receive spiritual training from one of the troupe's members. Only after that do new members begin their artistic training, with the group leader himself. Three criteria are important for admission to the company: new members should be willing to pray according to the practices of born-again Christians, they must complete the spiritual training, and their artistic training must be successful. The process usually takes three months, and only the company's president will assess their aptitude with regard to the spiritual and the artistic fields. Members should be bilingual in French-Lingala, French-tshiLuba, or French-Swahili; proficiency in English is considered a plus. Since many novices are not fluent in French, the artistic association organizes lessons for them. Finally, the candidates must prepare three letters: one formally requesting the troupe leader's permission to join the group; one from a guardian acknowledging that his or her child is allowed to join the company; and one from the candidate's current pastor confirming that he or she is a "good Christian."

This emphasis on the Christian identity of the troupe's (potential) members does not exclude the role of ethnicity in recruiting new members for the troupe. All theater companies in the city and also their cultural products are undoubtedly influenced by some ethnic cultures to varying degrees. This often depends on the ethnic identity of the troupe's director. In most cases, the leader's ethnic identity attracts individuals of the same ethnic group, which inevitably shapes the troupe's cultural work. The Cinarc leader, for example, is of Kongo origin, while some of the troupe's more influential men have Luba roots. As a result, most Cinarc members belong to either the Kongo or Luba groups. Unsurprisingly, the Cinarc serials display a balance between Kongo and Luba practices: fictional characters frequently have Kongo or Luba names and speak kiKongo or tshiLuba, and the dances used in the serials are inspired by Luba or Kongo rites.

Family members often occupy the most important positions in these associations. In most theater companies (as in many other *écuries*), consanguinity remains an important tie determining the distribution of power within the group. In the case of Cinarc, the core of this troupe consists of consanguine brothers and cousins, and many actors complain that consanguine relatives receive the most important roles. Without exception, the leaders perform the leading parts in the serials, and because of this they become very popular with the audience.

The composition of the troupes reflects the patriarchal character of Kinshasa's society: women rarely lead theater companies (see figs. 3.2 and 3.3).[5] Cinarc, the Evangelists (Les Evangélistes), the Lions (Théâtre Simba), the Stars of Africa (Les Étoiles de l'Afrique), and the Trumpet (La Trompette) are the names of some of the troupes that appear on television, but generally these drama groups are better known as "the group of [the screen name of its director]." Some examples are the troupe *ya Caleb* (the troupe of Caleb, referring to the fictional name of the Cinarc leader), or *les baCaleb,* troupe *ya Muyombe Gauche,* troupe *ya Sans Soucis,* and troupe *ya Devos* (*les Evangélistes*). The second most popular actor in any artistic association is generally a girl or woman who often plays the wife of the director's fictional character.

Most performers have no prior artistic experience when they join a troupe. Though some artists are active in other types of cultural production (such as singing in a choir) or have taken part in cultural activities organized in their schools, they all have to learn techniques of improvisation and behavior in front of a camera. For this purpose, Bienvenu organizes rehearsal sessions over a period of several weeks at which new members can observe the dramatic work of the more experienced artists. When the junior members finally begin to act, the troupe's director corrects them.

An interesting evolution characterizes the roles allotted to new members. At first they are relegated to small scenes that disrupt the serials' narratives—commercial shots for commodities like shampoo and food,

Figures 3.2. and 3.3. Cinarc men in discussion while Cinarc actresses wait (2006, © Katrien Pype)

or for stores or firms with which the company's leaders have contracts—requiring minimal acting skill. In a following stage, the actor is permitted to play the role of a sibling or child of one of a serial's protagonists. Once the troupe's director is convinced that the new performer has acquired the necessary dramatic skills, he creates a leading serial role for this player. This move, however, frequently leads to conflicts with other, more established artists who fear losing screen time and thus social prestige.[6]

The transmission of artistic ability from the troupe leader to the actors establishes his identity as an artistic father and constructs the others as his artistic children. Yet the type of fatherhood exerted by a troupe's leader is not at all limited to the teaching of dramatic skills. The directors of drama groups help their "children" socialize, adopt appropriate conduct in the urban space, and train themselves for their future roles as adults. The company's leader takes full responsibility for his actors' behavior both on and off stage, the latter probably being the more time-consuming task. As a result, troupe directors strive not only to mold the actors' performance but also to influence their social lives, social environment, and behavior in public spaces.

Food and housing also fall within the artistic father's sphere of responsibility. Each morning, Bienvenu gives his eldest sister money to buy food and cook it for the actors. Without exception, all actors are entitled to eat in Bienvenu's house, even those who are temporarily suspended from the screen. In some cases, Bienvenu houses certain actors. Ance, for example, who lives in a street dominated by Bana Bolafa, one of Kinshasa's most notorious fighting gangs, regularly seeks refuge in his president's home when police and military men are out arresting any boys and young men found in the surroundings of the Bana Bolafa headquarters.

Actors can also seek refuge in Bienvenu's house for a longer period. Patrick, for example, was living with the troupe's leader during fieldwork. He saw his mother only during the weekly services at the Church of the Holy Mountain, just a few streets away from her house. Bienvenu took Patrick in after he found out about a new job Patrick had taken. Since the salary Patrick earned as a newly initiated Cinarc member was insufficient to cover the needs of his family, Patrick accepted a job offer in the casino at Le Grand Hôtel (one of Kinshasa's biggest hotels, located in the residential area of Gombe). As Christians hold this to be a place where money, alcohol, and prostitutes go hand in hand—a "demonic" triad—Bienvenu ordered his actor to choose between working for God or continuing to serve the Devil. If Patrick chose God, Bienvenu promised, he would take Patrick into his home and feed and clothe him. The choice was easy, and Patrick found new shelter. As a resident of Bienvenu's compound, Patrick performs all kinds of chores; he is Bienvenu's driver and is sent around town to pick up people or goods, and at times he also functions as Bienvenu's bodyguard. Bienvenu's concern about the social worlds in which Patrick moved thus inspired the troupe's leader to host Patrick. In order to keep Patrick away from a "demonic" world, Bienvenu had to offer his artistic son the means to move out of it. Providing for the spiritual security of his pupils is only one of the various tasks of social fatherhood that Bienvenu performs for his artistic children.

The use of kinship terms is not uncommon when members of a drama group speak of fellow actors and church members. This creates a sense of belonging and enhances their sense of participating in a genuine family outside of the household and extended family. Most of the group's members see each other on a daily basis. Their participation in the rehearsals and recordings, regular attendance at television talk shows, encounters with fans, and visits to friendly church communities are all activities requiring a significant investment of time on the part of the actors.

The performers are also expected to share in the activities of the church. Like all other religious communities in the city, the troupe's church has a rigid program of activities, and full membership requires regular participation in the church's spiritual work. Because of these numerous activities, participating in a troupe like Cinarc is a nearly full-time engagement that removes the young members for long hours from the sphere of their guardians and relatives. While working in such close relationships, the actors cannot help but be cognizant of their fellow actors' personal problems, and in response they offer advice and financial assistance and attend each other's family rituals (weddings, funerals, celebrations on acquiring a *bac* or other diploma, and so on). For such family rituals, festivities related to the Cinarc group, and public performances, the actors and actresses incorporate a uniform cloth in their attire to signal the relatedness of the troupe's members. Members who do not have the means to buy the textile on their own undertake much effort to gather the needed money. Appearing in regular outfit would mean that others cannot see him or her as a real member of the group.

Finally, as a real father, the head of a drama group also endows his children with new, fictive names. It is exactly by these fictional names that the dramatic artists are known throughout the city. The artists will use this fictional name in all subsequent serials, regardless of the content of the narrative or the particular role their fictional character embodies.

Fiston "Chapy" Muzuma: From Rapper to Pastor

In an evangelizing drama group, an artistic father is often also a spiritual father (*tata ya Nzambe*). This is the case for the Cinarc group, in which Bienvenu has preached God's word to most of the actors. But for several Cinarc members, it is not Bienvenu but Chapy, Bievenu's maternal cousin, who is more of a spiritual father. Since Bienvenu is so involved in the serials' production process (writing scenarios, supervising the production of the serials) and public relations, he has delegated the task of caring for the newer members' spiritual welfare to other Cinarc members who are actively engaged in church activities. These actors, Chapy among them, are sometimes much younger than members put in their spiritual charge, but their ardent faith and intense engagement in the group's church accord them the status of spiritual elders. At times during the rehearsals, I witnessed how actors would turn to elders who would heal them by laying their hands on their heads or aching body zones, while the others continued to practice or take instruction from the president. Members could in fact discuss any physical afflictions and social problems with these spiritual fathers at any time.

Chapy wielded much authority over the other Cinarc members because of the training he was undergoing to become a pastor. He was by far the most ardent Christian of the Cinarc group and very frequently reprimanded other actors when he suspected them of unchristian behavior. The fire with which Chapy spoke about the spiritual battle was ignited by a personal tragedy, as he explained to me in a chain of interviews on his conversion. Here I produce a condensed version of his narrative.

> When I lived with my father, I prayed with him in the "*église apostolique*," a traditional church.[7] I already had God in me. But the moment my aunt took me into her home, she no longer allowed me to pray in that church. I returned to the world, for I was looking for freedom without responsibilities. You know, I was really a *moto ya mokili,* a man of the world. I used to be a rapper, and like the musicians of the world, I wore big shoes, I had an earring, and I was consistently talking in a violent way and with lots of gestures. I even straightened my hair. We had our rehearsal space in Kingabwa, and we were very popular with the girls—we had girlfriends all the time. And we sang like the American singers: about love—sexual love—drugs, and violence. Only when Bienvenu asked me to join Cinarc did I quit the band. But even in the serials I still liked to perform the role of a musician.
>
> At the age of 20 I enrolled at UNIKIN [University of Kinshasa]. We rented a house along with two other male friends, but the two others did not study much; they were always inviting girlfriends to visit. These girls looked for men. I had a fling with one girl from Mbanza Lemba by the name of Hélène, but I did not feel strongly for her. You know, even

our landlord asked us what we were doing: we were there to study, he reminded us. And you know, being students, we just answered "*Etali yo te* [none of your business]. As long as we pay you, you have nothing to say."

For Chapy, the moment when God spoke to him came after this girl-friend had an abortion. Because he and Hélène were "not stable" (meaning that they had no money, were not married, and did not have jobs), they were convinced they could not keep the baby. With some of his friends he brought the girl to a clinic in Kingabwa, where she had to stay for three days.

First, with one of the two friends, I visited a *féticheur* who lived in King-abwa. He started with incantations and, having asked me the name of the girl, he wrote it down on a piece of paper. He told me to bury this paper near a toilet. It had to stay there for three days. Afterwards, we would see that the pregnancy would disappear. It was a sacrifice for the Devil. We were not allowed to sleep during these three nights and had to refrain from eating during the daytime. The girl never knew that we visited this man because we did not entirely follow his prescription. That is also why the pregnancy did not go away. A few days later, the girl visited me and told me she had to have an abortion. She begged me to pay for it but I had no money. I remember the difficulties I encountered in trying to find the right amount. Then we went to a hospital in Kingabwa. This was the district that I knew best, as my rap orchestra rehearsed over there. The nurse was really nice. She helped us in committing a sinful act. She calmed us down and really helped us. The second day after the operation I was still looking for money although I had to pass an exam at university. Because of what happened, I could not attend the exam. I really suffered a lot to find the money, fifty dollars. A friend of mine even gave me a pair of new shoes so that I could offer them as a guarantee for the money that had not yet been paid. I never brought the remainder of the money, so the shoes have stayed there. I had to buy lots of medicines. I was really afraid that she would die. When Hélène got back home, she told her parents that she returned from a *matanga* (funeral ceremony)[8] of a family member of one of her closest friends. I urged her to take the medicines at my place so I could keep an eye on her. In the days she came to my place to take the medicine I started to think, and I told her I thought we had killed a human being. She started to cry. From that moment on I decided to abandon all sexual relationships with girls until I was married. Maybe God wanted me to "pass through" this moment, the better to "recoup" [*récupérer*][9] myself, because, as a child, I already prayed a lot but had gone back into the world.

As Chapy continued with his story, he insisted that nobody but those involved in this occurrence ever knew about it—no one except Clovis. Chapy felt ashamed, and during our talk he repeated several times that he had been an accomplice in the killing of a human being. He went on to say how and why he had informed Clovis about his biggest sin:

> It was when we were preparing our second serial. God talked to me through someone else. During our prayer session on Thursday evening, one of the actresses who no longer worked with us received a message from God saying that He would elevate us, that He wanted to talk to me. He had also informed her that I felt remorse and that I should talk to a *moto ya Nzambe* (a man of God) and confess. Only then would I be calm and succeed in my work. I was already working with the troupe and evangelizing at the time. But my mind kept on returning to what had happened a few years earlier. I started to speak in tongues—so heavily that Clovis, who guided the session, had to calm me down. After the prayer session, Clovis called me. I told him that I felt like the Devil was obstructing me from really praying, and I confessed. Since that day, it is as if God has forgiven me because it does not come to my mind any more.

It was obviously very difficult for Chapy to tell me about this sin. He still tried to block it from his mind and wanted to keep the information limited to as few people as possible. Even Bienvenu, his cousin and, according to Chapy his spiritual father, did not know. At the end of the interview he told me that whereas his story would in fact be good material for public confessions and for use in evangelization campaigns, he did not know if and when he would ever be able to speak about it in public. He referred to two Cinarc serials, *Apostasy* and *The End Times,* and the roles that the Cinarc actress Gemima had played in them. In both serials she is made pregnant by a false prophet and, with the man's financial assistance, has an abortion. In *Apostasy,* she loses her ovaries and becomes sterile as a consequence of the abortion. She meets with death in *The End Times.* So, Chapy concluded, the high stakes of this sin are clearly demonstrated in the serials and, in a way, his story has already been made public. Chapy's sinful life is the source of much shame, but his experience has also helped him persevere in his current endeavors: "It was a path that God had prepared for me. Now I can explain to youngsters in a very convincing way that alcohol, girls, and music are not good. It is where my energy and strength comes from. When I am with people of my age who do not walk with Jesus, I understand them. I have been there."

Chapy's narrative exemplifies the metaphorical boundaries that born-again Christians reproduce in their own biographies. As a (born-again) Christian, one has access to several realms of belonging: first, one or more local Christian communities; second, the larger Christian community in the city; and third, and very importantly, a global Christian community (cosmopolitan identity). For Kinshasa's Pentecostal youth, it is the first and second levels that are important. The notion of "community" I employ here is inspired by Anthony P. Cohen (1985), who defines it as a symbolic and contrastive concept. Cognizance of community resides in a sense of togetherness that depends on the consciousness of a boundary that marks one social group off from another. These communities and boundaries exist in people's minds and are constructed in their discourses and practices. The major practice that signifies membership in the Christian community is the ritual of baptism. City dwellers are also linguistically classified into contrasting categories. The first such dualism is that of "Christians" (Sg. *mukristu*) versus "pagans" (Sg. *mupagan*). In contrast to what one might expect, the children of God are identified not only through their personal beliefs and actions but also by the social world they live in. Those living with people who do not follow God's word, it is said, dwell with dead people and, accordingly, invite death into their own life and body.

A second set of categories divides the Christian community itself into "carnal Christians" or "Christians of the flesh" (*chrétiens charnels,* Li. *ba-chrétiens ya misuni*) and "real Christians" (*bachrétiens ya solo*). The first category is said to make up the majority of Kinshasa's Christians. Although these people attend the religious prayer gatherings and sing Christian songs, they are not entirely walking along Jesus's path. According to some Christians, these "Christians of the flesh" are "false Christians" and thus no better than "pagans." It is believed that the "carnal Christians" may well have Jesus in their life but continue to live according the "spirit of the flesh" (*selon l'esprit de la chair*). Such Christians are said to lie, drink beer, visit diviners, and have sexual relations before marriage, even though they attend church services and pray. Only when such people have completely given themselves to Jesus can renew their lives. Calling a person a "Christian of the flesh" is an insult, since it indicates that one does not consider the person to lead a morally acceptable life. Within the drama group, a few actors were often jokingly called "Christians of the flesh." These individuals consistently reacted in an emotional way and denied the insults.

A third distinction—"the old person" (*moto ya kala*) versus "the new person" (*moto ya sika*)—contrasts the personal past and present of individual believers. "Pagans are sleeping," it is said, for they are not leading a conscious life. Receiving Christ spiritually, that is, becoming receptive for the first time to the importance of the Holy Spirit in one's own life, is called "awakening" (*kolamuka*). In this way the Pentecostals draw boundaries not only in their society, in the world, and between Christians and others, but also in their private lives, between an "old," "pagan" self and the "new," "reborn Christian" self. When speaking about their lives before baptism, born-again Christians give the impression of talking about someone else. They speak of "*mon vieux X*" (*moto ya kala*), contrasting this person with a new phase in their life and with the "new person" (*moto ya sika*) they have become.

It is commonly assumed that becoming a Christian entails a thorough transformation of one's identity. This is reflected in the Lingala word for conversion: *bobongoli,* denoting transformation.[10] One's choices—of clothing, television programs, subjects of conversation, bodily behavior, management of emotions—are colored by this new Christian identity. Chapy's narrative shows how his lifestyle changed after he received Jesus. He used to be a rapper. Inspired by "the musicians of the world" (*ba-musiciens ya mokili*), he wore big shoes, had an earring, and was always talking in a violent way and with lots of gestures (hand movements). Once he was converted, his rapping business came to a rapid end, since these songs do not glorify or worship God. Since Chapy is reborn, he contends, he really feels Christ inside of him, which informs his control of his body: he now talks with humility and reserve and does not shout any more. By the time I knew him, he had been transformed into a very shy guy who even whispered instead of using his normal voice. "With our mouth we must honor God," he asserts. "In everything we do or say, we must glorify our master." Only when preaching, singing Christian songs, praying out loud, or casting out evil spirits does he use a loud voice. Christians should not be afraid, should not lose their temper, and should place all their hope and trust in God. In his view, this total surrender to God creates peace in the heart and distinguishes "pagans" from "Christians."

Chapy acknowledges in hindsight that at the moment when his maternal cousin Bienvenu asked him to join Cinarc, he was not yet a "real Christian" but a "Christian of the flesh." Feeling remorse, Chapy has changed his behavior and appearance totally. This occasionally proves bothersome to other residents of Bienvenu's house, where Chapy lives too: Chapy calls the family to pray together each morning from 6 to 7 A.M., and the spiritual guidance he provides then also gives him the opportunity to criticize their friends, their clothes, or any improper language they use.

The Pastor and *Maman Pasteur*

Ultimate spiritual parenthood for the members of a Christian theater company, however, resides within the couple of the pastor and his wife, who are considered to be their followers' spiritual parents (*baboti ya Nzambe*). The importance of the pastor and his spouse is reflected in practices at the end of a service or other spiritual activity. It is expected that all attendees at the gathering or ritual greet the couple. The pastor is allowed to ask private and, at times, unsettling questions of his children. He confronts them with their own doubts and indicates personal weaknesses where the Devil could profit or is already taking advantage. As a result of these conversations, the pastor knows a great deal about the private lives of the members of his church.

For an extensive part of my fieldwork, the Cinarc troupe was firmly embedded in the Holy Mountain revival church led by the *Pasteur* Gervais Tumbah, who, like the troupe's director, is also of Yombe origin (a subgroup among the Kongo ethnic group), albeit a few years older. His leadership in the church is founded on exactly the same grounds as Bienvenu's authority in the theater company: authority derives from a divine call of God and can accordingly be qualified as charismatic. Pastor Gervais recounted:

> In 1995 I was an active member in the church of the Resurrection [La Ré-surrection]. One day I saw a VHS tape of a South Korean prophet named Paulio Ngisho. He spoke about many things, but the main message of this videotaped sermon was "How to develop your communion with the Holy Spirit?" This tape revolutionized my life. It put fire in me. I was really touched by this program, and I started praying for two days. I fasted in order to receive God's message in a more clear way. There, God asked me to work for Him.

One year later Gervais led his first prayer group, and within a few years his church was born. The Church of the Holy Mountain, founded in 1998 and thus rather young, is still expanding, and it is representative of the religious renewal and expansion that the city today is undergoing. The main center of this particular religious community is located on the Rue des Poids Lourds (in the Kingabwa neighborhood of Limete borough). Kingabwa is a rather impoverished area of Limete, and for this reason Pastor Gervais sought to implant his church in the area. "Here, many souls need to be rescued," he states. In 2003, there were already two chapters in the vicinity of the main church, in Kingabwa Yaounde and Kingabwa Mombele.

The relationship between the church and the drama group was intense. The actors and the pastor considered the drama group to be a sixth ministry, and thus just one of the diverse church sections working for God. New actors had to become members of the Church of the Holy Mountain, and all of them needed to attend the Sunday services. Furthermore, those new actors who were not yet baptized as born-again Christians were necessarily baptized in this church. Sometimes the pastor gave a fictive name to the actor he baptized.

Only born-again actors who held an important position within another revival church were allowed to attend religious services in their own church, though they were expected to participate in Holy Mountain special events. Some of the Cinarc actors assumed roles with much responsibility in the Church of the Holy Mountain. Chapy and Clovis each led a Holy Mountain subchurch. Ndina, a young woman, sang in the church orchestra, and Doris led the children's gatherings during the Sunday services. Several other actresses served on Sunday morning as ushers (*protocol*), meaning that they dressed in the church uniform, directed people to their seats, and controlled the wanderings of the church attendees. For Pastor Gervais, the group was firmly embedded in the church workings. Bienvenu had to represent the drama group at the church board's meetings, which were always on Friday. When Bienvenu could not attend these meetings, the pastor publicly mentioned Bienvenu's absence at the next Sunday service and also punished him, either with a fine or by excluding Bienvenu temporarily from other board meetings.

Since Pastor Gervais did not yet have his own TV station (although he aspired very much to establish his own electronic church), he used the troupe as a mediator between the viewing audiences and his church. At times Pastor Gervais popped up in the narratives, always maintaining his own name and role of pastor. At other times, he addressed viewers in a monologue after the episode, framing the serial's message clearly in the spiritual battle. The church's intense involvement is also visible in the credits of the serials, which mentioned the church address and the pastor's name.

The interaction between the church and the drama group could never work without the strong appeal the pastor had for the young actors, a result of the social categories of the pastor and his wife (Maman Pasteur) being the role models that Christian boys and girls seek to mirror. More, the pastor and the pastor's wife have nowadays become the ideal types of masculinity and femininity in the city (see Pype 2007), for they combine several aspects of social success: others depend on them, and they enjoy material and financial wealth and occupy a privileged position with regard to the spiritual world. The pastor is the ultimate "strong man" (*moto ya makasi, homme fort*) in contemporary Kinshasa. *Pasteurs* acquire material goods such as cell phones, luxurious cars, and designer clothes from their followers and show off their opulence in public and semipublic spaces. The wealthier the pastor, the more he is believed to be in touch with God since his life of luxury is due to gifts of appreciation from satisfied followers. In their sermons, *pasteurs* talk enthusiastically about spiritual battles with Satan; they frequently jump up and down while preaching, just like *sportifs* warming up for a training session, or they punch the air with their fists, as if sparring with imaginary demons.

Furthermore, pastors are frequently invited to visit other regions of the country or the continent, or even the West. Statements like the following emphasize how easy it can become for a man of God to travel (something many Kinois long to do: leave their country and find a better life elsewhere, in particular in Europe): "When I was young I searched for several ways to get to Europe. I have looked for visas with a flashlight and larger lamps, but I did not find any. But now, since I work for God, I receive invitations. I now even must refuse an invitation to go to Cologne in Germany." Pastors are mobile and affluent, they enjoy material luxury, they have influence over others (their followers), and they are spiritually strong. Pastors thus combine the social appeal of politicians, businessmen, and *Sapeurs*, and they complement this with spiritual power.

The esteem of Christian leaders is reflected in the current greeting practices. Ardent Christians call each other "man of God" (Li. *moto ya Nzambe* or Fr. *homme de Dieu*), or alternatively "man of fire" (Fr. *homme de feu*). A Christian will frequently salute another with the words "Mangrokoto na yo, Frère X," accompanied with a particular handshake. The other then replies "Mangrokoto na yo mpe, Frère X." The term *mangrokoto* refers to one of the main heroes of young men in Kinshasa, the musician: it is a nickname for Papa Wemba, who is surnamed "*le grand prêtre mangrokoto*" ("the high priest mangrokoto"). Young Christian men change the interpretation of "*grand prêtre*" from a skilled musician to a "minister of God."

The pastor's wife occupies a pivotal role in the private lives of both younger and older women. Born-again Christian girls often turn to her with their personal problems. They imitate her clothing style and ask her advice on dress, looks, and social issues. In addition, the pastor's spouse leads the women's gatherings in the churches. During these gatherings, *Maman Pasteur* discusses the questions she has received in private, though respecting anonymity. She instructs girls on personal hygiene, appropriate social behavior, the Christian dress code, and management of emotions and desires. The female ideal professed in these encounters is grasped in the notion of "brides of Jesus" (*mwasi ya Yésu*). This notion has become pervasive in the city, to the extent that during the last part of my fieldwork, deceased adolescent girls and women were buried wearing a white veil, expressing their marriage with Jesus.

The Cinarc actresses refuted any assertion that their own mothers could function as their models or be the kind of woman whose life they would like to lead. Although these girls recognized that many women win social honor by taking care of their offspring on their own without any real help from husbands or lineage members, they still considered their mothers' lives too hard. They referred to the hardship of mothers who must work every day at the market trying to sell food, clothes, or other commodities, only to return home hungry and face the chore of preparing dinner or supervising the young girls who take over household tasks.

One Cinarc actress told why young girls admire the pastors' wives in the following way: "All girls long to become a *maman pasteur* because they notice that the pastors have 'a classy life': they travel to the United States, they are respected, have money and a nice car and wear beautiful clothes. Maman Pasteur is 'the first lady.' She also has her husband's full respect." A pastor's spouse thus becomes the ideal for young women because she is assumed to benefit from the privileges her husband's status lends: wealth, travel, and social respect. Furthermore, the girls take for granted that a pastor treats his wife with more respect than a regular Kinois man does.

Clovis Ikala: Setting Up a New Theater Company

As in all social relationships, conflicts may arise between troupes and churches. A few months before the final part of my fieldwork, a major struggle over authority splintered the Cinarc troupe into its original group and the new troupe Les Lévites.[11] The fracture followed a struggle between Bienvenu and Pastor Gervais. Various versions of the reasons for the split concurred. According to Bienvenu, he ceded from the Church of the Holy Mountain because Pastor Gervais had proclaimed himself the troupe's sole leader. Pastor Gervais continued to make these statements in sermons, which then spread through rumors in the community of Lemba. Additionally, Pastor Gervais needed the troupe to pay the tithe to the church. It meant that the money earned by the troupe (monthly salary at the TV station RTG@ and the donations of fans and sponsors, see below) had to be registered and checked by the pastor. The *pasteur* even ordered Bienvenu to inform him of all contacts with other spiritual advisors and to ask his permission if those spiritual leaders craved cooperation with the troupe. For Bienvenu, the problem thus resided in control over authority and money. He abandoned the church, and loyalty toward their leader led most of the Cinarc actors to follow him—although at that time they had no certainty about the cause of the divorce.

The *pasteur* recounted a completely different version of the story. Rumors about sexual relationships, lesbianism, alcohol abuse and internal disputes had reached the *pasteur*'s house, which made him pay a surprise visit to the troupe. Upon his arrival, he witnessed a fight between two actresses concerning a Congolese woman living in Europe (*mikiliste*), which confirmed his assumption that the actors were no longer leading a Christian life. The pastor demanded that the troupe retreat in the church to find God's path again. Bienvenu, however, had to decline the proposal. Lack of time was his main argument. Though, one might assume that this refusal was a strategy to deny the pastor's authority.

The conflict seemed to culminate at a point when Pastor Gervais warned Bienvenu via other persons that "he had the power of the word." Rumors spread that the pastor had already killed three people by cursing them. Most of the Cinarc actors advised Bienvenu to be careful in his encounters with the *pasteur*. Kinois are generally cautious so as to remain on good terms with spiritual leaders because they have supernatural powers. Rumors abound of pastors trying to poison or curse each other, and many believe these rumors to be true.

The rivalry between both charismatic leaders was fought out in the margins of the Cinarc serials: in the penultimate episode of *The Maquis Boys and Girls,* the *pasteur* appeared at the end of the serial and introduced himself as the troupe's sole spiritual leader (figs. 3.4 and 3.5). He gave some spiritual remarks about the content of the serial and invited all viewers to his church. The week after, the final episode opened with a monologue by Bienvenu who interpreted the serial in his terms and mentioned other spiritual leaders to whom he felt close and in turn invited the audience to assist the troupe's prayer gatherings in the rehearsal space. A few weeks later, when the break had become final, Bienvenu informed the audience during a scene in *The Heritage of Death* about the changes that had occurred.

Clovis, one of the leading Cinarc actors and an ardent Christian, followed Pastor Gervais. During the initial stage of my fieldwork, I had already noticed that Clovis and Pastor Gervais were very close. Often during sermons, the pastor would commend Clovis but decry Bienvenu's behavior. Clovis, who during my fieldwork came to lead the church subgroup (*cellule*) attached to the troupe, remained in the church and

Figures 3.4. and 3.5. Rivalry between the pastor and the troupe's leader on screen (screen shots from *The Maquis Boys and Girls*, © Cinarc)

created his own theater company. He recruited a whole range of new actors but managed to be left with some of the former Cinarc troupe who had not had the opportunity to obtain leading roles in Cinarc.[12]

The new troupe is called Les Lévites, according to the church orchestra. As Clovis told me, the name has symbolic meaning: "Lévite" refers to a biblical figure—one of Jacob's twelve sons, who led a group of people that worked for God. For Clovis, Lévi symbolizes total sacrifice for God. This is Clovis' narrative about the breakup:

> Bienvenu longed for an independent troupe, but this immediately means a rebellious troupe. Look at the Devil's behavior: he desired to be independent from God, he questioned God's authority. The same thing happens now with Bienvenu. I am sure he was inspired by the Devil. He only gave 5 percent of the income gained by RTG@, and before he gave it to the pastor we had many discussions. We really had to convince him to hand this amount of money over to the *pasteur*. These were signs that he did not fear God. As you have noticed, hardly anyone of the troupe prays now at [church of] the Holy Mountain. I wonder if they pray at all. Bienvenu has turned souls away from the church. Now, with my own troupe, I feel comfortable because I know that we are taking God's route.

The manner in which Clovis depicted Bienvenu as a fallen Christian is meaningful in this discussion. All parties questioned the Christian lifestyle and character of their opponents. In a Christian milieu, where Christianity governs both the individual and his social relations, attacks are directed at the foundation of identity: one's Christian conduct.

When Cinarc left the Church of the Holy Mountain, Bienvenu first went to the Winner's Chapel, and later on he and the troupe became affiliated with the church La Foi en Action (Faith in Action), headed by Pastor Flavien. The latter became the troupe's new spiritual leader.

Within his compound (Lemba Salongo) every Friday evening, Pastor Flavien organized prayer sessions for the troupe, at which fans and others were also welcome. The choice of Pastor Flavien as the new spiritual guide for the Cinarc group was undisputed: for the past three years, the troupe had frequently organized *maquis* (ritual seclusion to prepare a new serial) in his compound; he regularly visited them when filming and was frequently mentioned in the serials. In addition, he was one of Bienvenu's closest friends. During the Cinarc prayer sessions, he would often recall that Bienvenu had been a "real Christian" long before he had, thus confirming Bienvenu's spiritual seniority over his. As such, he posed no real threat to Bienvenu's authority.

Cinarc versus the Group of Muyombe Gauche: Rivalries among Troupes

In order to unite the multiple theater companies that appear on television, the Association of Independent Troupes of Popular Theater (ATITP) was created in 2003. Most of the leading TV drama groups in the city are represented in this committee, which sets out rules for the transfer of actors of one troupe to another, limits sponsorship, and controls the reputation and image of dramatic artists. Relationships fluctuate between the different companies in the city. Once-friendly troupes can suddenly become rivals for sponsors or actors.

Actors of one troupe appear sometimes in other theater companies' serials. These guest appearances reflect the friendly relationships between drama groups. Yet such performances are often performed without prior knowledge of one's leader. Ance, for example, regularly accepted invitations to perform in the serials of the troupe Esobe, but he never warned Bienvenu about it. He feared that his "father" would not give permission. Still, Ance really looked for invitations from other troupes, because the guest groups would pay him a small amount and the appearances offered Ance new chances to open up his network.

Performances in other groups are called *nzonzing* (moonlighting). The concept denotes *débrouillardise* (or synonym: *coop*), and is limited to the world of popular arts (in particular musicians and actors).[13] The word derives from the song *Nzingzong*, performed by the Kinois orchestra Bellabella. The song speaks about an adulterous wife. In the world of popular arts, the term indicates the work performed by musicians or actors outside of their own orchestra or drama group.

Most of Kinshasa's popular culture thrives upon competition between rival groups. The contest for social success is performed in publicly articulated and often mass-mediated discussions between *écuries*. These rambling arguments frequently contain insults and are known as *polémique* or *bakrètch*. They influence the relationships between the troupes as well as their cultural products. Cinarc's main opponent is the company of Muyombe Gauche, which the Cinarc actors and many other born-again Christians consider to be a "pagan" troupe. Many are convinced that Muyombe Gauche has plunged into the occult to achieve success. Cinarc experienced a victory over Muyombe Gauche when one of the latter's most popular performers joined the Cinarc group. Hughuette Ntambikila (known as Suza) was a very popular actress at the theater company of Muyombe Gauche, who had trained her since she was twelve years old. Bienvenu approached Hughuette and persuaded her to join Cinarc. From that day on, the rivalry between Cinarc and the Muyombe Gauche companies grew. In the serials and on talk shows, Muyombe Gauche provoked Bienvenu and insulted Hughuette. He announced in a talk show that he would bury Bienvenu's new girl, thus threatening to kill her. Muyombe Gauche realized his threats in a symbolic way in his serial *The African Life*. Hughuette had left Muyombe Gauche's troupe at the beginning of the recording of this serial, without any explication in the fictional storyline why one of the characters had disappeared. In the final episode of *The African Life*, Suza's relatives visit a cemetery in which we see her grave. Crying on her tomb, her relatives accuse her of having stolen someone else's husband and suggest that she deserved her death.

Half of the Cinarc crew objected to Hughuette's arrival in the troupe. Some in the Cinarc group disliked her for not being nicely dressed. She constantly wore short skirts and old clothes, and the Cinarc actresses rejected her for not appearing like a star. Others complained that Hughuette did not speak French, when one of the troupe's characteristics was its melting of French and Lingala. But most of the protest was directed at Hughuette's spiritual life: the actors did not believe she was a Christian, although she regularly showed up at the Sunday sermons and the troupe's prayer gatherings. One day, Hughuette was afflicted with a mystical disease. Bienvenu and the troupe's pastor, who had seen Muyombe Gauche's malediction on a talk show, discussed a proper cure. They accused her of not praying enough and therefore being vulnerable to Muyombe Gauche's maleficent powers. It came as no surprise for the Cinarc actors to learn that Muyombe Gauche had power over this young woman. In her initial months with the Cinarc troupe, she had confessed that she had been a lover of her artistic father. Through this, the actors thought that Muyombe Gauche had great power over Hughuette, and she was also the only gate through which he could manage to attack the Cinarc troupe.

Hughuette quit Cinarc early in 2006. The Cinarc actors were puzzled about her decision to leave. After some time she tried to join Cinarc again, but very quickly Bienvenu asked her to leave the group. A prophet had alerted him that one of the actresses had been looking for an *nganga* (traditional healer) to gain success. As the prophet could not give a specific name of a person, the leaders of the troupe sought whomever the Christian expert might have indicated. They remembered that Hughuette had been sent by her father to Boma (a provincial town in the province of Lower Congo). This raised suspicion among the leaders: for Christian Kinois, the Lower Congo is a region that is populated by many occult experts. The troupe's leaders suspected that the actress had consulted an *nganga* when she was in Boma. And this led Bienvenu not to accept her anymore in his troupe.

By the end of my fieldwork, Hughuette had appeared on several television spots on DigitalCongoWeb announcing that she had created her own troupe, called Les Nanas Lumière. The Cinarc actors mocked this name because they believed she was not a "real Christian" and her use of the word "light" (*lumière*) was merely a strategy to gain a following.

Mamy Moke and Her Lover

Joining a drama group is not that easy, since stardom in Kinshasa is, as I describe more fully in Chapter 5, often associated with occult practices and moral decay. Therefore, the morality of media and other stars of the city's popular culture is closely inspected and commented upon. Young performers, male and female alike, said they met with much resistance in their families when they first expressed their desire to become TV actors. The actresses in particular are constantly confronted with suspicion about sexual services and assumptions of the amorality of their worlds. Because they appear in public—a male space—associations with prostitution pop up immediately.[14] Their visibility in the masculine public sphere evokes public disapproval and fixes them in fragile social positions within the community at large. As a result, the actresses are constantly challenged to assert their Christian identity in both behavior and speech. Nene, for example, whose boyfriend had initiated the first rituals of "customary" marriage (presenting himself with an elder to her guardians and demanding they accept his suit to marry her) met with huge resistance from her boyfriend's relatives when they heard that she yearned to become a *vedette*. They even forbade her to continue this type of work. Only when Bienvenu personally assured her boyfriend's relatives that he would not give her any disrespectful roles (witch, prostitute, adulterous woman), and after he had emphasized that the serials were intended to evangelize the city, they reluctantly granted their permission. Pentecostalism, then, not only lends Nene access to the public sphere but it also provides her with a social shield to safeguard her honor.

Why, despite the social stigma attached to these public women, do young women decide to become actresses? La Fontaine, in an article about prostitution in Kinshasa, noted that *vedettes* are the ideal types of modern success, describing them as follows:[15]

> They are the outstandingly beautiful and vivacious women, elegant and elaborate in their dress, whose lovers are the most powerful and wealthy men of Kinshasa. They usually have only a few lovers who are regular clients and they will not entertain propositions from anyone who does not appear rich.... The *vedette* is well established financially. She usually lives in a modern house with good furniture and a high degree of material comfort. She employs a servant to do her domestic work and to cook, whom, according to rumo[u]r, she pays very little. Some *vedettes* live in expensive hotels or apartments in the formerly European part of town. Their clientele may include ministers, members of the diplomatic corps in Kinshasa, officials of the United Nations or European business men. (La Fontaine 1974: 99–100)

The young Christian girls and women that work(ed) for Cinarc are also attracted by the privileges this *vedette* status promises. This was brought home to me as I listened to a conversation among the actresses about a female host on one of Kinshasa's television channels. Some of them had noticed that this famous hostess did not appear on-screen anymore. One of the others told the group that this hostess now was housed in an apartment in the city center, waiting for her husband to arrange her documents for Europe. Apparently, a *mikiliste* had seen her on television and was charmed by her beauty (light skin), her French accent, and her elegant attire. He had investigated her reputation and proposed to marry her. After a few months, the couple was married. At the time of the conversation, the newlywed husband had returned to Europe and had lodged her in an apartment in the meantime. This news encouraged several Cinarc girls to continue their dramatic work. While some moments before they had been complaining about the low pay from their acting work, the news motivated the girls. Both male and female actors perceive appearing in public (on the screen) as a good strategy to attract more interesting marriage prospects.[16] However, marriage to a fan or admirer is still subject to social and religious exigencies.

One Cinarc actress, Mamy Moke, occupied a particular position within the troupe and best resembled La Fontaine's description of *vedettes*. She was admired for being the most beautiful and most skilled actress, an assessment confirmed by many other theater professionals in the city, who awarded her the ATITP prize for best actress in 2004 and 2005. The audience also liked her best; many men asked me for her phone number, inquired about her marital status, and begged me to help them to get in touch with her. Rumors about her private life abounded, and there was much suspicion and doubt about her "real Christian life", for she was the unmarried mother (*maman ya mwana*) of a son born before her arrival in the troupe. People also gossiped about her being a mistress (*deuxième bureau*). Although many thought she was not a "real Christian," hardly anyone spoke in a negative manner about her. The rumors were hard to verify, and only at the end of my fieldwork did Mamy Moke agree to speak with me about her sex life.

Throughout the course of my fieldwork, she had been associated with an older, wealthy, married man, whom I will call "Yaya José." The leading members of the Cinarc group could not disqualify the actress for the relationship with her sugar daddy because he was a "big man" who gave them money from time to time and frequently traveled to Europe, which suggested, they thought, that he could arrange a European producer for them. Every Monday evening, Yaya José's green Cherokee Jeep was parked at the compound where the theater company was filming. He would wait until Mamy Moke had finished her scenes before they took off together. Nobody ever remarked negatively on this relationship. In fact, sometimes the program schedule would be turned upside down because Yaya José had already arrived. Much information about this man was vague: he was in his fifties and worked for a cargo company, sending items from Europe to Kinshasa. It was also said that he was in a second marriage to a much younger wife in a community somewhere on the other side of town. Mamy Moke's "Yaya" (older sibling) provided her with many luxury items: she always had units on her mobile phone, every week she showed up with another hairstyle, and she wore the latest fashions. Everybody in the troupe knew that Yaya José was not really her "older brother," and that they had a sexual affair, but people were consistently very discreet about it.

By the end of the fieldwork, Yaya José was not showing up anymore, and people informed me that the relationship had come to an end. One of the signs was that she recycled her clothes more often. When I subtly asked Bienvenu about these rumors, he stated that he was the one who had asked her to end the relationship, as he considered it inappropriate for an evangelizing actress to display non-Christian behavior.

Then, very late in the course of my fieldwork, Mamy Moke agreed to talk to me about her Yaya. Mamy Moke's sudden openness to discussing her sex life with me did not so much derive from an increased feeling of trust toward me; rather it had more to do with the fact that the affair belonged to the past. She contended that she had dated Yaya José before joining the Cinarc company, and that upon her arrival in the drama group, the other Cinarc members invariably had expressed their disapproval of her behavior. At that time, however, she felt she could not end this relationship, since Yaya José not only provided her with money for clothes and food, but also paid her baby's medical expenses and her own school fees (at the time she was studying economics at UNI-KIN). When Mamy Moke ended the relationship she lost these financial benefits, dropped out of school, and had to turn to her relatives more frequently to cover expenses for her son. Her fellow artists encouraged her to fully embrace Jesus Christ. From then on, on a daily basis, Mamy Moke started to visit the revival church two houses down from hers. Instead of being involved with a married man, she stated, she is now Jesus's lover (*mwasi ya Jesus*).

Despite her unchristian attitude, the drama group did not suspend Mamy Moke because of her extreme popularity among the audience and her relation to Yaya José was beneficial for the group. In other cases, however, the troupe's leaders, with their strong affiliations to revival churches and their concern about safeguarding their image as "real Christians," are more rigid and follow the same stringent rules concerning sexuality that are also promoted in the churches.

Ance Luzolo: Boasting with a Contact

Apart from the intense relationships with leaders and fellow troupe members, another type of social relationship prevails in the life of young Kinois actors: "contacts" or "relations" (*les branchements, les relations*). These represent more fluid, temporary, superficial relationships with others. Ance, at age twenty one of the youngest Cinarc members, nicely demonstrates the ways in which actors enter into these loose but usually financially rewarding relationships.

Cinarc members frequently told me that Ance was not a "real Christian," but rather a "Christian of the flesh." They had noticed that the young man showed great interest in my work, and he always enthusiastically proposed to walk me home or to accompany me to any event. In a sense, the other Cinarc members feared that my friendship with Ance would pulverize the image of a solid and unified Christian group, which the Cinarc board energetically tried to transmit not only to their viewing audiences, but also to me. After all, Ance had joined the troupe only a few months before my arrival, and he still needed much spiritual guidance. Bienvenu once jokingly remarked that Ance had become my *petit* (smallboy). The joke was not that innocent, because it diminished the authority I could have attributed to Ance. The comment was immediately followed by an order that my religion-related questions be addressed to Chapy or him, but not to Ance. Probably much to Bienvenu's chagrin, I remained very much interested in how an apprentice of an evangelizing drama group became a Christian star.

As I show in Chapter 6, filming was regularly accompanied by discord as to the right direction the plot should take, and the actors did not always agree on the interpretation of certain scenes or images. In this, Ance and Chapy disagreed more than often than not. Because of Chapy's artistic and spiritual seniority, Ance could never really make any attempt to win Chapy over. Ance's subtle remarks, however, and the suppressed frustration when arising discussions were broken off before they could even begin, signaled to me that Cinarc was not at all a homogenous group, and that evangelization was a major practice even within the troupe. I still considered Ance a very important informant, and his religious uncertainty was only one of the reasons for me to continue planning and conducting interviews. Unlike other Cinarc members, this young man also talked rather openly about the money he earned, and he was the one who initially showed me the importance of contacts.

The network of contacts is called *le réseau*. The French origin of this idiom emphasizes the modern character of this mode of existence: in an urban setting, ties need to be forged outside of customary realms of belonging based on consanguinal and affinal kinship or territorial relatedness. Kinois seek to establish connections with as many people as possible, as attested by the much-heard expression "Relations, that is what counts in life." My informants never tired of emphasizing the importance of "having good relations" with everyone. The affirmation of the need to open and maintain connections with as many people as possible at first struck me as odd, for conversations with such "relations" were often minimal and there appeared to be little affinity in terms of common interests or other possible domains, based on Western concepts, in which individuals meet. However, the mere possession of people's phone numbers, and the act of exchanging these numbers without necessarily sharing a project or showing any intention of playing significant parts in each other's lives, are social practices that emphasize a plain need for "connecting."[17]

Those who aspire to become stars do this above all because they hope to connect with local "big men and women." Appearing on television becomes a strategy to expand possibilities of establishing contacts with others, in particular the viewers and the people to whom fans talk about their stars. Small favors and exchanges between spectators and actors are a key aspect of the social dynamics in Kinshasa's media world and are rendered possible by the closeness between television stars and Kinshasa's urbanites. Most TV actors use public transport, go to the market, and visit churches just as ordinary people do. In contrast to the few major music groups whose lead singers or musicians earn enough money to pay for their own car and driver, television actors earn almost nothing and accordingly, like most city dwellers, depend on their social network to survive. The status of stardom makes one visible in the street and enables one to establish contacts with a range of people wider than one's own small horizon of neighborhood, church community, and relatives.

The attraction between local elites and celebrities seems to be mutual, since political and social elites frequently ask to be mentioned by name[18] during the serials in order to enhance their personal prestige and reinforce their authority and position. This practice of name-dropping is not reserved to the fictional worlds of teleserials but also appears in local music production (White 1999). Kinois refer to this name-dropping as "throwing someone" (*kobwaka moto*). In a more abstract way, it is called the *mabanga* phenomenon (Sg. *libanga*), *mabanga* meaning (precious) stones or diamonds. Usually, the *mabanga* phenomenon is explained as strategy of *débrouillardise* within the help-yourself culture. It references the importance of one's name: by equating names with diamonds, Kinois thus emphasize the preciousness of names and their capacity to turn individuals into social beings larger than their physical entity. Mentioning someone's name converts that person's acts and qualities into a verbal discourse that circulates apart from him or her (cf. Munn 1986: 112). As Munn (1986: 111) suggests, fame (being talked about) is a "metaphorical body that ramifies as sound beyond the body." It allows for a spatio-temporal extension of the self. By paying for their names to be cited, the elites enhance their patron status. Many successful men and women deliberately seek out relationships with the actors, whose "power of the word" they can use for their self-promotion precisely because the television celebrities have such a wide audience. Usually, Kinshasa's important people initiate the exchange. But when a theater company is in need of money, the actors spontaneously praise the city's big men on the assumption that these "patrons" will see or hear of the mention and then contribute money. Often the young actors themselves try to become clients of big men and big women by presenting themselves, in phone calls and visits to their houses, as dependents of these patrons whose financial resources they hope to share in. The young artists have much more to offer their potential patrons than other youngsters: they can drop the names of their patrons in the televised episodes and other cultural performances, which of course allows the patrons' names to be heard all over town (and beyond, in the case of serials diffused on national television channels), thus raising the social cachet of the city's "big men and women."

Being mentioned by a TV actor in a media performance (in the teleserial, or in an interview in a TV show, or elsewhere when appearing in public) requires a counter-gift from the person whose name has been "thrown." We can speak in this context about "patronage."[19] The kind of patrons these young actors are engaged with are men and women of importance who ask to have their name cited in an episode, but they will never suggest a serial be created in order to enhance their social esteem.[20]

White (2008: 170–171) has described a similar strategy for gaining money among Kinois musicians, who during their performances often cite the same names the TV actors mention in their serials. White prefers to write about "sponsors" instead of "patrons," since most of the money providers in the music scene do not establish long-standing relationships with the musicians. I prefer to use the concept of patron because, first, it is closest to what the Kinois themselves use (Fr. *patron*); second, there is a sense of dependency inherent in the money transfer that goes beyond mere sponsorship; and finally, some TV actors do engage in long-standing relationships with the people whose names they cite.

The patron-client relationship between patrons and performers is more complex than sponsorship or a "*grand-petit*" relationship. As stars in the city, the actors occupy a privileged position that lifts them above the status of common people. For viewers, the actors are themselves big men; meanwhile they happily play the role of a *petit* in their relations with other big men and women who have won acclaim through commerce or politics. The players occupy dots, as it were, within a web of multiple relationships that bind them to both the "smallest people" and the "biggest persons" in town.

There is, however, some secrecy around these *mabanga*. First, face-to-face contact between the actors and these big men is rare. The latter frequently phone the artists, and after being mentioned they send one of their *petits* with a message of thanks and some money. Second, the actors are somewhat ambivalent about the practice of praising or citing people. At first, during our formal interviews, none of the actors would acknowledge that they actually "threw" people. Some argued that this would amount to a "selling of the art." The performers responded to questions in this regard with the same sense of shame that White has noted while researching *mabanga* in popular music (White 1998). Their front stage behavior (Goffman 1971[1959]) in our initial encounters demonstrated that they yearned to represent themselves as "real artists." They maintained that the references to patrons "ruined the story." However, the actors consistently referred to other theater companies where "one could hear one *libanga* after another," thus questioning the quality of their colleagues or competitors' serials. Sometimes the actors cited American films—most frequently *A Prince in New York*, starring Eddie Murphy—arguing, in their defense, that these big actors "drop" names: "Eddie Murphy mentioned Arnold Schwarzenegger in this film. If they can do it, why can't we?"

Most performers who are already well known to the public seek to secure rather long-standing individual relationships with patrons. Having one or more patrons is something to be proud of. Yet gendered differences persist in these patron-client relationships and determine the opportunities to establish them. Women are hampered in the search for individual patrons: fearful of losing honor or of being romantically linked to the persons mentioned by the audience and fellow actors, women are more reluctant to drop the names of big men. They tend, rather, to restrict themselves to citing family members or friends who are "socially harmless." Otherwise, they search for big women whose names they might drop. Unfortunately, as there are fewer big women than big men, actresses have only limited opportunities to access new networks.

Additional restrictions on the possibilities for citing people are inherent in the power relations of the drama group. First, *mabanga* reflect the internal hierarchal structure of a theater company. Big men are mentioned only by performers who are very successful or have already established a "name." The "bigger" the person who is mentioned, the more important the actor who mentions the person must be. In this way the social esteem of both parties, the actor who mentions the name and the person cited, is enhanced. Second, the relationships between the actors, cameramen, and image editors influence the final decision whether or not to keep the *mabanga* in the episode. When an episode is first broadcast, actors are often found expressing their discontent on learning that their *libanga* was cut. In several specific cases the performers complained that one particular actor, who was also responsible for production, intended to keep all the money, since his *libanga* consistently made it through the last cutting. Such occurrences often had repercussions on the relations between actors and their patrons, as the process of exchange was interrupted. The latter, dissatisfied because their name had not been mentioned, would fail to live up to their obligations as patrons, while the performers were deprived of desperately needed services.

Through Beti, a Cinarc actress, Ance had come in touch with a wealthy man whom he called "Didier Mpeti." This man was, in his view, a "big man," which Ance deduced from the fact that he traveled all the time and the fact that he was mentioned in many Congolese songs.

> He is "the sultan of Brussels." He is really a *grand prêtre*. I don't know exactly what he does in life, but I know that he has money. And he travels all the time. The first time we met he asked me: "What do you want?" I had no mobile phone at the time, so I asked him to buy one for me. I know that he was surprised that I asked him for a phone at our first meeting. He told me to get into his car, where I saw some piles of money that he gave to someone in Kauka. When I got out of the car, he gave me 5000 FC [then about 12 dollars]. He told me: "I am leaving for Europe very soon. I want you to 'throw' my name during my absence. My brothers will call me. As soon as I get back, I will look for you." I had no opportunity to "throw" him for a long time, but as soon as he was back I called him and told him to watch the following Thursday evening. In *Apostasy* I was in a shot with *frère* Patrice, who illegally arranged visas and travel to Europe. In the serial, I said: "You are a fraud. The only one I trust is Didier Mpeti, the Sultan of Brussels." I tried to call Didier Mpeti in Europe, but could not speak to him. Last week Beti told me Didier Mpeti's younger brother had called her and encouraged me to continue "throwing" him. I hope he will be here soon because I need money.

Beti, who was friends with Didier Mpeti's sister, Mi-Josée, had put Ance in touch with Didier Mpeti, a wealthy businessman who enjoyed a favorable status in Kinshasa because many urban dance musicians mentioned his name in their songs. Didier Mpeti gave Ance a blue suit and designer sunglasses. At the time of my conversation with Ance, he had only been able to cite his patron once. Ance, however, was convinced that in the future he would have more opportunities to mention him. Then, he would remind his patron that he preferred a mobile phone and maybe some money to start living on his own. Since Beti had been instrumental in finding Ance a patron, Ance was in a position of dependency toward her. Opening up new networks entails obligations of gratitude toward benefactors. Beti complained that she was normally entitled to receive a portion of the money or goods that Ance received from his patron, implying that Ance did not honor his obligations.

Conclusion

This chapter has shown how two types of "fictive kinship" (Pitt-Rivers 1968) overlap in an evangelizing theater company: artistic and spiritual kinship. The internal social relationships are based on artistic learning and spiritual training, which institutionalizes artistic and spiritual fatherhood and fraternity. Religious and artistic genealogies are traceable and often spelled out.

All fictive relationships established in associations are highly temporary, since people easily move from one *écurie* to another due to rivalries or a wish for better opportunities. Many male troupe members dream of leading their own drama groups and becoming leaders themselves. This is because the urban models of big men and leadership in voluntary associations correspond to a large extent to cultural aspirations of becoming an elder, according to which only elders can acquire full personhood. As De Boeck (1999) writes of the Aluund, becoming a person is a project that unfolds in time and space. Apart from the personal growth toward volition, intentionality, individual ambition, and self-consciousness, a social dimension contributes to the growth into a social person: "the more one becomes the focus of the social life of the kin group, the more one is given respect, but the more also, one becomes responsible for the redistribution and sharing of the goods that circulate in the kin group" (De Boeck 1999: 194). Whereas the mental evolution constitutes an adult, the growing insertion into the kin group, with increased responsibility for others, makes one a "patron" (ibid.: 197, see also for the baYaka Devisch 1993: 142). In addition, the new media technologies offer new ways of expanding individuals' social outreach. Mass media and the celebrity status that follows from appearing on-screen allow actors to become the focus of the social life in the city and beyond; thus the actors accumulate still more respect and responsibilities.

As already mentioned, membership and leadership in these voluntary organizations are highly temporal. People easily join and leave a group. This compels us to take a very flexible approach to the notion of "Christian." One should keep in mind that individuals not constantly act as ardent Christians. Rather, in one's lifespan there may be moments when one needs spiritual security and confirmation, but once fulfilled, totally or partially, that need disappears. One's religious life and intensity of religiosity vary over time as well. This is also one of the reasons why membership in revival churches fluctuates so: One can approach a pastor and attend sermons with much enthusiasm for several months, but after a while the intensity or the participation may diminish, either gradually or totally. From the vantage of these churches, the individual lapses into a "pagan" life or degrades to a "Christian of the flesh." However, this does not necessarily match the interpretation of those "fallen" individuals themselves.

Furthermore, this chapter has shown that it would be wrong to state that all Christian TV celebrities profess the apocalyptic ideology. For some, more prosaic reasons, such as making a livelihood and attracting potential marriage partners, are held to be more directly relevant than proselytizing. Yet neither necessary contradicts each other. Even those actors who are more concerned with their own survival, display, in their personal lives, a meticulous religious life, endorse the apocalyptic ideology, and never contradict the religious message their serials spread. It is in their public performance as Christians that their celebrity status attains an even higher level.

Notes

1. In the literature, this category of cunning people, deliberately and successfully trespassing boundaries between the moral and the immoral, the legal and the illegal, is better known as the *feyman*. On the notion of *feymen* see Malaquais (2001) and Ndjio (2008). In Kinshasa, this category is called the *Yankee* and is closely related to the *cowboy;* both types derive from American westerns that were shown in cinemas in the late colonial and early postcolonial period (De Boeck 2004: 39–40).

2. Several of the Cinarc fictional names are, for men, Caleb, Fataki, Luzolo, Makubakuba, Kuaku, and Paco, and for women, Caroline, Charlainne, Mambweni, Kuaku, Paco, Jeanne, Rebekkah, Deborah, etc. These names derive from biblical tales, ethnic epics, and the Western modern world, as well as from real individuals in the city to whom the troupe's leader feels obliged to show gratitude.

3. Most drama groups consist of young, i.e., unmarried, people. Once actors and actresses enter into matrimony, they usually refrain from acting. This is not so surprising, given the cultural association of play with youth.

4. A "shout" is a catchy phrase that is frequently repeated in the serials and often takes hold in the real world.

5. There are a few exceptions, one being Okapi, created in 2004. This group is headed by Shako, an important actress in the history of Kinshasa's television serials. She first worked with Tshitenge Tsana in Groupe Salongo and later joined Sans Soucis. Since 2006, Maman Alingi heads the troupe Théâtre Toli. Hughuette Ntambikila leads the group Les Nanas Lumière.

6. My participation in the Cinarc group followed the same route. I first appeared in a commercial; then small roles, such as a church member or the secretary of a business patron, were invented to insert me into the main storyline. After several months, Bienvenu created "my" serial (*Back to the Homestead*) with me in a leading role.

7. Chapy explains the Apostolo church, itself a derivation of Protestantism, as a "traditional" church. Here, interestingly, "tradition" does not merely denote "precolonial" or "premodern," but "pre-Pentecostal-charismatic."

8. This ceremony normally lasts three days. Relatives, neighbors, and close friends of the deceased, or friends of family members of the deceased, stay for three days in the compound where the ceremony takes place. Young girls often use this event as an excuse to go out and spend the night with their boyfriends.

9. Chapy here spoke of *récupérer,* which means to gain back, to retrieve again. The choice for this verb is probably inspired by the belief that all stems from a divine source. "Coming back" to God is thus both a salvation and a literal return.

10. This notion is not restricted to religious and spiritual life but may indicate other kinds of changes a person may undergo or pursue.

11. Fissions seem to be a constitutive feature of Kinshasa's popular culture. Music bands, for example, also continuously split into smaller ones (Tsambu 2004; White 2008).

12. Just like the actors, I saw myself forced to make a choice between Bienvenu and Clovis. Here is an excerpt from my field notes, written after the broadcast of the first episode of Les Lévites' first serial:

    This morning, I paid a visit to Bienvenu's house in order to prepare for tomorrow's festivities for '5 years Cinarc on television.' I was surprised to hear that Bienvenu already knew that the day before I had performed in a few scenes of the following episode of Clovis' serial. Bienvenu was obviously not pleased and asked me: 'Are you on my side or on his?' I was astonished and tried excusing myself: 'You know, Clovis came to my house Wednesday evening and talked to me about his new troupe. He asked me if I could join his troupe. I told him that I did not think that I had the time to join the troupe, and attend all the shootings. On this, Clovis promised me that I just had to arrange one hour so that I could make a small appearance in his serial.' There, Bienvenu interrupted me, saying that this is the way Clovis works: 'He is really sharp. He visits some of the actors in their house and promises them leading roles or money in order to take them away from me. But, he forgets that I have invested all my time in educating these young people. Did you see the spot he has made for his new serial? He has used images of some of my actors who have never left me. I was surprised to see them called his actors. They explained that Clovis had invited them to their prayer sessions and that he had filmed them over there. People are misled. And now that you are appearing in his serial, what will people think? They will say: "Oh, the white girl has left Caleb too."' Bienvenu wants to somehow ensure that I will appear in one of the following episodes of Cinarc. It is apparently meaningful to him that people see that I have not left Cinarc. (field notes, 27 May 2006)

13. See White (2008: 217–218) for a discussion of the moonlighting enacted by Kinshasa's musicians.

14. Abu-Lughod (1995) discusses the same attitude toward female performers in Egypt.

15. These *vedettes* are one type of "free woman" that La Fontaine (1974) encountered in Kinshasa. The other type of *femmes libre* are prostitutes in the European sense of the word (Pl. *balondoniennes, bamerengue*), which she calls *chambres d'hôtel* (La Fontaine 1974: 100) and describes as follows:

    They are said to be ready to accept any man who offers them their price and they have as many lovers as is feasible. Informants describe their appearance as slovenly, say they have little self-respect, and must find their clientele among the poorer men who give them little. They supplement their earnings by selling foodstuffs in the markets. In the evenings they sit in the more squalid bars, 'flamencos,' waiting for clients.... Their clientele is drawn from wage-earners who have little cash available except on pay-days, usually the middle and end of each month. They are said to fix their prices accordingly, charging according to what the market will bear at the time. The commercial nature of these transactions is thus clear and these women are generally scorned because they sell their bodies for money.

16. In his ethnography of an acting group in Lubumbashi during the 1980s, Fabian (1990: 123) also mentions that many of the actresses married well thanks to the fame they had acquired as an actress.

17. The beeping phenomenon can be considered in this respect. Beeping (*bip-page*) refers to the social practice in which a person calls another but allows the phone to ring only once. Not only is this an ingenious way of managing one's finances while using modern technology; it also emphasizes the need to maintain relations with people whom one does not regularly meet.

18. The phenomenon of dropping names is not to be confused with the advertisements that groups or actors sometimes make to promote such interests as commercial ventures (e.g., shops, boutiques, or cybercafes), *jours d'action* at local churches, or a school that a fellow spiritual leader has opened.

19. As mentioned above, in the Kinois sense, "patrons" are "big men" (or "big women") with a group of dependents around them. In the anthropology of art, however, the concept of "patron" is used to indicate wealthy individuals who commission works of art (Vansina 1984: 44–47; also Ben-Amos 1980; Perani and Wolff 1999). In the social context of Kinshasa's teleserials, the two senses are interlinked.

20. In the world of music production, however, the situation is different. Songs might be commissioned by individuals, who pay the artist for a song, and whose life might be appraised in the lyrics. Kinois know very well which songs have been ordered by what 'big person," and rumors about financial details or personal motivations of these cultural products circulate swiftly.

CHAPTER 4

Variations on Divine Afflatus

Artistic Inspiration, Special Effects, and Sermons

The Cinarc troupe films with a small digital camera owned by the channel RTG@. Each morning of a day of filming, one of the actors is sent to the channel's headquarters, located in the city center, to fetch the filming equipment. One Monday afternoon in January 2005, the actors were waiting as usual for the camera to arrive when I parked my car outside the compound where Bienvenu was living. It was already 4 P.M., and the troupe had not yet begun filming. As occurred frequently, Jef had only shown up around noon; then, claiming that he had no money to pay for the ride to the city center, he had to wait until Nadine returned from the market to receive the FC 500 that would allow him to take a public taxi from Lemba Terminus to the Avenue de Commerce and back. Just outside Bienvenu's tiny house, some of the actresses were braiding each other's hair, while Bienvenu, Clovis, Chapy, and Raph were eating inside. Nadine had prepared a considerable quantity of rice with a mixture of pondu (cooked manioc leaves) and tinned mackerel that could easily serve ten people, I guessed. I knew that whatever was left over would later be given to the actresses.

As was often the case, I was invited to sit inside with the men of the troupe. Teasing me, Bienvenu gave me a fork and said that eating from his plate would prove my respect for him. I noticed that the television was switched to the channel Nzondo TV, where the James Bond film *Goldfinger* was playing. Not much attention was paid to the film, because while eating the actors were discussing whether one particular actress had to be expelled from the group or not. Suddenly, Bienvenu glimpsed what was on the TV and, putting his fork on the table, exclaimed: "These are all lies." In the scene he had just seen, 007 was trying to avoid laser beams. He turned to me and asked: "Really, do you think this happens?" "This film is not about real life. These are lies!" he continued. For a moment I was struck dumb: I did not discern a difference between the special effects in Kinshasa's *maboke* and those used in the Bond film. Yet this James Bond film was not considered to be truthful; therefore, Bienvenu did not appreciate the film. Without being told to do so, Clovis immediately switched the channel. He halted at RTAE, Sony Kafuta's channel, which was beaming a music video clip by the Christian musician Aimé Nkanu. Some hours later Jef arrived, exclaiming that public transport was too hard these days and that the troupe really needed a car. Filming ended after midnight that day, and the next day a few other scenes had to be taped. Now Bienvenu had to rent a camera because the RTG@ equipment was reserved for another troupe.

I take this anecdote as an introduction into the diverse ways in which spiritual knowledge can be mediated and articulated. Mediation is here used in the sense of transmission: the transfer of messages from the Otherworld via sermons and Christian popular culture, as well as the transfer of spiritual powers via in-between figures such as pastors and TV actors. In particular, a discussion of the epistemological status of special effects in the Pentecostal melodrama will enable me to analyze divine afflatus and epiphany. For Kinois, veraciousness—representing what might be real—is an important criterion in evaluating visual products like films and television serials, and their own use of special effects does not cast their *maboke* as untruthful when considered against the backdrop of the religious world in which these are watched. Rather, as I discuss elsewhere (Pype 2011a), special effects share with dreams the possibility of epiphany, a glimpse into the invisible. The magical and the technological share one space and logic (de Vries and Weber 2001a: 28). In their search for the interfaces between media and religion, de Vries and Weber propose to speak of special effects in terms of miracles, and of miracles in terms of special effects (ibid.). I find it difficult to adopt the explanation of miracles as special effects, since it seems to trivialize the meaning and scope of religion (which the authors also acknowledge). The equation of special effects with miracles, on the other hand, seems to be warranted in Kinshasa's Christian popular culture. Here, the special effects and the social status of the Christian actor are inherently related to the spiritual knowledge conveyed in sermons and the figure of the pastor. Therefore, in this chapter, I will pay much attention to the charismatic authority of pastors and the revealing work of sermons as well.

During my conversations with the television actors, they recurrently stressed the real character of their serials and did not at all accept the label "fiction." It appeared that, according to local media aesthetics, the plotlines and characters had to be drawn from experiences really lived by either the actors themselves or the viewers. Events or dramatic persons that did not belong to the (spiritual and imaginative) life worlds of Kinois were not accepted. As a result of this, the line between reality and its representations became very thin. "The teleserials stick to reality!" it was frequently said. Through improvisation and the leader's artistic genius, new imaginary worlds were constructed out of the real material for purposes of instructions. So, what Kinois artists were doing was not producing fiction, but rather revealing and visualizing all dimensions of reality, its visible and invisible spheres.[1]

The insistence on the close rapport between reality and fiction is rooted in the Kinois epistemological understanding of reality and the experienced world, which is discussed in Chapter 2. The belief that the "Real" is located within the invisible indeed feeds a particular understanding of narration and the value accorded to the stories, their contents, and their messages. In Lingala, the word *lisapo* (pl. *masapo*) denotes "a report, coverage, news, story, tale, narrative, theater, fable, parable, short story, and novel" (Kawata 2003: 130). Firstly, these linguistic data confirm not just that there is no real distinction between "play" and "reality," but that both are invariably interlinked. Secondly, the point that I want to make here is that the factual or imaginative sources of these *masapo* are not meaningful, which cautions us not to transpose the label "fiction," with its Western significations, to oral and visual cultural products of the African continent. Consider what De Boeck (2004: 59) writes when discussing Kinshasa's imaginary and structures of attributing meaning: "the problems with notions such as 'fact' and 'fiction' is that they do not take into account the autochthonous experience of the realness of the double [the realm of the invisible], but risk reducing it to something unreal, a mere 'fantasy.'" The categorization into so-called real and unreal stories derives from a Western, enlightened episteme that locates reality and the truth in the physical and material. Concepts such as "fiction" and "reality" are culturally constructed and are inscribed within a particular interpretation of reality and the possibilities of representing it.[2]

The Christian Artist

In Kinshasa, it is said that "artists see the problems of the world." In local aesthetics, revelation is an important feature of good work. Artists are admired when they reveal certain things that ordinary people have not yet perceived. The idea that artistic creativity or inspiration and revelation are related is supported by linguistic information: the notions of both "retrieving inspiration" and "revealing" are included in the Lingala verb *kobimisa* (Kawata 2003: 16). This perpetuates beliefs dominant in other African societies (in the past, in rural worlds, and in urban contexts), where it is assumed that the artist occupies a special place in society because of his abilities to reveal, to make visible the unseen (Nooter 1993). Kinshasa's artists do not claim to make or create something ex nihilo; rather, they use the quotidian environment to make a song, a dance, or a theater play. One man who produces theater plays for development purposes contended that making a new cultural performance means adding something to something that already exists: "We begin with what we encounter in the streets. We can never begin working on a theme without opening our eyes to reality. We start with what we see and do something else with it." Through this reorganization of the visible, the artists reveal something that otherwise remains hidden.

According to the same actor, "*L'art eza molimo.*" This expression can be translated as "artistry is a spirit" or "artistry resides within the soul." It reflects the idea that creativity does not stem from the individual but originates in hidden realms. Such discourse denies virtuosity or technicity as the basis of good art, but it echoes long-standing approaches toward craftsmanship and artistry that locate creativity in a hidden supernatural realm and even require intense personal relationships with spirits (D'Azevedo 1973; Murphy 1998; Stone 1994). Three decades ago, Warren L. D'Azevedo (1973: 337) wrote about the "African artist": "The product of the archetypal artist is miraculous, and the artist is viewed essentially as a daring entrepreneur in the exchange of gifts between human society and a special supernatural realm." For Congo, for example, Alvin W. Wolfe (1955) described in a short piece how an Ngombe wood-carver acquired his skills. Ancestral spirits took the young man away to the forest, where he remained for several months. There the skills of making figurines were transmitted to him, and ancestors offered him the knowledge to endow the figurines with magical power. Also today, among Kinois, it is assumed that supernatural power and guidance are the basis of the wood-carver's craftsmanship. Though some wood-carvers explained to me that many of them still went to the forest to carve their figurines out of sight, nowadays most can be found working in the open air and in public places (fig. 4.1). That is not to say that the end or the diminution of the secret aura around wood carving has been paralleled by a loss of belief in spiritual agency on the part of the artists. Revival churches emphasize the presence of witchcraft in both the production of wood carving and in the artworks themselves. As a journalist noted, this stigmatization of the craft led to the disappearance of the art of sculpture in Kinshasa (Payne in the journal *L'Avenir,* 23 April 2007).

Figure 4.1. Wood-carvers at work on Lumumba Boulevard (2004, © Katrien Pype)

In a non-Christian context, a rich array of spirits is identified with the origin of craftsmanship, but among Kinshasa's Christians, it is held that only the Holy Spirit offers appropriate divine afflatus. Here, the normative "appropriate" is important. Many conveyed that several wood-carvers prefer to maintain bonds with demonic spirits instead of with the divine spirit. Singers, musicians, and choreographers are also located somewhere on the spiritual map outlined by Pentecostal leaders, which often leads to painstaking efforts by celebrities attempting to convince their audiences of their Christianity. This was one of the reasons why, during my first week of fieldwork with the Cinarc troupe, Anne Tshika, one of the elder actresses, could speak to the camera at length while the rest of the troupe was rearranging the living room in which they had just filmed. Overhearing Anne declaring that she was really a Christian and that people who doubted this should visit the troupe's church and witness with their own eyes that she really prayed and had no dealings with the occult, I asked Bienvenu for some information. Like me, he was listening attentively to the monologue. Whispering, he told me that Anne had begged for five minutes in which to speak. People were gossiping about her not being a Christian, and she wanted to end these rumors.

Concerned about the overall repute of the troupe, Bienvenu was allowing her to address the audience during the one-hour time slot that Cinarc occupied on the channel Tropicana TV. This was highly exceptional, because there were other platforms at hand in which the celebrities were able to clear such matters out, prime examples being the various talk shows. But Anne's case was serious enough to broadcast a short monologue at the end of the episode that the troupe had been shooting that day, which would air at the end of the week. At Bienvenu's request, the channel's editor inserted this clip just before the credits, that is, before viewers would be inclined to switch channels. Whether Anne's words had an effect on viewers' perceptions remains unclear. I would suspect they did not, because during the whole period of fieldwork people queried me repeatedly about Anne's spiritual connections. It did not help much that Anne continued playing occult roles such as witches, prostitutes, and paternal aunts. She often pressed Bienvenu for other roles, but he considered this to be her main talent. Anne could not do much to manage her off-screen reputation, other than frequently stating in public that she complied with Christian norms.

Kinois' suspicions that certain artists have occult dealings stem in part from perceptions about embodiment and imitation. There is an assumed rapport between a character and the artist (see Chapter 5). Glorifying human love and violence in songs and drama is, according to the born-again Christians, cultural work, which is not inspired by God but rather by the Devil. Moreover, it is commonly assumed that the most successful artists in the city draw their success from demonic alliances and activities (committing incest or human sacrifices; see White 2004).[3] Christian Kinois, non-artists and artists alike, claim that these performers have signed pacts with the Devil and married demons. On several occasions I heard that, for example, the three most successful *atalaku* (shouters, a typical function in Congo's urban dance music bands) in one of the most important bands (WMMM) owed their success to a pact with the Devil. As rumor had it, the *atalaku*s were buried in a coffin for three nights in N'Sele, on the outskirts of Kinshasa. A magician supposedly told them to do so if they yearned for success (wealth, money, and popularity). These beliefs in the occult as a source of musicians' immense popularity also apply to TV actors. People do not dare touch Muyombe Gauche, for example, and avoid looking him in the eyes when meeting him because they fear his supernatural powers: rumors indicate that this TV celebrity connives with the occult (Pype 2009a).

The Spirit of Improvisation

It is important to remind the reader that, for born-again Christians, the Holy Spirit has supplanted the role of other personal spirits that would otherwise be assumed to accompany artists, whisper tunes and lyrics into their ears, and guarantee success. Thus, though the revival churches do not deny any supernatural intervention in artistic creativity, they channel it according to their own scheme. Christian artists claim to appropriate divine afflatus during prayer sessions that are directed toward God or during dreams that are inspired by God. "Through his close contact with God, a Christian artist knows what people yearn for," one informant said. Or, "through him God reveals."[4]

Each Monday morning Bienvenu writes a summary of the episode of the serial that is to be filmed that week. Before going to bed on Sunday evenings, he prays to God and begs him for inspiration and assistance in working out of the story line. Bienvenu states that all the comments made by the audience, actors, and his relatives are mixed into subsequent episodes, but that God reveals to him, in dreams or during prayers, the way toward the story line. Based on short abstracts of the scenes provided by Bienvenu, the performers must fill out the scenes using their own imagination. For the individual actors as well, prayer is a key source of divine afflatus. Ance told of how God had inspired him to perform a scene the following day:

> One day Bienvenu had not asked me to play. That is why I stayed at home. Suddenly, as I was dozing off, I heard an inner voice telling me: "You will play at Tshim Lay.[5] And you will say: "The way you transfer money is very good. Why don't you transform your agency into a bank?" The next day, Bienvenu called me and said: "You will play tomorrow at Tshim Lay." And I have said everything that I had prepared at home.

If Ance feels dissatisfied with his performance, then he not only prays but also fasts for a few days. According to him, this is a recipe for success.

This emphasis on the divine inspiration explains why the first definitions of a good performer that I collected invariably referred to the actors' improvisation skills, and also why the troupe hardly rehearses the serials' scenes. Although Cinarc rented a rehearsal space, it was used more to pray than to do artistic work. And, more often than not, the troupe did not come together on the rehearsal days. Moreover, when they did, Bienvenu or some of the elders divided the actors into small groups of four to six, which had to improvise on themes such as "a daughter tells her father about her pregnancy," "a pastor seduces a girl in church," "a suitor and his uncle visit his girlfriend's father and initiate marriage negotiations," "a paternal aunt arrives from the village and joins her son's household." These matters recur in all *maboke,* sometimes as minor plots, sometimes as the main story lines. These improvisation sessions took place maybe once a month, each time taking between thirty minutes and one hour. It is questionable how far these moments prepared the actors for the real work.

"Our fetish is prayer," the Cinarc performers stated over and over again. The actors themselves held prayer to be the key to inspiration. This supernatural dimension should not be underestimated. As Anya Peterson Royce notes (2004: 14), Western culture places much value on virtuosity and has left us blunted to the transformative aspects of performances.[6] Knowing what to say and when to say it is an outcome of the actor's spiritual connection with the Holy Spirit. Prayer then transforms the actor into a medium through which the Holy Spirit speaks. And, as I will develop further in the following chapter when discussing the corporality of acting, this is the basic requirement for not only a good improvisation but also an ethically acceptable performance. For the evangelizing artists, the inspiration retrieved through prayer is the equivalent of *bomoyi* (life) and resembles the *onction* (power) that Christian spiritual leaders receive. It is this Christian power that enables artists to deliver good work. Divine afflatus helps them read and represent the world in such a way that their acting teaches people.

Improvisation seems also to be a key element in Pentecostals' performances beyond Kinshasa. In his study of Zambian Pentecostal preachers, Kirsch describes how the preparations for Sunday sermons allow space for "the inspiration of the moment" and sudden changes. Bible verses and even the preachers that will deliver the sermons all depend on the indications transmitted by the Holy Spirit during the meeting (Kirsch 2008: 213–225). The unpredictable is the manifestation of the divine, and Christians, be they pastors or proselytizing actors, need to be prepared to follow the divine orientations that an outsider might perceive as volatile or random. Christians hold that God has plans, and these might not always be comprehensible to humans. Total faith and surrender allow a complete implementation of God's intentions. Also, here, Pentecostal popular culture is an articulation of the constant emergence of divine powers.

The Pastor

Access to the divine, which opens up realms of secret knowledge, imbues the Christian artist with charismatic power and puts him in the same category of bearers of authority as the pastor. This is why my informants recurrently stated that the evangelizing teleserials reveal in the same way that pastors' sermons do. This assumption is also shared by the viewers. Explaining the success of Cinarc's *maboke*, the mother of the household in Lemba where I lived for some time said, "It is clear that these actors are inspired by God because their stories appeal to everyone, because everybody learns something out of it." Then she immediately compared them with successful *pasteurs*: "A real *pasteur* preaches on Sunday morning as if he talks to you personally, you never leave his service (*culte*) without having learned something about your personal situation." In order to further contextualize the lionization of Christian artists and the meaning of special effects, an exploration into the social and religious standing of the pastor is warranted.

Kinshasa's Christians pay successful spiritual leaders considerable respect, saying that their house is consecrated when a man of God visits them. He is sought out when personal or familial problems arise. Friends or relatives who have arrived from the village or from abroad are often introduced to their host's pastor, who invariably blesses the visitors and prays for them. My entrances into the Cinarc group and the Kongo family (my hosts in the Lemba community) followed the same scheme: as early as the first week of my work with the drama group, the players insisted that I attend the weekly worship (*culte*) at their church and explain my mission to their pastor. After my first Sunday service there, the pastor laid his hands on me and asked God to assist me in my work. The same goes for the Kongo family, with whom I stayed during the second half of my fieldwork. The family's mother expected me to accompany her on the first Sunday morning to the worship in her church (where her children also prayed), and afterward she urged me to speak with the pastor (see fig. 4.2). The same request was made over and over during my fieldwork: many of my other informants asked me to accompany them at least once to their church.

Both Christian artists and pastors are said to have "charisma" (*likabu*, 'gift'). Kinois use the concept of charisma in a way similar to that described by Max Weber. For Weber (1947: 329), charisma is a quality that sets an individual apart from ordinary people, who treat that person as being endowed with supernatural or exceptional powers or qualities. In Kinshasa, this word is often also used as proof of a given spiritual leader's supernatural abilities. Prophesying and performing faith healing and miracles confirm that a pastor possesses the necessary charisma. Drawing on Weber's definition, one would expect that all experts of the occult and the divine could be designated as charismatic. In Kinshasa's Pentecostal milieus, however, the quality of charisma appears to be set apart uniquely for Christian spiritual leaders and others gifted with a divine talent. Through these Christian leaders, the divine intervenes in quotidian life. For Kinshasa's Christians, the transcendence these "people of God" mobilize is totally opposed to the type of mystical ac-

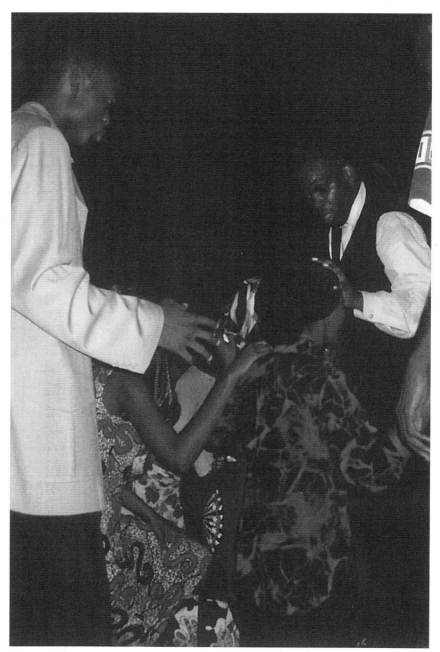

Figure 4.2. Pastor anointing followers (2005, © Katrien Pype)

tions that witches provoke. In the context of Kinshasa's Pentecostals, charismatic and mystical qualities thus become each other's opposites and refer to the two contrasting domains of the invisible.[7]

As Weber (1978: 230) writes, "the chief is often simply deserted if success deserts him." The leadership can be maintained only by proving supernatural capabilities and knowledge (Weber 1947: 329). Charisma is an inherently unstable category, since the exceptionality of the leader has to be proven again and again. In Kinshasa, pastors or leaders who fail to do so are suspected of having lost their privileged contact with the Holy Spirit. Expressions of such mistrust promptly travel around the city and stain the pastors' reputation; they then quickly lose followers and are left with an empty church. Kinshasa's spiritual leaders are very cognizant of this need for evidence, and they are often the first ones to speak about themselves as charismatic. During prayer meetings or sermons, Pastor Gervais frequently said, "Your pastor has enormous power," or "Your pastor has charisma," and then asked his followers to shout the word *charisme* three to five times. He furthermore often repeated miraculous interventions he had performed. This is totally in line with Weber's observation (1964: 227) that followers' loyalty and commitment is maintained as long as the leader "is able to retain their recognition by giving proofs." The following excerpt from my notes, taken during a prayer gathering of the theater group, illustrates how Pastor Gervais confirmed his supernatural powers:

> The gathering has nearly come to an end. There was not much ambiance during this session. I guess most of the actors were thinking about the upcoming *Mwana Mboka* elections. *Pasteur* Gervais has been annoyed with the rather reluctant singing, and he warns us that "those who are not serious about God will never succeed in what they desire." He presses the congregation to sing again, and this time he breaks into the song *Make a Miracle Happen* (*Sala likamwa*). After the song, he says that the Holy Spirit has informed him that some miracles are about to take place. Everyone with a particular problem will receive a solution, he promises: "Where death is present, it will be replaced by life." At this moment, one girl, who does not belong to the drama group but has been attending the service for a few weeks, begins to cry. Several boys rapidly position themselves behind her, just in time to catch her body that has begun to shiver. She is still in trance and making convulsions when the two boys carry her to the other side of the compound so that she does not interrupt the final part of this sermon. *Pasteur* Gervais comments that he saw a "spirit of sadness" (*molimo ya mawa*) leaving her body and encourages all of us to continue to pray. Afterwards he invites everyone with any kind of problems to come up to him, because "he feels that tonight the Holy Spirit is present, and He will act."
>
> The pastor promises the followers that "there where sickness reigns, he will dispel the disease and install peace." In order to confirm this claim,

he tells the community about miracles he himself has performed. In the same vein, the pastor speaks about invitations he has received to preach in Angola, Gabon, and even South Africa. Mentioning these foreign countries and informing the listeners about his successful passages should raise the esteem for the spiritual leader. He adds that people should seek to be in close contact with men of God, because their presence in one's life "can open doors" and even save one's life. In the following part of the sermon, the pastor summarizes his last visit to Brazzaville. He mentions that after one of the many preaching sessions he performed in a befriended church, a blind man came up to him, and told him that God had sent him to the "pastor of Kinshasa." Now, Pastor Gervais asks the group to repeat up to six times the question "What happened?" In these instances, the pastor is obviously playing a little game. Jokingly, he asks: "Do you really want to know? Show me, who wants to know the rest of the story?" People eagerly are waiting to hear the continuation of the event. They stand up, wave and shout "Tell us!" Encouraged by the enthusiastic response, Pastor Gervais recounts how he laid his hands on the man, prayed over him and asked him to return the following day. And, so the pastor says, the day after, the man arrived in the church without any companion. His sight was restored! Here, the pastor's words are fading out, people are clapping hands. The orchestra begins to play some music, inviting people to sing and dance. Calmly but with an enormous smile, the pastor approaches his chair and observes the dancing community.

Such tales about healing and miracles occurred very regularly in Pastor Gervais' sermons. Yet they invariably take place abroad: in Congo-Brazzaville, in Gabon and South Africa. Nobody seems to question the validity of these stories.

I often had the impression that the pastor was careful to tell stories that could not be verified by the congregation. After all, just as the reputation of an artist is subject to gossip and might be seriously taken into question, so a pastor's reputation can also be put to the test and even damaged. Lies, as well as rumors about making female followers pregnant or abusing his authority in another manner, are some of the reasons why a successful pastor can suddenly lose all esteem and be labeled a "false pastor" (*faux Pasteur*). In instances when there is no real occasion to verify the validity of the defamation, people test the *pasteurs* on their abilities to "know." I heard several stories about some *pasteurs* who were phoned during call-in television shows and unmasked as "false prophets." One young mother of the Lemba community told me that once, when she was watching a television show to which a Nigerian prophet had been invited, a male viewer called in to ask the prophet's blessing for his upcoming final exams. The prophet began to pray and stated that God had revealed to him that the caller would pass with an 86 percent mark. A few moments later, the same viewer called back with the message that he was a married man with children and was not going to be taking any exams. From that point on the Nigerian prophet was perceived to be a "false prophet." Significantly, there was no question as to the possibility of actually having such knowledge; rather, the access this particular person claimed to have with the divine was unmasked as false.

Knowing Secrets

An interesting twist occurred at the end of the conversation with the young woman in Lemba: according to her, the caller himself demonstrated possession of a spiritual gift—otherwise, how would he have known that the Nigerian man was a false prophet? "Real Christians" thus know more than others: they have access to hidden, secret information that others do not. Christian leaders confirm such suggestions time and again during sermons and in their evangelization campaigns on the street, in buses, on the radio and television. In the course of their sermons, *pasteurs* often ask their followers to repeat the phrase "Your pastor knows things." Sometimes they beg the whole community to repeat this phrase up to five times while waving their hands in the air. An excerpt of my field notes from a Sunday morning gathering at the Church of the Holy Mountain reads:

> *Pasteur* Gervais tells people that life is full of appearances. Shouting and waving with handkerchiefs, people acclaim their agreement. In a rather ironic tone he asks his followers why it is better to drive an old Mazda instead of a new Mercedes? He immediately answers his own question, saying that people very quickly become jealous if they notice what others possess. The problem is that people believe the things they see. According to him this is a problem. He again repeats that "one has to save one's appearances," and again, the listeners shout their agreement, clap their hands and say "Amen." *Pasteur* Gervais continues, stating that, in the end, everything must be interpreted in the light of the ongoing spiritual battle, which he defines as a battle between two spirits, the Holy Spirit against the Devil (and his demons). Every appearance, anything you see, is located in this battle. After explaining how the Devil might use false appearances, *Pasteur* Gervais says that the spirit of a pastor is superior to the spirit of other people and advises all of those present to come to him with problems of any kind.

In other instances, the pastor would break off his sermon and say:

> The Holy Spirit just told me that someone here has problems in his house-
> hold. In fact, that person might have doubted whether to join us tonight.
> But thanks to his belonging to God, he came to God's house. God wants
> you to know that He will take care of things. Who is it? Please come to
> see me after this session. We will speak about it. I will pray God to tell me
> more. You see, your pastor knows and will tell you.

Through such discourse, Pastor Gervais positioned himself as the
bearer of special knowledge. Receiving concrete information about the
divulgements proved to be rather difficult. The pastor and the persons
who were called by him would rarely share the content of the conversation. Yet some of my key informants told me on certain occasions what
the troupe's pastor or another spiritual leader had conveyed to them.
Several revelations could be summarized as "someone is preventing you
from getting married," "you do not find a job because you do not listen
to the right people," or "God wants you to convert truly; only then will
you achieve what you want." The knowledge these pastors share often
remains rather vague and may appear to be a culturally standardized
formula, which can acquire different meanings according to different
personal contexts. Yet this very game between knowing (or pretending
to know) and promising to show is an important strategy in the management of reputation in a society where authority is based on access to
sacred knowledge. The vagueness in the revelations discourse reminds
one of Michael Taussig's statement (1993: 273) that power flows not
from masking but from unmasking—or, at least, from the discourse
about one's capabilities of unmasking and the promises to do so. To
own secret knowledge, or to show that one does, is a form of power (Simmel 1965[1908]: 333–334, Nooter 1993: 58).

This bewildering game furthermore resonates with the rhetorical
management of secret knowledge in other African societies. Howard
Murphy (1981: 670) observed among the Kpelle (Liberia), for example,
that elders' skill in conveying the impression of having secret knowledge
is more important than the actual, concealed, content of the secrets
(Sg. *sekele*). Mary Nooter (1993: 57), who researched Luba art, another
dimension where secrecy is paramount, came to understand that the
power of the initiation secrets lay "not in their surrender, nor in the
disclosure of some 'within,' but in the strategies of concealment, and
in the tensions and boundaries they created among Luba people themselves and between Luba people and [herself]." She concludes that the

substance of the secrets was less important than "the social delineations resulting from their acquisition, ownership, and controlled revelation" (1993: 57–58). An often-cited expression in this regard is Jan Vansina's argument (1955: 138) that "the secret is empty": "the chief then called his village council and in their presence confessed that the secret of their initiation was that they had none."

The question of whether or not there is a secret is not relevant. All pastors with whom I spoke claimed firmly to know more than others. To be sure, the secret is out there, it travels in the social world, and many followers do believe that the charismatic leaders possess sacred knowledge. It is meaningful to understand what the content of the secret *could* be. As I described in Chapter 3, pastors promise that spiritual knowledge will help the born-again Christian read the spiritual condition of others and determine whether these others are life-giving or life-extracting beings. From an emic perspective, the secret centers on life (*bomoyi*) and the capacities that protect the flow of life. This is a perpetuation of the management of secrecy in non-Christian settings in Congo. In his discussion of secrecy in initiation and healing rituals among the Aluund, De Boeck mentions that the symbolism of the ritual practices transforms the human body into a secret (1995: 18). The same could be argued for Kinshasa's born-again Christians: insofar the secrets deal with the identification of one's double as divine or wicked, the bodies, as visible evidence of the double, are then the carriers of the secret of the flow of life. De Boeck described the Aluund rituals as highly charged with symbols relating to sexuality and food. Christians have marooned this sexual and social reproduction of their own group. If the indigenous initiation rituals displayed a concern for the perpetuation of the lineage, whose *bomoyi* was transmitted through blood, then it is no surprise that "life" was related to sexuality. In a Christian context, however, where discourse is centered on morality, "life" is primarily considered a spiritual entity not transmitted through biological reproduction, but through faith and social insertion in a patron-client relationship with a Christian leader.

Inspired by Simmel, the psychoanalyst Andreas Zempléni calls for a relational approach toward the construction of the secret, one that is felicitous for our discussion. In his view, three poles structure the practice of secrecy: the one who possesses the secret (*le détenteur*), the one to whom the secret is announced (*dépositaire*), and the one who is excluded from the secret knowledge yet to whom it is ultimately addressed (*destinataire*) (cf. Zempléni 1976: 313).[8] Born-again Christians, in particular the pastors, are said—or claim—to be the owners of the secret; they are the ones who will announce the secret content to those who convert, while their message is addressed to the pagans and the occult practitioners, whom they aim to convert.

It is also interesting to approach the spiritual knowledge and the revelations made by pastors, and Christian television actors as well, through the lens of "exposure" and "revelation" (Taussig 2003). "Revelation" remains within one particular perceptual mode of reality: revelation shows the hidden but does not undermine its secret, sacred, dangerous content. "Exposure" stands outside and uncovers the secret as false and hollow. Or, as Meyer (2003b: 203) notes, "the notion of exposure is part of a hierarchical perspective affirming the superiority of scientific thinking, which unmasks magic as false and based on mere superstition, the notion of revelation criticizes magic from within, thereby leaving intact the idiom itself." Discussing Ghanaian pastors and witchcraft films, Meyer contends that the pastors (and the video films) are engaged in revelatory work, not in exposure. Kinshasa's Christian experts do not question the existence or even the efficacy of witchcraft and magic, though they intend to disclose it. In this respect, we could say that the discourse described above certainly is revelatory. Yet these religious leaders are also engaged in undermining the power of witchcraft and its practitioners: they state and show in their dramatic performances that Jesus's power is stronger, and that "real Christians" cannot be affected by demonic forces, accordingly acclaiming their superiority over witchcraft. In this emic perspective, the revelatory work is understood as exposure.

The Pastor and the Diviner/Healer Compared

Nowadays, with the hegemony of Pentecostal-charismatic Christianity in Kinshasa's public culture, Christian leaders represent themselves as totally opposed to *féticheurs*. They designate the diviner and the healer and their clients into their Others, deploying idioms of witchcraft (eating life) when describing the practices of these agents. Whereas a diviner was customarily understood to "free" life (Devisch 1986: 130), in a Christian milieu all *banganga* are perceived to be "eaters of life"; different nuances of expertise among the Christians' adversaries are thus obliterated.

The relocation of these experts in the moral imagination is probably one of the most important transformations the social life worlds of the Congolese have undergone. Several texts on healing and divination in DR Congo and elsewhere in central Africa (Bekaert 2000; De Boeck 1991; Devisch 2004; MacGaffey 1986; Peek 1991; Stroeken 2004; Turner 1975) make clear that Kinshasa's born-again pastors perform roles similar to those of the diviner (*nganga m'bangu*) and the healer (*nganga n'kisi*). Though operating in distinctly different symbolic systems, all of these experts of the invisible share some meaningful characteristics: they articulate theories of evil and counteract fear and anxiety by imposing taboos, assigning meaning, and instructing their clients, though drawing from different meaning systems. In this respect—although in Kinshasa's Christian universe the pastor (in particular the prophet) is opposed to both the *féticheur* (general term for diviner and healer) and the witch—they are all included within one spiritual scheme. Pentecostal-charismatic Christianity accordingly offers a particular form of appropriation of the "foreign" religion into autochthonous structures of causality (MacGaffey 1986: 217–251; Tonda 2000).

How was this appropriation by Christian experts possible? Thirty years ago, Victor Turner indicated that divination and healing, as he encountered them among the Ndembu, were historical phenomena that might easily be transformed. He wrote: "All societies develop a need both for revelation and divination and construct appropriate cultural instruments for satisfying these needs.... [M]an cannot tolerate darkness; he must have light, whether it be the sunlight of revelation or the flaring torch of divination" (1975: 29). Turner thus understood divination as a collectively but timely approved response to a crisis in the life of the community (1975: 27). In his introduction to the study of divination, Philip M. Peek emphasizes the diversity in divinatory systems and divining processes (1991: 2). Echoing Turner, he writes: "Careful choices are made in each culture among many possible methods, mediums, and materials for divination" (1991: 12). The same author contends that divination systems "are not simply closed ideologies founded on religious beliefs" but are "dynamic systems of knowledge" (1991: 2). This openness and malleability of divination probably enabled it to be inserted easily within Pentecostal-charismatic Christianity. Ethnographies among the baYaka (Devisch 1993; 2004), the baSakata (Bekaert 2000), and the Aluund (De Boeck 1991) confirm that for a long time in most rural communities, healers and diviners embodied the stronghold of a society. Gradually, Christian symbols were incorporated. In her research on healing practitioners among the Nkanu, both in their autochthonous area and in Kinshasa, Creten (1996) displays how the Nkanu ritual specialists merged new Christian schemes within their symbolical actions and their etiology. Devisch (1986: 128, footnote) mentions the innovative category of an "exorcizing diviner" (*devin exorciste*), whose power derives from the knowledge of secret medicines and the Holy Spirit. Likewise, Bekaert observed that with Christianization, the role of ancestors in the divination process had been replaced by Jesus or Mary (2000: 278).

Both kinds of specialists (the indigenous experts and the Christian leaders) express a cosmological grid, but the similarities between the social roles and practices go much deeper. A profound and more thorough investigation of those categories is needed to better understand the analogies and divergences between pastors and diviners and healers within Kinshasa's complex symbolic system. The following proposal, based on a comparison of my field data about Christian spiritual leaders and academic sources on divination (Turner 1975; De Boeck 1991; De Boeck and Devisch 1994; Creten 1996; Bekaert 2000; Devisch 2004; Stroeken 2004; Winkelman and Peek 2004), can therefore be only an initial attempt to highlight a few striking similarities between these specialists.

In their ethnographic research on divination and healing in rural, peri-urban or even urban settings in Congo, De Boeck, Devisch, Creten, and Bekaert demonstrate that healing and divination aim to restore the stream of the life flow, that is, to reconnect the individual with the source of life. The same discourse is used in Kinshasa's Christian churches. Of the charismatic healing churches, for example, Devisch (1996: 567) writes, "healing is about alliance, being filled ... re-entering the full stream of life." In the Pentecostal-charismatic churches, a similar discourse is deployed: when a Christian filled with the Holy Spirit lays hands on someone, he or she reconnects with the Holy Spirit, who is ultimately the wind of life itself. However, when pastors restore the individual's spiritual balance, they do not aim to "unblock" the life flow by appeasing ancestral spirits and restoring harmony with agnatic and/or uterine lines, as would have been the case in autochthonous contexts. Rather, they seek to free the individual from evil and reconnect him or her with the divine source of life.

Like diviners, pastors are considered mediators between different worlds, and their role is to transmit messages and channel life-bearing forces between spirits and their followers. Devisch (2004: 262) writes that the diviner disavows any authorship of vision and judgment and pretends that whatever message he or she may be voicing stems from the divinatory forces at work in him or her, or in the divinatory media. Christian pastors frequently proclaim in their sermons that God is speaking through them. Like a diviner, the Christian leader attributes all authority to an exterior spirit, in casu the Holy Spirit, who uses the pastor's body and voice to pass on his messages.

The main transformation is in the identification of the external spirit. Whereas Devisch (2004: 252) and De Boeck (1991: 341-367) emphasize that the spirits working through the diviner are ancestral spirits, the dead, spiritual agencies, or other spirits evoked through witchcraft, Kinshasa's born-again Christians regard the pastor as a mediator between the human being and the Holy Spirit or demonic spirits.

Another common feature shared by diviners and the pastors is that their actions are directed against one and the same enemy: the witch. In his discussion on divination among the Ndembu, Victor Turner writes that the "reality" the diviner professes is "a secret war of all on all" (1975: 25). The diviner looks for secret causes of misfortune and restores disorder by ostracizing or physically punishing "the secret plotter," the witch (1975: 24–25). In the same vein, Devisch describes witchcraft as the anti-pole of divination (1986: 119). Just as the Yaka diviner must prove symbolically that he can withstand all sorcery and evil (Devisch 2004: 250–251) and accordingly master the life-giving powers (2004: 248), Kinshasa's born-again pastors claim that their spiritual forces are more powerful than those of witches. We could state that both the diviner and the pastor depend on the (real or imagined) existence of the witch: their actions are set in motion through the outcomes of witchcraft and aim to restore them.

The most important connection between the symbolic practices of diviners, healers, and pastors, however, is the emphasis on bringing what is hidden or unknown into the open. As Turner (1975: 211–212) wrote about Ndembu divination and healing, "the main theme of revealing the hidden is exemplified in all cults to cure persons afflicted by ancestor spirits with disease, reproductive disorders, or bad luck at hunting. The process of cure is essentially a process of what Ndembu call 'making known and visible' (*ku-solola*) or (*ku-mwekesa*) albeit in symbolic guise, the unknown and invisible agents of affliction." Disclosing what has previously been concealed is how Ndembu imagine divination. It uncovers hidden causes of ills brought about by designating immoral persons. According to Douglas and Stroeken, exactly the same concern for delving deeper into the "Real," instead of merely relying on "appearances," urges people to contact diviners (Douglas 1979: 129 in Winkelman and Peek 2004: 5; Stroeken 2004). As argued before, born-again Christians and their pastors too contend that appearances do not lead to the Real. The ancestor-related system and the ideology of born-again Christianity locate the Real elsewhere. According to Congolese autochthonous beliefs and certain charismatic healing churches in Kinshasa (as opposed to the mainstream and Pentecostal-charismatic Christian churches), ancestors symbolize the Real. In Kinshasa's born-again Christian context, however, the uncertainty about the whereabouts of the ancestors (see Chapter 2) already indicates that they cannot embody the Real.[9]

Special Effects as Visual Evidence

I now turn to the Christian actors' artistic work itself, the television serials. How must we understand the *maboke* as a reflection of the artists' privileged vision and the proof of their sacred knowledge? In what mode do the electronically mediated narratives produced by Christian artists evince their charisma? Which arguments do Kinois people use to imagine the Pentecostal melodrama as enmeshed in this particular configuration of the otherworldly secrecy and special knowledge?

The meaning of special effects or *trucage* is of interest in our discussion about media and glimpses of the Real, not only because of the compelling remark by Bienvenu with which I opened this chapter, but also when we consider that this kind of *trucage* is the only aesthetic technique that Kinshasa's artists use on the scenes once they have been filmed. Hardly any flashbacks or flash-forwards are inserted, but special effects are very common. These manipulated images are commonly understood to visualize the hidden world. The special effects are simulacra of what Christians consider miracles and occult practices, and they therefore appear in key scenes depicting such events as a performance of non-Christian dances, a visit to a "traditional" healer, cursing someone, or other moments of bewitchment. In *Kalaonga*, the female protagonist, a siren, attempts to seduce the married Caleb,* her friend's father. Spraying perfume on him, she gets him under her spell. He is suddenly charmed by her beauty, and after some flirting, she traps her father's friend in a kiss. In the moment when the two pairs of lips touch, the witch is able to capture Caleb's double. After having excused herself to the bathroom, she secretly locks his soul in a bottle by spitting the saliva.[10] Caleb's soul is visualized in a miniature of the regular Caleb, who can only jump up and down in agony, floating as he tries to free himself (figs. 4.3 and 4.4).

This special effect is not perceived as fantastic but appears to depict something quite possibly real and attains a high degree of verisimilitude to how witchcraft works. I went with Bienvenu to the TV studios, where an RTG@ employee, who was usually called when a tape had arrived, was doing the editing and mixing of that week's episode. Bienvenu commented on the scene that was being edited. In a serious tone, he said that this was how witches got hold of their victims—by putting put their spirits into food, drink, or perfume, as the *Kalaonga* serial shows. "We show on screen how this bewitchment takes place. But do not think that

*These moving images are available at http://www.berghahnbooks.com/title.php?rowtag=PypeMaking

Figures 4.3. and 4.4. The witch locks her victim's double in a bottle (screen shots *Kalaonga,* © Cinarc)

it is not true, because it is real," he continued. In an attempt to safeguard his Christian reputation, Bienvenu cleverly added that the Cinarc actors themselves do not possess the occult power necessary to visualize bewitchment and must therefore resort to *trucage.*

Research on African arts shows that the most important function of Africa's visual arts is to "act as a visual means of broadcasting secrecy—of publicly proclaiming the ownership of privileged information while protecting its contents" (Nooter 1993: 58). Most African art reveals by concealing (see also Hackett 1994; Murphy 1998), and the actual content of the secret is not betrayed. Masquerades, for example, and the dense but enigmatic iconography of visible arts, construct an aesthetic of "restricted access and partial perception" (Nooter 1993: 66). The secret "is always poised on the threshold of understanding and obscurity, of penetration and prohibition" (1993: 68). Assuming that these local cultural aesthetics still continue to influence local evaluations of good art, a question emerges: Are the special effects not in fact doing the opposite? In other words, how is it understood that the *maboke* extensively show occult work within these local aesthetic norms?

In my view, we can only understand the emphasis on special effects in Kinshasa's television serials if we take into account the transformation of Kinshasa's culture and the status that the visual has assumed in the appreciation of hiding and revealing. Colonization and Christianization altered the networks of meaning and people's relationships with the image, as Mbembe (1997: 152) notes in a discussion of "The Thing and Its Double." Alan P. Merriam, based on his observation of a village in the eastern Kasai region during the 1970s, remarked (1974) that the ongoing transformations in religion (i.e., increasing Christianization) were resulting in even more dramatic changes in visual art. The village was bereft of carved wooden figurines and masks, he reported; mask societies had died out, and no new masks were being carved. Whereas the emerging nationalist Mobutu ideology had given music and dance a boost, visual arts had experienced a tremendous decline because of a too apparent association with "traditional" religion. In a study on the meanings of *minkisi* (magical objects) among the baKongo, Wyatt Mac-Gaffey (1988: 189) observed that the use of *minkisi,* whose functions of government, healing and divination depended to a large extent on their visual effect, had been camouflaged in response to repressive action by secular and religious authorities. Moreover, when he compared the modern *minkisi* described by Laman, an ethnographer working in the first two decades of the twentieth century in the Lower Congo, with the *minkisi* of the early postcolonial baKongo society, he found the latter lacked the spectacular and dramatic qualities of their predecessors.

The innovations in representation that Merriam and MacGaffey point out were triggered by mainstream Christianity and modern ideologies like Mobutism. The monopoly of special effects in the Pentecostal melodrama is intrinsically related to the emergence of Pentecostalism and the new modalities of religious mediation (see Meyer 2006b: 435).[11] As Meyer (2006b: 439) argues, Pentecostal Christianity sets itself off against "traditional" religion, which asserts its rootedness in secrecy. She stresses that Christianity, in colonial missionary endeavors, was associated with light and public presence, while "traditional" religion was understood as hidden and wrapped in darkness.[12] In contrast to "traditional" religion, where entry to the Real behind the appearances was restricted to distinguished priests, Protestantism—and with it its flourishing offspring, Pentecostal-charismatic Christianity—made available to all the capacity to understand what lies behind the surface appearances. The "spirit of discernment," the gift of being able to retrace the spiritual bonds of people and their actions, connects with the camera's revelatory possibilities. This explains the salient use of special effects in Christian *maboke:* just as pastors explicate witchcraft and its actions in their sermons, the Pentecostal melodrama thematizes occult workings in its dramatization and visualizes this through special effects.

These data on special effects support Taussig's statement (1993: xiv) that new techniques of visual reproduction such as cinema and mass production of imagery may spark a rebirth, recharging, and retooling of the mimetic faculty, meaning the human ability to copy and imitate. While I reserve my discussion of the spiritual consequences of Kinshasa's mimetic performances for the next chapter, I want to pause here at the appropriation of electronic and digital media within the Pentecostal mimesis production.

Recently, the entanglement of visual media and religion, or the local use of modern technology to mediate and represent the otherworldly in different (Western and non-Western) societies, has inspired both anthropologists and theologians to embrace this modern terrain. It has taken a long time, however, for academics to acknowledge the influence of media on religious experiences. Only now are we observing the emergence of a body of literature dealing with the religious appropriation of modern technologies such as photography and other recording materials. The data range from spirit photography during the nineteenth century in the West to the religious reception of material from early and contemporary ethnographic encounters (among others Smith and Vokes 2008; Morris 2009). Before these, most researchers probably followed Heidegger's (1977) assertion that visual media technologies could only originate in the Western world, where knowledge and its acquisition, revelation, and articulation depend on visibility, and could only bring about the ruin of religious experience.

James Weiner (1997) argues that although these machineries embody Western concepts of representation, "visualism," and subjectivity, one may not take for granted that the material objects transfer these culturally dependent approaches to knowledge and its ability to be represented, into cultures governed by non-Western modes of knowledge and knowledge distribution. Relations between signs, concepts, and sociality are culturally dependent, Weiner maintains. A fine example is the perception of photomontage in Kenya. In a discussion of early photographic montage in 1960 in Lamu (Kenya), Heike Behrend (2009: 189) argues that the surrealistic collages that resulted from darkroom manipulation and manipulation by scissors and paste did not appear as strange or scandalous to the East African spectators. Rather, they linked up with artistic traditions such as the art of ornamental woodcarving, plasterwork in local architecture, embroidery, textiles, and calligraphy, and thus appeared as a continuation of these art forms.

Apart from artistic tradition, local religious beliefs also inform the production, manipulation, and reception of images. In the Lamu context, it was exactly the Islamic prohibitions of images that encouraged the photographer to experiment with collage. "Although the artist is not allowed to imitate Godly creation, he or she is accorded the freedom to experiment with the abstract depiction of various parts of God's world, and to recombine them within new ensembles," Behrend argues (2009: 189). Local perceptions of personhood and subjectivity also define the status of the image and what can be done with it. As I discuss in more detail in the following chapter, Congolese ethnographies emphasize that the soul of a human being can be captured in an image, be it one's shadow or photograph. Benjamin Smith and Richard Vokes (2008: 283) suggest a similar intimate, spiritual connection between religion and modern mimetic technology when they argue that in some Latin American and Australian societies, there is only one term to denote a photographic image and a ghost. Cultural anthropologists embarking on ethnographies of mass mediated realities nowadays start from the premise that transposing visual media to other societies that do not endorse the Western ontology behind these semiotic relations will have different consequences.

In one respect, research carried out by Bellman and Jules-Rosette (1977) in the 1970s proved that there is no universal grammar for filming events, though local metaphors and stylistic conventions may appropriate the medium. One of Jules-Rosette's most interesting discoveries was that her informants (the Bapostolo community in Kananga, Kasai province in Congo) filmed the singing congregation at length, frequently in close-up, while disregarding the pastor's sermon. This surprising emphasis on singing believers was visual evidence of the significance the Bapostolo accorded to singing as nourishing the body with divine power. This privileging of song may be contrasted with the gaze of a Western observer, whose main attention is oriented at the discursive instructions of sermons.

Although Bellman and Jules-Rosette's experimental work has not received much attention, most anthropologists accept that photographs and cinema have reshaped the way people perceive each other. Despite the introduction of these technologies in postcolonial African societies, an imaginary world remains and continues to impose a religious framework on the uses of figurative expressions (Mbembe 1997: 152). Behrend (2003: 131) has shown how, in an east African context, photography contributed substantially to the emergence of a modern, positivistic culture of realism but at the same time strengthened the latter's shadow side, the fantastic.[13] In Lamu, love magic was supposed to work through the combination of the pictures of the heads of two lovers: a young man's head in the heart of a famous Indian actress, and his lover's head as a shadow behind and below the lover's portrait (Behrend 2009: 198). The collage suggests the magical work of the image through the mediation of the portrait of the Indian actress, who appears as the ideal woman and brings the two lovers together.

Although I never encountered a similar, magical use of images among Kinshasa's Pentecostals, the spiritual efficacy of images and special effects seemed to be taken for granted. Still, given the overall spiritual confusion, my informants warned me that not all "special effects" are really special effects. Some of the *trucage* could be called "false special effects,"[14] even though this phrasing is never used in Kinshasa, since "false special effects" are not manipulated images and thus are not considered to be *trucage*. These images, "false special effects," do not derive from a spiritual knowledge that Christian artists have received through Christian rituals but are perceived to be the work of the Devil. The footage, then, is not considered to present a copy of reality but is "real"—part of the occult reality. I will take this point further in Chapter 5, when I discuss the performative powers of mass-mediated images, and especially when I point to the mystical influence of "false special effects" on spectators.

In the new literature dealing with the interface between religion and media, both theologians and anthropologists are beginning to acknowledge the importance of "mediatization and the technology it entails as a condition of possibility for all revelation" (de Vries and Weber 2001a: 28).[15] As analyzed in Chapter 2, spiritual vision ("peering into the occult realms") ultimately depends on connections with occult forces. The ability to "see" (or the lack thereof) is one marker of a person's spiritual identity. Concerned with equating miracles with special effects, de Vries and Weber (2001a: 23) try to illustrate the interface of the religious and the medium, the theological and the technological. Their insistence on the technicity of distinct phenomena like the miracle and the special effect would "correct a simplistic opposition between realms we only wish to be kept apart" (2001a: 28). However, the mass-mediated transmission of occult and sacred powers is not to be taken for granted. Each society has its own approach to mass media.

In an essay on mediums and electronic technology in northern Thailand, Rosalind Morris (2002: 289) rightly argues that "the aspiration of mediation is the disclosure of the Real, which otherwise cannot be contained in or by language." That is why human mediums, when they become possessed, speak via glossolalia and uncontrollable bodily gestures. Such phenomena express the linguistic untranslatability of the Real in the Thai context. Quoting Friedrich Kittler, a German researcher on the comparative history of technologies such as the typewriter, cinema, and gramophone, Morris argues that "noise," as in the scratching of gramophones or the fuzziness of the cinematic image, is the expression of the Real. Via sound and images, an immediate access to the Real is possible. The symbolic is circumvented; the Real appears with an unseen immediacy. In African Pentecostal communities, as well, it seems to be possible to capture the Real, or at least some of its manifestations. The realms of the technological and the theological are definitely not kept apart. Meyer (2009b: 119), for example, argues that for Ghanaian Pentecostals, video images of pastors' miracles serve as proof of their charisma, during which spectators watching the video are made into eyewitnesses of the pastors' spiritual powers. The performance of miracles and the celebration of vision, two key features of African Pentecostal Christianity (see Meyer 2009b: 120) produce an aesthetics that combines science, fiction, and irrationality and claims to offer true, and at times truthful, representations of the Real.

A fine example of the possibilities that new technologies provide for representing Kinois' approach to reality is a photo I took during a special prayer gathering organized by one of the troupe's spiritual leaders. In this event, which lasted two days, Pastor Flavien repeatedly promised to endow people with financial anointment. The services themselves were held on a sandy crossroad in Lemba Salongo Nord, just a two-minute walk from the church. For the occasion, plastic chairs and the electric music equipment were set up on the crossroad itself. No cars were hindered, since the roads in that area are too narrow for motor traffic. On each of the two days, the event began at sunset and lasted until after midnight. Singing, praying, and pronouncements of blessing appealed to the Holy Spirit to manifest itself. According to the participants, the Spirit's presence was physically felt: many people collapsed and "fell in spirits" to the floor. I was able to take some pictures (fig. 4.5.) on the first day, and on the following morning, when Chapy came to my house for one of our long interviews, I showed him some of the pictures I already had downloaded onto my portable computer. While downloading, I noticed a vertical orange streak blurring the image in

Figure 4.5. The divine fire captured in a photo during a prayer vigil (2006, © Katrien Pype)

most of these pictures. Something technical had gone wrong, I thought, and my first thought was to erase them. But then, because I knew that Chapy would be disappointed if he could not have a look at the shots before I deleted them, I decided to keep them for a while.

Much to my surprise, the pictures impassioned Chapy, who told me the orange lines were "the pillar of fire" (Fr. *la colonne de feu*, Li. *likonzi ya moto*) of the Holy Spirit. He convinced me not to erase them, and I felt I was on the trail of something special. When I arrived at the crossroad that afternoon, I encountered JC and Nene, who already had heard about the pictures and wanted copies. In the end, the pictures testified to miracles of healing and proved that the troupe's pastor had the power to evoke the Holy Spirit. What we encounter here is the insertion of technology into the religious world. In contrast to the human being, whose eyes that can easily be fooled and are also limited to the world of the tangible, the technological apparatus can provide humans with alternative, morally legitimate tools to render visible what otherwise lingers in the dark, or what can only be accessed by gifted, charismatic, or mystical individuals.

These data are similar to what Meyer observed in Ghana, where technology can "operate like the eyes of the priest, witch and magician": film can "offer a deeper vision than the one provided by one's own eyes, a vision similar to the special eyes of 'traditional' priests and the so-called 'spirit of discernment' which allows Christian preachers to penetrate into the realm of darkness" (Meyer 2003a: 27–28). The camera provides people with the viewpoint of God (Meyer 2003b: 215) and accordingly claims the ultimate power of revelation (2003b: 220).

Conclusion: Special Effects and Melodrama

In Kinshasa, all discourse about the invisible is imbued with secrecy and exclusivity. Pastors and other Christian leaders promise potential converts the possibility of attaining "divine spiritual knowledge." The pastor and the community of born-again Christians thus lay claim to a knowledge superior to that of non-Christians. Secrets are created and transmitted in an attempt to construct and maintain boundaries between Christians and their others, and also to enlarge the born-again Christian community. The promise of appropriating spiritual wisdom is, then, one of the most effective strategies these Christian spiritual leaders use to bind their followers to themselves. The aesthetics of the Pentecostal melodrama are embedded in this game between revealing and hiding. In line with the Protestant emphasis on disclosing the hidden to all, special effects contribute to the discernment of the good and the bad, the true and the false, the divine and the wicked.

Finishing this section on the revelatory function of visual media, I want to reflect on the genre of the melodrama itself. It could be argued that it is precisely melodrama that, as an art form, best fits Kinshasa's (or sub-Saharan urban Africa's) emphasis on the occult (also Meyer 2004b: 100). Brooks describes the melodrama as a mode of excess. The main message of the melodrama is that a hidden realm of reality governs the world, and the articulation of this hidden world, worded by Brooks as "a play of signs" (1976: 28), constitutes the melodrama. The novel writers Brooks examines, in his work on the melodramatic imagination, use a play of metaphors and metonyms to verbalize the hidden. All these signs have a depth of symbolic meaning: they are mere signifiers, but their spectacular or visual interaction weighs heavily. In contrast to nineteenth-century novels, which used the interior monologue to express the invisible—located in the individual's psychological interior—Kinshasa's serials (like Ghanaian and Nigerian witchcraft films) emphasize the demonic, which is manifested through special effects.

We must pose the question about the historical and cultural emergence of the melodrama and the use of special effects in contemporary Kinshasa. The *Salongo* serials produced during Mobutu's reign also exploited special effects, though not to the same extent as the present serials do. It is precisely the Pentecostal-charismatic Christian emphasis on vision, that is, on seeing and showing the real behind the appearances, that encourages Christian producers to insert *trucage* in their serials. Genres such as sermons and evangelizing TV serials share the same revelatory space. They originate from the invisible, and render it visual via images and/or discourse. As mentioned, special effects are not only meaningful within the *maboke* or in the sphere of the proselytizing project. *Trucage* also lays claim to the spiritual superiority of the Christian artists and thus contributes to the perceived morality of the TV group and its status within Kinshasa's celebrity world, a subject to which I turn in the next chapter.

Finally, the data in this chapter have indicated various "bodies" of religious mediation: the pastor, the diviner, the healer and the evangelizing artist all have privileged access to spiritual worlds. Divine mediation, as it has been shown, does not "fall" on the Christian leader/follower. Rather, prayer seems to be the necessary technique to prepare the medium for the transfer of divine knowledge. Here, it becomes clear the divine mediation is something that requires the agency of the Christian subject.

Notes

1. Meyer observed the same stress on reality in the reception of Ghanaian films—films that have much in common with Nigerian films: "Many films start with the short notice 'Based on a true story,' and this is what people actually expect from cinema. I noticed a strong dislike for science-fiction and other 'fantastic' stories (many people assured me that films as *E. T.* and *Jurassic Park* would not do well in Ghana).... People clearly judge particular films against the background of their understanding of the medium as such and continuously ask the question whether what they see may be true" (Meyer 2003a: 26–27).

2. These approaches are not unique to Kinshasa. Stephanie Newell (2002: 3), who also observed the strong affinities between African urban literature, gossip, conversations, and quotidian talk, creates the word "quasi-fictions" to characterize the real component of texts belonging to African popular culture in general. With "quasi-fictions" (instead of "quasi-*reality*") Newell raises the idea that African tales and narratives are not perceived as fictitious.

3. Kinois display the same attitude toward politicians, sportsmen, and other successful leaders in society.

4. In line with Thomas J. Csordas's (1994) rationalization of knowledge of charismatic healers in the North American movement of the Charismatic Catholic Renewal, we can rationalize the mystical knowledge of Kinshasa's Christian pastors: they know what people want to hear because they share the same habitus.

5. Tshim Lay is a local communications and money transfer agency and an important sponsor of Kinshasa's popular culture. Musicians and important television artists regularly "throw" this company's name. Cinarc and a few other groups go there every week to film scenes and make advertisements for the company.

6. I acknowledge Kelly Askew for pressing me to elaborate on Royce's distinction between virtuosity and artistry.

7. Similarly, miracles (*likamwi, likamwisi,* derived from *kokamwisa,* 'to astound') are performed by charismatic persons, while their counterpart, the concepts of the "mystique" and "magic," are only used in the context of the occult.

8. For an application of this grid on secrecy in Aluund initation and healing rituals, see De Boeck (1991: 283; 1995: 11, 13).

9. However, the mere fact that Kinois consult both types of experts (Christians and diviners) indicates that, at least among ordinary Kinois, there is still some puzzlement about the localization of the Real.

10. Locking people in bottles is very popular in east African photography. It refers to beliefs that spirits are stored, contained in objects. According to Farris Thompson, around 1700 in DR Congo, people placed bottles near trees in order to summon the dead and ask them for protection over the dwellings (in Behrend 2009: 202). The special effect in *Kalaonga* might be influenced by these local beliefs of containing spirits. But it is probably inspired by a very similar scene in the Nigerian film *Living in Bondage,* which has been shown on Kinshasa's screens from time to time. I wish to thank Matthias Krings for pointing out this similarity to me.

11. Curiously, a particular set of the colonial films produced by the missionaries de Vloo and Verstegen in the Congo exploited *trucage* and special effects to give the illusion of magical and divine powers. This small category of films dif-

fered largely from the other colonial films produced in the Congo, although they were highly popular among the colonized (Ramirez and Rolot 1985: 407–410).

12. Writing about the baYaka, Devisch (1991: 298) observes: "super-vision is seen as an essential attribute of sorcerers and chiefs."

13. Similar observations stem from research in Australian aboriginal communities, where video technologies themselves are manipulated in order to transmit knowledge in the same way as do paintings, rituals, and legends (Deger 2006), and social practices of viewing and circulating these video products reflect long-standing cautiousness and concerns about the management of secret knowledge (Ginsburg 2006).

14. I thank Sten Hagberg for pointing me at this.

15. Writing about Western scholarly traditions neglecting visual arts in general, Rosalind Hackett (1994: 301) suggests that the Protestant backgrounds of many scholars of African religions have privileged written texts over visual symbols.

CHAPTER 5

Mimesis in Motion

Embodied Experiences of Performers and Spectators

It was December 2004. The serial *The Open Tomb* had just begun, and Anne was already, once again, the victim of her role. She was at the time starring as a witch in the role of an adulterous woman who had made the trip from Mbuyi-Mayi to Kinshasa. There, her character, Theresia, started an affair with Makubakuba, her best friend's husband, and consulted a *féticheur* to kill Maman Jeanne, her best friend. As a result of the invisible law of exchange with the occult (implying that the one who receives something from the occult world becomes a witch in turn), Theresia became a witch who could bridge the invisible and the visible worlds as well as take on the appearance of others. In one episode, Theresia appeared as Maman Jeanne and bewitched the latter's children. A few days after the episode was broadcast, Anne went to another part of the city, Yolo, on an errand. When she stepped out of the car, some children who thought Anne really was Theresia insulted her and threw stones at her. Anne escaped only by fleeing into an open compound where she was out of sight of the children. This event, in which the children clearly conflated the actress with her TV persona was not an isolated case. People would frequently stop me and ask: "Theresia is really a witch. That actress is a witch herself, no?" Around the same time, Anne's family began to suffer repeated insults in public. They endured the stigma these roles inflicted on her, and several times I heard Anne complaining about the roles of wicked persons she usually had to perform. She longed to play the role of the pastor's wife or some other decent part that would allow her to walk around the city in peace.

Anne's experiences introduce the concept that performers cross boundaries between the supernatural and the human world when imitating evil and wicked characters. According to Frances Harding (2002: 2), this transgression is common to all forms of (cultural) performance, but in Africa, danger consistently lurks in the performing moment because "these boundaries cannot be crossed either in ordinary guise, nor permanently, without invoking life-threatening sanctions of death, social ostracization or physical affliction." Wole Soyinka, the Nigerian dramaturge, wrote about this bridge between several worlds and realities as "the transitional yet inchoate matrix of death and becoming" (1976: 142 in Harding 2002: 2). Today in Kinshasa, cultural performances, including those that imitate real-life experiences, are not spiritually neutral. When exhibiting the work of the Devil on stage, the actors are believed to take great risks that resemble the spiritual jeopardy Christian spiritual leaders must face. Therefore, TV actors regularly perform religious rituals that are said to "strengthen the soul" (*kolenda molimo*).

In this chapter, the concerns of the Yolo children who threw stones at Theresia/Anne and Anne herself are taken seriously by zooming in on the various transgressions between the palpable and the invisible that are actualized when acting and when watching the performances. The data thus allow us to delve deeper into the various mediating modes of popular culture. The body—of both the performer and the spectator—will be identified as an important channel for spiritual powers.[1] Dance, bodily imitation, songs, and expressions (be they uttered in the frame of a fictive universe or in the "reality" modus) set in motion visual and aural modes through which invisible forces can travel, and via which identities are constructed in the earthly realm. The spiritual confusion described in the previous chapters and the uncertainty and indeterminacy that accompany it also seep through in the work and lives of the television actors and their spectators.

Going into Seclusion

Like many other TV drama groups in Kinshasa, Cinarc organizes special prayer sessions at which participating members not only seek inspiration but also solicit spiritual guidance and protection. These sessions are held twice a week, during the Sunday services at the church and, midweek, at the private compound of the Cinarc leader. In addition, when approaching the end of the production of a serial, the drama group withdraws for two or three days (often from Friday evenings until Sunday mornings or afternoons) to the compound of a befriended church or prayer group to prepare the next story. If at any point one of the troupe's members senses an attack by the Devil, the acting company as a whole decides to do some serious introspection during the withdrawal (*maquis*). Frequently they will refrain from eating, though most time is spent praying because prayer, it is believed, is the only weapon the actors hold. During these sessions, the rituals performed are the same as those used by other, non-artistic Christians to enter into dialogue with the divine: prayers, Christian songs and dances, Bible teachings, exorcism rituals, confessions, and eventually prophecies. These actions belong to a stock set of Pentecostal rituals.

The seclusions invariably follow the same structure. From the first night onward, throughout the retreat, the Christians worship God in songs and dances and ask him to strengthen their souls so that they might be preserved from spiritual harm. Singing and dancing often lasts until 2 or 3 A.M. At dawn, around 5 A.M., the participants hold another prayer session. Saturday morning, time is spent on dramatic work such as distributing the roles, filling out characters, or brainstorming alternative plots. Sometimes these preparations are interrupted by other engagements such as the staging of a play in a neighboring school or church. Some members of the group might also go to television studios to participate in talk shows. Those who are not performing or have not been invited to the television studios remain in the compound either to prepare meals or to continue with rehearsals, which are nevertheless constantly interrupted by breaks for prayer.

During this period of isolation, there may be incidents that eventually inspire the Cinarc company to drop the idea of the story line chosen for the current TV drama and start all over again with a new script and a fresh story. Other *maquis* evolve better and promise good work and success. The following abstract is a synopsis of one of the withdrawals in which I participated.

11–13 March 2005 (Friday–Sunday)

Jef and Chapy want the Cinarc actors to go on a retreat because the troupe is planning a new serial called *The Nanas Benz*. There are also a number of other reasons for them to go into seclusion. Fans have been complaining about the lack of creativity in the *maboke,* and rumors have spread that not all Cinarc actors are "real Christians", since there have been so many scenes in which the actors dance urban dances and drink beer. Jef and Chapy are worried about the reputation of the group. They think some criticisms are well founded because a few actors have been misbehaving recently. Anne showed up drunk at the weekly prayer gathering, and Hughuette, Ance, and Carine do not regularly attend the praying events any more. In order to put a stop to the criticism, all the actors are expected to renew their divine forces. During the three days of seclusion they must ask God's forgiveness for their misbehavior and request his help in ensuring the success of the theater company. Further, in a few weeks' time the Mwana Mboka trophies will be awarded, and the Cinarc actors are convinced that they deserve this prize. During the retreat they will persistently pray that they will win this trophy. In short, the main arguments for this withdrawal are centered on healing, becoming inspired, and influencing reality.

We have gathered in the CEFAC compound[2] in Mbinza, in the neighborhood called "cité Baudouin," located in the green Mbinza hills. Three families are living in the first house, while the two other houses on the premises are rented for special prayer gatherings. The empty swimming pool—now a garbage dump—reminds many of the bygone glory of colonial times or even the time under Mobutu's regime. Most Cinarc members will sleep on the floor in one of many rooms in the middle house. In the vicinity of this setting is a party hall, where wedding parties and other festivities are held on weekends. During our weekend of seclusion, we can overhear recordings of Céline Dion alternated with Koffi Olomide, the tradi-modern music of Tshala Mwana, or the religious music of L'Or Mbongo until 5 A.M. From compounds in the neighborhood, we also hear other prayer groups speaking in tongues and singing.

On Friday evening, the actors and actresses make their way to the compound and look for their sleeping places, which are gender segregated. Bienvenu and the *bampaka* (the eldest of the group) sleep in the first house. The actors then await instructions. They are led by Chapy and JC, who, being in charge of the religious rituals in these three days of spiritual work, are primarily *hommes de Dieu* and only secondarily performers during the seclusion.

Bienvenu welcomes the group to the compound and begins by reminding them that all success stems from God. In recent months, however, the troupe has taken a route that has distanced it from God. He reprimands the actors for paying too much attention to their fans and patrons, and even says that most of them have abandoned God. The purpose of the gathering is to ask God to forgive them and to honor him, because it is above all for him that Cinarc exists. Bienvenu turns the meeting over to his younger cousin, Chapy, who immediately orders the others to pray.

The prayer sessions are briefly interrupted by some preaching, after which everybody starts praying out loud again. Some kneel, others walk around gesticulating wildly, and some begin to sing. About ten minutes later, Chapy claps his hands. The Christians know this is a sign that they need to end their prayers and listen to the announcement of the new theme for the subsequent round of prayers, which continues for several hours more. The prayer sessions are frequently disrupted by spontaneous bouts of fervent singing, which it is Chapy's job to subdue. There is no electricity, and the only light comes from a few candles. The music is accompanied by rhythmic ticking on empty cola bottles and clapping. During these prayer sessions, the artists also pray for the divine blessing to descend upon their leader.

On the first night, the prayers come to an end at 4 A.M. The prayer session follows a different pattern on the second night: at around 10 P.M., Chapy announces that the group will pray in shifts through the night. He splits the artists into several groups of three or four that will carry on with the spiritual work (praying and singing), each for about an hour. Chapy and JC lead these small prayer groups, which meet on the porch while the others are sleeping. It surprises me how the others manage to sleep while a constantly changing group of people loudly prays and sings only a few meters away.

When Chapy and JC feel they themselves need to take some rest, they write down, on a scrap of paper, a particular biblical passage that should guide the prayer session. My group has to pray from 2 A.M. until half past three. Nene, who leads my session, begins by asking forgiveness for our sins and requesting additional protection for the president of the group. Singing, clapping, and performing some dance steps help to pass the time while the others are resting or waiting for their turn to do the spiritual work.

Around 6.30 A.M., when the last group has finished its praying session, Chapy wakes everybody up. Washing is performed quickly, since JC and Chapy urge all of the artists to start dancing and clapping once again. Most of the artists are drowsy. This session lasts until around 9 A.M. and is rich with spiritual activity: three actresses fall into a trance and need to be delivered of evil spirits. During such moments, the whole troupe gathers around the actresses lying on the ground. The actors who are responsible for spiritual work in churches, including Chapy and JC but also Eric, Paco, and Nene, lead the exorcism rituals; they are assisted by the other actors, who are praying hard. Another actress prophesies. Her divine words, in which God promises success but demands unity, are noted down by one Cinarc member.

At 9 A.M., the group disperses and goes home.

The TV actors, as well as others in Kinshasa, feel these retreats are necessary because their work, which ultimately aims at exposing the Devil's strategies, angers him. As I mentioned in Chapter 2, the Devil's major weapon is secrecy, and it is held that he does not like people to know what he is up to, or when his workings are uncovered. One of his reactions is to send demons and witches to the acting company in order to diminish their success and the scope of their work exposing his machinations. One of these malefactors' strategies is to weaken the unity of the group. Christian TV actors may therefore be suspicious when new artists seek to join the group. A case occurring just a few months before I arrived in the Cinarc troupe illustrates this point. A youth of eighteen had shown interest in becoming a member of the group but was unmasked during a weekly prayer meeting. One of the Cinarc members received a divine message that the Devil was in their midst. The teenager confessed and left the group.

Another strategy of the Devil, and one that aroused more concern among the players, entails the artists' possession by the demons and wicked characters they have imitated. One of the artists explained this in the following way: "The Devil is all around. Demons can attack you. If you look carefully, there are lots of actors who are HIV positive. Many among them are dead because of AIDS, because they have not been careful. When you play the role of a bad person, you have to hang on to God." Not praying enough, sleeping too much, being lazy, and imitating the fictional character while not on stage or in rehearsal all constitute moments of inattentiveness in which the Devil can conquer the soul of the actor. Possession takes place in the world of the invisible but has visible effects: uneasiness, failure in an undertaking, or illness. An actor may even be stalked by the character he or she has embodied. Bienvenu very discreetly related a story about an actress who played the role of a prostitute. She became very proficient in embodying this character, but, according to the Cinarc leader, she did not pray sufficiently. When the serial was finished, people noticed that the actress had taken over the behavior of those women of loose morals: she continued wearing short skirts and using heavy makeup and even had sexual relationships with men. During this time she became pregnant. She was not allowed to act during her pregnancy, and only after purification rituals in the church was she allowed to return to Cinarc. Bienvenu interpreted the pregnancy as a result of the interference of the fictional character in the actress's life offstage. It was assumed that she had awakened the "spirit of illicit sexual behavior" (*kindumba*) by acting.

Bienvenu was therefore careful to assign the roles of prostitutes, witches, fools, demons, and sirens only to people who had a "strong soul" (*molimo makasi*), something that can only be acquired through ardent prayer and demonstration of a "real" Christian way of life.[3] If the group's spiritual leaders doubt the spiritual strength of one of their actors, they decide to augment the spiritual activities of the whole troupe.

Mimesis and Possession

The notion of artists becoming possessed by the embodied spirit is embedded in local religious beliefs and practices of possession.[4] Possession is a pervasive topic in anthropological literature on sub-Saharan societies (see Beattie and Middleton 1969; Behrend and Luig 1999; Boddy 1989; Lambek 1981; Sharp 1993). For Kinshasa's born-again Christians, possession is a symptom of witchcraft. I have not come across accounts of performers who became possessed by positively valued characters such as the pastor or the successful businessman. The performers yearn—and sometimes fight—to embody these roles, because they are cognizant that the audience transposes the performed identity to the social and spiritual identity of the performer. The outcomes of the imitations of the socially successful and thus positively valued positions are never a problem. This should be underlined, because in the following discussion I am focusing on the imitation of occult characters.

For Kinois, imitation is never "free" and innocent because it engages the soul. Christian role players prepare to guard their spiritual safety with prayers: they summon the Holy Spirit to possess their soul and accordingly to prevent their soul from being taken by any demons they imitate or render present in their performances. Not only mimetic actions but also spoken words might have a dangerous effect. In Kinshasa, words (Sg. *liloba*) are believed to mark people's lives and experiences. Therefore, religious performances such as prayers, songs, confessions, chasing out the Devil, speaking in tongues, and prophecies are salient. These invariably vest much power in the Word. From an etic point of view, the discursive acts can be understood as constructing reality and selves. For Kinois themselves, however, the power of the Word finds its meaning in the context of a reality filled with invisible forces. Via prayers and popular genres like songs and Kinshasa's *maboke* (which are more spoken dramas than in Europe), words are the instruments to "awaken spirits" or even to invite spirits. Both in non-Christian African religious practices (Peek 1994) and in the theologies of charismatic Christianity (Coleman 1996; 2000: 117–142), much weight is given to the outcomes of discursive acts. Although these religious systems have different stances on the ways in which religiosity can be mediated, the belief in the illocutionary effect of words found in many ethnographies of so-called traditional African societies is very much in line with the charismatic stance on the power of the Word, which derives above all from unmediated access to the divine, as promoted in Protestant and Protestant-inspired movements (see Kalu 2008: 249–270).

Therefore, beliefs about the danger of cultural performances are by no means limited to dramatic imitations but also structure dances and discursive performances like songs. Rumors abound regarding musicians who have been bewitched through the songs they sing. And the itinerant musicians, who make music on demand from their audience in public spaces like parks or restaurants (fig. 5.1), are reluctant to sing certain songs. The song "Maya," originally by Carlito, is said to be a particularly bewitching song (*chanson fétish*). The song's protagonist, Maya, is believed to be a female spirit—a siren—with whom the original singer had a sexual affair. Singing this song might awaken the siren.

The influential monograph *Mimesis and Alterity,* written by Michael Taussig (1993), inspires a fuller apprehension of Kinois' perceptions on the possibilities of becoming possessed through dramatic work. The author defines mimesis as a desire-driven practice of becoming what is imitated and performed. Studying mimetic practices of Cuna Indians, who made fun of colonials in mimetic performance, Taussig (1993: 21) discerns two essential aspects in the mimetic work: the imitation and the sensuous, palpable connection established through the act of imitating that creates a link between the body of the perceiver and the perceived. Outstanding mimetic work may assume the character and power of the original (1993: xiii). The closer the image of the copy is to the

Figure 5.1. Itinerant musicians (2005, © Katrien Pype)

original, the more easily the power of the original can transfer to the copy, Taussig writes. Mimesis creates webs of copy and contact, image and bodily involvement of the perceiver in the image. Using Frazer's concept of "sympathetic magic," in which laws of similarity allow the magician to act on the world through symbols, Taussig explains the link between the copied and the copier: by copying something, the copier brings the copied into the physical world (1993: 106). Duplication accordingly entails invocation. And the artist creates a bridge between the original and the copy.

What do the aforementioned observations inform us about Kinshasa's Christians' perceptions of the nature of "acting," "imitating," and "performing"? The data indicate that two distinct definitions of mimesis are combined in this urban African Christian poetics of representation. Firstly, "acting" equals "becoming," and secondly, when the performers have prayed enough, "acting" is merely "simulating" without altering or modifying the artists' being. Prayer is the only device that distinguishes the two different notions of mimesis. In the first instance, there is the belief that embodying and imitating particular behavior collapses, for the time being, the mimetic work with actual becoming. In the case of possession, this can have more permanent effects once the performance is over. The second approach denies the involvement of spiritual (and later psychological) effects on the performer and merely acknowledges the superficial, visual, technical imitation of behavior and people.

This analysis questions Fritz Kramer's distinction between a European and an African mimesis. In *The Red Fez: Art and Spirit Possession in Africa*, Kramer (1993: 247–250) defines "European mimesis" as mere *poeisis*, one based on the technical skills of copying and aping the Real as naturally as possible. For "African mimesis," by contrast, he describes possession as the quintessence of the mimetic work. Kramer seems to attribute one particular definition of mimesis to "the African people." While research on the aesthetics and technicity of mimetic performances in Africa adds nuance to Kramer's sharp categorization (see Stoller 1995), in this literature possession remains an important precondition for African performance to be considered "good." From an emic point of view, Kinshasa's born-again Christians discern between two different approaches toward mimesis: either performance, of which the quality derives to a large extent from the performer's technicity, or possession, where entranced performers are led by invisible spiritual agencies. These are differentiated through Christian rituals. Taking an etic perspective, we can question how far the actors, once they are protected by prayers that evoke the Holy Spirit, are not possessed. This pertains to the narrow meaning attributed to "possession" in charismatic circles in Kinshasa, where it is the outcome of witchcraft. Being filled with the Holy Spirit, by contrast, is not perceived as a condition of possession.

Acting versus Not-Acting

The line between actors merely imitating the wicked characters and others performing for the Devil (either as a consequence of the roles they embody or because they are possessed with impure spirits) is very thin. The movement is one from "acting" (pure imitation) to "not-acting" (possession). It is assumed it is difficult to perceive whether a performer is merely acting out a role, or has in fact become the role (either because he or she is possessed as a result of the mimetic work or because he or she arrived on the scene as a witch). Just as suspicions as to other people's intentions and spiritual affiliations govern social relations (see Chapter 2), the same doubts and suspicion dominate the perception of the dramatic work, including the serials, precisely because "appearances deceive." Outstanding dramatic performances may be the result of "real wicked practices." Muyombe Gauche, for example, was said to know all too well how to embody the role of a witch. According to some, he was not merely imitating a witch but was one himself. Meanwhile, confusion is always possible between "acting" and "becoming" and merely imitating a character or action, or between reality and pretense. There is always the possibility of "becoming" the witch, the demon, or the wicked character. Religious performances, such as prayer, are technologies actors employ to create a boundary between "mere play" and the "actually becoming," the "acting" and the "not-acting" (Kirby 1972) within the dramatic work.

A text on the African artist by Harding helps us to grasp the gradual shift between the two kinds of mimesis. Harding draws heavily on Michael Kirby's acting theory, which spelled out a continuum between "acting" ("to feign, to simulate, to represent, to impersonate"—a process in which the self of the actor is suspended) and "performing" (in which the performers tend to be "nobody or nothing else than themselves") (Kirby 1972: 3).[5] The concepts of "acting" and "not-acting" are the two opposite poles of a continuum of human presentations of the self that comprises subtle distinctions between degrees of performance of an Other, of alterity, and of self-performance.

When actors are in character, they pretend to be someone or something else. However, in the African dramatic context, in which the transgression of the material and the spiritual is always at hand, Kirby's distinction between actors and performers proves to be rather complex since it does not always entail the presentation of the self; sometimes, rather, spirits are governing the performances. How then do we understand the bodily involvement of the artist? Harding has inserted a third category, the "stagehands," exemplified by mask wearers in masquerades: the boys wearing the masks are "stagehands" in that their body is used to support the "central character," the spirit, who is the actual performer (Harding 1999: 119). The spirit stages itself in the performance and thus performs. Transposing this to Kinshasa's context, we could state that the artists who have prayed sufficiently, and whose spiritual being is not afflicted by the character they embody, operate as "actors." The case is different for the mimetic activity of those artists who become possessed by the spirit of the character they play. Here, the spirit is perceived as the performer—who presents him- or herself the way he or she is, while the artist works as a stagehand—whose body is then merely a support for the central, performing character (the spirit). When we consider that "outstanding performances" follow the workings of the Holy Spirit, we can assume that the best performers are, at least during the moment of the performance, the stagehand of the Holy Spirit.

Who knows whether a certain actor is really acting or is actually the stagehand of evil spirits, or whether a "fictional character" is performing, or whether it is the Holy Spirit that is presenting itself? Only those with privileged vision can discern between artists who rely on prayer and those who are of the dark world and accordingly do not imitate wicked characters but are really what they play.

In interaction with their audiences, the artists frequently have to reply to questions that echo the local beliefs that imitating is copying and becoming. Most of these questions point at the spiritual condition of the actor's double; sometimes spectators even encourage particular TV actors to pray harder. In other cases the artists are victims of social violence of all kinds, ranging from gossip and guessing at the spiritual state of the actors to throwing stones Empathy, disgust, disapproval, and admiration of the fictional characters are some of the main affects viewers experience, not only while watching television serials but also when encountering the actors who embody these characters in real life. Artists who embody evil characters especially experience hardship when merely walking around town during the period when the episodes are aired, and sometimes even their family members are scolded. This identification of actors with their fictional alter ego forces them to repeat again and again that the roles they embody do not coincide with their personal lives and have no impact on their double. Several times, in talk shows and during interviews at the end of an episode or serial, I observed that actors who played the roles of devilish characters dissociated themselves from their roles by stressing that they were "real Christians" and that their dramatic work was only theater (*kaka theater*).

Christian spiritual leaders, in particular those closely connected to troupes, perpetuate the cultural perception of "imitating" can lead to "becoming," while similarly promoting the possibility of mere pretense, of imitating something without having any spiritual effects on the imitator. During weekly prayer gatherings, the leaders criticize the actors when they notice that the latter are getting carried away by their success and neglecting their spiritual life. In their teachings, they give priority to the contact with the invisible that has been established through the imitation of certain characters and practices. The following is an excerpt of a sermon given by Maman Bibiche (the troupe's Maman Pasteur) at a weekly gathering of the Cinarc group:[6]

Tango ozoleka na écran,	When you appear on television,
okoya mpo chasser.	you are there to chase [away the impure spirits].
Y'okanisa eza kaka bahistoires.	You think those are only stories.
Sachez, na monde ya diable,	Be aware, in the world of the Devil,
il y a des histoires qui se passent!	things happen!
Et quand tu vas terminer la scène	And when you leave when you have
tu sors.	finished your scene,
il est là; il t'attend	he is there; He waits for you,
parce que oyebi okolivré ye en spectacle.	because you have shown him in the play.
Comme la Bible nous dit:	As the Bible tells us:
"olakisi baoeuvres na ye na libanda	"When you show his work in public
ye mpe en retour akoya mpo à attaquer yo."	he too, in return, he can attack you."
Quand tu veilles ou pas	Whether or not you are alert
omini que outi	it may happen that when you leave [the scene]
oza bien,	all goes well,
mais une fois obimi:	but once you have left [the stage]
ofungoli kaka porte:	you open a door:
o petit chéri(e), aza libanda,	oh, my sweetheart, s/he is outside,
azokozela yo.	s/he waits for you.
Okei kotambola lisusu na badésordres!	You start to walk around in disorder!
Yeba que le diable sera là!	Know that the Devil will be there!
Ce n'est pas Yésu qui sera là!	It is not Jesus who will be there!
"Parce que ayebi	"Because He knows
que chrétien auti kosala mosala na Ngai	that this Christian man has worked for me
apesi Ngai lukumu.	he has honored Me.

O nga naza acteur, te,	Oh, I am an actor,
eloko te	I have no problem,
mpo na etikali déjà na television. "	because I appear on television."
yo okimi ndenge oza wana	You flee in that way
Il va souffler ce qu'il veut.	He will whisper what he wants.
Il fait ça de toi oyo alingi.	He will make you do what he wants.
Mosala oyo bino bozala,	The work that you do,
eza mosala moko ya pasi,	it is a difficult job,
parce que boza provoquer royaume ya diable.	because you are provoking the Devil.
Eza mosala ya pamba pamba te.	It is not a light-hearted job.
Eza mosala moko bozomema croix.	It is one kind of job in which you are carrying a cross.
Même tango bozali kotambola	Even when you are walking
na Nkombo ya Yêsu Christu,	in Jesus's name,
tomema croix.	we carry a cross.
C'est la croix au nom de Yêsu Christu.	It is the cross in the Name of Jesus Christ.
Quand le diable te voit,	When the Devil sees you,
il voit la croix sur toi.	he sees the cross you wear.
Et ezali remarkable:	And it is clear:
partout oyo ozali kozala	wherever you go
akoyeba quand akoattaquer yo,	he will know when he will attack you,
il y aura des gens,	there will be others,
comme quand Yêsu Christ portait la croix.	as when Jesus carried the cross.
Bato mosusu bazalaki	There were others
bazoyekola ye mawa.	who sensed his pain.
Bato mosusu babandaki kotiola ye.	Other people mocked with him.
Batu mosusu babandaki bakracher sur ye.	Other people started to spit on him.

The pastor and his wife warned the players over and over again with regard to the dangers they confront in their work. The Christian leaders constantly frame the mimetic work within the context of a spiritual battle and thus try to control the mimetic performances, on and off stage.

Dance

The danger of imitation is not at all restricted to the world of TV actors but also influences the religious discourse about song and dance. The revival churches make a distinction between "good dances" (*mabino malamu*) and "bad dances" (*mabino mabe*) (see Pype 2006). The first group consists of dances that glorify the Christian God. These are often invented by church orchestras, so the most apt moments to enact these dances therefore occur during Christian gatherings, though Christians also perform "good dances" at all kinds of parties (fig. 5.2). By contrast, the "bad dances" are those that did not originate in the Christian popular culture but thrive within the world of *La Kinoiserie*, and accordingly are often danced in bars, where seduction of the other gender is the main goal of the dance. In Pentecostal discourse, Christian dances invigorate the performer with spiritual life (*bomoyi*), while "bad dances" may trigger witchcraft.

The choice of particular sorts and pieces of music, and of the dances that accompany the fictive characters and events, resonates with the Pentecostal interpretations of dance. When representing Christians and their leaders, the actors will either sing religious songs or set their dialogues to scores of religious music by Adorons l'Eternel, José Nzita, or other popular Christian groups or artists. The Cinarc troupe has itself also invented Christian dances. One, for example, is Open Heaven, We Want to Enter (*Pasola Lola, Tolingi Tokati*), which uses the bodily gestures of pounding manioc into flour, a familiar movement in ethnic and folkloric dances. The divine words render these "demonic" movements safe, it is said.

Music by baWerra, Papa Wemba, and other urban singers is played in the screened dramas when the scenario represents pagans drinking

Figure 5.2. Women dancing in church (2003, © Katrien Pype)

beer and flirting with women—in sum, the Kinoiserie life world. In a few instances the Cinarc company has even created new "bad" dances for its own purposes. This was the case for *The Nanas Benz,* "my" telenarrative. The serial depicts the efforts of a siren, Reine Love (played by me), to attack the households of Christian spiritual leaders. Offering cars, money, and luxurious items to five wealthy women (the "Nanas Benz"), she expects these women to seduce the leaders of a Pentecostal-char-ismatic church "because her sleep has been lacking due to the prayer vigils." In the course of the various episodes, the five women frequently meet their demonic patron in her house, where they inform her of their attempts to make the young men of God fall into sin. Each time these meetings end with a "bad" dance. The siren and her female accomplices engage in a circle-dance around a small table in the siren's living room. While bending a bit at the knees, shaking the pelvis and pushing out the buttocks, the Nanas Benz sing "Orobokibo. Exaggerate with the silly things" (*Orobokibo. Apusa bozoba. Orobokibo. Apusa bozoba*).

The lyrics for the dance were created by the group's leader, who re-ceived his inspiration in Nigeria. As he told the other actors and also the public during talk shows, during a long stay in that west African country he learned that prostitutes, after having sex with a client, frequently ask each other: "Did he push the hole?" This is expressed as "*Orobokibo,*" for which the Lingala equivalent, "*Apusa bozoba,*" expresses that idea that sinful acts are being performed. The dance movements were no doubt inspired by the *fwenge* dance,[7] which was in vogue in Kinshasa at the time of filming this serial. *Fwenge* is a kiKongo word for "pelvis," and female dancers perform the dance with their backs directed to the audi-ence, making circles with their hips and buttocks and ending by push-ing them up and toward the public. Evangelizing Christians considered *fwenge* a "bad dance" because it was invented and performed by a popu-lar dance music band that does not glorify the Christian God.

Though the actresses very much enjoyed performing the *fwenge* dance, a few events during the recordings reminded the whole troupe of the "demonic" nature of this dance and the evil powers that could be awakened by it. The most compelling event happened the night the troupe filmed the dance for the first time. It was already after midnight when the actors prepared to record the scene in which the Nanas Benz would meet their siren, played by me. When the group finally began to film the scene, one of the actresses came dangerously close to me with a turkey skewer she was eating, leaving a small wound at the outer corner of my left eye. All present—not least I myself—were shocked. Some of the actresses started yelling; others began to sing a Christian song. Bien-venu took me aside and disclosed this near-accident as a warning from the occult world. According to the troupe's leader, the Devil was showing me that he was not pleased with my role. I had to pray harder, he said. Here, I was confronted with my assumed lack of spiritual strength.

The mere nature of the role pushed me to reflect more thoroughly on the social impact of the dramatic work, in particular when asocial characters are embodied. It surely led me pondering the social risk a researcher can and/or should take in participation. It was obvious that, playing the role of a character that crosses the boundaries of normal and abnormal behavior, I was amplifying my ambivalent status in Kinshasa. Before taking up the role in *The Nanas Benz*, I had asked for advice from a family with which I had become friendly in an early stage of my fieldwork. The family head, Mr. Six, leads a theater company that produces development-oriented dramatic performances. Over time, my relationship with Mr. Six transformed into a daughter-parent one, and I greatly valued his opinion. He saw no major reasons for me to reject the role: I was already familiar to Kinshasa's viewers, and I had also had the opportunity to explain my activities with the troupe on several television shows. Nevertheless, the Six children did not approve of this "demonic" role. During the production and broadcast of the serial, the Six children often told me that I was helping the Devil, and they asked me to stop playing that role and work for God again. Their complaints made me cognizant of the difficult choices an anthropologist has to make when doing participant-observation. Yet their reactions also helped me to gain a more profound understanding of the social positioning of dramatic actors, a position that is partly determined by their fictive alter egos.

Spectators and the Sacred

It was not only the actors who were worried by the *Orobokibo* dance discussed above. Audience reactions showed that the spectators too felt uncomfortable with the dance. After a few episodes of *The Nanas Benz* were broadcast, several viewers expressed a fear of becoming bewitched while watching the actors perform dances originating in the dark worlds. The Cinarc leaders received repeated requests to stop portraying this dance. Furthermore, the inclusion of these kinds of performances in Cinarc TV productions caused people to increasingly question the Christian character of the Cinarc actors. In response to the public expressions of doubt, Bienvenu decided to integrate more Christian songs into the scripts. In the following serial, *Mayimona*, for example, some actors were cast as members of a religious band and were shown rehearsing certain religious songs. Particular scenes with the main character of that TV drama, again a siren, were even accompanied by clips of Christian music at times: the music served to spread the divine power that would balance out the devilish power depicted in the dance.

In the following part of this chapter I will explain the audience's fear of becoming possessed by viewing "bad dances" on television. Research on visual genres like painting with Christian themes, or like statuettes elsewhere in Congo, illustrates that visual representations are more than signs and are believed by those who purchase them to have magical potency and spiritual qualities (Jewsiewicki 1991: 130; Jules-Rosette 1984: 223; see also for Africa in general Hackett 1994: 298). For the Kinois, the invisible and external power that leads to the portrayal or representation in any artwork permeates not only the producer but also the artwork itself and its spectators. The Kinois then apprehend the practice of viewing as a particular moment of spiritual importance, one that generates an experience of the otherworldly or a spiritual transformation, such as possession or superhuman power. Research confirms that these experiences are not unique to Kinshasa's spectators but can be observed among Pentecostal-charismatic audiences elsewhere in sub-Saharan Africa (e.g., de Witte 2005; Meyer 2006a; 2006b) as well as among practitioners of other religions (Hackett 1998; Hirschkind 2001; Lyons 1990; Pinney 2002; Schulz 2003; Stout and Buddenbaum 1996; Tomaselli 1996; vande Port 2006).

In order to comprehend the particular viewing experiences of Kinshasa's Christians, the concept "embodied spectatorship," put forward in phenomenologically inspired media studies (Marks 2000; Sobchack 2004), offers a useful approach. Researchers of film and cinema that take a phenomenological perspective give priority to the interactive character of film and viewer: the viewer is not a passive agent who "witnesses cinema as through a frame, window, or mirror, but the viewer shares and performs cinematic space dialogically" (Marks 2000: 150). The following explorations deal less with the representations themselves than with the mediation between the images and the electronic material, and between the viewers and the footage. Images and human bodies interact and sometimes merge in the activity of watching. New sensorial regimes are activated, producing new modes of knowledge and altering the contemplator's being.

Mediating Divine Power through Television

Western rational thinking does not accept the coexistence of magic and science—technology, on the one hand, and aura or the uncanny on the other. But for Kinshasa's born-again Christians, the two are commensurable.⁸ "The satellite orbiting around the planet Saturn is controlled by the Antichrist. He will reign without rebels [without opposition]. Are you aware of this? Do you know this? I have the impression you did not know it. The satellite will serve the Antichrist and help to prepare his coming reign." This was Pastor Gervais's closing remark in a sermon one Sunday morning. He interprets this aspect of ultramodern technology within the context of a global spiritual battle between God and the Devil. His utterance does not stand alone. In Kinshasa, technological devices such as television, telephones, and the Internet are appropriated through a local cultural logic of witchcraft and magic. They are often jokingly called "the witchcraft of the white men" (*sorcellerie ya bamindele*) and are contrasted with "the witchcraft of the Africans" (Fr. *sorcellerie des Africains,* Li. *kindoki ya biso*). The latter refers to "traditional" magical acts as performed by magicians, "traditional healers," and customary chiefs.

Yet the distinction between the two types of witchcraft does not imply that the first one is not included in the spiritual battle. First, modern technology inspires Kinois to describe interactions between the visible and the invisible: witches bewitch others in order to install "antennae" in their homes. Being able to deliver or free someone from evil spirits is often expressed as "knowing the code to unblock a new cell phone" (*aza na code ya dévérouillage*).⁹ In Kinshasa's churches of the Holy Spirit (which are more in tune with ancestral traditions than are Pentecostal-charismatic churches), contact with the Holy Spirit is compared to the way a telephone or the television apparatus captures voices or images: "the entranced person repeatedly yells 'hallo, hallo' as if speaking on the telephone" (Devisch 1996: 566).

Second, it is assumed that the materiality of modern communication technologies does not impede the channeling of otherworldly forces but facilitates it. In Kinois' thinking about the human being, a person's double can be captured by technology. This is not a new phenomenon. Mirrors, the surface of water, and photographs are media used in "traditional" divinatory and occult practices, my informants stated. In light of the concepts of the human being, the double or the soul, which is present in one's shadow, can also be found in any image of the human being, for instance in a photograph. A French-Lingala/Lingala-French dictionary gives the following definitions for "image," *Elili:* (1) animated or non-animated image, photo, shadow, portrait, symbol; (2) invisible material body or visible material body (*nzoto*); *Elilingi:* (1) shade, shadow; (2) face, photo, image, television (Kawata 2003: 62, author's translation). There is thus a meaningful overlap in the words for image, portrait, photo, symbol, or television (animated image) and the invisible body of a person or thing. Customarily, diviners and "traditional healers" are said to use photographs of people to work on them, for good or for bad. In the religious imagination of born-again Christians, however, modern technological mimetic products like pictures are, significantly, used only for evil purposes. This discourse contrasts slightly with Behrend's (2003) observations among Christians in Kenya and Uganda, where both good and evil powers can be produced and transmitted through photography. In these two different contexts (east African Christians and Kinshasa's Pentecostals), the technological apparatus is used in differentiated ways as an instrument of enchantment to perform magic to do healing work.[10]

Practices in Kinshasa's local media worlds show that *pasteurs* and their followers use mass media to transmit the divine power containing the wind of life (*bomoyi*).[11] All religious TV channels feature programs in which the audience is invited to pray along with the hosts, and accordingly with the imagined community that is created through watching the same programs. Several confessional television stations hold special prayer moments for their audience. The channel CVV, for example, shows sober cards with the words "morning prayer" (*prière matinal*), "noon prayer" (*prière du midi*), or "evening prayer" (*prière du soir*) in the morning between 7:00 A.M. and 7:30 A.M., at noon between 12:30 P.M. and 1:00 P.M. and in the evening from 9:00 P.M. until 9:30 P.M., respectively (fig. 5.3). The TV viewers hear some men (rarely women) speaking in tongues and announcing themes to pray for.

Programs in which *pasteurs* or other spiritual leaders, seated in a small studio, invite the onlookers to participate in prayers by touching the screen with their hands are frequent. Some state that one's hands must actually touch the screen, while others contend that one's palms only need be brought upwards, as one would do in church in the presence of the pastor. Mothers with sick babies, students preparing for their exams, or others—for various reasons—bring their hands close to the television

Figure 5.3. Screen shot of evening prayer (2006, © Katrien Pype)

set and accordingly transform their domestic space into a religious space where the life force can be transmitted to them from a distance. If prayers are to be done for people who are not in the living room, then the *pasteurs* invite viewers to place a glass of water on the television set so that it becomes imbued with the divine power.[12] This water should be drunk afterward by the one for whom the prayers were intended. Sometimes viewers are invited to shout "*au Nom de Yésu*" ("In the name of Jesus") out loud in their living room. The hosts (*animateurs*) promise that calling Jesus's name out loud is a supernatural dialogue. The Holy Spirit will *décoder* (interpret) it and then send the divine power into the living room in response. *Pasteurs* are also often able to heal through mobile phones. The act of praying, especially for the purpose of chasing impure spirits through the Word, is the most important element in this ritual work and does not require the physical proximity of the participants. Whether the spoken word is channeled through electronic media or is uttered in person does not have an effect on the outcome of the prayers.

The mediation of divine powers is mostly clear in television programs that are intended to heal spectators. Such shows, which are numerous, share a similar format and structure: a pastor or other charismatic leader, sometimes alone, sometimes accompanied by other Christian leaders, sits in a studio facing the camera and inviting spectators to call in. Callers mostly consult these television hosts about domestic problems.[13] An example of the ways in which private sessions with Christian counselors occur through television is offered in the call-in program *Esther's Prayer* (*La Prière d'Esther*). The show is aired on NzondoTV, a confessional TV station belonging to the Arch of Noah, a church headed by Dennis Lessie. One of the oldest charismatic mass churches in the city, it has established several chapters in most of Kinshasa's townships. Hosted by a woman (Maman Josiane) who also is on the church's staff and coordinates the women's activities there, the television show is closely connected to activities within the church setting. I watched a live broadcast of the program in Kinshasa. Dressed in a beautiful yellow Senegalese-style dress, her hair braided according to the latest trends, and adorned with a gold necklace and impressive gold earrings, Maman Josiane suggested through her appearance that she was blessed by God's powers. Her assistant, a younger woman who seemed to be in her early thirties, was dressed in a different, more modest style: she wore black trousers, a red blouse, and hair extensions emulating a European style, which one easily can find at any of Kinshasa's markets. In their adornment, both women appealed to different age sets and classes.

The camera was fixed on the two women, who were seated on luxurious white chairs upholstered in blue velvet. The women were only filmed from the upper waist up, except when the assistant stood up and walked behind the two chairs while praying out loud. The studio was otherwise modestly furnished: a small table with plastic flowers and two microphones, each directed at one of the women, functioned as a desk.

Behind the women hung a naïve painting of a beach and palm trees, the kind one finds in the homes of an older generation of elite Congolese groups. The lower left corner of the screen featured the title of the show, *Esther's Prayer* (*Prière d'Ester*), and Maman Josiane's private phone number. People were continuously invited to call in and communicate their problems. It was mostly women who phoned, frequently to seek a solution for infertility, though other afflictions (like fever and insanity) and personal problems (such as job loss and marital problems) were discussed as well. The following is a transcription of a conversation between Maman Josiane and a female caller:

(Host): Good day, maman.

(Caller): Good day, maman. I live in Kalemie.[14]

(Host): Amen.

(Caller): I have a problem with my fathers.[15] I have been ill for about five years. It was really a battle. The battle is over now. And I want to go back to my husband. My husband refuses until today, so I stay here. Now my husband has problems over there, he has a wife [with a high social status].

(Host): Maman. God is great. You, come to our church. I want people like him, who have a woman in their house. I want people like this, like that man. I think that your husband, at this very moment, our God is waking him up. He touches your husband. Our God has no fetish. Come, let God do miracles. Maman, touch the television. We will pray for you in the name of Jesus the Messiah. God of miracles! Look how you have lost your husband … chase away his plans … chase everything … in the Name of Jesus! Chase his plans! Show them, God!

While Maman Josiane prayed, she shouted these words and gesticulated a great deal with her arms. Her assistant left her chair and started praying out loud. During the whole conversation, both women were very emotional, and the religious work apparently demanded a lot of energy. They constantly wiped the sweat from their faces with tissues. No doubt the tiny studio and the spotlights increased the heat, but the intense bodily involvement of both women in the healing process warmed them as well. After this call, three other women called in (one with a child with fever, another who had no time to go to church and asked to receive divine power, the third in need of a job), followed by two men. The first requested healing for his wife, who had a "husband of the night" (an impure spirit that causes sexual problems), and the second feared that his wife was a witch. At the end of the show (after ten callers in total), Maman Josiane had very nearly lost her voice but concluded by inviting those callers who had not been able to get on the air to come to the church compound during the afternoon. I visited the church premises that afternoon and saw that many women had come. Most had brought small children and were waiting for a private audience with Maman Josiane. I talked with some women, who told me that they had seen the show at noon and would now beg Maman Josiane to pray for them and/or their children.

Trying to understand how the actual healing could occur via television, I was told that viewers are expected to have the faith to receive the power of Jesus through television. Nobody could actually explain how this force is transmitted, but my informants all insisted on the need for faith and the power of the Word. They emphasized how calmness and peace came over their bodies when watching Maman Josiane's program.[16] These sensations, which echo the feelings of being in trance or receiving the divine power via immediate bodily contact, are also felt when touching the television screen or when drinking water that has been sanctified through television. I will have more to say about the meaning of these sensations, but for now we need only to note that such practices indicate that mass media contribute to the consolidation and the enlargement of the Christian community not only through the broadcasting of religious narratives and taped sermons, but also through the shared bodily sensations that are the outcomes of the transfer of divine invisible powers. It is precisely the emphasis on the viewers' altered emotional states that suggests that the construction of a Christian audience does not derive primarily from modified convictions and ideas among the viewers, but more from intimate sensations that go beyond the discursive. Nonetheless, the persistent association of these experiences with Christian speech, such as "in the Name of Jesus" and biblical verses, means that Christian television hosts must carefully manage their effects on the viewing community. Finally, these data show that Kinshasa's Christian spectators are not passive receptors of the charismatic teachings. Rather, by phoning call-in shows and petitioning for healing, or by complaining about the potential destructive effects of the filmed images, Kinshasa's viewing audiences actively participate in the charismatization of mass media.

Television and the Transfer of Demonic Power

In general, charismatic Christians classify television programs according to the two spheres of the invisible: divine TV programs (which are considered to be "good") and demonic broadcastings ("bad"). "Good" programs demystify Satan's strategies and are imbued with divine power, while others are perceived as the work of the Devil, and thus carry demonic forces. In the latter case, it is believed that the art director or the actors have received creative inspiration from the Devil in the production of their programs, or that they have engaged in fetishistic activities in order to gain money and popularity. By contrast, it is said that television programs that demystify Satan's strategies have the same revealing intent as Christian teachings and expose the Devil's works. Spiritual leaders accentuate again and again that only those viewers who hang on to God—and their opponents (witch doctors and witches)—possess the spiritual knowledge that allows them to distinguish between morally acceptable broadcastings and those in which demonic power is transmitted.

Most American films, video clips of worldly musicians, horror films, pornographic films, Ninja films, American wrestling shows, Chinese martial arts films, and science fiction films are classed as the type of television programs that are considered spiritually unsafe. Teachings about music video clips of urban songs and American wrestling shows are of utmost interest, because these are probably the two most viewed television programs in Kinshasa. The demonization of video clips of songs that are not produced within the Christian milieu is an important means to control the social and emotional lives of born-again Christians and opens up a politics of pedagogy. Spiritual leaders denounce parents who do not change TV channels airing music video clips of urban singers, which in a Christian context are designated as "worldly," "demonic," or "pagan," or who encourage their children to dance along. They warn that Christians who behave this way make their domestic space into a diabolical living room, accordingly exposing their children to evil spirits. Gaining control over these dances and over the reception of the urban music video clips is very difficult for the Christian leaders, because for Kinois, imitating these dances means apprehending Kinshasa's prevalent notions of beauty, rhythm, and bodily techniques.[17]

American wrestling shows are among the most popular televised programs, and almost all television channels screen them. Having watched a bout on one channel, people quickly change to another station to follow the same or another fight. Kinois—young and old, men and women—never tire of watching these programs.[18] Although their popularity may be due to a representation of Kinshasa's ideal of masculinity (the strong fighter as a hero, Pype 2007), these dramatic shows fall well within the dominant Christian paradigm of the Good God versus the Bad Devil.[19] Let me first give a brief description of one of the many occasions on which I followed the broadcast of an American wrestling show with the Cinarc actors. The show was called *Armaggedon,* and we saw one clash in a series called "The Battle of the Sexes." The contest pitted

Trish, a muscular young white woman with long blond hair, against Lita, a white brunette dressed in leather trousers and a black shirt. Trish wore a short skirt, a tight shirt that accentuated her breasts, and heavy boots. The masculinity of the fight contrasted with the extremely feminine appearance of the female fighters. The show started with a disagreement between the two young women in the dressing room, where a so-called hidden camera showed viewers how they had a heated argument that soon became physical. The two women were apparently fighting over a man, Christian, often shown in close-up, who observed the argument from a distance. The spectators in the arena watched everything on big screens and urged the two contestants to fight out their argument in the ring. Encouraged by the audience, the women climbed into the ring and immediately began sparring. Flouting the rules, they stomped on and bated each other, tore at each other's hair, jumped out of the ring, and continued on the side. When the (male) referee tried to convince them to come back to the ring, both women attacked him. Two men, Christian being one of them, quickly appeared and rescued the referee, which ultimately led to a real battle of the sexes. Suddenly, the alliances changed: Trish and Christian were now fighting Lita and Chris Jerico, who would finally win the battle.

The spectacle was simultaneously interpreted by a duo of French-speaking commentators, but for me, it was rather difficult to follow the comments because two of the Cinarc actors were constantly talking. Jef, an ardent Christian, begged to change the channel, but the others did not allow him to do so. Discontented, he went on to say that the Devil played a significant role in these kinds of shows. Without a doubt, references to the Devil and the Apocalypse (as in the title *Armageddon*) contribute to the popularity of these kinds of shows in Kinshasa. According to some Christians, these shows are examples of how life will be when the Devil reigns: violence will rule, and there will no longer be any law and order. Moreover, those who try to safeguard the rules (the referee) will lose all authority. Pentecostal leaders, although they also watch these shows, warn that these fighters are possessed with "the spirit of the fight" (*molimo ya litumba*) and that watching these shows might transfer these spirits to the spectators, which could result in aggressive behavior in Kinshasa's public and private spaces.

Visuality and the Senses

Several explanations enable us to understand the demarcation between "Christian" and "demonic" images. A first explanation relates to a specific representation of personhood and self. American series and films show how people faced with problems are able to overcome all kinds of obstacles by means of their personal character alone. Chapy criticized this: "When we have a problem, we get in touch with our *pasteur.* In those films of the Devil, people experiencing difficulties try to solve their own problems. They try to use their own power, which is devilish. They should instead show us to depend on God in order to solve our problems." Another reason to designate certain television programs as evil resides within the social relations in domestic space that inform the reception of television programs. In Kinshasa, watching television is a social activity. Rarely does a person sit alone in front of the television set. Social rules pertaining to age, gender, and other structures of authority allocation dictate who decides which television programs are watched. Sometimes Christians refuse to watch films that they consider to be demonic, and conflicts may arise over the decision as to which channel to be watched. "Real Christians" flee the living room. Chapy, for example, when he is in disagreement with the choice of program, simply walks off to his room and reads the Bible. Others, like Jef in the description of the American wrestling show above, however, try to change the television channel. If they are unsuccessful, they take the minor conflict arising out of this opposition between preferences as a first indicator of the devilish nature of these programs. Both these arguments deal less with the particular images or visual representations than with the possibility of disturbing social harmony. The selection of "good" and "bad" television shows is an exercise of power over experiences of the self within the individual world as well as the larger social world.

But probably most importantly, Christians and their leaders denounce the "demonic" genres because of these programs' emotional effects on viewers. Watching films activates certain emotions that trigger spiritual processes and transfer spiritual knowledge. "Being struck" by a serial was often worded as "being touched." "God touched me (*esimbi ngai*) through the *maboke*," people say. One Cinarc actress said of a TV production by the Christian group The Evangelists: "Last week, when I watched the final episode of the *maboke* of the Evangelists troupe, I was really touched because the *télédramatique* had really shown how someone who used to lead a Christian life was suddenly brought to lead a life of sin. I felt afraid; I feared that this might happen to me too. I am sure God has touched many people with this story." Chapy confirmed that God can also touch people through TV dramas that do not have an explicit Christian content: "Sometimes a serial of Muyombe Gauche can touch me. The Bible tells us: God can use anyone to talk to you. And indeed, there have been stories made by Muyombe Gauche that made me think." Some Cinarc informants stated that whereas watching Cinarc's plays did not arouse any asocial or unsettling feelings, and that the productions by Muyombe Gauche's group, whose leader the proselytizing TV actors regard as an occult artist, have a horrendous bearing on the emotional state of the spectator. These informants describe how, in such instances, they have to pray that the demonic spirits are not transmitted to the viewer.

Watching pornographic films or programs in which violence is celebrated results in the disturbance of a personal emotional balance. This sense of emotional and physical disorder is interpreted as the result of an impure spirit that pushes the viewer to commit sinful acts. One actor told me that he has not watched any Western films since 1995, when he saw *Child's Play*[20] on television, because through this horror film he had become possessed with a demonic spirit. He said: "That day, when I was watching that film, I sensed an evil spirit entering in my body. It had taken over my body and started to trouble me. I got angry with the children in the compound, I started to slap them in the face. This spirit really possessed me. Since that day, I have decided not to watch *bafilm ya bamindele* [white men's films] anymore."

The emotional imprint of the television programs is the most significant indicator of their spiritual source and value. When the spectators feel calm and experience a sensation of warmth, they know that the show or program comes from God. If the viewer feels agitated, afraid, or sexually excited, then Christians believe the television program is part of the Devil's work. Laura U. Marks's inspiring book on intercultural cinema, *The Skin of the Film: Intercultural Cinema, Embodiment, and the Senses* (2000), offers us an interesting perspective on the bodily effects of the filmed image on its audience. In the preface to her book (2000: xi), she argues that "vision can be tactile." Marks is concerned with both the representation of the senses and visceral, embodied knowledge *in* the films as the *sensuous reception* of these films, which she coins as "haptic" or "tactile visuality."[21]

"The ideal relationship between viewer and image in optical visuality tends to be one of mastery, in which the viewer isolates and comprehends the objects of vision. The ideal relationship between viewer and image in haptic visuality is one of mutuality, in which the viewer is more likely to lose herself in the image, to lose her sense of proportion," Marks contends (2000: 184). The author draws attention to the way an embodied and visceral knowledge is transmitted onto the beholder through the images: "tactile visuality draws on the mimetic knowledge that does not posit a gulf between subject and object, or the spectator and the world of a film" (2000: 151). Optical visuality, or how vision is usually perceived, sees things from a distance; viewer and image are separate, and the viewer's subjectivity is not transformed by the mere experience of looking (2000: 162). Haptical visuality, by contrast, "tends to move over the surface rather than to plunge into illusionistic depth" (2000: 162). According to Marks, in mainstream Western cinema and in particular in research on Western spectatorship, the optical mode dominates. She argues that mainstream Western society privileges the visual and discards the implication of the other senses in the viewing experience. This does not deny the possibility of Western viewers participating emotionally in the fictional events or characters' experiences. Yet the sensorial aspects of seeing, invariably present in the experience of looking and watching, tend not to be considered in the discourse of Western film producers and viewers. Often, a transfer of knowledge is promoted via intellectual reflections on the viewed images. Producers of feminist-inspired and intercultural cinema do not feel at ease with the dominant Western paradigm and subvert or even provoke the experience of watching through the insertion of haptic images, which are images that activate the senses for a fuller comprehension of the represented. They appraise the body's involvement both in the image and in the experience of the onlooker. Reflections on the viewing practice are then directed not merely by what has been shown, but also by the sensations that the viewers experience during the act of watching. Visceral modes of gaining knowledge are elected.

Marks's research has been embraced by anthropologists (e.g., Deger 2006) who support the idea that not all societies consider the visual to be the dominant mode of gaining knowledge. Dealing with the Indian concept of *darshan*, which refers to Hindu belief to the fact that followers need to see printed images of their deities and need to be seen by their gods in order to be fed with divine energy, Christopher Pinney has coined the concept of "corpothetic" consumption of images. "[T]he devotee's gaze, the proximity of his or her heart, and a whole repertoire of bodily performances in front of the image (breaking coconuts, lighting incense sticks, folding hands, shaking small bells, the utterance of mantras)" transform "pieces of paper [with images of deities] into powerful deities" (Pinney 2002: 364). Image and spectator share one zone—a space of visual mutuality—and feed each other, altering each other mutually into divine entities through which divine power flows.

The data described above on the apocalyptic signification of the filmed image in Kinshasa can easily be wedded to Marks's concept of "tactical visuality" or Pinney's "corpothetic consumption" of images. In the viewing context in Kinshasa, the perception of the images establishes a sensuous contact between the spectator and the footage. Emotions of joy, conviviality, calmness, and control, as well as anxiety, distress, jealousy, and despair, can be transposed onto the viewer. It is exactly in such a sensuous contact with the image that invisible powers are said to be transferred.

Could the television set then acquire a fetish quality? MacGaffey's ethnographies on the mediation of the fetish's uncanny powers through a particular looking modality encourage the equation of the moving images (as containers and diffusers of otherworldly powers) with a fetish. Comparing baKongo's *minkisi* as magical objects and as art objects (when displayed in galleries and museums), MacGaffey (1988) opposes dissimilar-looking contexts and concomitant different magical potentialities of the power objects. In a gallery, the social relationship remains in the control of the observer, whose gaze dominates the object, its perception, and its significance. This static condition of the *minkisi* in this locus of "art" contrasts with the kinetic context in which baKongo people interact with their fetish objects. He writes: "[T]he visible object … is intended to be seen as a container of forces, like djinn in a bottle, sealed, knotted, stuffed; the nature of the seeing identifies an autonomous personality that is as it were latent in the objects and is aroused by the relationship but is not fully constrained by it" (1988: 202–203). MacGaffey's distinction between looking at *minkisi* in a museum and experiencing one in the original social context can be wedded to Marks's opposition of optical and tactile visuality. Magical effects of fetishes depend on the looking context and the disposition of a viewer who imagines him- or herself as enmeshed in a world with otherworldly agentive forces. The promotion of the world as a space of a spiritual warfare, therefore, also encourages Kinshasa's born-again Christians to attribute particular meanings to the tactile experiences in the reception of dramatic performances, even when mass-mediated.

The television set can acquire only a fetish-*like* quality, because it is not a container of invisible spirits. This echoes Kirsch's observations about the spiritual power of the Bible among Pentecostal Zambians (Kirsch 2008: 137–143). In a thoughtful discussion of the intermediary power of the Bible, Kirsch points out that the Scriptures themselves do not hold any divine agency or potency, exactly because the Holy Spirit cannot be "stored" or contained (2008: 138). By contrast, Zambians hold that demonic powers can be preserved in material objects such as herbs and ritualistic paraphernalia. For Kinshasa's Pentecostals, a human's soul can be captured and locked up (e.g., in a bottle), but demons and other spirits (including the Holy Spirit) seem to be attached *to* people, objects, and places without necessarily being fixed *in* them. In Chapter 2, I indicated that places receive their spiritual identity because of the presence of certain demons, but these can always be chased away or invoked by prayers and other activities. Places are thus not "possessed" by spiritual forces; rather, they are visited by these spiritual forces, which transform the spiritual quality of that particular place. The same goes for humans: when indicating whether one is a Christian, people often say that this person is/walks *with the Holy Spirit* (*aza na Molimo Mosantu*) or *with demons* (*aza na bademon*). The same is true of objects such as the television set, the camera, perfume, lipstick, pens, notebooks, and so on. These objects carry spirits and acquire spiritual power because of their attachment to the invisible. The spiritual effects of images that are broadcast via the camera, words that are written with a bewitched pen, or the scent of perfume emanating from a non-Christian person all depend on the sources—the origins of the objects and the spiritual powers that surround these—and not on the objects themselves.

Recapturing Aura

In Kinshasa, the television set and the programs screened are thus assumed to be potential "technologies of enchantment," to use a phrase of Alfred Gell (1992). I showed above how the otherworldly is preserved or even inserted in Kinshasa's mass-mediated life worlds. While several ethnographies of African Pentecostal popular culture suggest that this is a common phenomenon in sub-Saharan African communities, ethnographies of other religions deny this possibility. In her discussion on videotaped recordings of mediums in northern Thailand, Morris (2002: 390) clearly states that "[t]he body appears in the video as a material signifier, the evidence of possession, but the video does not give access to the presence of the spirit. It defers that presence endlessly." Why do certain religions allow for mass-mediated transmission of sacred powers while others apparently do not? Although Morris argues that the dream of mass mediation in the age of electronification is a pure transmission (one in which no medium such as the body is needed), and that glimpses of the Real can manifest in the aural and visual "noise" (see Chapter 4), she emphasizes the spectralization of spirit possession and identifies the use of videoed mediums in trance as mere archives. Here, Morris thus implicitly agrees with Walter Benjamin's popular thesis that the otherworldly, that is, the magical—or aura—disappears when electronic technology is used.

The data collected among Kinshasa's Pentecostals suggest otherwise, and they even compel us to reconsider Benjamin's popular thesis. In Benjamin's influential work, "The Work of Art in the Age of Mechanical Reproduction" (1999 [1935]), Benjamin described aura as "the unique phenomenon of a distance." The experience of a distant power, character, or event may engender a feeling of awe in the contemplator. In modern times, he states, aura is threatened. His article laments the early twentieth-century West's transition from a "traditional" society, as he terms it, to a "modern" society where masses increasingly replace the individual. In Benjamin's view, the transformation of subject and subjectivity is also reflected in the technological progress of modernity. Benjamin contended that the mechanical (re-)production of artworks or of images obviated the authentic or original power that a craftsman invested in the work of art.

If we consider aura in Kinshasa's world as the experience of the invisible, whether that be divine or demonic, then my data on the perception of special effects (see Chapter 4) and on embodied spectatorship deny Benjamin's popular hypothesis that mechanical (re-)production erases the mediation of aura and thus call for attention to the magical uses of technology and of the ascription of uncanny powers to local and foreign television programs.

Benjamin's texts themselves hold two important remarks that make a differentiated view of his popular thesis necessary. First, the author emphasized that within "traditional" societies, the power inherent in art objects derived from the artist himself and the religious world in which the art object was born. The conditions of time and space (the ritualistic and religious origin and deployment of the art objects) preserved or enabled the presence of aura. Now, in Kinshasa's context, where not only the Pentecostal melodrama but also numerous other television programs are embedded in an evangelization campaign or deployed as means of healing and instructing, one can apprehend how the Holy can be transmitted via mass-mediated programs. The classification of the visual texts is invariably related to the source of inspiration of the producers, the performers of the programs. These observations relate to Gell's research on the magical qualities of a canoe board. Writing about why the display of a canoe board on the Trobriand Islands can render the beholder weak and without self-control, Gell (1992: 46) states that it is not the spectacular display of colors that enchants the onlooker but the fact that the canoe owner "had access to the services of a carver whose artistic prowess is also the result of his access to superior carving magic." This leads Gell to conclude: "It is the way an art object is *construed* as having come into the world which is the source of the power such objects have over us—their *becoming* rather than their being" (1992: 46, author's emphasis). Gell's stress on the process of production to explain the presence or absence of otherworldly powers is also valid for Kinshasa's born-again Christians' distinction between "good" and "bad" television programs. I therefore devoted much attention in the previous chapter to the inspiration and the sources of artistic knowledge of Kinshasa's performers.

A second remark that nuances Benjamin's thesis from within his own writings is spelled out by Sudeep Dasgupta (2006). In a dense and eloquently written article on India's visual culture and the emergence of religion in its visual public sphere, Dasgupta argues that Benjamin, in his earlier essays, mentioned that "the work of art when released from its place in a changeable tradition ... is not left to free-float outside the grasp of aura. It is re-embedded in 'the particular situation' of its reception, and, in the process is 'reactivated'" (2006: 256). Benjamin acknowledged that aura could be reconstructed or reinserted. The perception of Kinshasa's Christians that certain foreign (nonlocal) media works are accompanied by holy or demonic powers indicates that viewers in different social and cultural settings attribute new meanings and add new values to the programs and their content, producers, and performers. The inscription of global images in the apocalyptic ideology undermines the theorem that assumes a dominance of technology over culture.

Framing to Protect

Now I will turn back to the television serials themselves. Throughout this book, the evangelizing teleserials have been described as inherently melodramatic. Melodrama is characterized by its strong focus on the emotionality of the fictive characters as well as its address to the sentiments of the audience (see Pype forthcoming b). Larkin (2008: 190) writes of Nigerian films, which constitute an important source of inspiration for Kinshasa's TV actors, that "[t]hese images and narratives are provocations designed to scandalize and disgust. Through that bodily reaction moral reactions are provoked and social ethics publicized.... [The underlying] truth is experienced through the bodily response of revulsion. These are genres designed to generate physical effects. Like the Holy Spirit, they come in to take over your body."

Via an aesthetics of pain and terror, both Nigerian films and Kinshasa's teleserials trigger a haptical visual mode. However, it is not taken for granted that the divine knowledge the proselytizing actors intend to transmit via the images actually reaches the viewers. Nene and Chapy argued that spectators should already be in a relationship with the benign otherworldly in order to perceive the whole message behind the dramas, that is, the divine knowledge that is conveyed. Only then they can receive the deepest message ("the truth") embedded in the TV serials.

Such a remark echoes Kirsch's observations that, according to Pentecostals in Zambia, the Bible in itself does not transmit the divine power: "uninstructed and irreligious readers would be confused by the complexity and metaphorical language of the Bible, would not know how to proceed in their scriptural readings, and would be even less capable of interpreting it" (Kirsch 2008: 137–138). This again suggests that texts in themselves, be they printed or audiovisual, do not *contain* the spiritual power. The spiritual world of the readers/spectators is what allows for the channeling of spiritual knowledge and healing through the words and images.

The Cinarc actors discerned multiple levels on which people can watch their *maboke:* (a) as simply stories, not transcending entertainment; (b) as lessons in morality; and (c) as divine messages, this last being the most difficult for Western observers to apprehend. Only "real Christians" are said to be able to capture the divine message, just as only they are able to perceive the invisible fire. Anyone can watch the TV dramas, but Christians who are *with God* are touched in a more specific way and feel the divine power when viewing these serials. This diversification in the viewing experience challenges the idea of "the audience." Kinshasa's evangelizing TV artists clearly do not conceive of their viewers as one homogenous community. They even produce the *maboke* with diverging audiences in mind. Aware of the fact that not all of their spectators are "real Christians," the viewers can either merely be entertained while watching the *maboke* or they can be fed with the divine life that the Christian music and the biblical verses uttered in the fictional contexts of the melodramas transfer to the watching community.

These local approaches to the status of image and sound and the mediating role of television in the diffusion of uncanny powers influence the format of the serials' episodes and explain the repeated citations of biblical verses—two features of the Pentecostal melodrama that will be discussed now. First, out of concern about the spiritual effect of certain images, dances, and songs, Christian performers have created a framework that orients the spirits of the viewers toward the divine world: when an episode of their productions starts, viewers watch images of the actors underscored by a two-minute excerpt from a Christian song (frequently a song by Adorons l'Eternel, a popular religious band in Kinshasa). The lyrics, in French, advise viewers to place all confidence in the Holy One. The musicians advise viewers not to rely on their own wisdom and knowledge but to acknowledge God's omnipotence:

Mets ta confiance à l'Éternel.	Lay all your trust in the Eternal.
Ne t'appuie pas sur ta propre sagesse.	Do not rely on your own knowledge.

En toute chose, reconnaît	In all things, acknowledge
Il aplanira, Il aplanira tes sentiers.	He will smooth, He will smooth your paths.
Alors, dans tous tes problèmes,	So, in all your problems,
Il faut mettre confiance à l'Éternel	Lay all your trust in the Eternal
Parce que c'est Lui qui arrange ton	Because He is the one who sets out
chemin.	your path.

The words comfort and console those who are experiencing hardship, and the lyrics may trigger an awareness of the Holy Spirit in the minds of the viewers and accordingly spur them to live according to Christian rules. At the end of the episode, when the names of the actors and spiritual advisors and addresses are communicated, the same song is played again. Viewers frequently sing along, thus opening their soul to the Holy. This enables them to view the story as a religious lesson or a sermon without running the risk of their soul being attacked. There are striking parallels between this structure of the Pentecostal melodrama and the format of Kinshasa's Pentecostal rituals (prayer gatherings, sermons, testimonies of witches, acts of blessing, baptism, marriage, and funerals). These rituals consistently begin and end with religious songs in the worship of God accompanied by drumming or taped electronic music. This is the most essential part of the ritual, for singing is considered to be the main device for altering the soul, averting it from material reality and steering it toward the Holy. The opening and ending of the Christian TV dramas reflect the framing of Christian rituals.

The second important characteristic of the Christian serials is their continuous reference to the Bible and strong tendency toward biblical exegesis. The important instructive role of the Bible justifies its frequent citation in the TV dramas and elsewhere among Christians. Sometimes a key biblical verse around which the serial evolves is indicated in one of the screen's corners. One example is the verse 2 Thessalonians 2:3, a reference shown as a subtitle on the screen during the episodes of the Cinarc serial *Apostasy*. Chapy reasoned:

> The Bible says that preceding the Antichrist's arrival there will be a time of apostasy. People will abandon their faith and will turn to all kinds of storytellers. This is a sign of the Apocalypse. We are living this now. People listen to fables. Even in the church people prefer to listen to tales about the village and witchcraft instead of listening to biblical stories. When we [actors] speak about the same things, we always want people to read the Bible because the Bible explains what we perceive.

More frequent, however, is the use of references to biblical verses in the TV dramas. I observed how people noted down these biblical references while watching the *maboke*, or picked up their Bibles to read a certain phrase over again—practices that also characterize people's behavior when following sermons in church compounds. Accordingly, while watching religious programs, Kinois sometimes display the same behavior as in church. Such behavior is stimulated through the religious format of the programs. The fact that the message of God is electronically mediated and delivered in the form of fictionalized narratives does not diminish its authenticity.

Christian actors are furthermore convinced that the power of the Word is also at work during the broadcasting of their plays. Said Nene: "I am sure that Chapy's [biblical] references have a spiritual bearing. You know, sometimes miracles happen in the living room. The Word can produce a lot. Hearing is stronger than reading. And the more you read the Bible, the more you will be struck by the power of the Word of the Bible. These references speak to the souls of the viewers, and this will have consequences."

Closing Notes: Mediating Performances

This chapter has shown that, for Kinois, cultural performances have a spiritual effect. It is argued that while a person is acting, impure spirits can abuse the dramatic performance to possess the body, either out of anger because their strategies have been revealed, or because the actors themselves have invited these spirits to possess them. Dancing, a bodily activity that easily switches back and forth among joy, desire, and seduction, is represented as the most dangerous action. These beliefs influence both role distribution and the selection of music to accompany the images of the Pentecostal melodrama.

Considerable attention has been devoted to the preservation of the reality of the uncanny in mass-mediated stories and electronic images and sounds. While the shift from live to televised performance is of course significant (Hobart 2002), audiovisual recording does not diminish the spiritual presence or effects of performances. Here, we can pick up Hobart's expression that televised theater in Bali is dead (in contrast to stage plays) (Hobart 2002), now adding a Congolese twist to it: TV drama in Kinshasa is very much *alive,* for uncanny forces animate it. Among Kinshasa's born-again Christians, mimetic technology is appropriated within an enchanted universe. In Chapter 4, I agreed with

Meyer's (2003b) argument that there is no real difference between the *pasteur*—or even the diviner—who "sees" in the other world and the television set because all three (pastor, diviner, and television) render visible the invisible. The data on the media's potency to mediate uncanny powers allow us even to extend this statement: all three facilitate the flow of these forces as well.

The charismatic instructions conjuring a spiritual world in Kinshasa's viewing settings remind us not only that the meaning and value of electronically mediated programs derive from the broadcast content but that, and probably especially, the most important meaning structures at play in the spectators' life worlds also assign sense to mass-media narratives and images. The ways in which people perceive moving images, relate to the displayed events and characters, and regard their fellow audience members are historically and culturally specific and can only be understood through empirical research. As Barber notes, audiences are not all the same, but they are historical products (1997b: 348).[22] Furthermore, audiences exist only by virtue of performers. The offered ethnographic material is evidence that TV actors mediate much more than mere messages to their audiences: invisible powers are transmitted as well. Moreover, invisible powers are *always* present in the performance or are constantly guiding the performance.

The ethnographic material in this chapter allows me to extend the discussion of mediation between visible and invisible worlds by pointing to three important issues. First, the body plays a crucial role in the mediation of invisible powers. Performing and contemplating cultural performances, whether live or mass-mediated, are activities that allow the movement of invisible entities and the circulation of otherworldly powers. Both TV actors and audiences can become possessed by demonic spirits or by the Holy Spirit. Emotions and passions are essential players in this channeling of powers. In an essay on the role of emotions in Kinshasa's Pentecostalism and its popular culture (Pype forthcoming b), I identify anger, hatred, and jealousy as primordial emotions that can trigger witchcraft. Also, as has been shown, watching the melodramas and acting in them evoke various sensations. Emotions are ultimately bodily, but at the same time they also escape any material fixation. Emotions themselves occupy this vague zone between the material and the immaterial, the visible and the invisible. Perhaps this is one of the reasons why emotions are singled out in Pentecostal discourse on how individuals themselves can open their body to the Holy Spirit and close it to the Devil (Pype forthcoming b).[23]

Second, recall that in Kinshasa's context, mediation between the material and the otherworldly is *never* seen as neutral; nor can the interaction between the spiritual and the thisworldly be *totally* controlled by humans. Following the strong moral partition between the "good" and the "bad," audiences, fellow actors, and pastors constantly question whether the connections established through the cultural performances are tying the viewers to the Christian God or to the Devil. Pentecostals experience continuous exchange between the visible and the otherworldly, in which invisible agents (demonic spirits and the Holy Spirit) *actively* take part. At times, the agency of demonic spirits can overtake the whole performance. The potential for setting demonic flows in action has strong ramifications for the personal and public identities of evangelizing television actors. A wide range of ritual techniques must be activated in order to make sure that the "right" powers are channeled. These techniques influence both the actors' life worlds (in their cultural work and in their individual religious life) and the aesthetics of the teleserials.

Given the spiritual confusion that reigns in Kinshasa (Chapter 2) and the risks that actors take when embodying the roles of witches and their victims, it becomes clear that the nature of the mediation performed by the actors is often questioned. Whether they channel demonic entities or the Holy Spirit, the actors are not in control of themselves in the acting moment. Their bodies become the playground of invisible entities that use the materiality of the body to spread their powers. In the performance, mass-mediated or not, uncanny forces spill over into the audience. It should be emphasized that this approach toward the production of cultural performances and the viewing experience does not necessarily eliminate human agency. Through the performance of Christian rituals, actors and viewers attempt to control the powers they channel and receive. And when questioned by their audiences, actors refer to these techniques in order to prove their Christian identity.

Finally, the focus on the possible effects on the viewers allows me again to argue against the strong distinction between performers and spectators. In the performance and the broadcast, a "zone of sensory mutuality" (Pinney 2002: 355) is established between the actors, their viewers, and even the spiritual world. This means that if an actor (or a pastor, for that matter) is possessed by evil spirits, then these will easily transfer to the viewing audience. The mediating act is perceived as literally binding performers and audiences together.

Notes

1. In her reflection on religious mediation, Meyer (2009a: 23) argues that "the body itself is not just there, but inscribed via religious and other sensational forms, and via structures of repetition."

2. CEFAC is the abbreviation for the *Centre d'épanouissement des familles chrétiennes* (Center for the Development of Christian Families).

3. One's spiritual life is, of course, only one of the factors that guide the troupes' leaders in distributing roles. Personal relations, rivalries, amities, and a performer's popularity also inform the companies' heads' decisions on which role a certain actor should perform.

4. Significantly, the Lingala word for "possession" (*bo-ndoki*) is the abstract term of "witchcraft" (*ki-ndoki*).

5. Harding considers Kirby's theory relevant for African dramatic performances since "it avoids the sociological overlap between 'sacred' and 'secular,' 'old' and 'new,' 'ritual' and 'drama,' and focuses instead on the craft of performing in its several modes" (1999: 121).

6. Thursday's prayer gathering in Avenue Yambi, 18 March 2004.

7. The dance was created by Roi David, *atalaku* ("shouter") in Wenge Musica Maison Mère music band. One choreographer informed me that the *fwenge* dance is inspired by Manyanga dances. Manyanga, a subgroup of the ethnic baKongo group, reside on both banks of the Congo River. The Manyanga living in Congo-Brazzaville are renowned for their dances. Most Kinois were unaware of the "traditional" source inspiring this dance.

8. Early ethnographers in Congo also met with the commensurability between magic and Western technology. In a footnote of an interview on magic and sorcery with an old Christian Mongo couple, Gustaaf Hulstaert writes that one of the informants points out that the recording material captures their words, which could later on be used for witchcraft such as a magician does (1971: 161, footnote 12).

9. Vande Port (2006) noted the same insertion of the vocabulary of mass media into the religious imagination in Brazil.

10. Interestingly, Behrend (2003) discloses the active role of Europeans in the domestication of photography within religious practices and experiences.

11. Others have observed similar religious practices mediated through mass media. De Witte (2005), for example, describes how Ghanaian pastors mediate the power of the Holy Spirit to the spectators at home.

12. Campos (1999) has observed the same rituals among Neo-Pentecostals in Brasilia (Campos 1999 cited in vande Port 2006: 444–445).

13. Public matters like political crises and economic issues are addressed in other kinds of media formats in which experts debate with the religious hosts. These shows, however, usually do not involve active audience participation.

14. Kalemie is a city in the east of DR Congo, located on the west coast of Lake Tanganyika. As the phone conversation unfolds, it becomes clear that the caller has come to Kinshasa for medical reasons.

15. The caller is speaking about her husband and her own father. She equates her husband with paternal authority.

16. It is interesting to draw a parallel here with research on technology and religious experiences elsewhere in Africa. For a Cairene setting, Hirschkind (2001) has studied how states of moral being may be evoked by cassette technology. His data show that the illocutionary power of words is preserved when archived in recording modes such as cassettes.

17. Without exception, Kinois encourage small children to imitate the dance sequences shown in music video clips. Children who refuse or do not perform

exactly as they should are punished harshly, which indicates the emphasis Kinois people put on the body and its manipulations.

18. In contrast to the live organized wrestling combats around the city, which are attended by a dominantly male public, the televised American championship wrestling matches are eagerly watched by both men and women. The gendered difference resides in the first instance in the spaces in which this reception takes place: a sports field is a masculine site, while the living room is predominantly a feminine space.

19. Another reason why these shows are very popular may also be due to their melodramatic mode; see Barthes (1987 [1957]) and Levi (1997) on the melodramatic aspects of wrestling.

20. *Child's Play* is a horror film based on the novel by Stephen King.

21. The concepts of "haptical" and "optical visuality" are inspired by nineteenth-century art historian Aloïs Riegl's distinction between "haptic" and "optical" images. Riegl borrowed the term "haptic" from physiology (from *haptein*, to fasten), since the term "tactile" might be taken too literally as "touching" (Iversen 1993: 170, cited in Marks 2000: 162).

22. See also Spitulnik (2002), who calls for a deep contextual approach to audiences.

23. Emotions are also seen as important triggers for witchcraft in other African settings; see Evans-Pritchard (1937), who argues that antisocial feelings such as envy, anger, jealousy, and hatred are necessary catalysts for witchcraft.

CHAPTER 6

The Right Road

*Moral Movements, Confessions,
and the Christian Subject*

This chapter explores issues such as the production of Christian selves and the role of confessions and deliverance rituals therein, and also the ways in which these are represented in the Pentecostal melodrama. Pentecostal churches promote an array of techniques of the self (Foucault 1988)[1] that produce "subjects of God." The techniques of the self impact personal public appearance, body care, thoughts, and self-perception (see Bayart 1998; Marshall-Fratani and Péclard 2002: 9). These techniques require considerable investment from the person involved, which at first glance gives the impression of emphasizing the conscience and agency of subjects with their own rights, duties, and obligations as born-again Christians. These techniques could be related to the Protestant understanding of the individual as an autonomous and self-responsible unit. Kinshasa's Pentecostals also attach much importance to the contribution of social and spiritual Others when it comes to defining and producing the subject. Given the constant intervention of otherworldly spirits in the lives of Christians and non-Christians, it is difficult to accept the image of the self-governing subject in this context.

The analysis contributes to the overall theme of mediation, since rituals—both as intercession and as intervention—are tools of mediation. It is probably in this chapter that the transformative goal of mediation will be most clear. As indicated in the introduction to this book, inherent in any act of mediation is an urge or a desire for a change, be it the end of conflict, the attainment of a new identity, or the possession of new knowledge. Ritual techniques such as prayer, baptism, deliverance rituals, and confessions produce new identities, individual and collective. Healing and purification are the main reasons why sinners confess and why intervention of the Holy Spirit is required.

Before questioning how and why Pentecostal technologies of the self allow the intervention of the Holy Spirit, it is important to understand how the person is situated in the apocalyptic experience. Also, if the tele-serials are understood to aim at changing Kinshasa's society, we need to look at the ways in which the person's positioning is fictionalized in the evangelizing serials. To address these issues, I will touch on two inter-related themes: the moral evolution ("moral movement") of the fictional protagonists and the significance of confessions and deliverance rituals in the closures of the TV dramas.

In the description of the fictionalization of these theological concepts, and in particular in reproducing conversations the Cinarc actors had while filming the *maboke* and reflecting on the scenes, it will become clear that issues such as personal responsibility, the potentiality of being healed, and the agency of spiritual agencies are not ready-made. Rather, these are subject to disagreement and beg for continuous reflection and definition. I regard the debates surrounding the fictionalization of these issues as they occurred during filming as moments in which Christians co-construct the apocalyptic imagination.

"I Am a Sinner"

According to the leaders of revival churches, most Kinois are sinners (Sg. *moto ya lisumu*), even most of them who consider themselves to be Christians. During the Sunday services, or at any other teaching moment, audiences are accused of not leading a Christian life. These accusations can be conveyed in different ways. Here, I present two of the main techniques that Pastor Gervais used when laying blame on his followers. At times, the pastor spoke in a strong tone, bolstered by an angry look that pierced the souls of the congregation, and with one finger in the air warned people about the openings they created the day before when they were dancing in a nightclub, drinking beer, or having sex. At other moments, head bent, the pastor sighed, laughed a bit, and after a long silence said: "I don't know anymore. You know … how many times do I have to tell you…," expressing that by his lights he had fulfilled his task, but the gathered Christians had not followed his instructions.

He often alternated both styles; they could even occur successively during a single predication. But each time, the same idea was conveyed: the flock appeared to be Christian, but they all knew that they were sinning, except maybe on Sunday mornings or at other moments when in church. And even then, many in church used the service meetings to show off their expensive attire or to gossip, two major sins. No one ever denied the pastors' accusations during the services. Rather, some cheered, expressing agreement.

For a Western observer, it is difficult to understand why the Christians did not correct their pastor or counter his accusations. A first possible explanation draws on Joel Robbins's insightful study of millennial Christianity in a Papua New Guinean society (2004). The general social, religious, and political instability and insecurity that Kinois are enduring has stirred up the ways in which Kinois define themselves. Social life is broken down, there is unease with regard to ethnic identity, and people struggle between the moralities of various religious models (traditional systems and different types of Christianity). This all leads to confusion concerning one's positioning within the family, the role of the ethnic group in one's life, and the right religious world to adhere to. We could state that, quoting Robbins (2004: 249) there is "no other identity besides that of sinner which they are so secure."

Another explanation can be found in the public role of Christianity and the comfort zone it creates for the Christians. Pastors do not merely identify individuals as sinners; they also claim to have the solution or remedy, that is, deliverance and anointment. If we situate "sinfulness" among the various other undesirable conditions that Kinois can endure, then we see that sinfulness is the only one for which a cure is within reach. In contrast to, for example, unemployment, illness, or poverty, one easily can recover from "being a sinner" without having to incur serious debt for the cure to take place. This means that agreeing to be a sinner opens up a perspective on the future. By uttering the words "I am a sinner," Christians not only acknowledge wrongdoing but immediately activate change. They distance themselves from certain behaviors and thus set themselves on the road that changes an unwanted condition into a favorable one.

I, however, found the insistence on declaring myself a sinner most difficult. At times, Chapy asked me to identify myself as a sinner. At the beginning of fieldwork, I tried to change the direction of the conversation by posing linguistic and theological questions about sin and sinners, but I could not maintain this attitude for long. After a few months, I felt obliged to state that I was a sinner too. Here I narrate the occasion on which I confessed:

March 2004. For a few weeks now, I have met Chapy on Monday mornings around 10 A.M. in Bienvenu's compound on Avenue Vemba. Our meetings were scheduled at that time because, before ten, Chapy was following a seminar in a Pentecostal center in Limete. And, after our meeting, the

Cinarc troupe started filming. During all our sessions, Chapy had given me theological instructions about born-again Christianity, God and the world. I noted everything down, but I was more interested in his experiences with the invisible. All my questions were detoured by references to the Bible. This bothered me, because I felt that I was not receiving personal reflections, and finally, after two months, I vented these frustrations to Chapy. He replied: "What I have been doing is trying to persuade you about the work of the Devil. Very early on, you told us that you do not believe the Devil exists. And when we asked you to pray with us, you pray like a Catholic. You must pray out loud and summon God to enter your body. Only then, will you understand what we experience and what we try to do in our serials." I knew Chapy was inviting me to accept the Devil as the mastermind of all evil and to confess that I was a sinner. I forced myself to say the words: "I accept that the Devil exists and that he is present in Kinshasa and in my life." Chapy smiled and said: "I know this was not easy for you, but you will see, your life will become less chaotic now, *ma soeur.* Say now that you accept Jesus in your life." As soon as I had uttered this last sentence, he walked over to Bienvenu, who was preparing the afternoon film session, and told him what had just happened. The latter came up to me and congratulated me.

Identifying myself as a sinner meant humiliating myself. At least, that was how I felt about it. I confessed to finding pleasure in living according to my own will and desires, and in saying that this was a sin, I acknowledged having done wrong. Even today, as a private person, I cannot fully accept my own words. I also doubt whether I acted in an ethically correct way—was my lie a "white lie" or not? Despite the moral torment I felt (and keep on feeling) about my words, this moment had invaluable consequences for fieldwork. Suddenly a rapport was established, and my meetings with Chapy changed. Our weekly conversations became much more personal, even though Chapy always kept the Bible at hand and I still had to read certain passages during the interview sessions. What was new and exciting was that the following meetings invariably dealt with the question of "How does one go from sinner to rescued Christian?" and developed from biblical teachings into lessons in individual morality, models of the Christian subject, and moral guidelines for the composition of my social network.

I was not cognizant of this at the time, but in rereading the notes I took during these renewed weekly instructions, I came to understand that Chapy's teachings were not far removed from the sermons and the Pentecostal melodramas themselves, which all presented similar routes to a better morality. These routes, the "right" moral movement, constitute the best entry to the Pentecostals' understanding of the Christian (sinful) subject.

Moral Movement

"Moral movement" (Fernandez 1979; 1982) denotes a society's normative idea of moral evolution, which expresses how people imagine a current "bad moral situation" and the means to attain "a good moral situation" (1979: 59). Among Kinshasa's born-again Christians, moral movement is captured in the metaphor of the "right path" (*nzela malamu*). Lyrics of Christian songs frequently use the trope of "the road." "Jesus, You Are My Way" ("*Yésu, nzela na ngai*") and "Show Me the Way" ("*Lakisa nzela*") are some examples of religious songs. Being a Christian is described as "walking with Jesus" (*kotambola na Yésu*). Christian morality is thus articulated in terms of a journey that departs from one condition and aims to arrive at another: what Kinshasa's Christians want to or should achieve leads away from the bad, the insecure, and the evil toward health, calm, prosperity, and fortune, which all are signs of one's purity. The "right" movement abandons chaos, disorder, and instability, conditions that are captured in the concept of "death" (*liwa*), in favor of peace, order, tranquility, and coolness (*kimia*). The opposite of the ideal moral movement is expressed in the Lingala verb "*kopendwa*," which denotes both a public show of non-Christian behavior and losing one's way in a very concrete sense.

The "correct path" is a pervasive image in Kinshasa's overall public culture. Not at all limited to the imaginary of Christians, it relates to more long-standing local notions of health and well-being. Creten, for example, mentions the importance of the binary couple "rest" and "movement" for sustaining one's social identity, health, and well-being in Nkanu culture (1996: 411–425).[2] Titles of CDs produced by so-called "pagan" musicians in Kinshasa translate their moral concerns in a similar way, good examples being *The Direct Road* (*Droit chemin,* by Fally Ipupa, 2006) and *This Is the Way for Solution* (*C'est par là, la solution,* by Didier Lacoste, 2007).

One of the most promoted and also most exercised techniques to attain the "good" is prayer. Chapy explained this to me in terms of the idiom of the Holy Spirit as "breath" or "wind." Praying equates with breathing (*kopema ya molimo,* breathing in a spiritual way). The fixed structure of the prayer rituals follows this metaphor. First one breathes out in order to enable all negative things to leave the body. Breathing in then refills the body with energy. This movement of breathing out or expelling "bad air" (*mopepe mabe*) and replacing it with "divine air" (*mopepe malamu*) is reflected in the articulation of components of Kinshasa's prayer gatherings. Ideally, a prayer session consists of the following stages, which born-again Christians have internalized:

1. thanking God (*kotonda Nzambe*)
2. confessing/asking forgiveness (*kotubela*)
3. asking for protection (*kosenga ebateli*)
4. inviting the Holy Spirit (to enter your body) (*kobenga Molimo Mosantu*)
5. expressing personal desires, goals, and longings (*koloba mposa na yo*)
6. chasing demons (performing deliverance rituals) (*kobimisa ba-démons,* Li. Pl. *mabiki*).

In the second phase of the prayers, Christians confess their sins to God. This confession has a threefold structure: (a) acknowledging and voicing one's sins; (b) thanking God for his presence and constant love; and (c) denouncing sin by chasing it away (*kobimisa masumu*). These three actions call the Holy Spirit down upon the supplicant.

Prayer is perceived as a technology of the construction of the Christian subject because the presence of the Holy Spirit heals (*kobikisa*), purifies, or cleanses body and soul (*kopetola, kosukola molima*) and also inspires and instructs (*koteya*). Next to praying, dancing and singing for God (thus uttering Christian words underscored by bodily gestures) also trigger affective dispositions of calmness and coolness. Kinois Christians contend that all these performances "feed the soul" (*eleyisa molimo*).

The Holy Spirit has the agency to transform the person into what I call a "Christian self."[3] My informants consistently emphasized that this is not a permanent condition but a state that must be renewed time and again. It is assumed that humans are fallible; therefore they should, from time to time, perform prayers and other Christian rituals, such as deliverance rituals and confessions, to become pure again. Thus these rituals not only permeate religious activities but also fashion daily life and pervade social encounters. Most born-again Christians begin the day with prayers, either in the church or in their own home. They attend sermons on Sundays, while healing services and teaching for the young, women, new mothers, or the ill take place on other days of the week. Leaving the house, beginning a meal, or engaging in a serious conversation also requires the presence of the Holy Spirit. Most of the formal interviews with my key informants began and ended with prayers. Sometimes prayers are enacted rather quickly in silence (as when consuming offered food); at other times they can be lengthy and include singing, dancing, and ultimately a trance, which is a state of possession by the Holy Spirit.

Agency and Morality

Christian discourse in Kinshasa has it that good and evil are external sources that come to nest within the person. This is shown most spectacularly in the healing moments in the churches where evil spirits are chased out. During moments of "being with evil spirits" (*kozala na bademons*), the possessed bodies give voice to the spirit(s) that inhabit(s) them. Spiritual leaders frequently engage in conversation with this/ these spirit/s in order to identify the degree of possession, the origin of the possession, and any evil acts that may already have been performed. In deliverance rituals, the spirits' discourse is standardized. As soon as the possessed person falls down and begins to shiver like a snake, the spirit cries out, saying, "This is my body. This is my house. I will not leave this body." In the ensuing dialogue with the spirits, the spiritual leaders repeatedly invoke the name of Jesus and so drive out the evil spirits. The people surrounding the possessed and the healer(s) also break into loud, fervent prayer, for they need to protect their own souls from being possessed by the now homeless spirits.

The exact effect of the external powers struck me most when listening to Jef's account of the first fictional character (Julien) he ever performed:

> I was a financial director of an enterprise and married to Deborah. My parents came from the village to Kinshasa with my little sister. I had no idea that they were witches. They began to tell Deborah that I had another woman. You know, with witches, it always happens like that. I was seduced. As I was not really a Christian, I could be seduced. I had a so-called friend who invited me to bars. This man led me into errors. I have done many immoral things. I spent the night in bars, and slept with other women, even with prostitutes. The witches know how to direct people and make you do things that are not good. During my time of erring, they prepared me to end in the cooking pot. Luckily, my wife prayed a lot. That is how I was saved in the end.

In Jef's account, the absence of any individual agency on the part of his fictional alter ego (Julien) is significant in our discussion of the imagination of evil and the Christian subject. Julien is portrayed as a victim without any will or intentionality, and witches are held responsible for his erring and immorality. Even Julien's sexual acts with other women are not interpreted as the result of desire or lust but rather as the outcome of an absence of any Christian spiritual stronghold. In the end, it is his wife's spiritual work that mediates between her sinful husband and the divine, ultimately saving Julien.

How must we make sense of the emphasis in Pentecostal discourse on one's moral movement when the agency of evil spirits and higher powers like God and the Devil is taken for granted? And to what extent is the Christian subject a self-governing person? In the discourse of born-again Christians, a tension is consistently manifested between impersonal agents (demons and Satan), personal agents (the whole range of witches and their victims), and the individual's self-rule. Pastors state that God inspires all good things, sends people to earth, and decides when to take their souls back. At the same time, born-again Christians contend, "salvation is individual." People themselves must be conscious of their acts and take full responsibility for their decisions. A Western bias may comprehend all these statements and beliefs as discordant. For Kinshasa's born-again Christians, however, the notions of an individual's autonomy (to walk the "right road") and the limitation of his or her self-rule by higher invisible forces are not perceived as contradicting each other. Christians argue that only people who connect with God are totally free, and that Jesus "frees" people (*abikisi bato*). The choice to deliver oneself to the Christian God does not at all limit one's freedom and self-rule. To be governed by the Holy Spirit means to control one's own passions and actions and achieve one's release from sorcerers, witches, and demons. This freedom is accordingly considered in spiritual terms. For the Pentecostals, voluntary submission to the Holy Spirit does not contradict the sense of autonomy.

In sum, it deserves special mention that although God and the Devil are imagined to govern the world, human beings are not presented as mere puppets of those Actors. This point comes to the fore in understanding explanations of man's destiny (*ndaka*). Sermons continuously repeat that God has a destiny (*mukano ya Nzambe*) for each person. This destiny is hidden and only revealed when one prays to God. It is taken for granted that God wants only good things for humans: he wants his people to be healthy, to have a family, and to prosper. To realize this potentiality, a person should consciously choose to take Jesus's path. Here resides the autonomy and the agency of the human being: a man or woman has responsibility for his or her own life and thus can influence whether or not God's plan will be realized.

The repeated stress on the interconnections between the human being, external spirits, and the social environment indicates that Pentecostal Christianity does not promote a totally self-governing person. Rather, the person is interlinked with social others and via them connected with spiritual others, all of whom influence one's well-being. The Christian person in Kinshasa is therefore to a high degree "dividual." The concept of "dividuality" has come to denote a mode of personhood that perceives persons as "relational and divisible entities." McKim Marriott (1976) and Marilyn Strathern (1988) point out that this kind of subjectivity is antagonistic to "the individual," which both authors identify as the hegemonic perception of human beings in Western societies. The strict division between "societies with dividuals" and "societies with individuals" has been critiqued by Edward LiPuma (1998). First, he argues that "the individual" as a closed and bounded entity is merely an ideological construction that does not reflect how people in the West experience their identity. Second, and of utmost importance for the continuation of my analysis, LiPuma points out that in all societies there exist both individual and dividual aspects of personhood (1998: 56).

In the mindset of born-again Christians, the "subject" is defined by the spiritual qualities of the person's double. A "Christian" has a self (a soul), which is completed by "Christian" social persons when he or she dwells in "pure" spiritual surroundings. This subject is composed of dividual and individual aspects. "Christians of the flesh," the middle category between "pagans" and "real Christians," are also said to have a self, though the complementing parts constitute a mixture of "evil" and "Christian" origin. Their dividuality is qualified by the "pagan" and "Christian" social milieus in which they move about. "Pagans" and bewitched people are considered to lack any self because they are totally controlled by "impure spirits." Kinshasa's Pentecostals interpret "pagans" as "animals," living beings lacking any individuality, will of their own, or self-governance.

The moral movement a Christian should take can be explained in terms of a reconfiguration of the social and invisible components of one's double and a revitalization of one's autonomy. Recall that, in Jef's account of his fictional alter ego, it was in the end the efforts of Julien's wife that saved him. Accordingly, Julien transformed from a being without a self to a person with a pure social and spiritual entourage. The Christian person in his social environment, his wife, helped bring Julien back to humanity. One's social environment thus determines one's spiritual health. For this reason pastors do not focus on the predestination of the person as an individual but instead speak at length about the individual's self-rule, the ability to choose what road to take, and the importance of the Christian social environment. Christians are encouraged to examine closely the religious identity of their relatives, the co-tenants in the compound, their colleagues at school or at work, their friends, and others in their life worlds. Born-again Christians are summoned either to convert "pagans," or to distance themselves from any who stubbornly refuse to become Christian. This often leads to strife among relatives or people living together, as "Christians" and "non-Christians" typically cohabit within a compound. Even within families, usually not all members are born-again Christians; some may be Catholic while others pray at revival churches, and still others do not pray at all. I observed how born-again Christians were often very harsh on neighbors, relatives, and friends who did not consistently go to church, or who appeared to be "Christians of the flesh." Born-again Christians often make a point of inviting their "pagan" children, siblings, and friends to church. These invitations frequently turn into repeated requests to attend services, something that is taken as nagging by those who do not much feel like joining the prayer groups. Born-again Christians, however, do not like to take no for an answer and expect a good reason for any refusal. No matter what excuse a "pagan" might give, it rarely suffices for an awakened Christian.

Moral Movements in the Serials

Now that I have limned the contours of the "Christian subject" and the social paths that lead to it, I turn my gaze upon the teleserials. How is all this charted in TV fiction? In his study of epics in the northern Kongo area, John Janzen (1992) differentiates between "conjunctive" and "disjunctive" tales, a distinction that offers us an interesting starting point from which to approach the morality and agency of the fictive protagonists. Janzen defines narratives with a "conjunctive ending" as stories in which the characters eventually assimilate the "normal" social and moral order. Although tricksters (protagonists in epics) constantly violate the moral code of society (via murder, incest, or cannibalism), their ambiguous status is resolved and solutions are offered for their social integration. In the end, the trickster becomes cognizant of his/her asocial behavior and shows remorse.

A powerful example of a Cinarc *maboke* with a conjunctive ending is the serial *The Nanas Benz*. Five women, guided by the wishes of their siren and the demon Orobokibo, cause the downfall of four of their five spiritual leaders. Only Caleb gives the impression of being able to resist. In order to corrupt him as well, the five women follow him to Lubumbashi, where a prophet has invited him to attend an evangelization campaign. In a rather farcical scene, Theresia, the Nana Benz assigned to capture Caleb, tries to corrupt him: she awaits him at his hotel in Lubumbashi, and when he tries to send her away she fakes a sudden pain in her knee.

Being a caring man, Caleb helps her to his room so she can rest her legs. Once there, however, her knee is suddenly cured and she engages in a seductive dance. Caleb manages to flee, and Theresia returns to the other four women, who eagerly await her report only to hear of her failure to corrupt Caleb. The scene concludes:

> While the women gather in the hotel lobby in Lubumbashi, Pastor Chapy, in Kinshasa, is praying. He asks God for protection against the occult attacks that have ruined the households of his fellow leaders in the church. Thousands of kilometers to the east, the women fall victim to God's devouring fire. As a result Melina, who is somehow punished to a greater degree than the other women, loses her eyesight. The women are baffled by this sudden affliction and decide to return to Kinshasa immediately. There they search for Pasteur Chapy, who invites them to his church. The women confess to the occult work they have been engaged in. They spell out that Madame Love, a siren, had ordered them to corrupt the men and that, after her departure, the demon Orobokibo had taken over. The women confess that their mission was to cause the downfall of spiritual leaders' families but express that they now wish to put an end to their evil ways. Fearing the vengeance of the dark world, the Nanas Benz ask Pasteur Chapy for spiritual protection. He prays for them and restores Melina's eyesight. In the end, the spiritual men who had fallen victim to these women are confronted with the Nanas Benz. The latter expose their plot. The women finally accept Jesus, whose power is stronger than that of Madame Love and Orobokibo. The wives of the spiritual leaders are at last pleased to have an explanation for the bizarre behavior of their husbands. Peace, order and harmony are thus restored.

As this brief synopsis indicates, the serial finishes with the women reflecting on the consequences of their own actions and acquiring insight into their immoral behavior. The Nanas Benz learn that righteous moral conduct does not follow from obeying demons and sirens but comes only from God. Compliance with good social behavior, stemming from this kind of relocation on the moral map, marks the end of the narrative.

Other stories have more tragic endings. In these cases, the witch does not repent and is consequently punished by God. These stories can be called "disjunctive" because the evildoers do not acquire a sense of sociality and therefore remain a threat to the social order. Theresia's tragic death in *The Open Tomb* illustrates this kind of closure:

> Makubakuba and Theresia travel to Mbuji-Mayi, where a meeting with Makubakuba's elders is expected to solve the problems Makubakuba's

children are facing. His children, and even his siblings in Kinshasa, have accused Theresia, his new wife, of being at the root of the death of his first wife, the loss of his children's documents for travel to Europe, Caleb's madness, and the mysterious illness afflicting his two youngest daughters.

In the course of the family meeting, Theresia displays a lack of respect for Makubakuba's elders. Totally disinterested in the proceedings, she looks the elders straight in the eye, replies in an aggressive manner, and, instead of offering a chicken to be cut open for haruspication, throws a turkey down in the midst of the group. All these signs lead Makubakuba's elders to conclude that Theresia is indeed the origin of his misfortune. Theresia, however, rejects this conclusion and storms out of the meeting. While she is walking back home, lightning suddenly strikes her, and she dies.

Most sinners, however, are able to be socially reinserted thanks to the pastors' teachings of the biblical Word and the power of Jesus. Sometimes it is rather difficult to identify one serial as conjunctive or disjunctive. The many fictional characters and the multiple plotlines have different outcomes, thus producing a mixture of disjunctive and conjunctive closures. For example, although the protagonist's death in *The Open Tomb* gives her plotline a disjunctive closure, her two sisters, Melina and Monica, accept Jesus Christ, and their souls are saved.

A Modern Purification?

Concerning Theresia's tragic death in *The Open Tomb*, some questions arise. Why does Theresia die? Can she not confess and accept Jesus, just as her sisters do? While filming Theresia's sudden death, I queried Bienvenu, Jef, and Raph, who was holding the camera, about the harsh fate they had determined for Theresia. Two explanations were offered. For one, I had to keep in mind that Theresia had committed adultery (*ekobo*), which is an unforgivable sin. Furthermore, two weeks before, the troupe had filmed a scene in which Theresia introduced witchcraft to her own sisters. It was clear to them that this woman stubbornly refused to accept Jesus. The combination of these wrongs reflected an evil that could no longer be put right by God without consequences. When I steered the conversation into a discussion of the role of lightning in Theresia's death, there was suddenly less unanimity. Some actors, especially those of Luba origin, were convinced that lightning is a manifestation of God, while Bienvenu, Jef, and Raph held that the Luba ancestors were avenging Theresia's disrespect for the family tradition. The latter interpretation placed the Luba ancestors on the same level as the demonic agencies, while the Luba players themselves saw no distinction between the desires of the Luba ancestors and God's will.[4]

In the first instance, we can interpret these opposing viewpoints as the outcome of Luba members' efforts to identify themselves as Christians in contrast to the opinions of non-Luba members who regarded this interpretation of lightning as diabolical. We also learn that Christian ideology has not totally replaced or diabolized more long-standing, "traditional" values and thinking. It furthermore reminds us again of the fact that a group of born-again Christians participating in an evangelizing troupe does not form a complete unity. The meanings of the fictionalized actions and characters are often under discussion and are not necessarily shared by all the players of the company.

Moreover, there is undoubtedly distance between the ideology portrayed in the serials and the convictions of the performers themselves when considering the origin of evil. This point was brought home to me when I queried my informants about their interpretations of the closure of *Dilemma,* which was filmed in my absence. The narrative initially deals with the marriage choice Caleb faces: should he marry the young girl Monica, whom he loves but whom his parents dislike, or should he follow his parents' wish and marry Charlainne? After three episodes, a subplot takes over a thread that the Cinarc leader had initially devised: Monica enters into an incestuous relationship with her father, Fataki. Caught in the act by the domestic servant and his other three children, Fataki kills them all. The *maboke* closes with Fataki being arrested by a police officer and taken to prison. Monica pleads guilty to incest in front of a pastor and is exorcised. Her deliverance from the impure spirits confirms the agency of exterior maleficent powers in the misfortune of Fataki's household.

Several questions arise: Why did the performers insert a police arrest and an exorcising ritual? And why are these two distinct technologies of restoration (sanction and purification) distributed over different protagonists? Why does *Dilemma* not show Fataki's deliverance from impure spirits, for example?

In light of the prominent role given to spirits in influencing human actions, it is imperative to analyze the representation of invisible agents in the *Dilemma* serial. In contrast to other Cinarc *maboke,* this serial does not make extensive use of special effects to visualize the possession of evil spirits, nor, for that matter, does the theme of evil spirits dominate the episodes. Only two scenes stand out in this regard. One scene depicts Fataki in his office immediately after he has murdered his children.

It is shown how this successful businessman hears "mystical" sounds, created by special effects that resemble the sounds of computer games (Nintendo). Ance explained that these sounds should be interpreted as signs of his murdered children and their desire to punish their father for their deaths. Bienvenu and Chapy (the Cinarc leader and his cousin), on the other hand, attributed the noises to demons that had come to possess him.

Though these different understandings of the assumed intervention of spirit agents are worth exploring further, the paucity of references to the invisible world in this serial, as a whole, is surprising. When watching copies of the episodes in Kinshasa, I assumed that *Dilemma* portrayed a subject responsible for her own acts and their consequences. In addition, it is one of the few telenarratives that sends an evildoer to prison. Discussions with the actors about this particular closure revealed that they did not share the same interpretation of the outcome. Serge Kayumbi, the actor in the role of Fataki, whose improvisation skills had significantly altered the main plot, argued that his fictive alter ego had committed a crime (*bobe*) and therefore had to be punished according to the law (*mobeko*). Since the beginning of fieldwork, I had noticed that this particular actor always seemed to take a rational approach toward the group's work on television, and here, totally in line with the impression I already had, he focused on the murders and identified Fataki as a criminal. Furthermore, Serge did not consider evil spirits to have instigated the criminal behavior but pointed to Fataki's personal physical desires as the cause of the offence. Serge also sympathized with Ance's interpretation of the mystical sounds, defining them as reactions of the deceased children's spirits rather than a confirmation of Fataki's cohabitation with the dark world. Most other members of the acting company disagreed with this interpretation, however. The troupe's leader, who was a more ardent Christian than most, gave a totally different explanation. According to him, the most important "bad" act of Fataki was not the murder but the incest. He interpreted the consequent murders as a logical outcome of sinful behavior. Bienvenu thus identified Fataki in the first instance as a sinner; his criminal identity was then only secondary to his sins.

Surprisingly then, the actors somehow decided not to save Fataki from his demons but to send him to prison. According to Bienvenu, they could not allow him to be saved, because, as he argued adamantly, "we need to show people that there are certain sins that cannot be redeemed. If we would say that killing can be restored through praying and converting to God, then … we need to show people that they should stop this kind of life, and show them 'Look how you will end. You will be imprisoned and you will go to hell.' Even if we did not say so, he will go to hell."

I could not have anticipated the actors' ultimate accusations. In their reflections on the genealogy of evil presented in this narrative, all the actors agreed that Deborah, the mother, was in fact responsible for "having opened a door" to evil spirits, thus mitigating Fataki's transgression.[5] Although Deborah had not committed any sinful act, according to the Cinarc actors, her encouragements to her daughters to dress in seductive clothing, thus arousing her husband and pushing him to fantasize about their daughters' bodies, was the ultimate origin of all evil. Nene contended: "The Devil does not ask your permission to live with you. God does." Referring to Apocalypse 3:20 ("Look, here I am in front of your door and I knock. If someone hears my voice, and offers himself to me, I will be with him and he will be with me."),[6] Nene contrasted God's distance with the Devil's unrequested intrusion. Yet, as she reminded me, "in order for the Devil to succeed, someone has to give access. Monica gave access to the Devil, by way of her mother, because her mother bought her 'bad clothes.'"

Due to an internal conflict, Nadine, who performed the role of Deborah, was suspended for six weeks. This disrupted the filming scheme seriously. Her character returned only in the two final episodes and did not receive much screen time. As a result, the actors' reflections on evil did not dwell much on Deborah's evilness. The serial instead inspired the evangelizing artists to contemplate the merits of a sanction like imprisonment and standardized Christian techniques of restoration and purification. So, when Nene talked about Deborah's part in the spread of evil in her household, she immediately added that Fataki was possessed by the demons that used Monica, but he himself already had the "demon of sexual desire" (*molimo ya mposa*) within him. She held both the evil spirits and Fataki himself responsible for the old man's immoral behavior. For most ardent Christians, the person is also responsible for allowing these spirits to enter the body and the household, and only deliverance from these demons can purify the person and the community. Therefore, as Nene pointed out, one must be aware that Fataki's soul cannot be healed in prison.

Though most Kinois, including Nene, would agree that this modern correctional institution has many advantages, she reminded me of the fact that wardens merely confine the prisoners and do not care for the spiritual needs of the human person. Nene was nevertheless sure that, in prison, Fataki would have much time to reflect on his deeds and would, or at least would be expected to, become conscious of his wrongdoing. For this young Christian actress, as well as for Bienvenu and even

Serge (who seemed to attribute more agency to persons than his fellow performers did), the prison is a place where people become conscious (*kozwa mayele*), especially considering the frequent visits by evangelizers and pastors to the city's prisons. The Christian actors mentioned that this modern institution, where punishment is translated into physical confinement, could turn into a space in which human beings who are "on the wrong road" have the chance to reconnect with the divine. As to prove this possibility, the Cinarc actors referred to Kinshasa's best-known "worldly singer," Papa Wemba, who converted to Christianity during his months in a Parisian prison. All Cinarc members agreed that "many people get in touch with God" in prison.

Leaving aside the offscreen musings about Fataki's fate and focusing on the narrative of the *Dilemma* serial, we discern that two kinds of modern subjects are represented: the character of Fataki stands for a subject defined as a "citizen," subordinated to legislative justice; Monica, Fataki's partner in crime, on the other hand, is depicted as a "Christian subject" because of her prime interaction with a spiritual world. It is the latter aspect that receives remarkable emphasis in the *maboke:* although the serial depicts Fataki's arrest by a policeman, it does not linger on his fate.[7] Instead, lengthy scenes are devoted to Monica's destiny: it is shown how she is delivered, how she identifies herself as a sinner, and how she confesses her sins.

The decision to depict Monica's salvation demonstrates that, for the Christian actors, the spiritual restoration of the person is of more concern to them than the correction offered by Western judiciary procedures and incarceration. We can understand the preference for Monica's religious purification if we consider the role of the reconfiguration of one's double in the Pentecostal definition of the "Christian subject." As mentioned earlier in this chapter, much attention is given to the dividuality of a Christian person, and the right moral movement relates to the cleansing of one's soul. Confinement in prison encloses the human being, silences dividuality, and ignores the connection between the person and external influences. Deliverance rituals change the quality of the external components that to a large degree constitute the person. In the end, the Christian rituals reconfigure the composites of the human being and transform the person into a "Christian."

Confessions

Plots of the Pentecostal melodramas frequently end with confessions so as to produce a conjunctive closure. Confessions do not only appear in the *maboke:* the confession was probably the ritual that I observed most in the religious meetings. I also encountered a fascination for the confession in Kinois' viewing preferences. On extremely popular talk shows like *Jerry Springer* and the Walloon copy *Ca va se savoir*, people confess in public—to relatives, colleagues, friends, or other individuals from their network—to having committed incest or adultery, or having fathered a child with one's mother-in-law, and so on. What does the confession teach us about the Christian subject and about Kinshasa's society?

Christian spiritual leaders and their followers claim that the older purification rites no longer hold. Pastor Gervais commented on this shift in a sermon:

> Before, in the village, if something had been stolen, and there was doubt as to the perpetrator, between four persons accused of thievery for example, then all of them had to wash their hands, because water purified. But what people did not know is that the water also has a power of death. So even if you wash your hands with water, your sin will continue to follow you. You must make peace with your God.

The pastor here devalued the autochthonous purification rituals as demonic, possessing "the power of death." In a Christian context, evil behavior means trespassing the prohibitions defined in the Ten Commandments. "Performing evil" is then formulated as "to sin" (*kosuma*, Fr. *pécher*). The noun "*lisumu*" is related to the kiKongo verb "*kosuma*," which originally denotes, in a non-Christian society, "to defile a charm, or its priest, by breaking one of the rules that set it [him] apart as the embodiment of a specific power" (MacGaffey 1986: 158–159). Carl Sundberg, writing about Christians in Congo-Brazzaville, points to how Christian missionaries introduced the idea of "guilt" and "sin" and how this is intimately related to a dualistic worldview in which people are held to affiliate either with God or with the Devil.

> With the Bible and Christian beliefs, different notions of sin and reconciliation entered the scene. For the missionary, the *minkisi* and the practices related to *banganaga* and *bandoki* were the worst possible expressions of superstition or pagan cult.... What Christianity brought was the idea that sin was primarily an activity directed against god. Muntu [the human being], however, already lived in a relation with god and had never had the idea of a need for reconciliation with *nzambi*. He belonged to *nzambi* and could not step outside this togetherness. (Sundberg 2000: 72–73)

Sundberg's quotation demonstrates that Christianization introduced the possibility of a new relationship to God. From this we could expect that reconciliation is only needed in a vertical relationship with the divine ("make peace with God," as the pastor stated). This assumption, however, is not supported by the practices of reconciliation as enacted among Kinshasa's born-again Christians. Christian leaders demand that evildoers confess their sins and ask forgiveness in dialogue with both the divine and the social community. Most confessions are made in public; in church settings or on television witches and others regularly confess their wanderings in the nocturnal realm or wicked activities they have undertaken, even naming their victims. Repentant protagonists in the teleserials also confess in front of a group.

The analysis of the representation of confessions in *The Heritage of Death* explores the balance between individual and social restoration initiated by the confession.* This Cinarc serial, broadcast on RTG@ from January to March 2006, deals with relations among the children of Fataki, a polygamous Luba man who lies dying in a hospital. The title has a double meaning, which only gradually becomes clear in the successive episodes. At first, it appears as if this *maboke* will deal with the distribution of the dying old man's business and properties among the children of his two wives. The children of the first wife (Theresia) have not been to school, have hardly mastered French, and do not dress fashionably. Deborah's offspring, by contrast, obtained academic degrees, traveled abroad, and are fluent in French. Consequently, their father gave important positions to Caleb and Charlainne, the two eldest in this second household. Now that Fataki lies dying, Deborah's children claim the inheritance because of their skills and experience. Theresia and her children, however, reckon that the children of the first wife should benefit from Fataki's company. A third group claims his goods as well: Fataki's Luba siblings have flown in from the Kasai region and, following Luba custom, expect Fataki's houses, cars, money, and business should be divided among his brothers and sisters, leaving his wives and children empty-handed.

Five episodes later Fataki recovers, and the serial moves away from the issue of rightful successors. More attention is now paid to Deborah's occult activities. As the story unfolds, it becomes clear that the privileges Deborah's children are enjoying stem from an occult bond Deborah entered into with the *féticheur* Etcho Bendo back at the beginning of her marriage. From this point on, the title receives a new interpretation. The actors now state that *The Heritage of Death* hints at the consequences that bonds with the dark world bring about in the physical world: Fataki is faced with the madness of his son, the death of another son, the blindness of one of his daughters, and several illnesses in the family. In the last episode two other deaths occur due to poisoning.

*These moving images are available at http://www.berghahnbooks.com/title.php?rowtag=
PypeMaking

Maman Deborah, one of Fataki's two wives, portrays the subjectivity of evil, how evil is experienced, and how remorse (*bomima*) can gradually come about. One monologue in the seventh episode of the TV drama is particularly crucial. This scene depicts Deborah, who has left her husband's compound and fled to her sister's house, where she confesses she is the origin of all the misfortune in her family. The next scene shows Deborah touring the city. There are many pauses between her words, and her body language indicates how difficult it is for her to acknowledge the effects of her deeds. Tears roll down her cheeks, and the despair is easy to read in her eyes. Close-ups of her face heighten the importance of this scene, in which Deborah gains consciousness of her deeds and comes to feel remorse. Deborah's monologue is at once both a prayer and confession to God: "My God. The problems that I have created, they have brought problems into my life. The power that I looked for has begun to ruin me. I am living with these problems: Caroline has become blind, Lewis has died..." Here the scene fades out, suggesting that her monologue continues for some time.

Deborah's plea to God for forgiveness does not alone suffice to make her a Christian again: deliverance and confession are also required. The following scene depicts Deborah in Caleb's house, where the pastor and some of her own children have gathered. Caleb introduces the pastor to his mother; her children have been praying with the pastor each day in order to find a solution for the difficulties they have had in their households. Deborah, however, contests the authority of Pastor Chapy, who in her eyes is only a *mwana moke,* a small child. "How can an adult woman like her listen to a child?" she claims. Her rejection of Chapy's authority is related to the generational difference between herself and this young man. She explicitly refers to the Protestant missionaries, who were all "men with beards." When Deborah attempts to leave, the pastor tells everyone that God is revealing to him at that very moment that Deborah is the cause of all the misfortune. These words incite the children to pray. Pastor Chapy approaches the woman. The invisible divine fire invoked by those praying blows Deborah off her feet; she falls on the ground while the evil spirit, shouting *"Nakei"* (I am leaving), exits her body. At the same moment, one of the possessed daughters, Caroline, regains her sight. In the following scene Deborah gathers her children, her sister, and the pastor together and tells the group that she is willing to confess (figs. 6.1–4). Breaking into tears, she embarks on an emotional confession with the words: "I am a sinner" (*Naza moto ya massumu*). Her confession relates how she is at the root of Caroline's blindness, Caleb's madness, and Melina's death. She reveals her link with the *nganga* Etcho Bondo. All the misfortune, illness and disputes that have occurred in

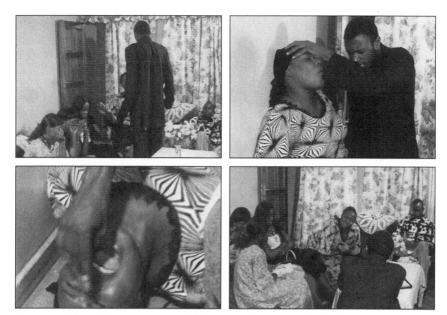

Figures 6.1., 6.2., 6.3. and 6.4. Pastor Chapy heals Deborah, who then confesses (screen shots from *The Heritage of Death,* © Cinarc)

the family are the outcomes of this occult bond. She also informs the others about the circumstances of Charlainne's death. Her children are astonished: they all had never thought that their own mother would be the cause of death and suffering. Pastor Chapy, however, is not surprised; and, according to him, God has already forgiven her. The scene ends with a collective prayer that aims at protecting Deborah's soul.

The scenario concludes with Fataki leaving the hospital and assembling his wives and all of his children. Kiodo, the insane son, has abandoned his *kizengi* (fool) fashion of speaking.[8] He, too, confesses his wicked acts and identifies himself as the origin of Caroline's blindness and Caleb's madness, promising to refrain from all witchcraft in the future. The final scene depicts a feast among the children of the two co-wives. The women and their offspring dance to Christian music and promise to cooperate with each other so that the family enterprise will become a fruitful business.

Becoming Conscious

In the above, it is shown that in order to halt the chain of misfortune and to restore peace and order, one must confess. Confessions contribute to the fabric of the Christian subject because these are indispensable steps in the process of "becoming conscious" (*kozwa mayele*). Consciousness—*mayele*—resides in the heart and denotes intelligence and knowledge but also manners, behaviors, character, and "spirit." It also can mean cleverness or cunning. In the context of confessing, *mayele* has more to do with morality and proper social conduct. Taking Foucault's line of interpretation of Christian technologies of the self (1988), confessions constitute the modern subject, for they trigger psychological exploration. From this Western point of view one can consider the confessional act on an individual level: poking around in one's memories and constructing a story about one's sins constitutes a particular consciousness that creates an individuality, one in which the speaker takes on responsibility for his or her actions.

A related discursive ritual among Kinshasa's Pentecostals is the soul healing (*cure d'âme*). Once people express the desire to become a born-again Christian, they are expected to undergo this. Soul healings consist of one or more private sessions with a spiritual leader in which the confessor constructs a narrative about his or her personal life history, indicating moments of disagreement, enmity, joy, bad luck, love, sexual relationships, and so on. A young prophet who frequently guides these sessions spoke about the practice in the following way: "At the beginning of a soul healing, many people say that they do not understand how they became jealous. But they are responsible, they were feeling the jealousy, and they let it rule their lives. They opened the door. In the soul healing, they suddenly remember where and how they opened that door." Soul healing sessions are key to the process of becoming conscious of sins, possible moments in which the speaker has connected with the dark world. "Becoming conscious," then, does not merely denote gaining knowledge about what has happened or getting clarity about one's personal emotional past, but also underlines—crucially, for Kinshasa's born-again Christians—the expectation that the knowledge retrieved in these discursive moments should help a person control his or her heart, which, because of the purification of the dividual subject, in turn leads to a purification of his or her social environment. Therefore, soul healings are often followed by public confessions and requests for forgiveness.

In emic discourse, it is said that the exploration of one's personal past must disclose difficulties and discord as the result of "unconscious" or "conscious witchcraft." This distinction between "conscious witchcraft" (Fr. *la sorcellerie consciente*, Li. *kindoki ya kondima*, "accepted witchcraft") and "unconscious witchcraft" (Fr. *la sorcellerie inconsciente*, Li. *kindoki ya bopesi*, "given witchcraft")[9] refers to the cognizance and intentions of the witch. "*Sorcellerie consciente*" denotes the consciousness of the person who knows that bad things happen through him- or herself. Frequently, jealousy, anger, and hatred are emotions that set witchcraft in motion (see Pype forthcoming b). In the serial *The Open Tomb*, for example, Deborah contacts an *nganga* in order to gain influence over Fataki and her co-wife. Her act is inspired by a quest for power, a desire to control her husband and to benefit, more than her co-wife, from Fataki's wealth. "Unconscious witchcraft," on the other hand, refers to people such as child witches, who are the victims of witchcraft (Kiodo in *The Heritage of Death* being one instance of this type). Due to mystical bonds these persons themselves become witches even though they are unaware of it. They too are required to undergo a soul healing to unravel the intrusion of the occult into their lives.[10]

The distinction between "conscious" and "unconscious witchcraft" has bearing on the understanding of urban sociality and individuality. First, with regard to sociality, the mere possibility of a person possessing "unconscious witchcraft" cautions Christians to view all others in their life worlds as potential enemies, as having evil inside. Christians are thus encouraged to monitor the speech and behavior of others in order to discover where they are positioned on the moral map. Meanwhile, this distinction also inspires Christians to engage in a process of continuous self-reflection and does not inflict shame on people who acknowledge the past involvement of evil spirits in their lives.

We must be wary of transposing a Western psychological meaning of consciousness onto the setting of Kinshasa's Christians. "Consciousness" is a cultural variable that is historical and dynamic (see Lutz 1992). In Kinshasa, Pentecostal churches invest a lot of time and energy in the construction of a particular kind of self and personhood in which the very concept of consciousness is utilized and manipulated. Pastor Gervais said in church: "God has created man with *mayele* (a conscience). He has shown him the tree of knowledge about good and evil. But, when the Devil enters into our life, he sows a doubt. The lines between good and evil are no longer clear. He makes us doubt God's goodness and even his existence." The pastor's sermon immediately moved to the social environment, and he preached that once the lines between good and evil are blurred, it is extremely difficult to know on whom to rely. In the pastor's discourse, spiritual knowledge, human agency, social trust, and extra-human actions are intertwined. If we can take the pastor's talk as indicative of the apocalyptic imagination of consciousness, then *mayele* means both "conscience," or the ability to evaluate one's actions as morally wrong or right, and the "self-awareness" of one's relations to others, both socially and spiritually. The interconnectedness of the person with invisible others, social others, and society at large is prioritized.

Confessions not only hold spiritual significance for the speaker but also bear on the social environment: publicly acknowledging one's evil acts triggers among the audience an awareness of the origin of distress and hardship the confessor might have experienced and situates him or her back in the Christian community. Given the pivotal role of the confessions in the closures of the telenarratives, the *maboke* transmit the message that human beings make their worlds—that their own speech and actions can restore society.[11]

The Mediating Role of Speech

Language is an important mediator between the human realm and the invisible. People's public articulation of their sins and distancing from such behavior produces new selves. Words are important mediators of identities and intersubjective relationships. Words construct ties with the otherworldly and physical others. In the act of speaking, audiences are immediately implied. As soon as words are expressed, a social identity is made manifest. Much has been said and written about the "performative power of the word" in Africa, and lately also in a charismatic context. Curses and maledictions (*balakela mabe,* "promising bad things") are discursive acts with illocutionary or even magical potency. In the context of Kinshasa's born-again Christians, it is argued that the Devil takes advantage of "bad words" and uses these in order to accomplish his mission. "Words bind people" (*maloba bakangaka bato*), it is argued.

The productive work of confessions does not mean that the words have an unambiguously performative force (Searle 1969). Rather, the role of the audience—the addressees of the public confessions—in accepting the request of forgiveness is primordial. I found in particular many parallels between Pentecostals' practices that construct the subject and ethnographies of more local, ethnicity-related spirit possession cults in Kinshasa such as Ellen Corin's (1998) discussion of the *zebola,* a female spirit possession cult among the Mongo that is also enacted in Kinshasa, and René Devisch's (1998) study of *mbwoolu,* a Yaka healing cult that also takes place in Congo's capital city. Through dance and song, the *zebola* cult offers women with all kinds of illnesses the possibility to engage with spirits of deceased Mongo women. *Mbwoolu* is performed in cases of fever, nightmares and anxiety, and loss of self-esteem.

Both Corin and Devisch point to the social role of the discourse uttered by the possessing spirits, who speak out as soon as the patient has entered in a condition of trance (*zebola*) and prayer (*mbwoolu*). Devisch

(1998: 127) writes in this regard that "speech weaves a tissue of life." Corin analyzes two important moments in the chain of words: in the first moment, the spirit reveals the woman's vulnerable position within society: people gossip about her, and she endures feelings of jealousy or has other complaints. This offers an explanation of why evil spirits have been able to intrude in the patient's life. In a second move, the narrative reveals the conflicts, transgressions, and events that have been set in motion through the spirit. Both types of narrative (which Corin calls "divination narrative") and the narrative evolution as well can easily be transposed onto the confessions among born-again Christians. In *The Open Tomb,* for instance, Deborah begins her confession by explaining why she sought out the *nganga.* This is followed by a list of the effects that her occult actions have caused: several of her co-wife's children died, her co-wife's son became insane and transformed into a witch himself, Deborah's own son became mad, her daughter lost her eyesight, and another daughter was killed. Confessions thus offer Pentecostals the possibility of reframing their problems and desires in a narrative form and situating them in a historical frame in the same way that the *zebola* ritual offers women a means to reconstruct themselves as persons (Corin 1998: 95). Or, as Devisch (1998: 154) words it for the *mbwoolu* patients: "This prayer is essentially a route of initial identification as a process of self, allowing the initiate to assume his biography and his multiple social roles at the heart of a drama that is partially extra human, paranormal, outside the normal and sacred."

Although Corin approaches the *zebola* ritual as a process of individualization, she describes a repositioning of the female patient in the social world as the main goal of the cult: "The goal is not the creation of autonomous, emancipated subjects, but to rework the relationships of *appartenance* of the person to her world" (1998: 100). The same goes for the *mbwoolu* ritual which is not over until the patient can take up normal social life again (Devisch 1998: 142). The reworking of the person's relationships to others is also at play in the confessions of born-again Christians. Confessions tend to finish with pleas for forgiveness from God and the social group. These are seldom refused, so the confessor thus enters the social group again. In the act of confessing, the evildoer moves from being an outsider to an insider and aligns him- or herself with a particular set of Christian values, just as Deborah ultimately did in *The Heritage of Death* by acknowledging that her eagerness to gain her husband's total devotion as well as material benefits eventually caused illness and death. This shift, which accompanies a transformation in the confessing person's consciousness, reinstalls the social community and confirms its boundaries.

All this indicates that for Kinshasa's born-again Christians, the confession of evil not only has a personal effect but also serves to create society. Here, I wish to draw attention to the coincidence of deliverance rituals (which feed the subject with "divine life") and confessions in the Pentecostal melodramas. It marks the necessity of simultaneous individual purification and restoration of social relations, and points out that the shift to the "right" road undertaken by the individual needs to be complemented with the reinsertion of the Christian in the larger Christian community. To that extent, born-again Christianity accentuates that "life" for the individual and the future of society are interdependent.[12]

Among Kinshasa's Pentecostals, it is taken for granted that "words produce reality," that the spoken becomes materialized. This is also one of the reasons why those who confess speak out: in stating in public that one has become a Christian, one hopes that the Christian community will acknowledge this. Yet while confessions seem to be overt statements of one's sense of guilt and intention to reintroduce oneself in the Christian moral community, this cannot be taken for granted in an apocalyptic society such as Kinshasa. I observed how one evangelizer, who made a livelihood by traveling around Kinshasa's churches and recounting his confessions, was approached with much suspicion during one of his performances, in which bats were circling around his head. This occurred while the man was disclosing how he had married a *mami wata* (a female demon), who had demanded sacrifices such as the souls of unborn babies (he thus took responsibility for several miscarriages in his neighborhood). One could observe a gradual increase in singing and praying on the side of the audience. Afterwards, the pastor who had organized the event felt he had to apologize for having invited the man, and he subtly suggested a (new) deliverance to set the confessed man free.

This anecdote evidences that the power of the Word is limited, or even subsidiary, to the spiritual condition of the speaker. Confessions as such do not automatically create Christian selves—there can be a breach between the pronounced words and the inner state of the "confessee." It explains why the purification of the heart essentially precedes the confession. Furthermore, the disclosure of evil spirits' activities might even trigger demonic anger and incite the demons to take revenge. Confessing thus becomes a highly ambiguous event: it is intended to be a moment in which a renewed connection with the divine is materialized, but this requires a soul purified beforehand. Only with a pure heart are penitents able to become "real Christians" and also cleanse their social environment. Confessing with an impure heart, meanwhile, is a hazardous exercise in which the very same words produce new occult realities, experiences, and identities.

Conclusion

Mediation by the Holy Spirit: Transformation from Evil to Purity

What do the rituals of confession and exorcism tell us about contemporary notions of evil? In his analysis of discourses of evil, Parkin (1985a) makes a distinction between evil as "dirt" or "defilement" and evil as "entanglement" or "disorder." The first of these definitions interprets "bad behavior" (*mosala mabe*) as a contamination by evil that can be removed by means of sacrifices and cleansing operations, such as "traditional" healing rituals, witchcraft eradication movements, and Christian rituals of exorcism. The second notion understands "evil" as disarray or disorder created through an excess of a particular behavior that disturbs social balance. Here, confession and compensation serve to straighten the relationships out again and resolve social discord. The cultural definitions of evil as entanglement and as disorder can occur in one and the same society. Parkin describes Mary Douglas's famous characterization of social dirt as "matter out of place" (1969) precisely as a conflation of evil as disarray and defilement (Parkin 1985b: 240). The two approaches to evil are also conflated in the Kinshasa data. Deliverance rituals and confessions concur and sometimes even coincide, for at times the confession forms part of a deliverance ritual. When tracing back a genealogy of evil it becomes clear that there is ultimately a person who was first contaminated with "dirt" (invaded by an evil spirit). The inevitable consequence of this original contamination is "disorder" or social disturbance (conflicts and suffering).

The "dirt," or the evil spirits, is "modern dirt" belonging to Kinshasa's cosmopolitan society. In *The Heritage of Death,* Deborah's competition with her co-wife for Fataki's love is inspired by a concern for money that would have provided education and luxury for her children. In the serial *The Nanas Benz,* the five Nanas Benz women make a pact with Reine Love in return for expensive cars and a luxurious lifestyle. The ostentatious wealth of the *moziki* women in *The Moziki Women* also derives from a connection with the Devil. In an emic discourse, the love of money goes hand in hand with the spirits of jealousy and hatred, spirits that lead the "evil" protagonists to sacrifice their loved ones and in the end themselves. In *The Heritage of Death,* Deborah first sacrifices the children of her co-wife, but at a certain point her own children become victims of the occult attacks. Deborah can counter this spiral of death only by converting to Jesus. In *The Nanas Benz,* Melina becomes blind; Theresia dies in *The Open Tomb.* The serials thus point at individuals' desires to participate in the modern capitalist society at the expense of the social community. This, however, does not mean that the subjects, once converted, cannot attain wealth and a life of luxury. Kinshasa's pastors use the Bible to indicate the route to wealth. But the wealth must be shared through tithing, a practice transforming one's riches from unaccepted into divinely recognized. Those who give receive the special blessing of the Christian leaders.

Finally, this chapter has shown the mediating role of the Holy Spirit in moral movement, the individual's transformation from a life in chaos and disorder to the good, the orderly, and the healthy. Purification techniques that produce Christian subjects thus require the active involvement of the Holy Spirit, and a ritual such as the confession can find closure only when the audience has agreed to forgive the one confessing. A Christian self thus is never totally autonomous; rather, social and spiritual agents mediate one's Christian identity.

Melodrama and Rituals

The insertion of such rituals as confessions and deliverance rituals into fictional mass-mediated narratives urges us to rethink the boundaries and convergences between media, performance, and ritual.[13] This is all the more the case when we consider that, in Kinshasa's predominant Christian culture, the line between ritual, the arts, and television is quite fine. As we have seen, dance, drama, and music form a preponderant part of Pentecostal rituals and are in turn shown on television and frame public cultural performances such as dance events and plays in the service of development programs. I wish to elaborate on two aspects: the healing function of narrative and the representation of the Christian subject in a "modern" genre like the melodrama.

First, having narrowed down the focus to the Pentecostal melodrama, we notice, next to the simultaneity of ritual and the aesthetic, the common grounds on which the telenarratives and other Pentecostal rituals frame experience, construct reality, and accordingly produce a particular consciousness. The "healing" capacity of the Pentecostal melodrama derives from the particular character of the genre of melodrama itself. "Revealing the most real in the universe" and "purging society" are significant terms Brooks uses in describing the fundamental goals of the melodrama (see Chapter 2). His description highlights the fundamental aspects that the melodrama shares with Pentecostal-charismatic Christianity. Consider, for example, Pentecostals' oft-performed rituals: deliverances, sermons, and testimonies of former witches. All of these aim at localizing evil within society (people/places) and expelling it. It comes as no surprise, then, that according to Brooks (1976: 17), the melodrama resembles a ritual insofar as it deals with experiences of pain and suffering and with expelling their evil causes. Brooks (1976: 206) even remarks that melodrama offers a substitute for the rite of sacrifice, "an urging toward combat in life, an active, lucid confrontation of evil." Ritual work and the field of the aesthetic do not constitute distinct fields. If we accept that conversion rituals, rituals of exorcism, and confession are rites of re-origination in the divine Real (for they reconnect the individual with the Christian God and his work), then it is not that difficult to understand how serials aim at realizing purification on a societal or collective level. The fictional representations of the hardship in everyday life and the solutions offered through the purifying rituals aim precisely at reestablishing connections with the Holy, which is portrayed as restoring and life-creating.

Second, it has been argued that the melodrama as a genre introduces new, "modern" forms of subjectivity (Abu-Lughod 2002; Vasudevan 2000). As shown above, the Pentecostal melodramas give much weight to one's emotional life and the need to revision one's personal past and confess publicly. This, however, does not mean that a Western "individual" dwells in these narratives. The significance of one's affects and personal actions consistently derives from their relation to social and spiritual others. The individuality of the protagonists of the Pentecostal melodrama is subjected to society at large and ultimately to the invisible. In this respect, the "modernity" of the Pentecostal melodrama is not a secular modernity but one rooted in the blend of Christianity and more long-standing local understandings of the person and his or her positioning in society and the "Real."

In my view, it is exactly the dividuality of the Christian subject—the connection to the outer social environment—that renders the evangelizing mission of Pentecostal Christian leaders so ubiquitous and even intrusive, and that accounts for the incredible production of Christian songs and serials. Pentecostal Christianity, with its message that evil is all around, encourages the Christian subject to repeat time and again the Christian technologies of purification and restoration. Being a Christian is a never-ending affair that must be continuously made anew; the weight is rather on how to become Christian. This need to purify oneself again and again might well be the exact reason why the Pentecostal melodrama has become a genre. The same stories are told over and over again because it is believed that while Christians might fall, they can continuously renew themselves—just as the protagonists of the Pentecostal melodramas encounter difficulties during one narrative and are healed at the serial's closure, only to be confronted with new problems and seductions when a new story line begins the next week.

Notes

1. Foucault (1988: 17) defines "technologies of the self" as techniques "which permit individuals to effect by their own means or with the help of others a certain

number of operations on their own bodies and souls, thoughts, conduct, and way of being, so as to transform themselves in order to attain a certain state of happiness, purity, wisdom, perfection, or immortality."

2. The baNkanu are a subgroup of the Kongo group.

3. This concept is inspired by the concept of the "sacred self" studied by Thomas J. Csordas among American charismatic Catholics (1994).

4. In Chapter 8 I offer a more detailed discussion of the role of adultery and the interpretation of the serial's closure.

5. In this interpretation, it is curious to note how evil spirits are associated with the female gender. Women are considered to be the origin of all misfortune: they open the door to evil. I will deal with the gendered dimensions of witchcraft in Chapter 9.

6. In the *New International Version* the verse reads "Here I am! I stand at the door and knock. If anyone hears my voice and opens the door, I will come in and eat with him, and he with me."

7. The representation of Fataki's arrest and the offscreen discourse about his fate can lead us into another analysis that goes beyond the scope of this chapter: the Christians accept the authority of the police man, and thus (reminiscent of Althusser's elaboration (1971) of the interpellation made by a police officer, which constructs the hailed person as a subject of the state) recognize Kinois' identities as "citizens" subject to law. At the same time—and this came to the fore when I invited the actors to discuss Fataki's fate—every individual is also immersed in the otherworldly and, as a Christian, subject to God's authority, here embodied by the pastors. These data thus hint at the commensurability of citizenship and Christianity, the authority of both the state and the Christian God.

8. A *kizengi* speaks in an unintelligible manner, articulating poorly and forming ungrammatical sentences. His anomalous speech is the outcome of witchcraft (see Pype 2010).

9. MacGaffey (1986: 161) briefly mentions that "[b]a[K]ongo themselves attribute witchcraft to conscious or unconscious jealousy (*kimpala*), and much of their discussion of instances of alleged witchcraft is psychologically perceptive."

10. People with unconscious witchcraft meet with less social hostility than witches who act consciously. In the Pentecostal melodrama, elderly people (like Makubakuba in *The Devouring Fire*) who wish their children to follow ethnic customs but have no idea that they are doing wrong are frequently depicted as unconsciously possessing evil. In this respect, witchcraft accusations against elders are somehow neutralized by downplaying evil intentions. The context of intergenerational relations will be further explored in the following chapter.

11. These born-again Christians' emphasis on needing to confess for social reintegration displays many parallels with Bruce Kapferer's finding, in his discussion of representations of sorcery in Sri Lanka (1997: 161), that "consciousness is important for it is the seat of sociality and community."

12. The entanglement of the individual and the social also incites the Christians to engage in national politics. I will discuss this in *Chapter 7*.

13. Anthropologists increasingly study the erosion of the boundaries between television and ritual and acknowledge the intertwinement of media, performance, and ritual (Couldry 2002; Goethals 1981; Hughes-Freeland and Crain 1998; Liebes and Curran 1998; Lyons and Lyons 1987; Meyer and Moors 2006).

Opening Up the Country

Christian Popular Culture,
Generation Trouble, and Time

The previous chapters discussed the mediating role of rituals and the positionality of the body in the context of artistic performances. I touched briefly on the healing role of narrative when analyzing the transformative power of confessions in the churches. This chapter moves back into the zone of popular culture, itself a liminal space, in which alternative approaches to reality can be expressed. Both an Arestotelian and Turnerian perspective emphasize the cathartic role of narrative. The healing power of the public and of articulation of personal suffering, sometimes mass-mediated, has been amply documented elsewhere in Africa, especially in postwar zones or societies that have experienced drastic conflicts (among others McEachern 2002; Price 2007; Gobodo-Madikizela and van der Merwe 2009). In the early post-apartheid context, for example, Truth and Reconciliation Commission hearings provided arenas for narratives of self where South Africans processed and negotiated uncertainties and possibilities (McEachern 2002: xiii). The broadcasting of these hearings, alongside a whole range of other representational sites (theater, art exhibitions, and so on), sought to constitute "communities of witnessing," giving voice to those who were silenced during the apartheid period (McEachern 2002: 63). The mass mediation of these personal stories inspired collective narratives through which reconciliation and dispensation could be produced, thus establishing a new basis for national unity.

In the context of Kinshasa's teleserials, similar concerns about personal witnessing and collective attempts for healing and restoration are evident. In this chapter, I will show that the teleserials constitute spaces in which young Pentecostals plot their personal experiences, render them public via teleserials, and thus hope to produce a new reality for themselves as well as for their wider social environment. The "fun space"

(Werbner 1996) of the teleserials becomes a playground in which frustrations about gerontocratic rule and state inefficiency are visualized (often quite humorously), while the ultimate goal is to resolve the crisis that young Christians are enduring. Importantly, these narratives cannot be too far removed from reality; otherwise the mediating role of the fictional tales—their healing function—is immunized. Before analyzing the representation of elders and the critique on the state, I will first discuss the experience of the crisis and the tensions between young and old in the city.

The Difference between Existing and Living

On my first day of filming with Cinarc, the troupe's leader Bienvenu asked me about my impressions of Kinshasa and then, without waiting for my reply, immediately gave his own analysis of life in the city: "Here we do not live, we merely exist."[1] Bienvenu's tenor was ironic, and the context in which he uttered this expression clarifies the irony. We were in a clothing store in the shadow of the Belgian embassy. A sign above the display window promised the arrival of the latest Parisian fashion. From time to time, the Cinarc group filmed small scenes here while producing advertisements for this shop. It had just been raining, and the poor condition of the road, dotted with big puddles of water, made it difficult to cross the street without getting one's feet and clothes muddy. This particular street is quite busy and boasts numerous activities: a cultural center, Lebanese diamond shops, Indian clothing stores, and shops selling electronic equipment and modern communications technologies. All these form the backdrop of a space where young ambulant vendors loudly hawk their wares—ranging from chewing gum to sunglasses or clocks and mirrors—while money changers (*cambistes*) await clients on the pavement. This is the economic and diplomatic heart of Kinshasa, a vibrant space full of noise and movement. More than any other place in this vast city, the city center is home to all the promises of modernity: embassies can arrange visas for Western countries, shops display fancy clothes, and travel agencies foster dreams of countries like the United Arab Emirates, Kenya, Tanzania, South Africa, France, and Belgium. Cinarc's serials contribute to the imagination of the city center as a place of consumption, as most of the commercials inserted in the story lines are shot there.

That first day of fieldwork with the Cinarc group, I observed Bienvenu picking up a pair of shoes that cost $250 (U.S.). This price was well in excess of his budget, but Bienvenu could wear them for the shoot. His ironic tone at this moment—speaking on this site where an oneiric imagination of the West was momentarily materialized in the wearing of Lina's Parisian clothes—reveals the contradiction lurking between the city center's promises and the reality of life in the townships. Just for an instant, Bienvenu did not need the visa for France that he had been trying to get through both official and illegal channels, because in that moment he was in Paris, wearing the latest fashions and flirting with equally well-dressed girls.

But despite these moments of escape, reality in Kinshasa quickly returns in all its harshness. The distance between living and existing that Bienvenu spoke of does not reside merely in the acquisition of commodities but is more profound. Bienvenu explained to me later: "Here, in Kinshasa, there are no rules. People just do what they wish, and how they want it." This was his explanation of the crisis.[2] These words articulate the fundamental lack of meaning these young people perceive in their social relationships, their daily struggle to survive, and their experiences with the state.

The Congolese state and the urban government are not able to impose any clear rules on their citizens. But paradoxically, this incapacity, or absence, is very deeply felt by Kinshasa's young. During fieldwork, I heard numerous accounts of young men being beaten up at night by military men who, instead of offering security, were perpetrating violent acts on civilians. The looming threat of interference by state officials affected the mobility of Kinshasa's youth. Cinarc actors frequently slept over in Bienvenu's compound when filming continued until after midnight. And there was an ongoing risk of being taken by soldiers, who would release their hostages only in return for money, a watch, a mobile phone, or some other object the military men could then resell.[3]

Of critical importance here is that Bienvenu, in applying the notion of insecurity (*insécurité*) in the nation's historical course, transposed his analysis of the general political situation onto a larger spiritual frame. He defined a society without rules as a society led by the Devil, who enjoys chaos. "If God governed the country," Bienvenu continued, "the roads would be the same as they had been during colonial times." Such discourse resonates with a nostalgia that I encountered often among Kinois about the city's outlook during colonial times.[4] Many Kinois like to compare colonial Leopoldville with Paris. According to Bienvenu, the main reason for the deterioration of the city is the fact that the Congolese have chased God away. "It is time that we all ask God to come back to Congo," he claimed.

Unruly soldiers, an increasingly deplorable urban environment, and the lack of infrastructure (roads, electricity, water, and so on) are interpreted as physical outcomes of a spiritual battle. The same goes for the conditions of economic hardship. Jobs are difficult to find, even for the educated, and there is ongoing poverty; people perceive themselves as living in a "virtually wealthy" but underdeveloped country. The political transition seems to last forever, social relations are strained by suspicion, and the country is alienated from its "traditional" worlds (now diabolized by many).

In Bienvenu's words, the difference between living and existing resides in the presence or absence of rules to be obeyed. A society without rules means chaos (*mubulu*), where no "life" (*bomoyi*) is possible. The statement "We do not live, we merely exist" can be clarified by Robert Desjarlais's distinction between "experience" and "struggling along." Desjarlais defines these concepts as two phenomenal categories depicting two distinct ways of being. "Experience" entails coherence and a transcendent meaning of "tying things together through time" (1996: 87), whereas "struggling along" depicts the experience of displacement and unrest, of the inability to make sense of things, of not finding any way to blend encounters and moods into a meaningful narrative. The difference between these two modes of being rests on the kind of environment in which one lives: an absence of security and trust, but also the lack of an orientation toward the future or the profound experience of crisis, create a mode of "struggling along" (1996: 88).

Narrative helps to form the sense of temporal integration (Desjarlais 1996: 75), which activates the possibility of experience.[5] As De Boeck (1998: 31) has noted, the deeply felt crisis in Congo has opened up a symbolic space where multiple cultural forces, Christianity being only one of them, propound their narratives. Kinshasa's young Christians turn toward the Bible, which gives clear rules and instructs people on appropriate everyday behavior. The Holy Book is thus a reference not only about the invisible world but about the visible as well, and it guides them in their social encounters and expectations toward others. The centrality of the Bible in their life worlds is reflected in some of their practices: Bienvenu keeps two Bibles in his car, while many actresses carry a Bible (in a few instances only the New Testament) in their handbag and some of the youths regularly walk around carrying the Bible ostentatiously in their hands. Pressed by the hopes of evangelizing me as well, several Cinarc actors repeatedly begged me to show them my own Bible. For a long time, I had to confess that I had none. This admission always met with much insistence on their part that I either purchase one myself or ask for it as a gift.

Kinshasa's born-again Christians embrace the New Testament as a key scenario for a prosperous future, while the Old Testament is associated with African customs. In its rejection of the older books, this generation of Christians distances itself from older Christians, who, as I learned during conversations with several older relatives of my key informants, saw no reason to discard these texts. Older people frequently invoked certain passages of the Old Testament to defend customary practices, in particular when discussing polygamy. One of my neighbors, an older Catholic Luba woman, reminded me that "polygamy exists in the Bible, so if it is there, then it must be good." Her son, who was firmly spreading the health-wealth-and-faith gospel, manifestly could not agree. This differentiated approach toward the Bible and its different books reflects both a generational division and diverging approaches toward long-standing local customs. This incongruity between the young charismatic artists and older Catholics offers us a glimpse into the diverse Christianities at play in Kinshasa. As I mentioned in Chapter 1, if scholars currently are concerned to fashion a comparative anthropology of Christianity (Cannell 2006; Robbins 2007), then attention should be devoted to the variegated Christianities within one society. Not only does Christianity mean different things in different places; it can also carry various qualities and meanings at a single time in a single place.

When debating the merits of the Old and the New Testaments, what is at stake in the oppositional reflections is societal competition. However, this does not mean that the opposed groups (youth versus elders) support homogeneous readings of the Bible. I could not help but notice, when listening to Kinshasa's Christians, young and old, how the fixity of the Bible quickly vaporizes in the face of the predicaments of life in Kinshasa and all the uncertainties they entail. One such occasion was a sermon delivered by Chapy, who in our interviews had always severely jettisoned the Old Testament. Much to my surprise, I observed during the sermon that Chapy was portraying the Old Testament character David as an example to follow. When confronted with my query about what seemed to me a contradiction, Chapy did not take it seriously and waved it away. Here again, we encounter inconsistency in born-again Christians' expressions and articulations of their interpretation of proper Christianity. The evangelizers with the loudest voices, the best rhetorical skills, and the most airtime on TV and radio tap into this weak spot of Kinshasa's Christians and, skillfully reusing the ashes of colonial Christianity while adding modern capitalist feats, compose in bits and pieces their own kind of Christianity, which in turn feeds into the variegated forms of Christianity that the followers themselves configure.

The Generation Trouble

Kinshasa's young refer to their lives as intensely "chaotic"—both in a spiritual sense, due to the reign of the Devil, and in a social sense, due to a lack of social norms. By promoting Christian rules and order, the Christians refute those who have installed chaos. According to the Christian youth, the elder generations are to blame. "We are Christians, but our parents are not," the fictional character Julien claims firmly in *The Devouring Fire,* expressing the origin of the "generation trouble"[6] Kinshasa's youth is experiencing.

Why do the youth point at their elders? MacGaffey (1986: 83) noted for the baKongo that fathers and relatives are responsible for their children's success in life. Success for young Kinois means being able to attend school, finding a job, and being able to marry (gathering the bride price). Due to the economic crisis, however, most relatives are in no position to provide these conditions. Many parents are jobless; mothers usually provide some money for food, but even young boys and girls are expected to find money elsewhere to pay for expenses such as food, transport, school fees, telephone cards, and clothing. Both young men and women assume the general culture of *débrouillardise,* that is, solving one's own problems, and they appear to enjoy even more success than most family heads, or even the majority of the active adult population, in adapting to the informal economy (De Boeck 2004: 190).[7] Financially deprived, many young men and women question whether they will ever be able to marry. Boys in particular doubt whether they will find enough money to pay the bride price for their future spouses. Furthermore, young Cinarc actors often blamed the lack of parental control for the increase in prostitution (in large part what would in Western terms be called "child prostitution") and the phenomenon of street children. Their discourse resonates with Anastase Nzeza Bilakela's argument (2004: 23) that the fend-for-yourself or even for-your-family ethos has pushed many Kinois to corruption, theft, extortion, collusion, embezzlement, fraud, counterfeiting, and prostitution.[8]

"We are our own fathers. So young and yet so old, that makes me think, you know. We are our own mothers. So young and serious, but that will change,"[9] sings Corneille in his hit song "Parce qu'on vient de loin." I met many young people who spontaneously repeated the verses of this extremely popular song when discussing the role of their parents. These lyrics very well express the fundamental disappointment of Kinshasa's young in their parents and in the elder generations as a whole. In all this, I do not wish to point solely to the recent crisis as the origin of the distrust between youth and elders. Decades of corrupt political governance have also contributed to a large extent to the social fissure between generations. Mobutu's authenticity program offered a new paternal figure, embodied by the nation's leader and the state (Devisch 1995: 602–603; Nzongola-Ntalaja 1979: 609; Schatzberg 2001). I found the idiom of Mobutu as father of all Zairians perpetuated in the appellation still used of the present generation of young Congolese, "children of Mobutu" (*bana Mobutu*), called thus because they were born during Mobutu's reign. In one of his speeches, Mobutu explicitly advised youth: "if your father bothers you, punch him in the nose" (*soki a sakani beta ye kanon*) (Nzeza Bilakela 2004: 22). It rather quickly became evident, however, that the Zairian/Congolese state could not perform its parental duties (Trefon 2004).

Many households in the city hold a number of children—sometimes with many different parents or from other, non-related families—living together in the same compound and growing up without the image of the father in everyday life (see Mbembe 1985: 22, who generalizes this pattern for the whole of central Africa). Whereas many Kinois people speak of the solidarity that the larger family can provide (during preparations for marriage arrangements and funerals, for example), they invariably point at the cracks that this stereotype holds nowadays. Family elders are said to be hypocritical, appearing in their children's lives only once the latter have known success. Many informants complained that neither their parents nor their lineage relations had performed their duties of paying school fees or assisted in their upbringing until they had more chances at a mature age to provide for themselves. These remarks confirm Mbembe's argument that the "myth of the African family" masks quotidian realities of conflict and abandonment (1985: 20). The absence of the lineage in the life of the young became very clear to me when I asked Ance what ethnic group he belonged to. He could not reply; only the next day did he tell me that his mother had said he was muKongo.

The Young, the Old, and the City

The economic and political crisis acts along with the climate of spiritual and social distrust to upset the norms of intergenerational encounters. However, older notions continue to structure what is assumed to be "good behavior" and the allocation of authority. Who is a "child," an "adult," or a "youth" in the customary point of view? The concepts of "childhood" (*bomwana*) and "adulthood" (*bokolo*) have both relative and absolute meanings in Kinshasa. In its absolute sense, the term "child" denotes someone who is not yet married, entailing the perception that this person is not yet "responsible" for someone else. One is considered either a child (*mwana*) or an adult (*mukolo*). Unmarried couples living together (*yaka tofanda*, "come and let's co-habit") only achieve adult status once they produce offspring, while the growing category of "teenage mothers" (Li. Pl. *bamaman ya mwana*, Fr. *filles-mères*) occupies the boundary zone between childhood and adulthood. Only upon marriage will they fully cross this border.

In the relative sense, the social distinction is based on one's situational position on the axis of childhood and adulthood: a younger person, although he might be married and have children, is still seen as being subordinate to an older person. Women tend to marry at a much younger age than men do, so it might be expected that women achieve adult status earlier than men do. Full adulthood, however, is something that only men can achieve. Even when a girl marries and thus becomes a woman, she becomes the *petit* (*leki*) of her husband, to whom she will always be in a subordinate position.

In this relative idiom, "youth" does not exist as a social category. *Bolenge, bonzenga,* and *bopalanga* are Lingala words that denote youth as a life stage in between childhood and adulthood, but "young people" are still "*children* with beauty and splendor" (Kawata 2003: 35, author's emphasis). Furthermore, in this "traditional" view, youth is primarily seen as a male life phase. One dictionary (Kawata 2003: 35, author's translation) gives the following definitions for the term *bonzenga:* "(1) beauty, splendor; (2) adolescence (for boys)." Girls are thus regarded as children who cannot reach adolescence.

The cultural logic behind this idiom localizes elders (*bakulutu, bampaka, bamokolo*) closer to the origin of the life flow, which gives rise to a social code demanding that elders be treated with politeness (*bokonde*), respect (*botosi*), and deference (*bobangi*). Moreover, children and young people should never correct or contradict elders. Customarily, children and youth are said to relate to elders as listening relates to speaking (Devisch 1991: 295). As Devisch notes, listening is constitutive of social personhood, for learning to listen amounts to "an acceptance of the order of society and culture" (ibid.). Being polite means at once to fear (*kobanga*), to humiliate oneself (*komitikisa*), and to show respect (*kopesa botosi*). "The ear can never surpass the head" (*matoyi baleki moto te*) goes one proverb, pithily articulating that social hierarchy should be respected. The reason why children (including adolescents) should listen attentively to the words of gray-haired people is symbolically expressed in a proverb, "The elders have seen the sun long before you" (*Bamikolo bamona moyi liboso na bino*). Meanwhile, young Kinois jokingly complement this proverb with the saying: "The mouth of an old man speaks the truth, but it smells bad" (*Monoko ya nkulutu elobi ya solo, kasi ezobima nsolo mabe*).

My young informants agree that elders have much more experience, but they immediately add that former generations were ignorant of the World Wide Web, that their education had not attained the level of current schooling, or that scientific research often denies what the elders proclaim. Youth hereby state that they possess "other" or "modern knowledge" (*mayele ya sika*, "new knowledge"), derived from Western institutions and acquired through schooling and electronic media (such as the Internet and television). This gives them the right to speak. Educated young Kinois in particular boast that they have acquired scientific knowledge stemming from foreign worlds through "democratic" means (inasmuch as anyone can enter a cybercafe, watch television, or go to school), in contrast to the possession of secret and therefore esoteric knowledge, which one acquires only at a relatively late age and through occult means. Such persuasions push young Kinois to no longer obey the ideal prescriptions of how young people should behave in the presence of elders.

A new, modern idiom about "youth," is now increasingly dominant, not only affecting the social relations between younger and older people but also transforming the quality of social prestige attributed to the categories of "elderhood" and "youth." The life stage "youth" has come to be considered more powerful because of the privileges young people encounter on the formal economic market. Young men and women now not only outnumber elders in the society at large, they are socially and economically very influential: job offerings with foreign NGOs or companies are primarily addressed to youth in school who then fill the vacant positions, have incomes, and bring home the money. Other important money-generating activities in which young people generally engage—like petty commerce or brokering economic transactions (among them prostitution, fraud, and extortion)—are more lucrative than the efforts made by their parents or elder relatives. This has resulted in the emergence of a separate social category. Whereas in the first social idiom there was no room for a stage such as youth, since it is incorporated into the phase of "childhood," the new idiom privileges youth, for which the French "*jeunesse*" is usually used. The term "*jeune*" has, next to *beauty* and *elegance* (already inherent in the synonym *bonzenga*), come to emphasize *future* (*ndaka*).

This second notion of "youth" is an identity relating to several political aspects of "modernity" at large and to specific cultural features of Kinshasa's modernity in particular. School registration and attendance as well as participation in youth clubs and movements are among the mechanisms set up by the colonial administration that served to construct "youth" as a fixed social category (cf. Tshimanga 2001). Alongside these modern institutions, which have profoundly disrupted more "traditional" practices of evolving personhood, a new sense of urbanity and the concept of *Kinoiserie* have contributed to the emergence of a particular symbolic meaning of "youth" in present-day Kinshasa. My informants often said, "a man may be married, but when he acts breezy and cool, like Papa Wemba, well, that is *un jeune;* it's a question of style." Older men who dress fashionably, discuss popular contemporary musicians, or frequent the bars and clubs are said to have a "young" spirit.

Spatial occupation and body culture reveal "the spirit of youth." *La Kinoiserie* sits much better with youth than with elders. The urban ambiance tends to obfuscate the spatial distinctions between young and old, which leads to disturbing intrusions as Kinshasa's (male) youth encounter difficulties coping with the shifting borders between generations. As long as adults pay for food and drinks, lend them clothes, offer them rides in their cars, or help them get into private bars, young people seek the company of these "fake old men" (*bafaux vieux*), as the young call them.[10] However, as soon as these "youthful adults" appear to compete with the young in the sexual domain, all respect is lost. It is particularly in the sexual sphere that youth feel threatened by their elders, since the latter's financial capabilities usually exceed those of the young boys, money being one of the main weapons in the game of seduction (see infra Chapter 9). "Old people have to remain in their corner, the younger ones must stay in their places, and so the young will respect the elders" (*Bavieux, il faut baza na coin na bango, bapetit il faut baza na place ya bango. Nde bapetit bakotosa bavieux*), said one adolescent.

Men especially want to be called *jeune*, although an article in a local newspaper (2006) denounced the fact that even for women today, "youth" and a youthful appearance (dress and company) have become more attractive than the status of being a married woman:

> As young women (*les femmes-jeunes*) become more educated and bureaucratic, they wish to be addressed as madame or mademoiselle and constantly want young people around them…. With their bleached skin and perfect makeup, these women always look beautiful, especially when they are away from home. (*L'Avenir*, 18 February 2006, author's translation)[11]

The author of the item lamented the growing number of married women who no longer wish to identify with the image of the reproducing and child-rearing woman. These women, even after having had children, do not dress like mothers but strive to look young and beautiful—by bleaching their skin, for example. In the article, the journalist emphasizes that the primary world of identification for these women is no longer at home but is located outside, where they hang out with youngsters instead of their contemporaries or other women who are married and older. At least for that particular group of married women, the ideal of youth—achieved through imitating teenagers or looking like them—becomes paramount in the way these women stage themselves in public.[12]

To conclude this section on the difficult relations between young and old, I wish to emphasize the entwinement of the notions "youth" and "future." With the emergence of "youth" as an important social group and its associations with urban sociality and economic privileges, the importance of "elderhood" as the ultimate social goal is denied. The social identity of "youth," inserted between childhood and adulthood, postpones the process of becoming an elder and even denies the desirability of that status in a postcolonial urban setting.

Although the young may often provide some household income, they are still considered subalterns in Kinshasa. All unmarried men and women are subordinate to elders who are responsible for them and whom they should obey. As such, young people are hardly well positioned to criticize their (social) parents, let alone society as a whole. Thus, despite the recent shifts in society's perceptions of youth, adult men still "have the word," and "children" (including youth) are expected to listen to the voices of the elders. Nevertheless, an old proverb aligning children and youth with play offers them room to defend their portrayals of parents and older generations in the serials. "A child too can beat the drums, and the elders will dance" ("*Mwana moke abetaka mbunda bakolo mpe babini*"), it is said. The very existence of this proverb from the village seems to grant the young the right to confront the elders. In line with this proverb, which confines the mastery of the young over the elders to the realm of dance, young Kinois have monopolized the site of popular culture to articulate their aspirations and vent their frustrations. According to Mamadou Diouf, this orientation of youth to popular culture would appear to be a general pattern for Africa. He depicts songs, theater and other products of popular culture as "masks of the voice of African youth" (2005: 231).

What happens within these ludic spaces? During rehearsals and improvisation sessions, the Cinarc leader would encourage new actors or rather shy members of the group to "steal the word" (*koyiba liloba*): "You have to know how to steal the word" (*il faut koyeba koyiba*), he would often counsel them. This statement reflects the fact that during these sessions, the actors with the most experience tended to talk all the time and thus determined the development of the scenarios. Their monopolization of the process paralyzed the new and younger members of the troupe and gave the latter little opportunity to join in the dialogue or direct the story line. In my view, this expression can be related to the sphere of the serials as a whole within the gerontocratic society that Kinshasa still is: young people must be cunning in order to "steal the word." They are prevented from speaking about domestic and public politics. The space of popular culture, particularly that of troupe rehearsals or television airings, is a disguised site in which young Kinois can express themselves, have a voice, and capture the word.

My understanding of the television serials as a site for giving voices to the voiceless is profoundly influenced by other scholars who attach great value to spaces within society that are not seen as politically relevant, if one is to adhere to Western-rational approaches to the public sphere. In a discussion of Pakistani immigrants in Manchester, Pnina Werbner (1996: 56) argues that symbolic discourses on social identities, moral behavior, and politics are created, negotiated, and elaborated in social spaces marked by gaiety, humor, music, and laughter. She introduces the notion of "fun space," which she identifies as such occasions as sports events, wedding ceremonies, and watching films. Werbner links these fun events with the struggle of subalterns such as women and youth to acquire a voice within the Manchester Pakistani immigrants' public sphere. In Kinshasa, popular theater is a public zone in which, through mockery and parody, actors distance themselves from the older generations. In the humoristic reversal of the real, regular behavior is subjected to satire and critiqued.

In a similar vein, Peter Probst has analyzed theatrical performances during rituals as a zone in the public sphere. In line with Habermas's notion of "discursive *Öffentlichkeit*," which emerged with the publication of popular magazines that provided Europe's first "citizens" with a forum to discuss common, namely political and economic, issues, Probst (2002) has introduced the notion of "performative *Öffentlichkeit*," stressing the role of the body and performances in expressing opinions on public matters. If we acknowledge the political role of dance and theater as enacted in political rallies or awareness-raising campaigns on human rights, democracy, and health issues, then we can also understand Kinshasa's television serials as occupying a zone within a performative public sphere where a Pentecostal morality is negotiated.

Acting and the projection of their imagined worlds provide safe arenas in which the young can vent their frustrations. We can thus label these serials as "moments of freedom," which are defined by Fabian (1998: 133) as "acts of creation and negation." However, in contrast to the Jamaa movement, the Shaba popular paintings, and Lubumbashi's sites of freedom during colonialism and early postcolonialism, Kinshasa's serials do not speak out against the government or (foreign) employers (or even missions) so much as they confront—rather in line with the Pentecostal melodrama's focus on domestic conflicts—the lineage elders and authority-bearers in their own families.

Elders as Witches

According to young Pentecostals, the "paganism," that is, the sinfulness of the elders, is the reason for the hardship the young are experiencing. A recurring expression among Kinshasa's young people runs: "The word of elder people is like the word of a *féticheur*" (*Lilobi bakulutu, bilobi banganga*). It refers to the magical power of elders' speech: what they say can become reality, just as a diviner can produce the future through his words. Significant in the Pentecostal context is the fact that the youths equate elders with *féticheurs:* elderly people are perceived as being no different from occult experts.[13]

In the Pentecostal melodramas, special effects are frequently used to portray these elders as bewitched persons. An example in this regard is the scene in which Paco's parents intend to teach their son's *ketyul* (fiancée)[14] how to be with a man, especially proper sexual conduct. In line with Congolese associations between dance and sexuality, Paco's parents invite their son's *ketyul* to show them how she dances a Yanzi dance, which is also performed to glorify the Yanzi ancestors. It does not take long for the elders to join in the dance, during which the viewer observes, by means of special effects, spirits entering into the dancing bodies. For Kinois, as mentioned before, these special effects are accepted methods for demonstrating how the realm of the Devil pervades the visible realm of reality. Here, via this technique, a clear association is drawn between ancestors and demonic activities. The scene moves to its climax when Paco and a female member of his church enter his home and witness this scene, which from their vantage is a pagan performance. Their faces show terror and disgust, since they regard the music and the accompanying dance as glorifications of the Devil (*bokumisi na Satana*). After switching off the music, Paco and the young woman clap their hands to call attention, extend their arms toward the three "pagans," and shout "In the Name of Jesus!" accordingly chasing away the evil spirits invoked by the performance.

Witchcraft idiom is a powerful yet indirect site for venting frustration. And popular culture offers a culturally appropriate site to express the feelings of dissatisfaction and adversity that set the occult apparatus in motion. In the serials, these accusations are combined with another indirect technology, laughter. Walking in a manner too slow for the urban rhythm, speaking in broken French or combining their Lingala with words from the vernacular, and poorly dressed, these fictional elders elicit ridicule and mockery time and again as actors are performing these roles and spectators watch the scenes. The humor derives chiefly from the imagination of elders as ill-adapted to urban life and visibly not in step with urban style, something which the young are capable of. In this way the elders' authority is subverted and solidarity among the young emerges (see Van Dijk 2000; 2001).

These observations regarding ludic action beg a comparison with Mbembe's (1997) analysis of the pervasive force of laughter in subverting political power in Africa. Mbembe describes how, in Cameroon, derision, obscene humor, and political cartoons serve to strip political leaders of their authority in moments of laughter—but nevertheless, this mockery does not incite political transformations. The humor evoked by the fictional characters in Kinshasa's serials is as ineffective in undermining or transcending the power of the gerontocracy as are Mbembe's mocking postcolonial subjects. To achieve an effect, Kinshasa's young Christians need to align with Christian leaders.

Despite the question whether these symbolic acts of resistance have a "real" effect, it should be stressed that associating "pagans" and elders with the Devil, on the one hand, and born-again Christians with God, on the other, significantly transforms the religious meaning and social value of the past (*eleki*) and present (*lelo*). The Devil occupies the realm of the past with its gerontocracy, while the Christian God and his followers (mostly youth) are directed to the future. In the young Pentecostals' mindset, "the village" (which many of them have never visited) and "the elders" constitute an association of evil forces that belong to the realm of the past, one that no longer has any meaning for the future that Kinshasa's young Christians long to inhabit. The future these youngsters aim to realize is a destiny (*ndaka*)[15] given by God, and it is attainable only when a Christian approach to development is embraced. Only God's will should be enacted: lineage obligations or restrictions are considered hindrances to the realization of God's master plan.

The threat perceived to be emanating from the village and the past might be explained by the centrality of the village in prevailing views of Congolese society and culture. Resonating with the general cultural extraversion of Kinshasa's public culture, Christianity promises a religious utopia by establishing a connection with the Holy Spirit, which is an external force that does not reside within the hands of the elders or the "traditional" past (see Van Dijk 1998: 166–169 for the Malawian context).

Serials as Witchcraft Accusations

Even though it may appear paradoxical at first, the occurrence in the teleserials of the "bad girl" (*mwasi mabe, mwasi ya Satana*), another witch type alongside the elders, is intrinsically related to the critique of the elder generation. The "bad girl" depicts an adolescent girl with occult powers[16] who does not belong to the earthly realm of reality but inhabits a demonic world (fig. 7.1). This "child of the night"[17] appears as á normal child during the day, but the diabolical spirit governing her body and soul transforms her into an adult at night. Examples in case are the Cinarc serials *Kalaonga* and *Mayimona.** The latter showcases the occult work of Mayimona, who was presented to a traditional chief immediately after birth, which in the urban Pentecostal imaginary links her to the Devil. Kalaonga, in turn, has been sent to earth by the Devil or a major demon. Both story lines begin when the girls are adolescents and depict how the teenagers attempt to break up Christian marriages, using witchcraft to seduce their victims and eliminate their rivals.

This witch type of the "bad girl" connects with an icon of central African aesthetics: the Mami Wata, a seductive female water spirit. Kinois frequently speak about the "bad girl" as a "siren" (*sirène*), a synonym used more often than "Mami Wata." In central and west African popular painting, the Mami Wata is usually represented as a young woman

Figure 7.1. A "bad girl" (screen shot from *Kalaonga,* © Cinarc)

*These moving images are available at http://www.berghahnbooks.com/title.php?rowtag=PypeMaking

with light skin and long dark hair, sometimes adorned with the tail of a mermaid. According to my informants, young women in particular are believed to be the incarnation of this water spirit. Henry Drewal, Johannes Fabian, and others who have discussed the Mami Wata phenomenon, as found elsewhere in Congo and Africa, explain the construction of the Mami Wata as the articulation of African modernity:[18] the siren personifies unattainable and exquisite beauty, vanity, jealousy, sexuality, romantic or maternal love, and limitless good fortune—not health, long life, or progeny, but riches: material and monetary wealth (Drewal 1996: 311).

Following Meyer (2003a), we could typify Mami Wata as the imaginative outcome of postcolonial cosmopolitanism:[19] in her appearance, the siren resembles Indian women and is adorned with Western consumer goods (a watch and silver and gold jewelry).

The same iconography of the Mami Wata appears in Kinshasa's *maboke*. In the serial *Kalaonga*, the protagonist is invariably beautifully dressed, has paler skin than others, is self-assured, wears expensive jewelry, and possesses the latest fashionable commodities (especially new brands of mobile phones). The cosmopolitan appearance of this fictive character seems to be necessary: during the broadcast of the serial *Mayimona*, people congratulated Bienvenu on his decision to give the role of Mayimona to this particular actress, who had lighter skin than the others.

In contrast to what Drewal (1996) writes about Mami Wata as a free, unencumbered spirit of nature detached from any social bonds, Christians in Kinshasa have inserted the siren in an occult social world where she is only one of many demonic spirits[20] and is entrenched in apocalyptic approaches to witchcraft. This representation of the "bad girl" pertains to transformations in the social structures of authority, respect, and distance.[21] Kalaonga uses her body to manipulate older men for money and other commodities. Her sexuality enables her to become a modern consumer: she extracts money from numerous married men—money they would be spending on food, rent, and health care for their own families. As such, young women like Kalaonga not only enjoy modernity more than men do but also threaten the social equilibrium that highly values matrimonial harmony. Their bodies and spiritual forces combine to endanger the masculine powers in the public and private domains of the city. Crucially, the "bad girl" reflects the modern and urban dispositions of young single women: extremely mobile, they do not remain in their homes but create networks outside the family and escape the control of patriarchal structures. This interpretation of the "bad girl" as related to economic and gender structures has been inspired by writings of Misty Bastian (2001; 2002), whose analysis of female teen witches

(Mami Wata–like characters) in Nigerian cartoons, gossip, and the social imaginary at large points to two important societal conditions that are also relevant in the context of Kinshasa. First, the female gender of teen witches merges with threats experienced by masculine city dwellers in a postcolonial city: these girls/women expose the weakening grip of masculine and gerontocratic authority. Second, the imagination of the female teen witch who becomes the "ultimate consumer" (Bastian 2002: 21)[22] relates to the twists of capitalism in Africa. Bastian considers the appearance of this stereotype of wicked girls to be a strategy for taming this category of young women. It is shown that only Christians (particularly males) are able to dominate the "bad girl." The social imaginary accordingly "puts" the teen witch "back in her place" (Bastian 2001: 88).

When scrutinizing the origin of evil among female teen witches in Kinshasa's serials, we observe that the young performers offer a particular explanation about the occult identity of these teen witches: they lay blame for the young women's evil identities on the girls' mothers. In the two serials *Kalaonga* and *Mayimona,* the teen witches' parents (especially mothers) are accused of having "opened a door." Mayimona is a child blessed by "traditional" healers and diviners who introduced (demonic) water spirits into the baby's body. In the case of Kalaonga, Maman Jeanne made a pact with demons during her pregnancy (fig. 7.2).

Figure 7.2. Maman Jeanne visits a diviner* (screen shot from *Kalaonga,* © Cinarc)

*These moving images are available at http://www.berghahnbooks.com/title.php?rowtag= PypeMaking

The sorrow, pain, and death that "bad girls" are said to produce, are presented as the outcomes of the occult exchanges triggered by the bad girls' own mother.

These fictionalized etiologies of evil are informative about Kinshasa's social relations and the life worlds of born-again Christians. Although these fictive stories are rooted within Kinshasa's Christian social imaginary, we should not forget that they are produced by a specific group of city dwellers who seek to reply to gerontocratic power holders through these serials. The young TV actors blame their parents and the elder generation for luring their children into the occult world. In their perspective, many young people in Kinshasa today are possessed by evil spirits because of their parents' wrongdoing. Nadine, who performed the role of Deborah (Mayimona's mother), told the following story:

> There are many Mayimonas in Kinshasa. I know one girl in my neighborhood, Righini. Her skin was rather pale, so a real beauty. She became a prostitute in the city.[23] The way she dressed did not please the mothers in the neighborhood. Furthermore, she had a bad disposition, and, unsurprisingly, her parents chased her away from home. One day I had the opportunity to talk to her about Jesus Christ. I took her with me to an evangelization campaign being held one street away from my home. When we started praying she was touched by the Holy Spirit. She fell to the ground and began to testify. I was the pastor's assistant so I heard everything she said. Her father's voice emanated from her body saying: "I am her husband. You do not have the right to set her free. I am the owner of this body. You may not touch her because I have sacrificed her." When we stopped praying she had been set free, and she abandoned her former lifestyle for a moment. Before this she had been her father's slave. Her father had sacrificed her for either wealth or success with women.

These accusations directed at the parents are understandable to us only if we consider that the producers of the serials are young urban men and women who wish to advance their own generation. In the production of their dramas, then, they accuse their relatives, in particular their mothers,[24] of contributing to the expansion of evil. But, as Deborah's account shows, fathers may also be condemned for "destroying" these teenagers. Popular culture can be understood as a space in which urban youth direct accusations against the elders. The TV dramas show that neither the young nor modernity is to blame for the demonic identity of the youngsters, but that the evil twin of elders and "tradition" should be held accountable.

The Healing Power of Narrative

There is no drama without tragedy, and unsurprisingly the young actors frequently select traumatic events from their own personal life histories to be portrayed in the scenarios. Under the roof of the serial, these painful experiences are interpreted within the framework of a Pentecostal imaginary. The ongoing production of the genre of the Pentecostal melodrama is part of young Pentecostals' inveterate attempts to frame their experiences in a coherent way. By taking up the issues of their personal pasts, these young Christians offer themselves and the city a place to articulate their memories. Although the serials are not perfect dramatizations of how the actors experienced the past, they are an ingenious reworking and immediate reframing of the young's own personal pasts, which, once brought into the public space of television, are lifted to an urban collective level.

Kinshasa's Cinderella

I document this with information about the generation of the Cinarc serial *Caroline and Poupette*, which dealt with certain traumatic events experienced by one of the performers, Beti, alias Caroline. When Bienvenu announced the idea of the new serial *Caroline and Poupette*, he stated that it would be "Beti's story."[25] Although the personal events took place in the early 1990s, the story line resituates them for the viewers in a more contemporary setting reflective of the year 2004. This did not matter much to the actors, since in their opinion nothing had changed (*ebongoli te*), though some contended that "things had even gone worse" (*ependwi*).

In the serial Beti herself plays the leading role of Caroline. At the time *Caroline and Poupette* was being filmed, Beti was nineteen years old and lived with her old maternal grandmother, who was over seventy, in the latter's compound in Kauka, near the Kimbanguist University. The youngest girl in a family of six children, Beti became an orphan at the age of twelve. A year after her mother died, her father remarried, to his deceased wife's sister.[26] Six years later her father also died—poisoned by Mobutu, it was said. Beti had no idea what position her father occupied in the Mobutu government, but she knew that he was close to Mobutu, which explained the wealth her family enjoyed during Mobutu's reign. During that time, Beti's siblings were sent to Europe to study, and her grandmother was even among the most influential women in Mobutu's entourage.

Later, poverty struck. Beti could no longer travel to Europe to study and even had great difficulty obtaining her secondary school diploma. As she herself had to pay the fees for her final year of secondary school, it took her three years to finish. Still, with her income from braiding hair for friends, family, and other clients, along with the money she earns from acting, Beti managed to wear fashionable clothes and even to put aside some savings. She wished to pursue her education and study accounting, but that proved to be too expensive; by the time my fieldwork ended, Beti had begun training in a beauty salon in Limete, learning to dye hair and apply makeup. The most upsetting part of her life history was reserved to memories about her aunt. After her father's death, Beti remained in the home of her aunt/stepmother and her three children. Although Beti mentions that her aunt did not treat her as badly as the fictive character Theresia did in *Caronline and Poupette,* she was never treated equally by her stepmother. Because of that, she would never like her.

Beti was always very secretive about her life story, and it appeared that social constraints prevented her from complaining about her situation. "Everybody suffered during Mobutu's regime," she explained, adding that everyone had endured some loss or another under his rule. The serial *Caroline and Poupette* provided Beti with a good motive to talk about her past, in particular on television talk shows where hosts and callers longed to hear about the similarities and differences between the serial and Beti's private life. Beti was very grateful to Bienvenu for offering her this leading role and for being able to tell her personal history. Some Kinois, however, did not approve of Beti making her life story public because they knew that Beti's real aunt would likely be confronted as a result of the serial being aired.

As much as a year after filming and airing the serial, a period in which Beti played several other roles, she still considered this leading role in *Caroline and Poupette* the most meaningful character she had ever portrayed. This was above all, she said, because it had given her contacts (see Chapter 3). But it was not just the leading role and the contacts that were significant. "It was me who played my story," she said. "Even if in subsequent episodes the story no longer dealt with my past, I was still invited by people to tell what had happened to me. People knew that this serial was inspired by my own life, and this gave me the opportunity to speak with people about it." The act of publicly recounting what had happened was extremely meaningful. Beti was allowed to skip rehearsals and even prayer meetings during the weeks the serial was broadcast, for Bienvenu did not want her to miss any opportunity to talk about her private experiences. In doing so, Beti repeatedly framed her biography within the Pentecostal narrative, saying that "God needs people to treat each other in a good, decent way," and that "if you are badly treated, you should pray to God, for He will hear your prayers and will make life better. Look at me, how I am good now. I have no problems; life has changed since I have received Jesus Christ." Each time, the conversation ended with "*Nzambe akopambela yo*" ("May God bless you"), and Beti saying the same to the caller or host.

Although Beti's story can be read as a reflection on her personal past, she and the Cinarc group at large wished to expand the dramatic events to reflect the experience of many Kinois. The actors regarded this urban Cinderella story as an admonition, both to Beti's real aunt and to all the other households in which orphans were badly treated.

Serials and Collective Healing

Explaining the private sources of the *Caroline and Poupette* serial, I have shown that, through the reenactment of their personal dramas within the plot of the Pentecostal melodrama, the young actors scrutinize their family life within a Pentecostal frame. But the meaning of the teleserials is not at all limited to the individual lives of the TV actors themselves. When the serial's episodes are shown on television, the dramatic work leaves the personal arena and is endowed with social significance. Hosts of televised talk shows invite their viewers to call and comment on currently running serials. Apart from questions about the actors' private lives, the topics of the calls are very much centered on the correspondence between certain fictional events and "real" dramatic events in the spectators' lives as well. It was striking to hear how the conversations between Beti and the calling viewers followed the same structure: the callers first congratulated Beti and thanked her for being so courageous, implying that speaking in public as a victim demands much strength. Often, then, the callers began to tell their own, similar stories.

The cultural public sphere that is generated through the airing of the episodes reveals that many Kinois share the mental suffering and bodily pain depicted in the serials' imagined worlds. Through a transfer to their own private experiential worlds and pasts, Kinshasa's viewers identified with Beti's cathartic experience. And like many other serials, *Caroline and Poupette* featured a narrative that offered both producers and spectators moments and means to resignify personal life worlds.

In all this, Kinshasa's spectators are not merely passive receivers of the teledramas. The particular conditions of production enable the audience also to participate in the unfolding of the story lines. As mentioned earlier, the drama groups film only one episode a week, which is immediately broadcast the same week. The storyline can go in all directions, and the audience participates in directing the plots. People call in to television shows, ring the actors' private numbers, or even stop the actors in public places to say how they think a specific serial should evolve and eventually end. During the production of the serial *Caroline and Poupette,* for example, I observed how a girl of about sixteen stopped Bienvenu at a gas station. After expressing to him how much she cared for Poupette, who was still in hospital at the time, she told him that he should cure her and marry her, because "that is what the poor girl deserves, no?" Bienvenu replied that he would think about it. Back in the car, he told me that whereas the girl had given him an interesting hint, social constraints prevented his fictional character from marrying Poupette, since his own sister played this role. Nevertheless, in the episode filmed three weeks later, Poupette was miraculously healed by a pastor that Bienvenu had brought in, and her recovery was celebrated at a party during which Caleb proposed to Caroline.

A second case illustrates how viewers yearn to merge their own private experiences with the fictional worlds. In the first episode of the serial *The Open Tomb* (eight were still to follow), a wealthy Luba man became involved in an extramarital affair with his wife's best friend. Following the airing of this episode, Luise, one of the Cinarc actresses, reported to the fellow actors that her brother had been approached by a young Christian who knew that his sister was acting with Cinarc: after just two episodes of *The Open Tomb,* the man had recognized his own familial problems in the story plot that was unfolding on the screen. Apparently, his brother had taken a second wife, and just as in the serial, this second wife was his first wife's best friend. Very soon, however, the young man's family identified the new wife as a witch, whom they held responsible for the death of her co-wife and the sterility of all of the co-wife's children. At this point in the serial, the plot of the *The Open Tomb* narrative prescribed the death of Maman Jeanne, Makubakuba's first wife. Luise added that her brother's friend had requested that the story line evolve in the same way as the "real" story, so that the wicked wife would come to recognize her evil deeds. Bienvenu followed this line when finalizing the serial *The Open Tomb.*

These examples indicate how Kinshasa's audience takes part in the construction of the narratives. The serials are not a product of the imagination of the young actors alone; spectators participate in the creative process as well, thereby generating a common narrative dealing with collective experiences of trauma and crisis. The therapeutic value of these serials, for both their makers and their audiences, should not be underestimated. Moreover, and in view of television's capacity to inspire reflection on personal experiences, the serials constitute a technology of memory construction that ties together those who share these experiences. Viewing or discussing the episodes and especially congratulating the actors on their work are social practices that provide a space for communitas within the Christian community. These discursive moments unite viewers and actors in relation to the hardships of the fictional/real pasts and presents they share, and create consensus with regard to Christian values.

Past, Present, and Future

Fictional reenactments are not mere representations of reality. They are above all selections, a characteristic that Kenneth Burke (1962) attributes to narrative in general. In selecting and constructing the narratives, the narrative labor unfolds, meaning that events are interwoven with characters, motives, situations, and actions (Antze 1996: 6; Garro and Mattingly 2000: 1; Munn 1996; Pollock 2000: 109; Ricoeur 1984). This work of story-making relates immediately to the making of identities and the generating of knowledge of selves. The emplotment (Ricoeur 1984) of the present seizes on events from different times and worlds and weaves them into a meaningful story line that transforms lived uncertainties into moments that are decisive for the evolution of the plot (Rapport and Overing 2000: 283–290). Such stories not only reshape the past and the present; they also "create new paths for the future" (Capps and Ochs 1995: 176). Concerning the production of Kinshasa's TV dramas, this means that we encounter young Kinois involved in an interpretive and practical struggle to understand life and direct it toward a future. In the final part of this chapter, I will first compare the quality of time represented in Kinshasa's telenarratives with the Nigerian and Ghanaian films and then juxtapose the representation of time in Kinshasa's *maboke* with some offscreen practices that produce time.

Kinshasa's television serials struggle primarily with the periods of the present and a very recent past. The fictional reality of the serials ultimately goes back to the moments of conception, pregnancy, and birth of the fictive characters, but not beyond. The narratives show how the maleficent practices of parents (especially mothers) and living grandparents shape the afflictions and misfortunes of the protagonists' fictional present. The time period spanning the origin of evil practices and their consequences reflects a particular approach to the past that is ultimately different from that portrayed in most west African witchcraft films. The latter not only deal with personal memories, they also frequently locate the origins of human misfortune in a past reaching back several generations or even to a mythic "ancestral" time. Bonds made by ancestors or great-grandparents in a far removed past continue to influence the experiences and lived realities in the fictional present of the Nigerian and Ghanaian films.

The denial of the influence of ancestral forces or the silencing of the distant past in Kinshasa's teleserials resonates with the discourse of Kinshasa's Pentecostal-charismatic leaders, who—when digging into the private pasts of individuals—do not point to the demonic activities of ancestors but rather to sorcerous practices enacted by persons in one's social environment. These are held responsible for determining daily life in the present.

This "break with the past" (Meyer 1998) depicted in the Pentecostal melodrama shares many similarities with the "cultural de-mnemoniza-tion" documented by Van Dijk among born-again Christians in Malawi (2000: 14). As in urban Malawi, Kinshasa's born-agains reject traditional initiation rituals and dealings with traditional healers because these could lead the individual in the realm of the elder generations. He writes that "[l]ong, binding threads are seen to be have been woven by the older generation through their dealings with evil powers, which still affect the activities of relatives in the present" (Van Dijk 2000: 15). Interestingly, when my informants were asked about the plausibility of the occult heritage of ancestral bonds as depicted in Nigerian films, they did not refute the effectiveness of ancient demonic dealings. In the young born-again Christians' imagination, present distress can indeed be the outcome of older devilish bonds. The fact that this relation is not exploited in their teleserials is indicative of the social competition between generations as described above, and it also ties in with the emphasis on the present, to which I will turn now.

A common critique on Pentecostal churches is that they direct all attention to the otherworldly, thus minimizing believers' suffering and relegating salvation and well-being to the hereafter. However, after listening to my informants and also analyzing the predications and witch testimonies, the view that revival churches are solely directed toward a celestial future does not hold. Rather, born-again Christians are very much anchored in the here and now (also Ellis and ter Haar 2004; Maxwell 2000; Meyer 1995; Van Dijk 1998).

During mass religious meetings that I attended in the run-up to the national elections, people prayed by the thousands that Jesus Christ would descend on Congo, that he would keep the city safe during the precarious days of voting, and that a good leader would be chosen. The numerous prayer gatherings and healing services were defined in such terms as "prayer of the nation" (*prière de la nation*) and "Christians take part in the political process" (*Les chrétiens participent à la politique natio-nale*). Similar events were organized by small-scale prayer groups meeting either in private homes or in smaller churches, by bigger churches within the neighborhoods, or by various religious leaders across the city in football stadiums or on community grounds. At all of these meetings, the preachers repeatedly equated the individual with the nation and stressed that progress and national development would only be realized when the country and its inhabitants were delivered from Satan.

All these activities of pastors and other charismatic leaders on the political and economic domain spur me to argue that Pentecostal-charismatic Christianity has an effect that should be taken seriously. Of course it is difficult to see a causal relation between pastors' discourses and incentives and the national political world. An argument against my claim here could be that the city has not improved significantly on an economic level since these churches usurped the city's public sphere. I agree with Gifford (2004: 196), who concludes his investigation of the public role of Ghana's charismatic Christianity by saying that "there is no simple link between a religion and its public effects." Though the significance and the effects of these churches are visible in the private lives of the followers, they reach far beyond the symbolic work of giving sense and attaching meaning to one's condition. Women set up boutiques with money gathered in the church group; young and old went out to vote on 30 July 2006 because their pastor had encouraged them to do so; people were able to pay a doctor's bill or to contribute to a bride-price thanks to networks established in the churches, and so on. The revival churches foster the circulation of money and incite individuals to become consumers, producers, and political actors (as voters). These outcomes all hold major significance for the individual: they can mean the difference between life and death, celibacy or marriage, or, though less dramatic, going to bed with a hungry stomach or not.[27] Arguing that the revival churches do not have a "public effect" is, in my view, inspired by a too-rigid analytic approach that keeps the private and the public separate. But these two domains are interwoven. There is no public without its private persons, whose public identities ("roles") are to a large extent inspired by personal desires and motives. As I show in the following section, this is exactly the terrain on which charismatic Christians in Kinshasa are operating.

The Nation and the Individual

Religious leaders expressing their political opinions, engaging with political leaders, and even taking political roles in government literally embodied the entwinement of the political and the spiritual.[28] As mentioned above, in the weeks preceding the first democratic elections (July 2006), numerous "men and women of God" became candidates for seats in the national parliament. In the same period, many television channels aired discussion programs on themes such as "Christianity and the nation" or "religious leaders and national politics," in which Christian leaders outlined what political programs should be undertaken by the next president and his government. Other Christians invited political candidates to come to their churches because, as these Christians leaders stated, they possessed the gift of discernment and were capable of identifying those candidates who were on God's side and those who were governed by demonic forces and intentions. Pentecostals constantly performed deliverance rituals. These events express a concern to untie, or unblock (*kofungola*) the nation from the grip of evil.[29] Prayer over individuals and laying hands on them served to liberate the Kinois, and by extension the Congolese people as a whole, from demons. Prayer aimed to "heal the country" (*kobikisa mboka*) or "open up the country" (*bafungoli mboka*) (fig. 7.3). In line with the witchcraft metaphor, in which a bewitched person is said to be locked up (*bakangi ye*), prayer was a key to open the lock, to untie the bonds. The best way to heal the country was, according to many, to minimize the number of people who practiced demonic activities by converting the population to Christianity.[30] To that effect, Christians also voluntarily preached

Figure 7.3. Announcement for a prayer event (2005, © Katrien Pype)

in the city's prisons and among prostitutes. They were convinced that spreading Jesus's word to sinners would redeem these individuals' lives, render the city safer, "unblock" economic development activities, and "open up the country."

Born-again Christians' engagement with the present and the future coincides with an emphasis on the unity of the individual and the social. The affinity between the private and the collective receives much attention in Pentecostal discourse and practice alike and encourages the Christian community to act both spiritually and politically. This identification of the individual and the collective connects with long-standing autochthonous perspectives on the individual's participation in the larger group (the village and/or the lineage). In a discussion on solidarity within lineages, Ruytinx (1969: 18) writes that "the vital potentiality of an individual and that of a collectivity with which the latter relates, depend on each other." De Boeck (2004: 118), inspired by his ethnographic work among the Aluund, contends that metaphors of tying and knotting, used to indicate the degree of the individual's physical and social health, also refer to the continuation of the descent group and the perpetuation of the community. Born-again Christians are called to change—convert—on a personal level, which is expected to have repercussions on a wider, collective level. A Christian has the duty and the power to purify both private and public experience. The results of this spiritual healing are economic (jobs), social (marriage without problems), and political (the end of corruption, a new democracy).

The Christians' imagination of time and the engagement of bornagain Christian leaders with the present inspire the Christian TV actors to present conversions, deliverance rituals, and confessions in the serials' closures. Only to an outsider unfamiliar with Christian leaders' deep involvement with the crisis might the importance of conversion in the plotlines of the serials come as a surprise. Meanwhile, for all who produce and watch the post-Mobutu serials, the main potential for development is believed to reside in "spiritual development" (*nkola ya molimo*). *Maboke* in which this Christian solution is not represented are discredited by evangelizing actors and the larger viewing audience. The productions of Cinarc's main rival, Muyombe Gauche's group, for example, were at times refuted for showing too many scenes of occult activities and accordingly privileging the demonic over the Christian message.[31]

Nene, a female Cinarc performer who regularly performs deliverance rituals for children and teenagers, was very confident of the role that Christian spiritual leaders and prayer rituals played in healing the nation. For her, Christianity was far more meaningful than political parties:

The political parties do not share the same agenda. But in all the churches, we all read the same word of God. The *pasteurs* have the same way of preaching. They do not differentiate when preaching to audiences of the UDPS or PPRD,[32] but everyone listening hears the same story. There is only one Bible that unites all people and even all politicians of different persuasions. But be aware that it is neither the *pasteur* nor the politicians who invite us to behave properly and work honestly for the progress of the nation, it is God who calls us, speaking through the *pasteurs*. Furthermore, how many Kinois are aware of the national laws? Hardly any, but many of them know that God's law should be followed.

Nene concluded:

Prayer has a big impact, because everything that is physical has its beginnings in the spiritual. Because, the Bible says, in Chronicles: "If my people speak my name, and if they pray, I will cure their country." And in our, the Congolese, case, if we do not hold on to God there will never be a solution.

It is interesting to follow how Nene spoke about the democratic multiparty system, which had been introduced just a few years before, as a weakness. In the view of many Kinois, the end of Mobutu's strong political program and the takeoff of the democratization process had fragmented society. Where unity once reigned, a plurality of voices had now installed chaos. Nene imagined the Holy Book as more influential than the country's constitution in her experience,[33] a view shared by many ardent young Christians. Biblical injunctions are far better known to the populace than juridical obligations and restrictions. Basing themselves on this foreign text, Kinshasa's Christians try to reconstruct their society into one where chaos makes place for order, and where people do not merely exist but are able to live. Nobody can deny that compared to national jurisdiction, the Bible is far better known by Kinshasa's young people, who constantly refer to biblical tales or characters, and Christianity's spokespersons undoubtedly command a greater measure of trust from the population than do state officials. Lack of trust in the national government pushes Kinois people to embrace God's promises.

Divine Promises

The orientation toward the future, framed within eschatological terms, is maintained through a discourse of promises (Sg. *elaka*) that wrench youth away from the grasp of both the gerontocracy and the state. In return for conversion, pastors promise converts stability, wealth, health, an identity, and life. Significantly, these promises do not always refer to an unreachable, heavenly future but often concern the near future, one that can start as soon as one converts or reconnects with the divine. This is how the pastor's wife reminded the Cinarc actors, during their weekly prayer gathering, about God's promise to his children:[34]

Soki oza na ndako ya Nzambe,	If you are in God's house,
soki oyambi Yésu,	if you have received Jesus,
oza na libota ya Nzambe.	you belong to God's family.
Oza na badroits nionso.	You are entitled to everything.
Soki oza na ndako ya tata na yo,	If you are in your father's house,
ozosukola kuna, ozoliya epai na ye.	you wash yourself there, and you eat.
Alors, na ndako ya Nzambe, eza	
ndenge moko.	Well, the same goes for God's house.
Tata ya yo apesi yo nionso.	Your Father will give you everything.
La bénédiction ya cieux eza na yo.	Heaven's blessing belongs to you.
Il faut seulement demander à Dieu.	You only have to ask God.
Soki olinga mbongo, libala,	If you want money, to get married,
akopesa yo!	He will give this to you!
Soki ozocomporter lokola mwana ya	
Nzambe	If you behave like a child of God
et soki oyebi Ye moko,	and if you only know Him,
soyez sûres, akopesa. Allelujah. (Amen)	then, know for certain, He will give it.
Alleluiah *(Amen)*	Alleluiah. (Amen)
…	…
Toza na droits nionso,	We have all the rights:
na kolata, na koliya,	to get dressed, to eat,
na libala, na mbongo,	to get married, to have money,
na sécurité, na santé,	to be safe, to have a good health.
Lokola mwana ya Nzambe	As a child of God,
toza na badroits nionso.	we are entitled to everything.

Providing food, organizing marriages, and offering money are tasks that, according to custom, fathers and/or uncles have to perform for their offspring. Christian leaders now usurp these familial obligations and repeatedly state that the Christian God has the power to take over. However, this does not happen unconditionally. It is invariably added that these promises will only be kept when the Christians maintain Christian standards of behavior.

In this discourse about Christian covenants, the Christian twist to the term *bokoli,* a word for "development," is crucial. The substantive *bokoli* (derived from the verb *kokola*) means "to ripen, obtain finality, or reach an endpoint, which is already latently present in something that needs time and social encouragement to fully realize itself" (Kawata 2003). In the Christian discourse on national development, it is said that the finality of the country (*suka ya mboka*) is prosperity on all levels, economically, politically, socially, and spiritually. Ardent Christians are thoroughly convinced that one day they will find a job, that they will marry, that their illness is only temporary, or that they are immune from any sorcerers' attacks on the part of relatives or unknown urbanites. At the beginning of my fieldwork, I was struck by Chapy's firm statement that in 2006 he would marry, although he himself wondered how he would find the money to pay the bride price. Nene's self-assured attitude surprised me too: she said that she knew that within two decades she would be one of the country's leading ladies. When I confronted them with the difficulties they might encounter in realizing these goals, both replied, in a very calm manner, that they knew what God's plan for them was, and that they were sure he would bring these projects to fruition.

Sometime later, I attended a service of the prayer group where Chapy preached. The theme of his sermon was "Whoever said that this was the end for you?" (*Qui t'as dit que c'est fini pour toi?*). Reading the story of Joseph (Genesis 37), Chapy spoke about the promises that God made and instructed the community that God has plans for all of his children:

> God is directed to the future. He has promised me many things. Those who suffer today should know that they will not suffer forever. Listen, be aware, each one of us has a promise, and we have to live according to that promise. If we lose faith, then everything is finished for us.... Be patient, because once God has made a promise he will make it come true.... Everything has its own time, the Bible says. God never forgets His promises.... This is your promise, you will be saved. His promise to you says that you will live.

Chapy's sermon lasted more than an hour and was frequently punctuated by shouts of joy from the audience expressing appreciation for his statements. His assurances that "nobody is lost," but that "God has reserved a future for every single one of them" were especially applauded. Chapy comforted all those present by ensuring them that they were in the right place: their future resided in the Christian community and not in the lineage or elsewhere in mundane spaces. God had promised each one of them a future, this gave all the young Christians abundant confidence about their futures, despite their own personal pasts and in contrast to the plight of the "pagans" who were just wandering about, still searching for a sense of belonging in the lineage, student groups, or elsewhere.

To conclude this section on the Christian covenant, I want to point at the tremendous social effects this discourse brings forth. After all, the claim of a promise not only structures the consciousness of Kinshasa's Christians, but it also diminishes the social significance of "generations," an important social means of structuring time, often with a conservative orientation. The gospel of health, wealth, and well-being denies the social ideal of becoming an "elder." The customary idea that previous generations should be regarded with much respect since they are closer to the origin of the life flow is discarded by the Christians' emphasis on a future within the Christian community. The proposition of "the Christian" as a new social ideal resonates with the new Christian signification of "life" (*bomoyi*), one that overrules the elder generations and thus the ancestors as well as serious mediators or even providers of "life." The boundaries set by born-again Christians between the converted and the non-converted articulate and construct a schism between those with a future and those without. In this respect, the past, elders, and "pagans" are all synonymous with death, while Christians, or the converted youth, are fed with life and possess a future. Such discourse should not at all be perceived as shallow talk; it finds very fecund ground in a youth-oriented city such as Kinshasa, where young people enjoy privileges in the economic domain and are often obliged to support their relatives financially. Christian leaders acknowledge the (potential) contribution of the young in the survival of the household and the reconstruction of the country, and this probably explains the appeal of the revival churches among Kinshasa's youth.

Conclusion: Youth, Christianity, and Development

In the current urban African context, characterized by political instability, economic crisis and social upheaval, most voluntary associations (NGOs, churches, and others—sometimes even in conjunction) are preoccupied with social change. Bayart et al. (1992) attribute enormous political value to Africa's youth associations. Explaining the pivotal role of youth in political protest, Bayart (1992: 94) writes, "[t]hey have nothing to lose, not from a traditional point of view, nor from a modern point of view." In contrast to women, who use several strategies to improve their familial and individual condition, Africa's postcolonial youth speak for a collective unit (ibid.). This also applies to Kinshasa's youth, who prefer to use popular expressive arts like theater, music, and paintings to participate in the political field. Their creativity turns them into political actors (see Tshimanga 2001: 297–299). Profoundly discontent with the postcolonial crisis, Africa's youth look to reconstruct their society. The Cinarc actors do this through TV dramas. In the space of television, they contribute in their own capable style to the reconstruction of the city and the nation. They aspire to attribute meaning to lived experiences and communicate their personal traumas and hardships. Through the translation of their private worlds in the Christian narrative, they seek for both themselves and their audiences to transcend the "existing mode" into the "living mode," a life where meaning and sense are created and articulated. In an informal and playful yet pervasive manner, the artists help to reestablish the city's morality.

Kinshasa's teleserials have always been engrossed with issues of development and progress (see Pype 2009a). Still, different political regimes favor distinct visual cultures and narratives. The general assumption that the nation and its citizens are bewitched imposes a particular idiom of development that does not derive from formal education, the acquisition of consumer goods, or monetary progress. A Bible-inspired key scenario for the individual and the larger collectivity is privileged, and the major routes toward progress and social transformation are exorcism rituals and conversion. The Pentecostal churches focus on the individual, whose responsibility in the development of the nation builds on the melodrama and accounts for its very successful evangelization campaign.

Notes

1. Bienvenu was speaking in French; there seems to be no Lingala equivalent for this expression. A similar expression is *Tokomi vivre lokola banyama* ("We have begun to lead a life like animals"—De Boeck, personal communication, April 2005), which has a particular resonance in a Christian discourse that equates "pagans" with animals.

2. The experience of crisis did not emerge in the 1990s but had already occurred during the colonial encounter and continued during the Zaire-state phase until post-Mobutu Congo (De Boeck 1998: 25; also White 2005: 66).

3. Despite disenchantment with the state and military violence, the figure of the soldier (*soda,* from French *soldat*) nonetheless remains one of the main hero-types for a subgroup of Kinshasa's male youth (see Pype 2007).

4. See De Boeck (1998) for a questioning of this play between forgetting the atrocities of the colonial project and emphasizing its local fruits.

5. Desjarlais is inspired by Paul Ricoeur (1984), for whom the main function of narrative is "humanizing time" because it portrays human experience. Also Fernandez (1986) and Ochs and Capps (2001) contend that creating narratives helps us to deal with reality.

6. Comaroff and Comaroff coin the notion of "generation trouble"—a concept inspired by Butler's "gender trouble"—but they aim to subvert the negative tones implicitly present in the concept of "trouble." They write, "It can also imply the productive unsettling of dominant epistemic regimes under the heat of desire, frustration or anger" (Comaroff and Comaroff 2005: 20).

7. The strategies adopted in this search are gendered: young men stroll about the city in search of an opportunity to strike a deal or a chance to provide services for others in exchange for money. They frequently take up retailing, selling items such as music, videotapes, clothes, mobile phones, and so on. Girls often engage in selling clothes and food items (small fried cakes, bread, meat, fish, manioc flour or fruit and vegetables). But they also become involved in sexual networks by attaching themselves to older men who pay for their school fees, clothes, or luxury items.

8. In their analysis of lexical innovations in Lubumbashi as a response to the crisis, Pierre Petit and Georges Mulumbwa Mutambwa (2005) have uncovered how corruption, cunning, and fraud are nowadays perceived as socially apt and accepted.

9. Original lyrics: Nous sommes nos propres pères. Si jeunes et pourtant si vieux, ça me fait penser, tu sais. Nous sommes nos propres mères. Si jeunes et sérieux, mais ça va changer.

10. Tonda (2002: 39) mentions a similar frustration among Brazzaville's young men in discussing their relationships with elders: according to the young, the elders, who want to date young women, need money. In order to gain the needed cash, these elders will use witchcraft to extract the financial profits of successful young men, whose potential girlfriends they thus steal.

11. "A Kinshasa: les mères sont toujours jeunes" (In Kinshasa, all mothers are young), written by Kito K.

12. The article in question may be a sign of the changing ways in which young married women relate to their primary tasks in producing and raising offspring. Being a wife and a mother confines these women to the home and the domestic sphere, but they increasingly long to forge new social relations and selves outside of the nuclear family.

13. Young Christians' accusations that elders possess witchcraft are a phenomenon that today also occurs in other urban and rural African societies (Tonda 2002; van der Geest 2002).

14. *Ketuyl* is kiYanzi, meaning literally "preferred marriage partner" according to Yanzi customs. This serial and the signification of the *ketuyl* in charismatic Christian contexts will be further explored in the following chapter.

15. *Ndaka* means at once future and destiny; see Chapter 6 for a religious explanation for this.

16. The presence of the "bad girl" as an important witch type also explains the popularity among Kinshasa's audiences of American series like *Buffy the Vampire Slayer,* which is regularly broadcast on several of Kinshasa's television channels. Each episode stages a battle between Buffy (an American teenage girl with supernatural powers) and demons. The overall frame of the serial is inspired by Western astrology, the New Age cult, and Christian demonology (all the spirits that attack Buffy are demons trying to destroy the earth). Buffy triumphs in each episode.

17. The "bad girl" must be seen in relation to the category of the child witch (Li. *mwana ya ndoki, mwana ya Satana,* Fr. *enfant sorcier*). In Kinshasa, children have

increasingly become victims of witchcraft accusations (see De Boeck 2005b). Two explanations for the evil nature of these children coexist: it is said that they either have been sent by the Devil—and thus possess evil forces from birth—or have become witches as a result of accepting gifts. Usually, this latter strategy of recruiting children for Evil only appears in the teleserials' subplots. By contrast, the wicked teenage girl (socially still a "child" since she is unmarried) often receives the leading role in a serial. As I explain further in the text, the girls' parents are invariably identified as the source of the girls' witchcraft. The narratives do not focus on the childhood of the young girls. Rather, their occult dealings are strongly connected to their sexuality; plots are set in motion when the "bad girl" reaches puberty.

18. It is, however, questionable in what sense we must understand "modernity." Does it mean "the first encounter with the white man" or does it refer to the implementation of the political, administrative, and religious colonial apparatus? See Jan Knappert's (1978) recordings of Woyo tales for an outline of "precolonial" female water spirits.

19. Meyer (2003a: 34) prefers to define her as "the spirit of modern consumerism."

20. Meyer (2003a: 29) has observed the same phenomenon in Ghana. Ghanaian films visualize a world at the bottom of the sea, which she calls "the land of affluence—in a word, America."

21. According to Isaac Shapera, who discussed the rise of the "modern girl" in South Africa, this type of femininity, which combines novel forms of intimacy with a strong desire for materialism, is the outcome of social transformations such as Christian schooling, labor migrancy, and the colonial cash economy (1933, cited in Thomas 2009: 51). Since her very first emergence, the "modern girl," as some authors call her (Thomas 2009), occupies an ambivalent status in society, worshipped and despised, a model and anti-model at once.

22. De Boeck (2005b: 191) generalizes the privilege of children (children and young people). He writes: "They [children] appear not only as passive consumers, as in the West, but also as major societal players with access to these new global economic fields, and frequently in direct opposition to the generations that precede them." There seems nevertheless to be a gendered difference: adolescent girls are the ultimate consumers, since their lovers raise their social status and accordingly their importance to these same lovers who are "capable" of transmitting these consumer goods to the teenagers.

23. "The city" (*ville*) denotes the city center, especially the area of the Boulevard 30 Juin.

24. Women appear to be the target of accusations more frequently than male elders. This is in line with what De Boeck (2005b: 203) has observed of the accusations made by witch children themselves, who mainly accuse women and maternal figures. De Boeck relates this gender bias to the socioeconomic shifts mediated by gender: women have increasingly absorbed more economic power outside the domestic sphere; this has augmented their power and authority in the home.

25. Each time a new member joins the Cinarc group, the troupe's leader questions the new actors, as he is concerned to know the personal life history of each of his children. As a "father," he should know everything about his children, Bienvenu explains. It is considered absolutely normal for him to use this information in the serials he creates.

26. Beti's relatives belong to the Mongo group. Sororate is practiced by the ba-Mongo, both in their home region in Equateur province and in Kinshasa.

27. I agree with David Maxwell's remark (2000) that the answer concerning the public outcomes of African Pentecostal Christianity should primarily be sought not on the macro level but in more intimate spheres, such as between genders and between generations.

28. Gifford (1994: 513) emphasizes the role of Christian churches in what he calls "the second liberation" of Africa, which took place throughout the continent in the late 1980s, when "the peoples of Africa tried to throw off the political systems that had come to serve them so badly."

29. This Christian approach to the nation's instability and corruption is not a recent religious innovation. As early as 1971, Bernard (1971: 154) wrote that Congolese prophetic movements (such as Kimbanguism, Église de la Foi, and others) proposed similar measures as "a fundamental remedy for the nation's trials: reveal the sorcerers, ban the fetishes, and pray to God."

30. All in all, a strange paradox inheres in the Pentecostals' actions. While the content of their practices and discursive genres emphasize the aim of preventing the impending Apocalypse, it can be argued that exactly the incessant repetition of the same message perpetuates its impossibility, or even the desire to continue the threat of the Apocalypse. Voiding the Apocalypse, or the threat thereof, would make the Christians' present response and actions redundant. The apocalyptic representation of time justifies the Christian leaders' presence and power, since they are represented as the only means of becoming free from this utterly pessimistic time view. Indeed, as Munn (1996: 109) writes, "control over time is not just a strategy of interaction; it is also a medium of hierarchic power and governance."

31. See Pype (2009a), where I discuss the reception of Muyombe Gauche's teleserials in light of national progress and development.

32. UDPS and PPRD are two Congolese political parties.

33. The national constitution has been modified several times, and for Kinois, older and newer versions coexist. People generally are quite unaware of their rights and duties. Foreign NGOs intent on educating the public tend to explain the constitution through the lens of Western human rights.

34. From a sermon given by the pastor's spouse during a meeting of the women's group of the Church of the Resurrection in Lemba, 19 January 2005.

CHAPTER 8

Marriage Comes from God

Negotiating Matrimony and Urban Sexuality (Part I)

Oh libala, libala, ewutaki na Nzambe eh
Oh libala, libala, esengo na likolo (2x)
Nzembo: *Libala kati na Yésu*
Oh, marriage comes from God,
Oh, marriage, it gives joy to those in heaven (2x)
Song: "Christian Marriage"
Best of Maman Théthé Djungandeke[1]
(Frequently played during marriage ceremonies)

In the TV serials, young Christians reflect not only on the state and intergenerational relationships but also on marriage and sexuality. The choice of marriage partners, erotic dreams, informal polygamy, and girls' attire are main themes of the *maboke*. In this chapter, I focus on discourse on and representations of arranged marriage, incest (*ekobo*), polygamy, and adultery (both *kindumba*), reserving my discussion of the various masculinities and femininities for the next chapter. Though other social phenomena such as formal polygamy, levirate, homosexuality, and AIDS also appear thematically in the *maboke,* these topics do not contribute to the serials' plots; such subject matters are more typically a focus in "theater for development." The reason for their minimal presence in the TV narratives is not so much that the practices do not occur in real life (they do), but that they are not the main concerns of Kinshasa's Christian youth. The serials' strong attention to marriage (*libala*) and preparation for it, in particular the choice of a suitable spouse, reflect Kinois youth's concern to enter into adulthood.

Gender Games in Kinshasa

Marriage (*libala*), love (*bolingo*), sexuality (*bosoni*), and intimacy (*ya es-eka*) are culturally and historically situated concepts, and the practices involved are likewise contingent on the political, social, and economic situation of the individuals involved (Thomas and Cole 2009: 29). Only recently have the complexities involved in matrimony and sexuality in Africa become the focus of attention (Cole and Thomas 2009). Since the colonial period, dramatic changes in matrimonial agreements and the expression of affection and "love" have emerged. This is in particular due to Christianity and the widespread distribution of printed and broadcast romantic fiction (Fuglesang 1994; Larkin 1997; Newell 2008; Fair 2009), which have allowed for a circulation of Western and non-Western ideas about courtship, the choice of sexual partners, and matrimonial communication. As Thomas and Cole (2009: 18) argue in the introduction to the edited volume *Love in Africa,* cinema, television, radio, and print magazines have a long history of shaping ideas and practices of courtship, love, and sexuality and "providing sentimental educations and encouraging public discussion of love" in Africa.

In the postcolony, gender relations in and outside of matrimony are extremely complex. In a city such as Kinshasa, where various kinds of cosmopolitanism are celebrated, the Christian churches obviously constitute only one of multiple forces that fashion gender and sexuality. In the Christians' discourse, their most overt opposite is the so-called *La Kinoiserie,* urban public culture (Chapter 2). The tunes of the music scene, with its suggestive dances and lyrics, celebrate the female body and (hetero-)sexual intercourse in the city's streets and the bars, terraces, and nightclubs. Yet a whole range of social, religious, and cultural worlds continue to define sexuality and matrimony and influence—according to distinct and at times opposing lines—sexual practices and discourse about these topics. Following Ortner (1996), I prefer to refer to the practices and discourses of the various worlds as "games." "Games" refer to cultural organization, the construction of social life, the webs of relationships and interactions between multiple, shifting, interrelated subject positions, and the agency of social actors (Ortner 1996: 14). The cultural organization frames and produces rules and codes, but people can also imagine or fantasize escapes and alternatives. As will become clear throughout this chapter, the co-presence of structures that prescribe certain behavior, as well as the fact that Kinois reflect on these structures and may decide to follow their rules or not, makes a "game" approach to the construction and experience of love, sexuality, and matrimony extremely compelling.

In particular, three gender games structure discourse about sexuality in Kinshasa: lineage-related codes prescribing rules for marriage and appropriate time-spaces for enacting sexuality; Christianity, in its diverse manifestations, imposing biblical norms and codes for man-woman encounters, sexual pleasure, and procreation; and the game of an urban hedonistic modernity, especially in its transmission of images of eroticism, romantic love, and new patterns of social behavior between the two genders through popular music and the mass media (television, music, and the Internet). The government could be identified as a fourth domain, but despite governmental initiatives to control public culture and to mold Kinois men and women into citizens honoring their country, city and national authorities have a rather minimal impact on gender practices.

Of course, this delineation of distinct cultural domains in which codes and values concerning matrimony and sexuality are transmitted does not imply that these different ideologies are totally opposed to one another. First, they continuously interact, shape each other, and transform according to new social and cultural realities. The Christian "gender game," for example, has superimposed itself upon lineage rules and practices and resignifies them. Second, a major meeting ground between the three games is the strong patriarchal tone stimulating men to continue to exert control over the sexuality of women (particularly wives and daughters). An often-heard credo in this respect states, "The Bible says: 'Wife, obey your husband, and he will love you'" (*Bible alobi*, *"maman, otosa mobali; alinga yo"*), thus rooting the husband's authority within the Christian belief system. In this and the following chapter, I intend to show that young evangelizing Christians are playing multiple gender games: though they prefer to follow the rules of born-again Christianity, they are confronted with the games of their lineages, which have their own rules; further, they are obliged to dialogue with the highly eroticized quality of a public Afromodernity.

Against Ethnic Endogamous Marriages: *Mayimona*

In the telenarrative *Mayimona*, Caleb's marriage with Charlainne is contested by his Luba relatives. In the first episode, the parents of Caleb and Mayimona talk about how Luba people should marry among themselves in order to retain wealth within their own ethnic group. Caleb is already married to Charlainne, a girl from the Bandundu region, but as this marital union has remained childless, Theresia, Caleb's mother, allows that her son should perhaps find a second wife with whom he could have offspring. Mayimona's mother Deborah agrees with Theresia, and the two women decide to thrust Mayimona on Caleb.

Their efforts are thwarted by Caleb, who really loves his wife and shows no interest in Mayimona. He has fully accepted his wife's children from a prior marriage as his own, and although he regrets that he has not fathered a child with Charlainne, he rejects polygamy as an unchristian option. In spite of this, Caleb's parents and his paternal aunt visit Caleb's house and insult Charlainne: they complain that the food she offers to her parents-in-law is tasteless, that she does not know how to please her husband, and above all that she is from Bandundu, a region where, according to Caleb's parents, people are destitute. The harassment continues in a subtler manner as well: Theresia arranges secret meetings between her son and Mayimona. Theresia, however, is unaware that Mayimona is a "bad girl" and does not notice how Mayimona bewitches Caleb on their first visit. Two episodes later, Caleb's relatives inform Charlainne that they are convinced she cannot offer their son a prosperous future. They announce to her that Mayimona will come into the home and from that moment on everybody should treat her as Caleb's real wife. Charlainne is faced with a stark choice: either she accepts a rival (*mbanda*), or she leaves the house. Not daring to object to her in-laws, Charlainne can only watch, with much sorrow and pain, as Mayimona arrives and immediately proceeds to take over Charlainne's role as spouse and housewife.

The introduction of this evil woman into Caleb's household sets the plot in motion: Mayimona persuades Caleb that Charlainne should be chased away and obliges him to take her to fancy restaurants, buy her nice clothing and spend all his money on her. In the meantime, Charlainne too falls victim to the witch's conniving: Mayimona takes on Charlainne's appearance and insults Caleb's parents, accordingly furthering their inclination to expel their son's wife. Mayimona also bewitches Charlainne's children and even spreads rumors about Charlainne having adulterous affairs, which leads her husband to lose faith in her. Throughout this time, Charlainne is supported by her brother, Pastor Chapy, by the godparents of her religious marriage, and by the Christian singer Marie Missamu.[2] These four help her to retain her faith in the Bible and the Christian God. Their efforts falter, however, and in the end both Charlainne and Caleb die as a result of occult attacks initiated by Mayimona, who is herself ultimately punished by death as well.

This central plot is mirrored by a minor thread depicting the state of affairs in Fataki's household. Fataki, married to Melina, succumbs to the charms of one of Mayimona's friends, Nora. Like Mayimona, Nora is a member of a demonic group of young "bad girls" who try to seduce married men. When Nora becomes pregnant, her relatives drop her at Fataki's doorstep. Melina, a woman of ardent faith, manages to save her house and protect it from Nora's evil influences by intensifying her spiritual work. The final episode shows Melina's house covered by a spiritual fire that protects it.

The *Mayimona* story is more than a tale about rivalries between co-spouses. It deals with interference by non-Christians in a Christian marriage. The efforts of Theresia, who is obviously concerned about the absence of grandchildren, introduce a spirit of death, hosted by Mayimona, into Caleb's household. It is thus shown how relatives who do not consider God's will also endanger, sometimes unknowingly, Christian households.

As his sister Charlainne faces her in-laws' attempts to impose a second wife on her husband, Pastor Chapy tries to comfort her with the words: "Do not fear, because you have a Christian marriage. What God has united, nobody can break apart. Even if Caleb's relatives show up, it is only God who can separate you" (*Mayimona,* fourth episode). Viewers follow how Charlainne loses faith, however, and how Caleb too eventually diverges from God's way as a result of listening to a "false pastor." Caleb, who initially does not accept a second wife, confides in Pastor Divioli, a "false prophet," who reminds him that the Old Testament is full of polygamous men. He himself, Divioli states, is married to seven women. Citing numerous biblical references, the "false prophet" manages to convince Caleb to accept the polygamous marriage. The scenes involving this "false pastor" are highly comedic, which for the audience immediately undermines the man's authority and the power of his words. Having decided to follow this man's advice, Caleb is held responsible for the misfortune that strikes his household. Both spouses eventually die because they did not cling to God, despite the efforts of Christians in their entourage who encouraged them to pray.

Melina's behavior contrasts sharply with Charlainne's reaction to the intrusion of a third person in her household: whereas Charlainne cries, despairs, and does not rely on God, Melina is depicted reading the Bible, citing biblical verses to her husband and her rival, and singing Christian songs. Instead of leaving her house (as Charlainne does), Melina does not cede her place as housewife. Furthermore, she remains firmly attached to her church and the church leader, whom she invites to her home and whose advice she follows.

The serial *Mayimona* introduces an important theme that constantly appears in Kinshasa's post-Mobutu *maboke:* the Christian couple is threatened by a coalition between elders, traditions (i.e., polygamy and preferential marriages prescribed by the lineage), and demonic forces. This coalition is represented as accidental: parents and elders are not always portrayed as agents of evil but at times as victims of the occult—Deborah, for instance, was unaware of the demonic outcome when she asked the lineage chief's blessing on the newborn Mayimona.

The choice to depict Luba people as representing the preference for lineage-related endogamous marriages ties in with other practices that many Kinois imagine to be representative for "the Luba." Generally, this ethnic group is known for feeling a great sense of pride of belonging to "the Luba community." The Cinarc head, a muKongo man, explained to me that "Luba people," reputed to be the wealthiest people in Kinshasa, are equally known for their penchant to keep wealth within the group. I would frequently hear, during casual conversations about the role of ethnicity in contemporary Kinshasa, that the Luba's refusal to share their resources with other groups stems from their arrogance and their imagined superiority over other Congolese groups. Some of the Luba actresses confirmed these statements. They recalled how during their childhood, their parents often reminded their brothers that non-Luba girls had a bad reputation and that only Luba girls were virtuous. According to these actresses, such instructions were solely inspired by the Luba's concern to protect their own riches.

There is much to say about the representation of ethnic groups and the homogenizing work about ethnicity that is currently going on in Kinshasa. The point that I want to make here is that the idea of a unified Luba group is an illusion, though it serves the Christians' efforts to construct an Other, a group, and even a cultural trend to which they can be opposed. The opposition is not between "Luba people" and "non-Luba people"; rather, the category of "Luba people" should be read as a construction that here denotes the epitome of a group that promotes "tradition," which is then the Christians' Other.

Christian Leaders Intruding in the Marriage Process

Marriage politics as represented in Cinarc's *maboke* reflects the preferred marriage alliances of the Pentecostal community. Pentecostal leaders instruct their members to marry within the (Pentecostal) Christian community and underline the asocial outcomes of ethnic preferential marriage politics. Nowadays, pastors and the revival churches play a principal role in the different stages of the marriage process. The Christian community and its leaders are unmistakably present from the initial moment in the search for a marriage partner throughout the negotiations over the bride price between the marrying families to the phase of the marriage rituals and even beyond, sometimes mediating in matrimonial conflicts. The involvement of the Christian community in the marriage arrangements is significant because it competes with, and at times overrules, the authority of the extended family. Consider the following assertions heard during a church service at the Church of the Resurrection (Lemba) about marriage. The pastors posed the following questions: "Who marries people?" (*Nani abalisa?*), "Who gives the money [for the marriage preparations]?" (*Nani apesa mbongo?*), and "Who gives the bride price?" (*Nani a dotté?*). Each time, the congregation replied: "God!" (*Nzambe*). Both the church leaders and those in attendance denied the participation of relatives whose permission is needed in order to marry, who assist in collecting the money, and who retain authority over the in-married wife.[3]

Many informants stated that, in order to find a suitable marriage partner, one should go to the church and hang on to God. It is often jokingly said that young people only attend the churches to find marriage partners in the prayer groups or benefit from the active help of the spiritual leaders. But prayer gatherings facilitate encounters between the two sexes, and without a doubt they serve to enhance long-standing friendships between male and female youth. Furthermore, the Christian space itself functions as a primary grid by means of which "good girls" are selected. After all, among many Kinois boys Christian girls have a better reputation than girls who do not pray.

Pastors play an active part in the search for a future spouse and thus influence the marital choice. In their sermons at Sunday services and other religious gatherings, pastors frequently inform their followers that certain Congolese in the diaspora (whom they name and whose profile they sketch) have asked them to select a spouse for the young person in search of a partner. They also recurrently affirm marriage for those who are seeking it by declaring that the Holy Spirit whispers that certain individuals (again, naming them) stand on the verge of marriage. At times, *pasteurs* even promote certain individuals among their followers, stating that so-and-so is longing for a marriage partner and stressing his or her positive qualities. In these praises, the pastors usually refer to that person's spiritual work for God. Pastor Gervais once spoke about Clovis, his favorite Cinarc actor, in these terms: "Let me tell you, my brothers and sisters. Paco[4] is a man of God who will be lifted. The sister [to whom he will propose] should have a clear vision. If Paco proposes to marry somewhere,[5] she should not look at his shirt or his trousers but she must look at his inner person." When this same Christian leader predicts "this year one of us will get married," people clap their hands and wave kisses to him because he is confirming their dearest wish.

Of course, such discourse rather transparently seems an all-too-easy strategy to acquire followers. However, these words strike a very sensitive cord among Kinshasa's youth, who all long to get married. Many young men and women complained to me that their relatives did not talk about organizing a marriage for their son or daughter because that meant too many worries about money and even the likelihood of incurring debts. Only the *pasteur* offers Kinshasa's youth certain prospects of getting married. He encourages young men to pray so that they will find a good woman they can marry with a marriage payment that is not too high. As for the women, he promises that a wealthy man will cross each of their paths.

These leaders also shape new courting practices and direct the quest for a suitable marriage partner. To that extent, churches organize special days of instruction on engagement (*fiançailles*) at which they teach young people biblical norms and offer practical advice for selecting a suitable partner. This is, however, not a unidirectional practice: young people themselves also seek out pastors and ask them for advice on sexual matters and help in the choice of a marriage partner. The following is an excerpt from my field notes detailing a sermon given by the troupe's spiritual leader:

> *Pasteur* Gervais takes the microphone and begins speaking as soon as the clapping has died down. In his high-pitched voice he asks the congregation to repeat the phrase: "Your pastor knows how to take care of things." The group repeats this up to three times. Then he starts to explain what this statement means. The previous Sunday, after the weekly service, one of the young girls of the church community had asked to speak to him in private. "She had a *problème de luxe*," as he says jokingly. It appeared that the girl had been proposed to by three different young men. She had no idea whom to choose and asked her spiritual leader for advice. He tells the community that he has advised her not to pay any attention to their clothes, their cars, their diplomas or their frequent trips to South Africa. Instead she should investigate if the men pray and are real Christians. And she should ask God for help. While she is at prayer, God will indicate to her whom to choose, because, as he continues, "God has plans for you!" When he pronounces this phrase, everybody claps their hands again and starts waving at the pastor. The band begins to play, and the pastor invites everybody to dance for God.

The pastor no doubt mentioned this request for advice in order to promote himself as a much-solicited counselor. There is, however, no reason to distrust the veracity of his words: many young boys and girls contact pastors for clarification and guidance in the choice of marriage partners.

The demand that the girl's choice should depend on the religious identity of the suitor deserves emphasis. This restriction is part of the rules and obligations that the revival churches impose on the young: Christian leaders push their members to marry born-again Christians. A pamphlet distributed among couples preparing for their marriage in the Church La Colombe (Lemba, Massano neighborhood) offers the following guidelines concerning the choice of a marriage partner:[6]

1. The choice of a partner is of utmost importance. You can break off the engagement but not the marriage. Marriage is a conjugal life that cannot be restored [after a serious problem]. This choice is founded on the acceptance of Jesus Christ as Lord and Savior—life in Christ must be guided by the Holy Spirit.
2. Being born again: the baptism of the brother and the sister ensure that the marriage endures.
3. The support of the brother and the sister at the church.
4. Being committed to the church and its vision.

The following factors are called false criteria: a choice made by the family, regionalism (preferences for a marriage partner coming from the same region), tribalism (preference for a marriage partner belonging to the same ethnic group), tradition, material goods, financial capacities, beauty, and others.

The special emphasis on the role of the family, territorial affiliations, appearances, and modern consumerist desires as unfavorable guidelines manifests the churches' negation of Kinshasa's indigenous traditions, *La Kinoiserie*, and the desire for an insertion into the global capitalist economy. If a born-again Christian man or woman desires to marry a "pagan," the latter must be converted and baptized before the marriage preparations can start. Born-again Christians thus tend to contract endogamous marriages within the Pentecostal community. When a Catholic man courts a born-again Christian girl, the man is often required to join the Pentecostal church. If the suitor is not a reborn Christian, the partner will either decline the marriage process or convince the "pagan" to become a Christian.

The mounting influence of Christianity in the marriage process has altered the concept of betrothal or engagement. "Betrothal" (*bokangi lopango*), translated as "closing the compound," refers to the initial step of the marriage process, in which the suitor presents the girl's guardians with a bottle of strong drink (often whiskey) and offers them a letter asking their consent to the marriage. Nowadays, for many born-again Christians, these lineage-related ceremonies mark only the beginning of the engagement, which for them culminates in and ends with the marriage ceremony in the church.[7] A concept of "Christian engagement" (*les fiançailles chrétiennes*) has entered the process; this now spans the period between the announcement in the church and the actual religious marriage ceremony.

During the *fiançailles*, the pair will complete religious courses on a suitable Christian conjugal life (*malongi*). The church leaders also choose a couple from the congregation to serve as godparents of the marriage (*baboti ya libala*, "the parents of the marriage," *parrain et marraine du mariage*). They are present during the *malongi* courses and become social and spiritual advisers for the engaged couple. A godfather guides the future groom, while the former's wife informs the future bride about all aspects of Christian matrimony. They are considered co-responsible for the success of the matrimonial union and are to be consulted regularly and asked for advice at different stages of the couple's marital life. The godparents thus complement the work of the pastors.

Incest Reconsidered: *The Devouring Fire*

Incest (*ekobo*) also has a prominent place in the discourse of born-again Christians and in the evangelizing serials. Understood in a narrow sense, incest denotes sexual contact between a father and his daughter. The Cinarc serial *Dilemma* thematizes this particular relationship, giving it a Pentecostal frame. The plot sets off with the skirt-chaser Fataki, who develops an unhealthy fascination with his daughter's body. He invites her to bars and takes her shopping for clothes, something mothers usually do for their children or men for their girlfriends. He insists that instead of calling him "*tata*" (father), she should call him "*papa chéri*," the form of address young girls use in speaking to married and older lovers. Though the serial does not show any sexual scenes, images of the father entering Monica's room at night and hastily leaving it suggest that there is a sexual side to their relationship. As the story unfolds, Monica takes over her mother's role in the household: she orders her siblings around, disobeys her mother, and replaces her mother by accompanying her father on familial visits. Monica becomes her mother's rival and lacks the respect that she as a daughter owes her parents, showing disrespect even toward her father. The serial not only displays the social consequences of the transgression of sexual distance between parents and their offspring but also hints at a spiritual dimension that is portrayed as the ultimate origin of the anomaly: demonic spirits are accountable for the transgression.[8]

The Devouring Fire, which the Cinarc troupe produced and broadcast between November 2004 and February 2005, touches more explicitly on the demonic nature of incest. In the final episode, Paco, a pastor in training, and Belinda, a girl from his church, conclude a marriage between their respective lineages. Over the course of the eleven preceding episodes, Paco has been confronted with a dilemma: whether to marry the girl his parents have chosen for him or the beautiful city girl, Belinda, whom he has already promised to marry. In the sixth episode of the story, Paco's parents try to convince him to marry his *ketyul*[9]—the preferred marriage partner according to Yanzi[10] cultural codes. They offer him US $900 to rent a luxurious apartment in the city center. But the young Christian man refuses, exclaiming: "*Eza ekobo. Nakobala ye te. Eglise na ngai endima te. Eza ekobo.*" ("This is incest. I will not marry her. My church does not allow me to marry her. It is incest."). His refusal is based on a church teaching that proclaims the practice to be incestuous, and his words reflect the gap between generations in the city.

The serial shows how his parents and his matrilineal descent group employ witchcraft to get their son to follow their rules. Their occult practices are countered by the constant efforts of Paco's fellow "men of God," who pray for him and his family. His colleagues encounter numerous obstacles in their campaign to lead Paco's family back to God's path. The elders' occult forces are so strong that in the seventh episode, Paco decides to abandon Belinda and to accept the young girl from the village (whom he has never met). Very soon Paco's family suffers from disaster and misfortune. There are quarrels within the extended family, and Paco's father (Makubakuba) loses his eyesight. Jef, Paco's friend and a strongly spiritual man, succeeds in bringing Paco back to Jesus's way and heals Makubakuba, restoring his sight through an exorcism ritual. As a result of this miracle, the old man accepts Jesus and decides that marriage practices according to lineage or ethnic rules are demonic. He then allows his son the freedom to choose the girl he desires to marry. The final scene, where Paco and Belinda become man and wife, depicts the victory of the young Pentecostals over the elder generations who still follow lineage-related marriage arrangements. Makubakuba, who arrives on the scene with his relatives and his son, now repents, saying: "I ask you to forgive me for everything that has happened. I am now converted. We are here to marry your daughter." The families withdraw to the living room to discuss the bride price while the young people wait outside.

Among Kinshasa's Christians, the practice of *kitshuili* is often mentioned when discussing incest. *Kitshuili* denotes the marriage preference of the Yanzi group, that is, marriage between a man and his matrilateral second cross-cousin. Although most Congolese groups practice preferential marriage arrangements, the baYanzi in particular are known in Kinshasa for continuing this practice in the city. Among Kinshasa's Christians, the Yanzi practice has become the epitome of incest and "traditional" marriage preferences in the same way that Luba endogamous marriages are most often mentioned when discussing ethnic concerns for boundary maintenance. Yet ideas of romantic love and the free choice of a marriage partner flourish among the young. As has been documented for other African postcolonial societies (Smith 2009; Cole and Thomas 2009), young Kinois associate these ideas of *bolingo* (love) and personal selection of marriage partners with being "modern." The concept of *kitshuili* has become the primary expression for "tradition" and the lineage forcing its members into prearranged marriages.[11]

The following is an example of how Christians essentialize "tradition" and deliberately transmit a negative image of it. According to the Yanzi men with whom I conducted a series of interviews about the representation of *kitshuili* in Kinshasa's teleserials, and based on an ethnography on Yanzi culture (de Plaen 1974), I learned that the Yanzi community practices two different matrimonial strategies. One is the preferential marriage of a man with his *ketyul,* namely the granddaughter of his mother's maternal uncle. He in turn is called the *ngatyul* of the young girl, "the owner of the girl." "Owning" entails duties such as providing food and clothes and providing all kinds of services to the parents of the girl, but it also affords the man the right to marry that particular girl. Payment of bride price is not necessary in this case, since the "owner" has usually bought food and paid for school fees and other necessities while his *ketyul* has been growing up.[12] The other strategy, marriage to someone who is not one's *ketyul,* is also permitted. In this case, the marriage is enacted with matrimonial services and the exchange of gifts that go to the family of the bride.

The preferential marriage structure (when an *ngatyul* marries his *ketyul*) reflects the Yanzi urge to find equilibrium between clans and lineages. According to Yanzi logic, the maternal grandfather owns his granddaughter because she is a reincarnation of his wife. He thus "possesses" his granddaughter/wife. Two generations after his own, he brings back into his family, who has had to pay for his marriage, a girl. The grandfather forgoes his right to marry his granddaughter (she is regarded as a reincarnation of his wife and is accordingly identified with her) and transmits her to the son of his sister's son, ideally, or to any other marriageable man of his lineage. In this way, the bride price that he, as a maternal uncle, assembles on behalf of the young men for whom he is responsible remains within the clan because he in turn is entitled to compensation for the young girl he owns.

Every Yanzi girl, then, has one or more *ngatyul* designated at her birth, just as all Yanzi men have a group of young women from whom they may choose a marriage partner without having to provide bride price. Yanzi rules also accept that a girl can marry a man other than her *ngatyul.* In that case, general marriage practices are followed: the suitor is presented, and a marriage ritual with the exchange of a bride price is held. In this case, the man transmits the marriage compensation not to her parents but to her *ngatyul;* he thus reimburses the costs (for school fees, medicine, or clothes) the *ngatyul* has incurred for his *ketyul.* It is said that he "buys" or redeems her from her owner.

Carine and Her Ngatyul

The Devouring Fire visualizes the biography of one of the troupe's actresses, Carine Massamba (screen name Mamy La Chatte), and narrates how Pentecostal ideology is used to "liberate" the young from gerontocratic rules. Carine is a young girl in her mid twenties who joined the Cinarc group in 1998 after seeing an announcement on a local television channel in which the president of the troupe called for Christian actors to join the group. When she came to the company, she had just re-converted to Christianity. Although she had been raised by Catholic parents, in her late teenage years she was drawn by "the call of the city," as she said herself, meaning that she had sexual relationships with men, drank alcohol, performed "worldly dances," and dressed like a "bad girl." In 1998, she aborted a love affair and became a born-again Christian. At the time she felt that she "had been ignoring God, and it was time to lead the life of a respectful girl." Her reconversion meant that she had to be baptized again, a ritual she underwent in the revival church affiliated with Cinarc.

As a Yanzi girl, Carine belonged to a *ngatyul* from birth. However, born and raised in Kinshasa, where lineage-related attachments, prescriptions, and codes tend to be forgotten, she was never cognizant of her relatedness to any *ngatyul.* The existence of a man "who owned her" came as a total surprise to her and her relatives a few years before the creation of the *Devouring Fire* serial. During the marriage ceremony of her eldest sister, Sylvie, when all the gifts and the money were handed over to the bride's family, a man sitting among her relatives suddenly stood up and announced: "My wife will not leave." He identified himself as Sylvie's *ngatyul* and demanded money. If the money were not produced, he would block the marriage. Everybody was astonished because both her parents and her brothers had completely forgotten about this practice. Yet he apparently did own her. At first, Sylvie's *ngatyul* was asking US $700. The two families negotiated on the spot and finally agreed on US $140. Only then, at the marriage of her oldest sister, was the *ketyul* practice explained to Carine.

When Carine talked to me about this event, she spoke about her *ngatyul* in a rather neutral way. She did not fear that her parents would oblige her to marry him, as they had themselves become born-again Christians two years before. Nevertheless, her *ngatyul* was real and would not disappear with conversion.

The serial *The Devouring Fire* was inspired by Carine's Yanzi background and explicitly created to persuade elders of the demonic nature of arranged marriages and of the necessity of endogamous Christian conjugal unions. Bienvenu Mutungilayi, one of the male leaders of the troupe, clears up their intentions for shooting *The Devouring Fire*:

> Evangelizing the city means that we have to show people how the Devil works. Sometimes our parents oblige us to follow certain rules, but they do not know that what they are doing is what the Devil wants. We have to show them that certain ancient practices from the village are in fact pagan. Carine is lucky her parents have become born-again Christians. They do not force her to marry this man in the village. But there are numerous other young women and men who follow the will of their elders. We have to reveal that their ideas are the Devil's work.

All born-again Christians acknowledge the mystical impact of such rules and attempt to avert them without offending the elders. "My husband will have to pay my *ngatyul* for me. If he does not, then we might encounter problems in our household," Carine said. These problems could range from infertility or incessant matrimonial disputes to financial problems and material loss. Urbanization and Christianization have not expelled beliefs about the mystical danger that might be triggered by trespassing lineage-related prescriptions.[13]

Carine did believe that some marriages between a *ketyul* and her *ngatyul* might well work, but she assumed these to be exceptions. She recalled a story she had heard about a couple in "the village" who married according to *kitshuili* convention. The daughters born from this union were never married, although they were already in their thirties. According to Carine, this was a consequence of the *kitshuili*, which she described as incestuous and a practice forbidden by God. The difficulty in finding suitors for these girls was in fact a matter of divine punishment.

When confronting the Yanzi preference for *ketyul* marriage with the Christian understanding of it, we observe two opposing interpretations of incest. As Guy de Plaen (1974: 64) remarks, *ketyul* practice enforces certain nuptial interdictions of behaviors that are not considered incestuous. For the Yanzi group, descent is reckoned only along the maternal line. Here, then, the maternal grandfather and his sister's children belong to the same bloodline, but his own granddaughter and her children do not; a woman and her female offspring may marry the men from the matrilineal descent line of her grandfather without committing incest. Born-again Christians, however, in line with Western kinship rules, follow a double lineal descent line that encompasses both "traditionally acknowledged" blood relatives and also those who, in "traditional" reckoning, do not belong to the same lineage. As a result, people who according to ethnic traditions do not belong to the same lineage now appear to be members of the same family. This has far-reaching consequences, since people who, following the lineage prescriptions, are preferred marriage partners now become prohibited partners.

The churches add a Christian meaning to incest and enlarge the group of prohibited sexual partners. Explaining the biblical prohibition of incest, Christians refer to the biblical verses Leviticus 18:6, "No one is to approach any close relative to have sexual relations," and, more explicitly, Leviticus 20:17, "And if a man shall take his sister, his father's daughter, or his mother's daughter, and see her nakedness, it is a wicked thing, and they shall be cut off in the sight of their people: he has uncovered his sister's nakedness, he shall bear his iniquity." This Christian resignification of incest is sustained by two important strategies. First, the new definition given to ethnic marriage preferences interprets these preferences as demonic. To underscore their argument, Christians refer to the misfortune that could occur when people did not obey the ethnic preferences. Traditionally, people have their own preferential marriage arrangements and structure sexual relationships according to cultural prohibitions. Violation of these taboos is commonly followed by all kinds of misfortune, understood as punishments, such as death, infertility, disease, or other kinds of bad luck. Creten, for example, mentions that Nkanu preferential marriages are obligatory in a few cases: a first son should marry his classificatory female father (FaSi) or a classificatory granddaughter of marriageable age who lacks suitors—if these required unions are not performed, then bewitchment is going to happen. In Kinshasa, many young people mention, and even fear, such punishments when not respecting the rules of their lineages. Christian leaders identify these occurrences of misfortune as evidence of elders' evil powers, thereby taking advantage of the young people's anxieties. Second, the new patterns in tracing descent are significant for the scope of these churches' success.[14] It is precisely this enlargement, rather than confinement, of the set of prohibited partners that assures the churches' success, since their rules do not cross-cut any prohibitions of the "traditional" incest definition.

Taking the discussion of incest one step further, we could state that these data show that the Christian churches transform marriage practices in Kinshasa into "complex structures" (Lévi-Strauss 1969). In contrast to societies that Lévi-Strauss termed "simple systems" where preferred marriage partners are indicated, the Christian churches do not point at particular categories that are preferred to marry with, but indicate the prohibited partners, the "pagans."[15]

Where does the need to reflect on the contours of "incest" come from? All Congolese kinship systems use classificatory kinship terminology to map out potential and prohibited sexual partners. In an urban context, youngsters do not always have much knowledge of their lineage affiliations and traditions. Blood relatedness and relations of avoidance are not always spelled out any more and thus have often ceased to structure social relations. The serial *Whose Blood?* (*Makila ya nani?*), produced by the acting company Sans Soucis in early 2005, reflects on this loss of social knowledge. The serial concerns a young couple who meet in one of Kinshasa's churches. Following Western modes of romance and sexuality, they fall in love and decide to marry. After all the necessary rituals have been performed, the couple waits for children for several years until the despairing wife finally seeks a pastor. The Holy Spirit reveals to the pastor that the union is doomed, for the spouses are classificatory siblings and have thus been committing incest. The case is not inconceivable if we consider the fact that some young people no longer know which ethnic group they belong to. In order to prevent such situations, Pentecostal churches conquer the opaque field of forbidden and potential marriage partners. Taking the mystical punishments of the lineages seriously and replying to the loss of social knowledge, new boundaries are erected to define sex and marriage, boundaries that used to be demarcated by the lineage.

Negotiating Adultery: *The Open Tomb*

Polygamy and adultery are two other themes that figure prominently in the *maboke*. From a Christian perspective, the two themes are inter-related, since they threaten the ideal of the nuclear family. Kinois are fond of citing the calculation "1 + 1 = 1," indicating both the unity of the couple and the rejection of any third intruding on the couple. In religious weddings, the cars used to transport the young couple are fre-quently decorated with this mathematical phrase. During the religious ritual, the pastor reminds the groom and bride of this as a divine law, and it is also often repeated during the party following the religious cer-emony. The main idea is that God has united two people in marriage. No other person is allowed to come between them.

The topic of adultery is also an omnipresent theme in Kinshasa's pub-lic culture, popular culture, and private conversations. Rumors about politicians, music stars, and actors who have sexual relations with their female employees, dancers, or the wives of their adversaries are told and retold. These stories invariably involve a warning: adultery leads to the death of at least one of the partners unless one confesses and un-dergoes rites of reparation in "the village." The high mortality among truck drivers commuting between Kinshasa and Tshipaka or other cities in the Kasai (home region of the Luba group) is frequently held to be the effect of adultery. This refers to the concept of *tshibao,* commonly represented among Kinois as a mystical law that punishes extramarital intercourse with a woman married to a Luba man (*la femme d'autrui,* Li. *mwasi ya mosusu*). Kinois jokingly advise foreigners not to have sexual affairs with Luba women. Here again, the Luba ethnic group appears as the Christian Kinois' Other.

Significantly, the definition of *tshibao* given by Kinois differs from the original Luba interpretation of *tshibao* as any grave transgression of social order. Murder, witchcraft directed against someone's health or well-being, theft, and wounding are also included in the Luba concept (Muteba 1987: 282–286). A *muena tshibao* is then a "criminal." In Kin-shasa, a *muena tshibao* more specifically denotes an "adulterer."

Although each lineage has its own rules and practices, such as those regarding preferential marriages, in the context of adultery the Luba have also become the prototype of a society that stubbornly holds on to its "traditions." Among the many groups in the country, the Luba are well known for their rigid safeguarding of the moral purity of in-mar-rying women. The ritual performed during Luba marriage ceremonies instates a mystical power that brings death to the adulterous wife unless she confesses. If the betrayed husband is cognizant of his wife's adultery but makes no attempt to repair the damage she has done, then death can befall him, too.[16] The *tshibao* phenomenon is a strategy that lineage elders of Luba groups deploy to control the sexuality of their in-married women in order to safeguard the continuation of their lineage. Immediately after the exchange of bride price, a ritual is enacted to mystically bind the in-married woman to the Luba group. The *bakoko* (elders) of the patrilineal group visit the newly arrived woman a few days after the ceremony. There they prepare a meal with food that they themselves have brought to the house. The wife must eat this meal while the elders utter the sacred pronouncement: "The wife cannot go out with another man, only with her own husband." Today, the cooking of a meal is no longer invariably performed among Luba in Kinshasa, but the speech and gifts still bind the in-married women to the mystical power of the Luba elders. One young woman related to me how, three days after she moved in with her new husband (following the religious marriage ceremony), his paternal aunts visited her and gave her some money. During the act of giving, one woman instructed her to obey her husband, to produce offspring for his family, and to be faithful to him. Through the power of speech and the gifts of the elders, these words set the *tshibao* rule in action.

The representatives of the patrilineage instruct the in-married wife that the man to whom she has been married is the only one from whom she can accept food, money, or sex. If she is ever offered money from a friend of her husband for transport or food, for example, she must decline—or, if she accepts, she must at least show the money to her husband and inform him of the source. The husband should then reflect on the relationship he has with the man: is he a rival or a friend? Nowadays in Kinshasa, young women marrying into Luba families may try to avoid this ritual, but this refusal leads to problems with their new families, who perceive their behavior as a sign of lack of devotion to the husband. In their attempts to escape from these binding mystical practices, the young women invoke Christianity, which demonizes these rituals.

In the "traditional" belief system, adultery upsets the exchanges between lineages and the balance within society. It is often interpreted in cosmological terms, requiring rituals of reparation that restore the flow of life.[17] In the Christian discourse on adultery, however, it is not the balance between lineages but the boundaries between Christians and non-Christians and the growth of the Christian community that are threatened by extramarital sex. Consequently, the Pentecostal melodrama emphasizes the occult, wicked dimension of adultery. An example of the apocalyptic understanding of adultery is manifest in the Cinarc production *The Open Tomb*.

The plot of the serial *The Open Tomb* is set in motion when Theresia and her four children arrive in Kinshasa. She has left her husband, whom she accuses of treating her badly, in Mbuji-Mayi. A friend from the village, Maman Jeanne, invites them to her home. Theresia is intrigued by this friend's husband, Makubakuba, a wealthy Luba businessman. In order to enjoy a share of his wealth, she needs to eliminate the friend, whom she now considers a rival. First she visits General, a *féticheur,* and invites her paternal aunt to join her in her home in Kinshasa. The viewer witnesses how Theresia's visits to the *féticheur* and the occult strategies of *tata mwasi* slowly help her gain influence over Makubakuba. Her aunt takes Theresia to the compound's toilets, where the two women invoke ancestral, and accordingly "evil," spirits and invite them into the house. These bad spirits afflict Maman Jeanne with the mystical disease *lesmbassu.* Theresia convinces Makubakuba that pastors will not be able to heal this disease, and she drags Maman Jeanne to her *féticheur,* who aggravates the suffering woman's condition and eventually kills her. Theresia's further efforts to strengthen her privileged relationship with Makubakuba include destroying the official documents of Makubakuba's children returned from Europe, canceling his daughter's marriage, and turning his son into a madman. The serial ends tragically: struck by lightening, Theresia falls to the ground and dies (figs. 8.1–4).

Figures 8.1., 8.2., 8.3., and 8.4. Theresia dies by lightning (screen shots from *The Open Tomb,* © Cinarc)

For most of Kinshasa's viewers, Theresia's extraordinary death is a sign of her occult identity and should be interpreted as God's punishment (see Chapter 6 for a discussion of this closure).

The troupe's leader initially had a conjunctive closure in mind for *The Open Tomb*. The scenario he had prepared the morning of the filming had Theresia feeling regret and accepting Jesus. But while the filming was going on, Bienvenu was in the city center settling problems with the boss of RTG@ and had left his eldest brother in charge. Jef, whose mother had remarried a Luba man, questioned out loud whether Theresia could be converted that easily. Anne Tshika, the performer in the role of Theresia and a Luba woman herself, joined in the conversation. She disagreed with Bienvenu's initial plan. With the consent of some of the other actors, they decided to modify the close of the serial in such a way that it reflected their view that the mystical rule of *tshibao* is so strong that even Jesus cannot counter it.

As not all the members of the Cinarc crew belong to the Luba group, many of the other actors were puzzled, finding it difficult to believe that Theresia could not convert and thus be spared a terrible death. Dorcaz Mbombo, another Cinarc actress of Luba origin, explained the law of *tshibao* to the non-Luba performers. Although Dorcaz was born and raised in Kinshasa and had never set foot on ancestral grounds, she displayed considerable conviction in her exposé on Luba culture. She contended that reversing the supernatural dangers evoked by the adulterous act necessitates the intervention of specialized persons and cleansing rituals that, according to many Luba youth, can only be performed "in the village," on the grounds of the ancestors, "where people know how to deal with these matters." The adulterous woman should confess in front of the lineage elders and undergo ritual cleansing. Only then can the mystical retribution of the ancestors be neutralized. Dorcaz then described the proceedings in the village:

> In the village, if a woman confesses she has committed adultery, she must leave her home naked the next morning at 5 o'clock and must walk to the market. There the old women may stone her. If a woman dies because of *tshibao*, it is said that all the spirits of the other women who have died because of *thsibao* get her. This is especially the case if a dying woman yells: "They are coming to get me, don't you see them?"

Dorcaz stated that the mystical revenge directs itself to turn back on the wrongdoers. If others have notified her husband about his wife's transgression, and if he does not take steps for ritual cleansing (*kosukola/kopetola mwasi, kolongola botutu*), then the mystical punishment falls on him for not having purified his home.

"In fact," Dorcaz continued, "these spiritual laws have effects in the lives of those who trespass them. Nowadays, times have changed, and not everybody thinks that these laws still function. But I tell you, each time somebody from the Kasai disobeys one of these laws, he or she will suddenly notice that certain things do not go right any more. These are things which still happen today, even here in Kinshasa." Dorcaz stressed that only girls and women who belong to the Luba of the Kasai, or women married to Luba men who have performed the *tshibao* ritual, are subject to this law.[18]

The plot of *The Open Tomb* evolves along the lines of Dorcaz's explanation. When Makubakuba witnesses the death of his wife, his son's descent into madness, the disappearance of his children's French passports, the mystical diseases of his stepchildren, and the breakup of his daughter's *fiançailles*, he turns to his brothers for advice. They recommend the Luba rites of reparation. Makubakuba obeys his brothers, who command him to return to their natal village in Mbuji-Mayi and seek the help of the lineage elders. Theresia and Makubakuba leave for "the village," where a family gathering is prepared. Kuaku, Theresia's first husband—whom she has not yet divorced—follows them. Makubakuba introduces Theresia as his new wife although he has not yet married her in the conventional Luba way. The elders inform them that a parley and divination will clarify the origin of the misfortunes they are experiencing.

The next day Theresia arrives with a turkey in order to solve the problem (*kokata likambo*, literally "to cut the problem"). Luba law, however, demands that she bring a rooster to prove her innocence. Theresia throws the turkey down in the midst of the lineage elders in a disrespectful way; this behavior identifies her as an adulterous woman. Kuaku and Makubakuba both decide to break with her. In the meantime, in Kinshasa, Theresia's two daughters fall ill. A mystical disease called "the disease of the cockroaches" (*maladie ya pese*)—the outcome of sorcerous attacks that their mother had directed at Makubakuba's offspring—is now redirected back on her own children. In order to avoid the maleficent power, Theresia's sisters, who have remained in Kinshasa, confess their wicked deeds, ask forgiveness of Makubakuba's children and God, and convert to Christianity. At the same time, far away, Theresia dies in a supernatural way through lightning.

In her argument, Dorcaz attacked the notion of patriarchy at the basis of these extreme mystical happenings: "It is consistently the women who are punished. You know, men have created these laws. These are satanic laws. People call them *sage* [wise]. Of course, the men who have created them have a special kind of knowledge, but the power they use does not stem from God. I am sure *tshibao* was brought about by the Devil. Tell me, do you think a *fidèle* [a Christian] can commit adultery?" Nevertheless, Dorcaz did not question the power of *tshibao.* Speaking with me afterward, Dorcaz gave me an example of how *tshibao* had operated in her own family context.

> The daughter of my aunt married a muSwahili. She already had a child before the marriage, and he had two children before he married her. Their union gave them two more. One day, the woman cheated on her husband. That evening, the man left the house, while his wife stayed in her room with the children. Suddenly a fire entered the room. Only the two children of this union and their clothes were burnt. The other children were left untouched by the fire, as were their clothes. The wife herself was very badly burnt but luckily God did not want her death. It is the *tshibao* that had come as a fire. It was a clever fire that knew how to distinguish between the clothes of the children of that union and the other children. As I pray, I tell you, this fire is diabolic.

The equation of ancestral anger with demonic action is central to this narrative. Along with the non-Luba members, Dorcaz regarded Jesus's power as stronger than the mystical power, although she emphasized the need for reparation. According to Bienvenu (a muKongo), confession and accepting Jesus could easily have saved Theresia. Chapy, as a Christian leader, agreed with him, for in his view, as soon as a woman has committed adultery she is tied to the Devil. Recalling a biblical passage, he contended that this sin could be expiated.

> If we read John Chapter 8 in the Bible, we learn how people brought an adulterous wife to Jesus. At that time the old law was still in effect, and this woman should have been punished severely. In fact, we can compare this old law with the *tshibao* taboo among the baLuba.... Well, they brought this woman to Jesus and asked him what to do. Jesus told them: those who have never committed a sin may start throwing stones. Nobody reacted; instead, they all left, young and old. Jesus wanted to show them that everybody commits sins, and this should not lead to those kinds of violent acts. He told the woman to leave and not to sin again.

Despite the difference in opinions and the varying interpretations as to whether the lightning was of divine or occult origin, the message the Cinarc productions convey is that adultery leads to death. In the serial *The Moziki Women,* televised the year before, adulterous men and women killed each other. Then, too, a discussion among the Cinarc members had played a part in determining the narrative's close. Bienvenu had asked the actors whether the adulterous men and women should die or merely be wounded. After discussing several alternative outcomes, the troupe's members agreed that one of the adulterous men would kill the others and then commit suicide. This, they believed, would best show how unchristian behavior destroys not only others but the wrongdoers themselves. In *The Moziki Women* narrative, the ethnic background of the fictional characters is not spelled out, accordingly avoiding the need to deal with the *tshibao* issue and the quandary with regard to the leveling of "traditional" powers through Jesus's name.

Although the eventual outcomes reflected the opinion of only a minority of the Cinarc members (the Luba actors), in these two telenarratives the troupe represented adultery as the only sin that cannot be restored through confession and conversion. In this respect the evangelizing *maboke* communicate a conviction that is harsher than what most of the actors and their spiritual leaders actually adhere to. If theater offers an exaggeration of real life, or if it needs extreme cases to prove its point, then it is understandable that the Cinarc actors make recourse to the Luba rules on adultery and its consequences. The reality of these punishments is not questioned among Kinshasa's born-again Christians, who, by contrast, invoke the authority of the Christian God to repudiate adultery. And due to its overt links with the management of the lineage, the *tshibao* phenomenon is identified as demonic, as the discussion about the closure of the production *The Open Tomb* has shown.

Concluding Notes: Playing the Games

Marriage in Kinshasa is an extremely complex field where frequently divergent and competing political and cultural forces are in play during the preparatory phase of choosing the right partner, in the decisive moments of financing and performing the marriage ceremonies, and in the conjugal life of the couple. Because choosing the right partner affects one's access to human and material resources, this quest is often the result of a struggle within the sexes and between generations (Parpart 1994: 243).

In previous chapters, I outlined how and why young Christians turn to the ideology of revival churches, in particular when resignifying witchcraft. Their sympathy for these churches accounts also for what marriage and sexuality concern. The churches offer the young newly defined kin terminologies and new marriage patterns that distance them from stated customary rules. The serials allow us to understand how revival churches transform the process of selecting marriage partners: they provide the born-again Christian community with new definitions of incest that exclude marriage partners who customarily could be considered preferential, resignify the mystical outcomes of adultery as demonic, and promote marriages within the Christian group.

Significantly, the dominant discourse of the Christian leaders and of the teleserials is not always reflected in the opinions and behavior of born-again Christians in everyday life. During the period of my fieldwork, Ndina, one of the Cinarc actresses, temporary left the troupe. She had been called back to her home region of Matadi to nurse her mother, who had suddenly fallen ill. A year after her departure, the news arrived in Kinshasa that Ndina's mother had died. Any hopes that the actress would soon return were put to rest when the troupe learned that her family had found a husband for their daughter, and that the couple was already preparing for marriage. Everyone was happy for her, for a marriage means entrance into full adulthood. Some, however, wondered whether their friend was happy with the man she was going to marry. Their reactions displayed an interesting mixture between the cultural ideal of marriage, which one has to perform to become a fully socially accepted person, and the Western ideal of the necessity of romantic love in a marriage. What surprised me most in the discourse of the Christian actors was their not-so-negative stance toward Ndina's relatives and their intervention in the marriage process. This points to the excess in fictional representations where the involvement of kin in urban marriage politics is jettisoned.

Furthermore, in the accounts that I heard about selecting a future bride and accepting a man for a husband, there is consistently a degree of choice. When a man prepares for marriage, he chooses the girl he desires to marry. Disregarding the preferences of relatives and family elders, Kinois men take the liberty of making their own choices, even if this leads to conflict in the lineage. On the girl's side there is always a degree of liberty as well. In the course of the marriage process, the girl repeatedly has to state that she accepts this boy as her husband. She also has several opportunities to express discontent at formal and informal occasions. In some cases where her own lineage does not approve of the suitor, the girl can even make serious efforts to convince her relatives of the choice she has made. Older ethnographies stress this relative degree of freedom in the choice of marriage partners, though they also mention prearranged and imposed marriages and thus present a balanced description of matrimonial politics of lineages authorities (see Mair 1969: 81–84). My young Christian informants, however, preferred to talk about the various impositions committed by the lineages, including withholding occasions on which individuals can seek their own partners. Their representation of "tradition" as compelling, and at times even exploitative, is a strategy to justify their sympathies with Christian leaders, whom they portray as helping them to break away from the constraints of the family and accordingly offering them autonomy.

Notes

1. Maman Théthé Djungandeke is known as a Christian musician. The lyrics (*Libala ewutaki na Nzambe*) are also sung by musicians who do not have an explicit religious profile, such as Tshala Mwana in her song *Petit Démon*, for example.

2. The appearance of the Christian singer Marie Missamu in the Cinarc serial is an illustration of the friendly relationships between Christian artists, singers, and actors. Marie Missamu occupies a fictional role within the serial, though she keeps the artist name by which she is known in the city.

3. Despite this dismissal of kin, Pentecostal leaders emphasize that the spouses' kin should be present during the religious marriage ceremony. The latter perform an active role in this ritual, as parents and other relatives are expected to express their agreement with the religious marriage.

4. The pastor used here the actor's screen name, by which he is best known in the city.

5. This is a literal translation of the French "*proposer quelque part,*" suggesting that place (or family) is more important than the person to whom one proposes.

6. Author's translation from the original in French.

7. Van Dijk (2004) observes a similar resignification of traditional marriage among Pentecostals in Ghana.

8. In Christian discourse, committing incest is a major sin and is considered animal-like behavior, which amounts to attributing humanity to "Christians" and animalism to "pagans." The metaphor of bestiality for incest is not unique to Christian discourse but also appears in indigenous representations of incestuous relationships.

9. Kinois variously speak of *ketyul, kinzudi,* and *kitshuili.* The latter term is far more common, although the academic literature more often gives the term *ketyul.*

10. The home region of the Yanzi group is Bandundu province.

11. People also frequently referred to Kongo marriage preferences, which show many similarities with the Yanzi arrangements (see Creten 1996: 352–370).

12. This practice of paying for food, education, and clothing of the girl to whom one is promised before her birth or during her childhood also occurs in other Congolese groups, such as the Aluund (De Boeck 1991: 231–232).

13. Creten (1996: 362), for example, describes bewitchment and cursing as possible consequences when preferential partners among the Nkanu do not marry.

14. Without a doubt, colonialism (by way of formal administration and evangelization) introduced this bilateral descent reckoning.

15. I do not imply that lineage-based marriage regulations totally conform to Lévi-Strauss's "simple structures." Creten (1996: 368), for example, indicated that the Nkanu marriage politics also entail prohibitions, and that they are

thus a mixture of "primitive" and "complex societies" (using Lévi-Strauss's vocabulary).

16. De Boeck (1991: 144) has noted the same logic for Aluund.

17. See for various Congolese groups: Yaka (Devisch 1993: 109–111), Aluund (De Boeck 1991: 144–146, 240–241; 1994), Lele (Douglas 1977[1963]: 109–110, 122–124, 217–219), Nkanu (Creten 1996: 175–176).

18. This also includes girls and women born and raised elsewhere but belonging to the ethnic group of the Luba of the Kasai.

CHAPTER 9

The Danger of Sex

Negotiating Matrimony and Urban Sexuality (Part II)

For Teresa de Lauretis, the definition and prescription of the ideal masculinities and femininities in a society are the outcome of semiotic work: meanings and values of "Man" and "Woman" emerge from signs and their interpretations. Gender is produced exactly in the act of representing. Or, to quote de Lauretis (1984: 9): "The representation falls together with presentation." In the construction and interpretation of signs, meanings and values of "manhood" and "womanhood" are shaped, and individual subjectivities are produced. This semiotic work takes place through a wide range of social and cultural technologies. Cinema, de Lauretis's main field of research, is one of these technologies; everyday practices and institutional discourses are other, interrelated technologies (de Lauretis 1987: 2). Inspired by Foucault's "technologies of the self" (1988), de Lauretis calls societal techniques that produce masculinities and femininities "technologies of gender."

As I will show, the evangelizing serials constitute one of many Christian technologies in which particular gendered and sexualized practices and identities are imbued with meaning. Furthermore, in line with the various social games at play in Kinshasa's post-Mobutu society, the Christian technologies of gender operate in a complex field where other cultural forces also transmit significations and moral values to the signifiers "man" and "woman."

Kindumba: Deviations from Accepted Sexual Practices

The regulation of sexuality is at the heart of the Pentecostal melodrama. The serials do not show explicit sexual scenes, but eroticization, sexual desire (*mposo*), and extramarital domestic sex frequently foreground the dramatic action. A wide range of extramarital sexual practices—understood from a Christian perspective as deviations—are grasped in the notion of *kindumba,* which derives from the Lingala word *ndumba.* The prototypical figure of the *ndumba* is the female protagonist in *La Kinoiserie.* This woman is normally single, uses her body to earn money, and thrives in an atmosphere of ambiance, a typical urban space-time setting. She is found drinking and dancing in bars and dresses provocatively in tight clothes that stress the shape of her body or miniskirts and short tops that reveal the upper legs and the navel (see Biaya 1996). Her male counterpart is *l'ambianceur,* a well-dressed man who enjoys going out, dancing, and drinking beer (Chapter 2).

Among Kongo groups, *ndumba* means "woman," and *kindumba* could best be translated as "femininity" (Creten 1996: 336). In literature on early colonial Léopoldville, the word *ndumba* referred to "a non-married woman." During colonial times the semantic content was extended as *ndumba* came to denote the sexual lives of unmarried women. C. Didier Gondola (1997: 68) writes that in the colonial city the word was used for women who, while remaining single, had more than one male partner at a time. The colonial administration allowed a restricted number of single women to live in the colonial city and entertain the colonial workers, often offering them sex. Nowadays, the word *ndumba* is translated as "prostitute" (Fr. *prostituée*) or "free woman" (Fr. *femme libre*), but its content transcends the categories of female sex workers and women living on their own. *Ndumba* now also denotes "promiscuous" women: married women committing adultery and unmarried women having sex.

In line with the semantic transformation of *ndumba,* the content of *kindumba* is enlarged and now denotes "asocial sexuality" or even "non-Christian sexuality" on the part of men or women. Although in general Kinois parlance *kindumba* can be performed by either gender, most of the discourse in the serials and outside the media world lays the emphasis on asocial female sexuality and often depicts men as victims of women's wicked acts and their evil nature.

A similar key concept in the construction of sexuality as professed in Kinshasa's Pentecostal-charismatic churches is *ekobo.* The Lingala word *ekobo* initially indicated incest in the sense of sexual intercourse with socially designated prohibited partners (see Chapter 8). In Kinshasa's Pentecostal churches, *ekobo* has now also come to encompass adultery, pornography, and prostitution. The semantic enlargement of both concepts (*kindumba* and *ekobo*) in Christian discourse reveals the scope of non-Christian sexuality and betrays the rigid attempts of the new religious communities to regulate sexuality and to promote the nuclear family unit as the sole social space in which sexuality can be enacted.

Figure 9.1. Detail from a mural in one of the bars in Lemba (2006, © Katrien Pype)

Sex in the City

Why do born-again Christians invest so much time and energy in the regulation of urbanites' sexual lives? And how do they construct sexuality? In the serial *The Devouring Fire,* Chapy, playing the role of a Christian leader, informs the audience about a newly published book *Sexuality Is Threatening Us* (*Le sexe nous menace*).[1] He summarizes the book's main message as follows: "Sexuality is a weapon of the Devil to bind people to him, to destroy social cohesion and to steal souls." He warns the audience that girls' nice body shapes or men's display of wealth should not encourage them to engage in sexual encounters.[2] In his short monologue, Chapy combines social politics, modern capitalism, and a spiritual understanding of sexuality. Money, sex, and witchcraft make up the core of an apocalyptic interpretation of sexuality.

Chapy explained to me, in a tone that oscillated between dejection and pugnacity, that he felt it necessary to mention this book because young Kinois are far too preoccupied with sex. According to him, it would be a difficult task to find a fourteen-year-old girl without any sexual experience. "Things were different in the times of our parents," he mused. In his view, it is abnormal that young people spend so much time on sex. With a tone of indignation he regretted that people were not following biblical rules, and he pointed me to the books of Exodus and Leviticus, where sexual intercourse is explained as an act restricted to married partners. For Chapy, the only solution to counter the sexual excesses of young urbanites is to bring them back to the Bible.

Chapy's comments are in line with the general promotion of sexual abstinence and virginity in the revival churches. If a girl who is active in the church (for example with the church band or the children's group) becomes pregnant, she will be suspended for the duration of her pregnancy. The same goes for the evangelizing drama groups. Just before my arrival one Cinarc actress had become pregnant. As soon as the troupe's leaders learned about her condition, she was asked to leave the group. After delivery the teenage mother attended rehearsals a few more times, but Bienvenu never encouraged her to join the drama group again. Christian leaders contend that pregnant girls (Sg. *maman ya mwana*) do not honor their entourage. They therefore hold that they cannot receive them into the house of God. During the period of suspension, the young mothers will frequently be closely monitored but also will receive financial assistance from the church members. They furthermore will be given spiritual assistance, something the ardent Christians consider more meaningful.

Chapy is not alone in observing an excess of sexuality in the city, nor is he overemphasizing the role of sexuality in Kinshasa's public culture. La Fontaine described the centrality of sexuality for social personhood when she studied the complex of masculinities and femininities in early postcolonial Kinshasa. As the author (1974: 97) noted, the social status of a man or woman was built chiefly on sexual success: "Sexual success, in men and women, demonstrates superiority over others." Having multiple wives and/or mistresses was regarded as the summit of a man's social prestige and derived in the first instance from one's appearance (*elili, ekeko*). Physical attractiveness (smartness of dress, clearness of skin, vitality) resulted in sexual success, earning the envy and admiration of others. La Fontaine argued that the successful man "wins prestige by having a numerous variety of attractive women as mistresses and the successful young woman has many lovers among important men" (ibid.). Social success thus meant being sexually active, a condition resulting from physical features. Today, not much has changed. This urban ideal of personhood and sexual prowess still flourishes. Kinois eagerly gossip about secret lovers and mistresses, and they frequently talk about their own appearance and that of others, even often encouraging men and women to adorn themselves in seductive and erotic ways.

It is exactly the culture of *La Kinoiserie* that celebrates sexuality and incites young Kinois to be sexually active. Modern urban music (which Christian discourse terms "music of the dark world," "music of the world," and "pagan music") is the soundtrack of the city's public culture, sparking dances enacted in public and in private. These popular dances are frequently explicitly provocative, in their names as well in the body movements that accompany them. The dances imitate sexual intercourse, although the official discourse of the choreographers or the leaders of the music groups contests these interpretations. In 2000, a censorship board was set up by the national government to monitor the lyrics and the images of music video clips. Overly explicit texts or movements are banned, and bands are forced to modify the lyrics and make the dances more decent. The censorship committee regularly orders the musicians to adjust their video clips or even rename their dances. As a result, different versions of one particular song or clip may circulate in the city at any one time: the censored version is shown on television, while versions that escape the government's control are available in music stores or distributed on tapes and DVDs. Examples of dances in vogue in Kinshasa during my fieldwork were *Nzoto ya maman elengi* (Felix Wazekwa), *Koyimbi ko* (Werrason), *Nkila mogrosso* (Papa Wemba), and *Sambara* (by Collège des Nobles). Although the singers make an effort to provide morally acceptable interpretations of the dances' names and movements, Kinois commonly interpret the official explanations about these dances as the singers' maneuvering to escape official reprimands, and they imagine the dances and lyrics primarily as evocations of sexuality. It is commonly assumed that Wazekwa sings about the physical pleasure that the body of a woman gives, Werrason dances the sexual act, Papa Wemba sings about a big penis, and Collège des Nobles imitates the act of masturbation. Provocative shouts generally accompany these dances, one example being "*Maman apesa sima, papa abeta tonga*" ("Mama is 'giving' the back so papa can start sewing"—Kofi Olomide).

These dances are enacted in bars, at concerts, in the streets, and in living rooms. Accordingly, all these spaces are transformed into feasts of sexual pleasure and erotic seduction. The movements are believed to display women's fecundity and enhance their sexual capacities. Men observe how young girls dance and read their dance skills as indicative of their sexual know-how. In the dances and the lyrics, patriarchy remains unchallenged: women dance to please men; their dancing bodies are consumed by male eyes. In this game of sexual hunting, girls are objects of masculine desire. Female urban singers such as Tshala Mwana might contest masculine violence within matrimony or men's insatiable sexual desire, but even she will never stage women as agents of their own sexual life.

Women's Attire

In the video clips of urban dance music, young women seduce the audience through their dance movements. These dancers frequently bleach their hair, wear Western-style clothes (sporty and chic, with tight trousers, short skirts, and tops that stress buttocks and breasts), and adorn their bodies with piercings (usually in the face, belly, or tongue). By contrast, video clips of Christian songs portray women in three-piece outfits or the Nigerian *bazins* (heavy, shiny cloth cut into a skirt and baggy shirt). These women consistently wear long skirts or dresses, never miniskirts or trousers.

The female urban dancers of Kinshasa's "worldly" bands inspire the tastes in fashion of many teenage girls, who imitate the dancers and parade about in the streets to attract the gaze of men, young and old. Because of such behavior, women's clothing has become one of the most obvious features of female identity that Christian churches attempt to control. Apparel is also a recurrent theme in the Pentecostal melodrama, for example in the serial *Dilemma* (discussed in Chapters 6 and 8), whose female protagonist, Monica, dresses in "bad clothes" (*bilamba mabe*). Each time she enters the living room her father is distracted by his daughter's shapely body, and this admiration turns into sexual desire. Neighbors and relatives of the household blame her mother for having bought her these clothes. Maman Deborah, Monica's mother, defends herself, arguing that she simply likes to offer her daughters the latest fashions, and that they are expected to display their beauty. Monica's fiancé, Caleb, and his parents, all born-again Christians, attempt to adjust her taste in clothing as well. Once when she shows up in a transparent blouse and skin-tight trousers, Julien, Caleb's father, asks his future daughter-in-law, "Which jungle do you come from?" In urban Christian discourse, the term "jungle" evokes "animal," which is synonymous with "pagan."

As indicated in Chapter 6, when Cinarc actors discussed the *Dilemma* serial, not only the father but the young girl and her mother as well were blamed for having "opened a door" to the Devil. This step inevitably led to the ultimate transgressive act, sex between father and daughter. It is important to draw attention to the way in which the Christian ideology has inserted fashionable Western garb worn by young girls into a frame of spiritual battle. It is said that these "bad clothes" render men weak and open the door to demons. The patriarchal ideology thus points at women as the source of evil.

The churches and the evangelizing performers invest much time and energy—not only on-screen but also in the real world—on the imposition of "good clothes" (*bilamba ya malamu*), meaning clothes that honor the person and her entourage and accordingly also God. An illustration of this occurred when the troupe was filming an episode of the *Mayimona* serial. A group of teenage girls was strolling down the street by a group of Cinarc actors who were waiting outside the compound where the Cinarc crew was filming. (So as not to overcrowd the private space of the family that had generously allowed Cinarc crew to use their home as a set, Bienvenu allowed only the actors whose scenes were being shot to enter the compound.) One of the teenage passers-by happened to be wearing a miniskirt. Mamy Moke, one of Cinarc's leading actresses, spotted the girl and crossed the street without hesitation. In a soft but firm voice, and without any introductory small talk, the TV personality told the girl not to wear that kind of skirt anymore, so as not to attract men. The young girl obviously felt ashamed to be reproved by a TV star. Looking at the ground and whispering—the best way to show someone respect in Kinshasa—she thanked Mamy Moke for her advice and continued on her way. The other Cinarc members remained silent during this brief exchange, but afterward they congratulated the actress, though they doubted whether the girl would in fact change her clothing style. "There is a lot of work to be done here," one of the others sighed.

It is important to add that Pentecostal-charismatic churches are not alone in trying to control women's attire. City authorities too consider some of the clothing worn by Kinshasa's women to be disrespectful. Concerned about the potential influence certain seductive garb may have on men, the government has several times attempted to impose a dress code. The campaign was called "tie your cloth" (*kanga liputa*). The expression refers more specifically to attempts to encourage young Kinois girls and women to forgo trousers and continue wearing the one-piece cloth that is wrapped around the hips and legs and knotted on the side, thus resembling a long skirt. On several occasions government officials and policemen have attacked women wearing trousers and even disrobed them. Such interventions from the state are, however, very sporadic and thus lack enduring significance.

The Danger of Sex

In the Christian discourse on clothing, sexuality is never far away. That discourse perceives the body as a part of God that should constantly be glorified and honored. Christians are called to honor their God by respecting their body and having sex only within a Christian marriage. They are taught that sexuality is pure only as long as it is confined to the setting of heterosexual marriage.[3] "You automatically become one body (*une seule chair, nzoto moko*). But, be aware, it is not only married couples who become one," the pastor's spouse said with much persuasion during the weekly prayer gathering with the drama group. "In sexual contact, there are also demons present, so if he or she hosts demons, they will enter into your body. The Bible says, the *onction* is transmittable; demons are as well!" In this discourse, sexual behavior outside of wedlock is represented as being more dangerous than conjugal sex, since there is consistently a chance that one's partner is an accomplice of the Devil. Bodily fluids such as semen, blood, and saliva might also transmit these spirits. To prevent harmful spiritual transgression, Pentecostal authorities advise young men and women not to touch their friends or fiancés. The body itself becomes a frontier for preserving the sacredness of sexuality. Within this Christian sphere, only God and one's husband or wife should perceive one's naked body (*bolumbu*). Of course, this reading of the spiritual implications of sexuality is not exclusively Christian. Customary thinking also displays a firm belief in the intrusion of spiritual qualities through the exchange of body liquids like semen and menstrual blood (see Bekaert 2000, Creten 1996, De Boeck 1991, and Devisch 1993). The demonization of the spiritual intrusions, however, is a product of the general apocalyptic imagination that has been installed since the mid 1990s.

The belief of an exchange of spirits through sex is more fully articulated in discussion of the phenomenon of the "Mario," a name given to unmarried men, frequently teenagers, who engage in sexual relationships with older, usually married, women. The phenomenon of older women seeking out beautiful, strong, healthy young men for sexual companionship was the topic of Kinshasa's first serial, *Small Chicken* (*Mwana Nsosu*), broadcast in 1981. More than thirty years later, it is still a common theme in local serials: in *The Moziki Women*, Maman Jeanne seduces her daughter's suitor, Chapy; and, in *The Nanas Benz*, Paco is seduced by the older Maman Jeanne, who promises him a nice car and clothes in return for his sexual services. These relationships are no longer a central topic of the post-Mobutu serials, though offscreen the actors talk about it a lot.

According to my informants, young boys need to be very careful, since women hunt for them in order to "steal their success" (*koyiba lupemba*) through sexual intercourse. One's success is held to be captured in a star, a spiritual entity. It is said that all men and women are born with a particular star (*minzoto*). This star, closely linked to one's soul, denotes the progress and social success that a person might possess. Only people with "four eyes" can perceive this star. It is assumed that through occult means, one can steal someone else's star to lift one's own success. In the fusion of body fluids, sexual partners exchange their stars. Hence popular discourse holds that older women sleep with younger men to steal their star. In this type of sexual encounter the women become younger by acquiring the young man's star. This popular notion seems to be gendered, as none of my informants could confirm the assumption of stealing a star as a motivation for sexual relationships between young girls and older men.[4] Although social anthropologists would be tempted to understand the condemnation of "Mario" relationships as a result of the intergenerational confusion these liaisons produce, born-again Christians emphasize the spiritual transgression of such sexual encounters.

A related and often recurring theme in Kinshasa's serials is the existence of "wives of the night" (Sg. *mwasi ya butu*). The teleserials use special effects to show how female spirits visit sleeping male characters, with whom they have sexual relations in the spirit world. From a Western point of view we would call these experiences erotic dreams. Kinois, however, and Christian leaders in particular, do not treat these visions as fantasies of the mind but as dangerous physical encounters with occult spirits (Pype 2011a). These beliefs relate to what has been described in ethnographies of Congolese groups. Devisch (1993: 98), for example, has documented that the baYaka consider erotic dreams inauspicious as they foretell divorce, witchcraft, or death. Among born-again Christians erotic dreams are perceived to be both a cause and an effect of witchcraft. It is said that erotic dreams are occasions for impure spirits to visit their partners, with whom they often have children in the world of the invisible.[5] A similar discourse is used to explain homosexuality. Men physically attracted to men are believed to be possessed by a female spirit. The reverse accounts for lesbian women. All these explanations indicate that, within the Pentecostal milieu, one's gender and sexuality are to a high degree defined by one's double, one's invisible complement to the self.

God's Men Making Meaning of Sex

In an interview I had with Nene on the subject of these spiritual liaisons, and in particular with regard to erotic dreams, she explained that one should immediately shout out Jesus's name to chase these evil spirits away. When I asked her whether she had already experienced this herself, she confessed that all her knowledge about occult spirits and their actions stemmed from the churches. This remark compelled me to examine the extent of the pastors' authority in the interpretation of sexual experiences.

The Pentecostal churches transmit their interpretation of sexuality and their vision of appropriate sexual behavior in various ways. In special weekly gatherings organized for women, the pastors—and more importantly, their spouses—lead sexual instruction sessions for adolescent Kinois girls and married women. Much of their teaching is coded in a gendered morality that redraws the boundaries between "good" and "bad" or "impure" sexual behavior. The strength of the sermons given by *maman pasteur* lies in her constant reference to conversations she has had with women during the week. Maman Bibiche once introduced the theme "husbands and wives of the night" as follows: "Today's theme is inspired by many complaints of women who told me that during the night they dreamt of having intercourse with other men. Some even dreamt of sleeping with a woman. I will tell you that these experiences have an invisible origin. These are bad spirits, which have entered into your body." In their structure and atmosphere, these sessions resemble the Sunday service: prayers, Christian songs, and Christian dances open and close the teaching portion of the service, during which the audience takes notes of the Bible verses cited by the speaker and her exposition. Women are then not so much blamed for being possessed by evil spirits but for enjoying their presence: "And you like it. You know that the only thing you should do is shout '*au nom de Jesus,*' but no, you do not do it. Why not? Because you like it!" I once heard the pastor's wife challenging her audience. In this way women are told that they can modify their situation, and that the church offers a solution to problems concerning infertility, frigidity, lack of sexual intercourse with one's husband, erotic fantasies, and masturbation.

Separate instructional sessions are organized for youth. Some include both genders, while others are aimed at young men and women independently. The Church of the Eternal Army, for example, holds a session each Wednesday called "Sons of Abraham" (Les Fils d'Abraham), while the girls of this church meet on Friday afternoons in meetings labeled "Daughters of Sarah" (Les Filles de Sarah). Both gatherings are filmed and then broadcast in different time slots on the church's own television channel, Radio-Television of the Eternal Army (RTAE). During these gender-specific meetings, the youth receive biblical and Christian instructions on aspects of gendered social behavior. The screened meetings address themes such as "How to recognize a Christian girl?" "How does the Devil work through clothes?" and "How does a Christian boy differ from a non-Christian boy in his speech?"

A second genre of mass-mediated programs on gender and sexuality is aired late in the evening or at night.[6] These are Christian shows dealing more explicitly with issues of sexuality, a prime example being *Matrimonial Harmony* (*Harmonie conjugale*).[7] One frequently hears facetious metaphors like "St. Joseph" for penis, "Internet" for vagina, "to connect" or "*kosala feti*"—to party—for sexual intercourse, and so on. This program is a public forum for discussing overtly sexual matters such as appropriate Christian positions during sexual intercourse, preparations for a woman to undergo deep penetration, or the whys and hows of oral sex. Such shows are addressed to both engaged and married couples.

Media broadcasts on matrimony and sexuality are extremely popular in Kinshasa and other African cities (Spronk 2009: 194; Graetz 2010). Rachel Spronk (2009: 203), who has studied print and audiovisual magazines in Kenya dealing with love, adultery, and sexuality, argues that the popularity of these media outlets follows the disappearance of various "traditional" counselors in the matters, such as the aunt. The same can be argued for Kinshasa's context, where many youth complained about the lack of sexual orientation provided by relatives (grandparents and aunts) who, they knew, had performed this function in their parents' generation. Here too, Kinshasa's pastors have taken over the role, using both physical and virtual gatherings to transmit their knowledge and values concerning love, intimacy, and the problems that can arise during one's sexual life.

The distinct time slots in which the two kinds of television programs on sexuality are broadcast reflect the local idea that sexuality ideally belongs to the night (*ya butu*). Furthermore, the distinct formats of the shows reveal the churches' varying attitudes with regard to the respective target audiences. The shows produced for an adolescent public—"youth"—stage adult Christian spiritual leaders seated at a desk, reading and expounding on biblical verses. In this exegesis, the adolescent audience is portrayed as unknowing, and in some instances even as "pagan." A hierarchy is established in the unidirectional transfer of knowledge from the screen to the viewer (who is often encouraged to take notes): the Christian leader knows all, while the audience knows nothing and should take in all the information by listening and watching carefully. In sharp contrast with this pattern, the late-night shows address married couples ("adults"). The talk show hosts, usually a man and a woman, respond to phone calls from spectators. Other viewers may weigh in on questions. This particular format gives the audience a voice and the chance to participate, thereby treating viewers and hosts as equal participants when touching on the "adult" topic of sexuality.

Similarly, the churches organize special gatherings to discuss the theme of sexuality. These meetings are open to engaged and married couples only, and admission is strictly controlled. In comparison, radio and television programs have far less control over the composition of their audiences. I noticed in the two houses where I lived during fieldwork that many adolescents are quite eager to watch these late-night shows and actively participate in the sort of debates on sexuality from which they are otherwise excluded.

The sophisticated formats in which issues such as dress code, matrimonial interaction, and also sexual proficiency can be discussed underscore that the politics of Pentecostal leaders regarding gender and sexuality are diversified according to the youth-adult paradigm. Further, the differentiated distribution of authority to speak on these matters is reflected in the spatial layout and the temporalities in which sexuality is discussed, in the church setting as well as in mass-mediated instruction sessions.

The evangelizing teleserials also partake in the instruction of accepted and disapproved sexuality. These TV dramas project multiple possibilities for man-woman sexual relationships, some of which are devalued and others more appreciated by the producers. A rich catalogue of deceit, manipulation, and cleverness is offered, as older oral literature in Africa (see Beidelman 1997; Verbeek 2006) also conveyed. Considerable attention is devoted to anomalies in courting and conjugal life, abuse of and between women and men, false promises, and pregnancy out of wedlock. Like city gossip, the tales describe society in its most perverse forms. In contrast to the cultural heroes of the *pasteur* and, by extension, his wife, men and women are depicted as egoistic humans who are easily seduced by demons. Sexuality, wealth, and beauty form a devilish triad endangering social order.

The Maquis Boys and Girls: Sex for Money

In the serial *The Maquis Boys and Girls,* the emphasis lies on two themes of urban sexuality: homosexuality (lesbianism)[8] and the commoditization of sexuality, also called the phenomenon of *kochina* (or "the three C's"—*chic-choc-chèque*).[9] The serial's six episodes recount the whereabouts of two groups of last year's pupils (a boys' and a girls' group) who retreat into the *maquis* to prepare for the final, state-organized exam to obtain a high school diploma. In this social withdrawal of high school students, boys and girls retire, in sexually segregated groups of five to eight or ten, to annexes of compounds in order to study during the two or three months before this final exam (usually held in June or July).

A subplot of the serial offers a political critique, showing how teachers and school directors set their own price for participation in the final exam. Pupils' parents complain about fluctuation in the prices and accuse the government of not controlling the corrupt teachers. However, this critique remains vague ("the government"), and the serial voices only general social complaints without putting the artists at any risk. Most attention is allotted to the sexual lives of the pupils in seclusion. The boys and girls, freed for a specific amount of time from parental or familial supervision, are shown to engage in illicit sexuality. This "unchristian" behavior is discussed in lengthy scenes that portray the *maquis* as a space of libertinage: it is a world of unbounded sexual activity, featuring perversions like lesbianism and even the spread of HIV. For most Cinarc actors, the sexual freedom in the *maquis* is an experienced reality. The Cinarc actress Nadine Massamba, for example, had been three months pregnant when she left her *maquis*. Like Nadine, most of the Cinarc members had entered the *maquis* in what they called their "old" and "pagan" life and felt they had to warn the public about the unchristian atmosphere of these youth camps.

In the serial, the Cinarc artists portray the boys and girls in the groups as a mixture of "pagans," "Christians of the flesh," and "real Christians," being a community where evangelization is probable. The non-

Christians are shown to be extremely intolerant of the Christians, preventing them from reading the Bible or saying their prayers out loud. In addition, the non-Christians disrespect God's men. At times, for example, they chase Pastor Chapy, who visits his sister in the *maquis*, or they begin to question the value of the biblical Word. Revenge, however, is sweet: in the end the "pagans" and the "false Christians" fail to obtain their diplomas. On the other hand, the "real Christians," who have understood the necessity of studying instead of engaging in sexual affairs and fights, have merited their diplomas.

Kochina, or the Commoditization of Love

In the same serial, Gemima and Caroline often leave the compound to meet Julien and Fataki, two older men (sugar daddies, *papa chéri, super-papa*) who turn out to be their friends' fathers. Colleagues with prosperous careers in an international communications office in the city center, the two men evoke a classy milieu with their apparel, cars, and accents when speaking French. Attracted by these signs of wealth, the two girls eagerly accept when, after a chance meeting, the men invite them to a restaurant and later take them to a hotel.

The sexual relationship between young teenage girls and older men is a common theme in Kinshasa's popular culture and elsewhere in Africa (Cole and Thomas 2009). It relates to a dominant feature of the scenery in the city's bars and hotels: one frequently sees girls as young as thirteen in the company of older men, having dinner and often drinking beer. Usually one notices how the girl sits uncomfortably, waiting for the beer or the dinner to be finished. She knows that people know that she is linked in a sexual way to the man she is with. People do not ask her questions, but if they know the man they will greet him. He might introduce her as his "niece" (*cousine*), but people know better.

These young girls embody the type of the "bad girl." They belong to the group of "*série 8*" or "*série 9,*" notably the girls born during the decades of the 1980s and 1990s who, at the time of fieldwork, were still adolescents in their late teens or early twenties. These girls are also called *kamoke sukali sukali* ("sugar sugar") or *fioti-fioti* (a word derived from kiKongo meaning "very small"). Men also refer to these girls as *katola-soif,* a kiKongo-French word group, which could best be translated as "thirst-quencher" (kiKongo: *katola*). They constitute the cohort of young women that govern the city's public image and discourse about urban women: young, mobile girls who stroll around the city in seductive clothes and exhibit their bodies during erotic dances. The relationships that men have with these girls differ from the notorious *deuxième bureau* ("second office") or the *tiroir* system ("shelves"). These bureaucratic metaphors for modern urban polygamous relationships denote long-standing extramarital sexual liaisons with women past adolescence. In such affairs, the men are expected to contribute financially to the housing, feeding, and clothing of their mistresses. Usually they do not take the *deuxième bureau* out to bars or do not appear in public with them. By contrast, they adore parading the young girls around in cars and bars, where they offer them money and luxurious commodities (particularly Western fashions and jewelry).

Turning back to the serial, the many publicity shots that intersperse *The Maquis Boys and Girls'* story line are embedded in this gift giving: sugar daddies take their young lovers to supermarkets, where they buy them products like Western-style clothes, food (milk cartons, French wine, chocolate, etc.) and hygiene products (shampoo, shower gel, perfume, etc.). Most of these commodities not only move the young girls into a global consumer world but also add to the girls' physical attractiveness. Furthermore, these gifts contribute to the girls' financial independence. For example, Caroline's own informal commercial activity (selling hair extensions) is initiated by a generous gift from Papa Julien.

More importantly, the serial successfully spells out how not only the girls but also the men benefit from these relationships. Julien and Fataki bring their young girlfriends to a luxurious hotel. After a lengthy visit to all the rooms and repeated mention of the address and the phone numbers of the hotel owners, the two men engage in a potlatch-like practice when seducing the girls: when Papa Fataki offers Gemima a necklace, Papa Julien replies, "Watch what I will do!" and gives his young girlfriend his mobile phone. From the men's perspective, these relationships are opportunities for a sexual life outside of matrimony and also occasions to behave like "big men" capable of bestowing gifts upon non-kin, hence heightening their social esteem.

The cultural phenomenon of young female lovers dating older, married, wealthy men originates in the cultural grid of sexualized social personhood: "A man with money is a real man, while a girl's body defines her femininity" (*Mobali mobali mbongo, mwasi mwasi nzoto*). The logically derived interaction between the two genders, then, involves the exchange of money for sex. These urban male-female relationships are based on the same principle as the practice of a man providing for the material needs of his future spouse. In urban centers, men claim the sexual services of these girls by paying for their school fees and giving them material objects. In general, giving gifts outside the context of the customary marriage ceremony is a way of making a claim on a woman's sexual services (see Collier and Rosaldo 1981: 286). The exchange of wealth for sex is thus not an urban invention but is based on more indigenous approaches concerning the regulation of sexuality and the choice of sexual partners. In the case of domestic work and financial contributions performed by the "owner" of a *ketiyul* (Chapter 8), the commoditization of sexual relationships clearly constitutes a large part of courting practices.

Nowadays, among Kinshasa's female youth, the most poignant manifestation of the interrelationship between money and love resides in the phenomenon *Chic-Choc-Chèque* (also called *3C*) and the practice of *kochina*.[10] Both practices refer to sexuality from a female perspective and could best be described as informal polyandry. Many teenage and adolescent girls are engaged in social relationships with multiple men, each of whom provides different services for the girl. This kind of transactional sexuality has been documented all over Africa (Cole and Thomas 2009). Urban unmarried girls use their body and sexuality to get their school fees paid, to dress well, to go out to fancy clubs, to have enough units on their mobile phones, and so on. These different men are typically kept apart and have no clue about their competitors. One man pays for her clothes (*chic*), another man is there to have sex with (*choque*), and she is dating a third man to pay her school fees (*chèque*). Biaya (2001) encountered the same practice in Senegal. For Dakar, Biaya (2001: 80) writes that this phenomenon is mostly observed on the university campus. In Kinshasa, the phenomenon is widespread and also includes girls who do not go to school.

As various people told me, conflicts frequently arise when one of the suitors learns about his rivals. As soon as the man the girl prefers has gathered enough money to pay the bride price, he supersedes his competitors. Meanwhile, a girl who has three different men paying for different services is not necessarily sleeping with all of them. Promises of waiting until they are certain of one another, excuses about menstruation, and giving men a hard time by meeting them in public spaces such as bars and avoiding going to hotels with them are tactics these girls often use to keep the men attached to them without actually having sex.

There is a slight difference between *kochina* and the *3C* phenomenon. *Kochina* is a pidgin Lingala word derived from the French verb *chiner*. A dictionary translates this as "to tease, to pull one's leg, to horse around," although it does not fully capture the exploitative intentions of the playful relationship. One informant explained the verb by referring to La Fontaine's fable of the raven and the fox: the raven manipulates the fox in such a way that he manages to steal the cheese from the fox's mouth. Similarly, young Kinois girls manipulate older men for financial means by promising these men sex but seldom engaging in it. A girl will often bring female peers or siblings to a date with an older man, thus preventing the man from inviting her to a hotel. She keeps the promise of sexual intercourse alive but delays it time after time. Such a girl is called a *muchina*. In this case the sex does not take place, making this practice less difficult for Christian girls who are attached to the preservation of their virginity.

Nevertheless, Christians harshly condemn these practices. From a Christian perspective, *kochina* is denounced as stealing. One female informant explained: "*Kochina* is prohibited in the Bible. It is theft. The Bible does not permit flatteries. Once I connect with a person for his money, I am a thief. There are three sins within the *kochina:* flatteries, lies and theft. The Bible forbids all three of them." Unsurprisingly, my Cinarc informants all condemned *kochina* and even referred to it as prostitution (*ekobo*). Still, most of them regarded the three C's as a general feature of urban sexual life for both single and married people. Interestingly, many of the young born-again Christians blamed parents for introducing their daughters into these sexual networks. They argued that girls were pushed by their parents to get in touch with older men, from whose money both the girls and their families could benefit.[11]

In line with the young Christians' general aversion to these sexual networks, the serial *The Maquis Boys and Girls* denounces this polyandry. The disapproval of *kochina* is primarily manifested in Gemima's character. Although Gemima is engaged to Caleb, she has sexual relations with several people: her teacher (to obtain good exam results), Fataki (to obtain luxury commodities), and JR, a *mikiliste* (to gain entrance to the world of Europeans). She furthermore has a lesbian relationship with Mamy. JR infects her with the HIV virus, which she transmits to Mamy and Fataki. As soon as her future husband learns about her HIV-positive status, he cancels the marriage preparations, emphasizing that he had invariably been faithful and reminding her of God's law that sexuality should be enacted within matrimony. In the close to the serial, Gemima, JR, and Fataki all die. The message is clear: if Gemima had refrained from sexual relationships, she would still be alive and able to/about to enter marriage.

Next to death, the serial also exposes the social damage that stems from the intergenerational imbalance inherent in these sexual relationships. The sexual partners confuse the ideal encounters between the generations and threaten conjugal unity. One of the Christian housewives in *The Maquis Boys and Girls* says: "I notice that the young girls do not fear old papas anymore." The verb "to fear" (*kobanga*) denotes both fear and respect, which is normally played out in standardized patterns of avoidance behavior, in view of creating physical distance. Furthermore, in several hilarious scenes Gemima and Caroline have to hide when the sugar daddies, looking for their lovers, encounter their own daughters in the *maquis*, or when a friend recognizes her father's watch on Caroline's wrist. All this leads the two young girls and the two fathers to lie, thus committing another Christian sin. The love affairs culminate in a crisis when Caroline learns that she is pregnant. Following a widespread custom dictating that unmarried pregnant women be dropped at the home of the baby's father until the baby's birth, Caroline's relatives arrive with the schoolgirl at Julien's house.

In discussing the topic of this polyandry, the Christian artists all denigrated the *Chic-Choc-Chèque* phenomenon on the basis of the abovementioned Christian arguments. As "Christians," they all stated, they could not enter into these kinds of relationships any more. Several of the actresses confessed of having benefited from lovers' gifts in return for sex, and some of them even had children born out of these relationships. However, they all firmly contended that these relationships belonged to the "pagan" lives they had led before they had come to know Jesus. Of course it was especially difficult to verify my informants' claims in this domain. I suspected a few of the girls of receiving, or having received, money and clothing from men. Chapter 3 details the case of Mamy Moke, who eventually talked to me about her relationship with an older, married man. The secrecy that generally attends these kinds of relationships hindered me from obtaining information that countered their public discourse. Another reason—probably the most important one—was that these actors and actresses invest great effort in protecting their public identity as "evangelizing Christians" and thus are even more inclined to hide these relationships.

The case is somehow different for the male actors, who frequently bring girls along to the filming sessions. These girls are introduced as their fans, their cousins, or even "sisters" from churches that they visit. If there is music around, the actors often start dancing with these girls to Christian music, though not to the "worldly" music. I also noticed how the men borrowed money from each other (and from the actresses) to pay for their female guests' food and drinks. (They gave these girls only soft drinks—never beer.) Though the particular joy and ambiance that accompanied these encounters betrayed flirting and courting, such gifts were easily dismissed as mere tokens of politeness and part of the public relations television stars should take care of. It is important to note that, for the actors, their identity as "Christian artists" provides them with ample opportunities to meet girls and to stage themselves as "big men" using the same strategy (the giving of gifts) that is shown in the serials.

Opposing Messages

Christian leaders constitute only one particular channel in the transmission of information and instruction concerning sexuality. Kinois teens are exposed to other values and norms that often contrast sharply with those propagated by the churches. Peers and popular media encourage young Kinois to be sexually active. As for parents, their advice is often confusing. I observed how one widowed mother, herself a born-again Christian, attempted to control her daughter's wanderings and social network. Although she was never informed of any lovers, the mother suspected that her daughter was sexually active. Through a game of concealing and lying, the girl managed to keep secret her affair with an older, unmarried man who regularly visited another family in the compound. Yet the daughter's behavior aroused suspicion nonetheless, whereupon her mother would harshly enjoin her not to act too familiar with this man, warning her that engaging in "stupid things" with him was unacceptable. Meanwhile, while gossiping with her daughter and another woman about another girl visiting a bachelor in the compound too frequently, this same mother repeated a few times that premarital sex was needed "in order to bind your lover to you." Her speech clearly echoed the correlation between sexual activity and social success described by La Fontaine (see above).

It is indeed very important to acknowledge that the city's logic of sexual lovers as indexes of social success and the precarious economy inciting young women to use their sexuality for money make it difficult, and sometimes even unfeasible, for young born-again Christians to remain sexually inactive until they are married. This was brought home to me when the Cinarc actress Nene confessed that she was shocked to hear some other actresses openly discuss how many times a month they had sex. When Nene told them that she had never even slept with her *fiancé*, nobody believed her and they all started laughing. This conversation disturbed Nene, who came to realize that the other girls were not as Christian as they hoped others would believe. For Nene, her virginity is what she is most proud of. The contrast with the other actresses in the drama group is striking: some girls were teenage mothers,[12] while rumors about others' sexual lives and partners abounded among the audience and the other group members.

These data present us with an image of the Christian drama group as a heterogeneous amalgam of "real Christians" and "Christians of the flesh" who jointly spread a Christian ideology that they themselves do not consistently follow in their own practices. The plurality of values and norms of gender and sexuality encourages the young Christian leaders to construct a particular public identity that does not necessarily coincide with their private identity. Thus we could state that Kinshasa's Christian TV actors are first of all Kinois and only secondarily "Christian."

Women and Social Power: *The Moziki Women* and *Vedettes*

All the practices and discourses described above produce a complex image of "womanhood" (*kimwasi*). The complexity derives from the much-polarized politics of representing Kinshasa's women. On the one hand, it depicts them as hardworking, ardent in their faith, and ingenious in finding ways for their households to survive in a precarious economy. This ideal type of woman is embodied by the married Christian wife. Her opposite is the jealous woman who manipulates her body and beauty to bind men (in particular married men) to her, often by making use of occult forces. Portrayals of such amoral women make up most of the lead roles in Kinshasa's moralizing TV dramas.

An example is *The Open Tomb,* in which only Theresia is identified as responsible for adultery. The *maboke* clearly indicates how, attracted by the promises of the capital city, she abandons her own husband in Mbuji-Mayi and longs for the privileges a sexual involvement with a wealthy (though married) Kinois man may offer. Her desire for material well-being and a better future for her own offspring encourages this woman to break up her best friend's marriage and steal her husband. Although Makubakuba agrees to the adulterous relationship (after several hesitations), it is the woman's efforts to gain this man that are emphasized in the serial. Makubakuba is depicted as the passive object of Theresia's egoistic longings and the occult work that she falls back on to fulfil them. The emphasis on her wrongdoings coincides with the patriarchal tone of the immorality of adultery, both in "traditional" beliefs and practices and in the Christian Pentecostal imaginations of matrimony and sexuality. Adultery by the man usually does not lead to divorce, but a straying wife is a critical problem (see Mair 1969: 3).

Kinois also take the wicked identity of women for granted. A proverb says, "To eat with a woman is to eat with a witch" (*Kolia na mwasi, kolia na ndoki*). Both male and female informants gave several arguments to sustain the idea that women are born witches. For instance, they held that jealousy, an emotion understood as both the cause and effect of occult action, is a typical female emotion. In the same vein, my informants would quote a proverb that expresses the idea of women as instigators of rupture and incongruity: "Women cannot build a village" (*Basi batongaka mboka te*), for their jealousy and quarrels render social harmony unattainable. Furthermore, they continue, does the Bible not inform us that Eve and the serpent conspired against Adam? In all this, it is said that women are much more in tune with the spiritual world than men are, which explains the more emotional attitude of woman and the more rational attitude of men. It was frequently related to me that women have an invisible power that men lack. According to one of my female informants, the Devil understood that he had to align with or conquer this innate female power in order to accomplish his mission. The discourse about women's occult connections is accordingly shaped by an amalgamation of Christianity and customary ideologies.[13]

While the category of "manhood" (*kimobali*) is problematized as well, Kinshasa is predominantly a masculine city (see Bernard 1972; De Boeck 2004).[14] The city seems to direct its (masculine) gaze at women, and even when men are accused of deviant or sinful behavior, it is often a woman (wife, mistress, or other female figure in the social vicinity) who is identified as the cause of all wrongs. It is probably no coincidence that the "bad boy" rarely occurs in the serials and is never granted the status of a protagonist.

The recurring staging of woman's (im)morality in the *maboke* indicates that "womanhood" is a constant matter of discussion constituting a field of contrasting images and emotions: a woman is at once adored and blamed, worshipped and despised. The incessant and firm attention to women's behavior derives from the central symbolic value of "womanhood" for society, power, and the future of society (see de Lauretis 1984; Rofel 1994). In postcolonial Kinshasa, female identity, with all its implications in the realms of matrimony and sexuality, faces acute dilemmas as the city undergoes rapid social transformation: intergenerational relationships are transforming ideas about "youth" and endangering gerontocratic privileges, and women's emancipation is not only presented through mass media and schooling but also encouraged in often aggressive NGO campaigns that question the "traditional" subordinate position of women and promote matrimonial behavior inspired by Western ideals of equality. Furthermore, young adolescent women create new identities and take up new social positions, thereby augmenting a relative sense of autonomy. These new roles frequently take them outside the domestic domain into schools and economic areas. All this gives rise to new cultural dilemmas about what counts as good moral behavior for girls and women. The main question is: Where are the contours of an accepted autonomy for women? The following section of this chapter will focus on the representation of women and the control of the actresses in the drama group.

Representing Ur ban Women's Associations

Urban women's associations are an important theme in Kinshasa's serials. Cinarc treated urban women's groupings in *The Moziki Women, The Nanas Benz,* and *Apostasy.* The serial *The Moziki Women* (January–March 2004), depicts a moziki group of eight wealthy women who gather weekly in a bar or in a private home, invariably a luxurious space. Moziki groups—women's associations renowned for their parties and conspicuous consumption of wealth—have been attacked by men since their earliest appearance. Suzanne Comhaire-Sylvain (1968: 265) quotes a letter (1948) by a reader, Henri Bongolo, chief of an unidentified neighborhood: "one of the factors that contribute the most to discredit the marriage in favo[u]r of prostitution are the innumerable women's associations." Thirty years later the Congolese researcher Katshay Tshilunga Ntambwe (1983) encouraged the same idea when he lamented that the moziki groups favored the infidelity of married women, since the display of wealth that these meetings required urged women to look for an additional man (*pneu de reserve,* "spare tire") who could provide them with money or luxury items like jewelry and expensive clothing. The author describes these associations as social spaces fostering competition between fellow moziki women through the social need to show up at each gathering in new clothing, jewelry, and perfume. Furthermore, the internal division into a particular subgroup of moziki women, whose members are identified as "moziki of the house" (*moziki ya ndako*) and have the right to be informed about all familial intimacy, often feeds conjugal conflicts through bad advice and jealousy.

Exactly the same negative perception of the moziki groups was conveyed in the Cinarc serial *The Moziki Women* twenty years later. All its female protagonists are "big women" (*basi ya kilo,* women with weight), or women with great social prestige: they occupy an important economic position that renders them financially independent from their husbands. Theresia works at the market, selling expensive Nigerian cloth; Mamy La Chatte works in a local phone center; and Charlainne runs a perfume shop. Their meetings are depicted as moments of conspicuous consumption: in weekly rotation, one of the women invites the other moziki members to share a meal by either inviting them to dinner at a restaurant or having their housemaids prepare ostentatious meals in their homes. These moziki meetings are presented as revolving around jewelry and clothes, thereby constituting a rivalry or competition between these women. Alcohol and "pagan" dances accompany these gatherings. Inevitably, in the serial, jealousy and hatred enter into these female networks, inciting the women to steal each other's husbands. Charlainne seduces Mamy La Chatte's husband, while Maman Jeanne dates Gemima's future son-in-law. Suspicion about these affairs mounts among the fellow moziki women, and the emerging conflicts eventually lead to death: Mamy La Chatte wrongly suspects Melina of dating her husband and kills her by poison. The end of the serial depicts a triple murder and a suicide: the soldier Paco catches his wife, Mamy La Chatte, with her lover in the corridor of a hotel and kills them both along with Charlainne, Mamy La Chatte's rival; he then commits suicide.

Two weeks after the broadcast of this serial's last episode, the female protagonists were invited onto the television program *Theater in the Townships* (*Théâtre en Cité*). This show welcomes performers to discuss and explain their fictional characters and the serials' narratives. Inspired by the upcoming International Women's Day on 8 March, the interviewer asked the actresses to articulate the main message of *The Moziki Women* for the female audience. Anne and Mamy Moke acknowledged the social and economic value of these female spaces, yet they also warned the audience that chaos could emerge from them if jealousy had a chance to enter. The actresses emphasized that women should not forget that their primary duty lay in the realm of the household, and that these female associations should by no means be privileged over the house and over domestic duties, such as caretaking of their children and husbands.

The fascination with these female associations led to another serial a year later, *The Nanas Benz* (March–June 2005). Influenced by the notorious Nanas Benz of Lomé (Togo), the serial again depicted a small group of five women with privileged positions, beautiful clothes, houses, cars, and jewelry. *The Moziki Women* had paid more attention to the negative social and domestic consequences of these associations, whereas *The Nanas Benz* strongly emphasized the occult origin of these women's riches, depicting the women characters as emissaries of the occult who, in exchange for money and other commodities, broke up the households of Christian leaders.

Cinarc's leader indicated that the inspiration for both serials (*The Moziki Women* and *The Nanas Benz*) stemmed from his personal memories: during his childhood, his mother had been part of a moziki group, which caused her to abandon domestic chores and leave the nurturing of her children to other relatives. He contended that his mother would frequently come home very late, penniless and drunk. "She neglected her children," he firmly stated.[15] In particular during the shootings of the *The Moziki Women*, Bienvenu repeatedly informed me that this serial was explicitly directed against his mother. The negative image he had constructed of his mother in his memory would now be presented in his serials.

Why did the troupe's leader consider these female spaces to be detrimental? What does it say about the status of "woman" and "womanhood"? In my view, the representation of the women's associations as islands of rivalry and the nonsocial displays a patriarchal anxiety about women's privileged social position when they compete with men in a men's world. Women's participation in the urban public sphere and in economic activities is fraught with social stigma, in particular in cases where it makes them more powerful than men. Several statements by the fictional characters in the serial *Apostasy* underscore this interpretation. While *The Moziki Women* and *The Nanas Benz* put more emphasis on the social consequences and give a spiritual interpretation to this "abnormal" position of women in a patriarchal society, *Apostasy* explicitly displays how these "heavy women" subvert the social logic of women as domestic beings controlled by their husbands.

In *Apostasy*, four women create a female group associated with Paco's church. Participation in this group, called Femmes-En-Action (FAC), consumes much time and money: the women gather daily, buy clothes for Pasteur Paco, and prepare for the visit of a Nigerian prophet. One searches for a house in which to lodge the prophet, another buys him a car, and others seek furniture, clothing, and food for their distinguished guest. The devotion to this women's group is total and thus threatens the primary tasks they should fulfill as mothers and wives. They no longer prepare food for their husbands, and they constantly seek nieces and other young girls to look after their children and even to replace their work in the household. When the men of their houses protest, these women contest their husbands' authority. This leads Julien (Deborah's husband) to ask a rhetorical question once his wife has left the house again: "Is she the man or am I the man of this house?" Kuaku refuses to take up the domestic work and informs Fataki (Theresia's husband), "You are a man, you should remain a man" (*Ozali mobali, otikali mobali*). The three complaining men are supported by Pastor Shekina, who contends that "a wife should in the first instance take care of her family."

The three serials depict how paid work, urban associations, and church groups create spaces for women that compete with their primary duties to husbands and children. The women have become "masculine women" (*basi mobali*).[16] This concept refers to women who have taken up the tasks and social roles of men and accordingly exert authority usually attributed to men.[17] The representation of these women expresses the gradual erosion of patriarchy. Domestic order is threatened by women's activities outside of the domestic sphere. Man and woman each have their specific role to play: men's is in the public sphere, while women should await them at home.

The Pentecostal churches offer an alternative to these types of "bad womanhood" and "bad associations": *maman pasteur,* the pastor's wife, and the church women's groups. The pastor's spouse is the ideal housewife. She has become the emblem of the virtuous and successful modern urban woman. Married, often with offspring, she encourages her husband in his social and spiritual work. She is strong in her faith (at times even stronger than her husband), has a group of female dependents surrounding her (the women of the church), and reaps all benefits of her husband's privileged status: she wears beautiful clothes, can travel, and is never short of money. She is *supermaman,* the mother of not only her own offspring but also of all the children and women of the church. Furthermore, the pastor's wife moves between the home and the church, thus shifting between the culturally accepted domestic interior and the religious space. As such, *maman pasteur* has become the most socially prestigious category in Kinshasa's female world, and it is also depicted as such in the telenarratives. Still, I would not call her the heroine of the Pentecostal melodrama, for she is never granted the leading role. The supporting role of this fictional character very well expresses the supporting role a woman ideally occupies in public and private life.

Of utmost importance in the signification of *maman pasteur* as the "best big woman" is the domestication of the moziki groups within the Christian social and spatial setting. At the Church of the Holy Mountain, this group was called the Women in Flames (Les Femmes de Flamme). Other churchwomen's groups are called the Daughters of Jesus, Women in Action, and so on. Women's groups belonging to the church and headed by pastor's spouses are considered spaces of solidarity, progress, and harmony. All churches organize special sessions for the women of the church. At regular intervals (often weekly), these groups meet, discuss personal difficulties, and try to explain these from a biblical perspective. In these religious female associations, the women also aid each other financially and share troubles concerning domestic and sexual issues (see above). These church groups accordingly incorporate and likewise perpetuate the urban women's groups. They divest the other female associations of their asocial reputation through the insertion of the group into the church structure.

The positive image of the wife's pastor does not necessarily grant a female pastor the utmost in social prestige. These leading women are also frequently subject to harsh social criticism, and they have to prove that they are above all excellent wives and mothers. Furthermore, even the Christian women's groups become spaces of rivalry and enmity. The mother of the second house where I lived never felt totally at ease in her women's church group, which she saw as dominated by Luba women. In her view, these women used the church setting as a space to show off. She, however, had to scrape money together for her children's studies and was not capable of regularly buying new outfits. Here again, the representations of Christian groups embellish reality to project a beneficial image of the Christian community.

Controlling the Actresses

The concern about women's authority and mobility also colors the social environments of the actresses. As I mentioned in Chapter 3 when discussing the life story of Mamy Moke, the morality of the city's media and other popular culture stars is closely inspected and commented upon. In particular two Cinarc actresses, Wallone Shongo and Dorcaz Mbombo, continuously had to defend themselves against their identification with "free women." Both actresses lived on their own, an atypical situation for young, unmarried Christian women.

This close eye on the social environment does much extend to male youth. Once he is regarded as a "youth," a young man is expected to leave the household and find living arrangements of his own, apart from his kin. Whereas young men can more easily leave the household of their childhood and live on their own, girls and young women tend to remain within the domestic spaces of their lineage. As a rule they live among kin until they are married, although it is also rare that a young woman lives with her own parents until the day of her marriage. At a fairly young age girls are sent to other households within the family group, where they are expected to take care of babies and infants or, in the absence of the mother of the house, perform the duties of the *femme ménagère*. Members of the kin group obviously control these young women in such situations. And although young women are increasingly mobile, they are expected to inform their guardians of their whereabouts. Young men, on the other hand, never have to ask permission. Only upon marriage does a Kinois girl leave the house of her lineage and join her husband. These gendered differences with regard to teenagers' mobility and control over their social lives derive from the cultural logic that defines the domestic space as a female space.

Disappointed after several marriage proposals—by "false lovers," as she called them in hindsight—Wallone (in her late thirties) regarded herself as too old to still be living with her married siblings. Well aware of public disapproval, and also attempting not to give her relatives any justification to call her back to the houses of the family, Wallone was very selective about the people she talked to and the places she visited. She furthermore had functions in several different revival churches. Thanks to her regular attendance at the religious services organized by the Cinarc group, nobody—neither the other group members nor the audience—questioned her Christian identity. She did not dress indecently, and no rumors were ever heard about promiscuity, something otherwise quite common in this milieu. Furthermore, when some of the Cinarc members experienced social problems, she was the one they turned to for advice. For that reason also, many called her "Maman Wallone." Wallone's Christian behavior contradicted the common stereotype of unmarried women living on their own as "prostitutes."

The case was different for Dorcaz Mbombo, a woman in her late twenties. She moved from her parents' compound to an annex during the period of my fieldwork. When I first met Dorcaz, she lived with her two sisters and the children of one of them in a compound in Kasa-Vubu. The three sisters were orphans; both their parents had died around 2000—from sorcery, it was said. Since then, Dorcaz had resolutely chosen to follow Jesus's path, even if this caused a rupture with her extended family. Custom among the Luba, the group to which Dorcaz belongs through her father, dictates that all the father's goods should be transferred to his siblings after his death. Dorcaz's father, however, had managed to merge "traditional," Christian, and Western worlds brilliantly: he bequeathed his furniture, a number of art objects, and the ownership of several compounds in the city to his three daughters. An official letter granted his two sisters, who were also living in the compound, the right to occupy his plot in Kasa-Vubu, one of Kinshasa's communities.

Unfortunately Dorcaz did not get along with her two aunts. She suspected them of being witches and told me several stories of how they were blocking her from progressing, and how they had even tried to kill her. "These women are very beautiful, well-dressed and friendly. You would never believe that they are witches. But they told me, 'You too will follow the way of your parents. We will eat you.' I don't like them any more, and I hate it that they will represent my family on the day of my marriage," Dorcaz said.[18] Some months before his death, her father had welcomed a pastor to the compound and allowed him to begin a church there. Fortunately, in Dorcaz's view, this small church continued to hold meetings in the compound after her parents' death, which served to neutralize her aunts' evil intentions for some time. However, one day the pastor informed the sisters that he had found a larger space for his growing religious community and would be leaving the compound. Around the same time, one of her sisters married and the other (the mother of two boys) procured a visa, planning to join her husband in Belgium. Fearing her aunts, Dorcaz assumed that her life would be in danger if she continued to live in the compound. She decided to move out of the family compound into a rented two-room annex elsewhere in the neighborhood. She left together with her sister's sons, who had stayed behind until their mother could arrange visas for them to join their parents in Belgium. Dorcaz fed and cared for the boys, took them to church, and supervised their school activities. She stated that if her aunts had been Christians she would not be living on her own.

Dorcaz was aware of the reputation of a "free woman," but she felt that the situation of this category of women had to be examined carefully because no one really knew why most were living on their own. She met many difficulties at the beginning of this period of living on her own. She related:

> Many people reacted badly when I informed them that I would live on my own. They said that I did it to receive men. But I really do not have the spirit of prostitution. If I had, then I would have prostituted myself already there where I lived before. But as I do not feel like talking to many people about my family problems, I shut up. I am now at an age to be a responsible person.

The reactions on the part of the community—both her kin and the fictive kin of the church congregation and the drama group—can be considered normal, for in the mindset of the Kinois, "free women" are the only category of females who live outside the control of the lineage and are, in a real sense, self-sustaining. Women are otherwise considered to be dependent for all their needs on men, whether fathers, brothers, or husbands. Even today, in a socioeconomic situation where many girls have college degrees and some even have well-paid jobs with NGOs or foreign enterprises, it remains difficult and socially unacceptable to believe that a woman living alone can afford to pay the rent for a studio or similar accommodation without offering sexual services.

Like most Congolese, Dorcaz is very discreet about the source of her earnings. People do not know that her ability to rent out several of her parents' houses provides her with a decent monthly income with which she can buy nice clothes, pay the rent for her own annex, and still afford her studies. When I confronted Chapy with Dorcaz's social problems, he responded:

When a girl lives alone, people will say that she is a prostitute because men can visit her whenever they want. If a girl wants to be respected, then she has to be married. Even if you have much money, or an important job, for example being a minister, you still need to have children and a husband. Otherwise, people will laugh at you and not respect you. By contrast, people will never laugh at a man. Today he may lack money, but tomorrow he can have a thousand dollars. A man's respect is in his pocket.

Varying social evaluations with regard to personal autonomy derive from the gendered societal conditions for the achievement of prestige (*lukumu*). "The honor of a woman resides in the marriage" (*Lukumu ya mwasi ezali makwela*), it is said, while "A man's honor stems from his money" (*Lukumu ya mobali ezali libunga*). In this respect, a young man living on his own proves to his relatives, the neighborhood, and his potential lovers that he is capable of being his own man, of paying the rent. A young woman living alone, on the other hand, goes against the ideal of a married woman. For Dorcaz, agreeing to live with her nephews did not just reflect a duty she as a relative was expected to perform; this situation also suited her because the presence of the children served to deflect the inevitable rumors and gossip. Socially regarded as these children's mother, Dorcaz escaped the full force of the stigma endured by women living on their own in Kinshasa.

Conclusion

Negotiations about Matrimony and Sexuality

In the previous chapter, I distinguished three gender games governed by the lineage, Christian churches, and the urban atmosphere. This demarcation is to a high degree informed by my informants' reflections and the serials' representations of the multiplicity of values and morals concerning gender and sexuality. Without a doubt, there is much diversity within and overlap among the three discerned domains. The Christian perpetuation of spiritual experiences and concepts is one example of the intersections between the ideology of born-again Christianity and local cultures. Nevertheless, the three games point at particular cultural vectors that seem to oppose one another.

The titles that I gave to this chapter and the preceding one speak of "negotiating" matrimony and urban sexuality. The negotiations take place on three different levels. First, in the competition for control over urban youth, church leaders and Christians deliberate over "customary" and "urban worldly" gendered practices. The qualifications of "Christian" and "demonic" relationships, prohibited partners, and right and wrong sexual behavior indicate that matrimony and sex open up spaces of conflict where competing signification systems play out. Love, sexuality, and conjugal alliances are not fixed domains, but they change and are at times contested (Thomas and Cole 2009). Because of the hegemony of Pentecostal Christianity in Kinshasa's public culture, the "customary" politics are losing the battle. Second, the young artists themselves use the teleserials as spaces to negotiate their opinions about love and sexuality as opposed to the demands of lineage elders and relatives. These negotiations, however, are not totally free: since the actors are known throughout the city as evangelizers, they have to adhere to the dominant Christian discourse. As mentioned above, Kinshasa's born-again Christians remain, above all, Kinois who are also playing gender games other than the Christian one. Yet in their public discourse, the Christian artists reproduce the hegemonic Christian stance on matrimony and sexuality in an attempt to construct their own identity and establish themselves as "Christians." Finally, I have also shown how young Kinois inform each other and discuss their own understandings of sex and marriage among themselves. This leads us to break down the concept of "African sexuality" as a homogenizing and essentializing notion that obscures the variations and controversies about sexuality among "Africans." This observation is in line with Jo Helle-Valle's (2004: 195) argument that "sexuality, both as practice and as a discursive theme, is (in Africa as elsewhere) many different things depending on the contexts it is part of and must hence always be analysed as part of such communicative contexts."

The Melodrama and the Feminine

Kinois consider serials, soap operas, and the more abstract genre of the melodrama as "feminine," and academics have tended to do the same. The emphasis on domestic matters and the overbearing emotional charge of these visual texts are said to make up the "feminine character" of the serials. And Kinois say that it is mainly women and children who follow the TV plays. People make this assumption because the house is the main space in which the serials are watched. Yet the qualification of the Pentecostal melodrama as a feminine media text is erroneous for a number of reasons. For one, the stories deal with matters that concern both sexes. Also, my observations confirm that men avidly follow these serials as well. The *maboke* trigger discussions about the serials' value and meaning for Kinois subjectivities among men and women, young and old, Christians and pagans. The serials and the discourses surrounding them blend the worlds of men and women. In addition, men occupy the most important positions in the drama groups, television studios, and churches, which means that while the so-called feminine genre of the melodrama broadcasts a masculine discourse on gender, it obscures the masculine power configurations and the patriarchal ideology that the serials convey.

Pentecostalism is the main ideology transmitted through the serials, but gender matters and sexuality are the topics the serials mainly focus on in order to fight against Satan. Kinshasa's serials are thus part of a wide range of Pentecostal and patriarchal technologies of gender (see de Lauretis 1984; 1987). The authorial voice of Pentecostal leaders in the post-Mobutu *maboke* leads me to agree with the conclusion of most feminist-inspired research (among others Abu-Lughod 1999; de Lauretis 1984; Mankekar 1999) that the arrangement of marriage and sexuality in mass-mediated fictional narratives is not value-free: with regard to the representation of gender, the staging of popular culture is far from autonomous. It does not lie outside the field of cultural power and domination but partakes in a complex process of fashioning identities, norms, and values.

Notes

1. The book was written by Godé Mungala Moke, a Christian leader living in Chapy's street. Besides being the author of evangelizing texts, this man is also a journalist, pastor, director of Christian radio stations, and organizer of Christian rallies, seminars, and biblical conferences.
2. "Girls are not the only instruments of seduction which the Devil uses in the church. Many boys and young men are also possessed with a demonic seducing force" (author's translation of a passage from the book *Le sexe nous menace*, p. 51). Note how the beginning of this quotation expresses the assumed connection between girls and the Devil.
3. "Heterosexual marriage" is a tautology in Kinshasa's context.
4. I can only speculate that this stems from the patriarchal ideology that values only a man's star.
5. One frequently hears talk of "husbands" and "wives of the night"—thus assuming that not only women but also men can fall victim to evil spirits—in the Pentecostal churches. None of the many Kinshasa serials that I have viewed ever portrayed a case of "husbands of the night."
6. Apart from religious radio and television broadcasts dealing with matrimony and sexuality, various "secular" radio and TV shows also deal with these issues, though without framing them in an explicit proselytizing discourse. During fieldwork, the most popular radio show, *JeudiMarius* on RTKM (2000–2005) and RagaFM (2005–2007), hosted by Marius Muhunga, dealt in particular with problems of love and sexuality in the city.

7. This show is broadcast on the radio channel RTP late on Friday evenings and aired on the RTP television station on Saturday nights (from 2:00 to 4:00 A.M.)

8. Homosexuality is not at all portrayed by the *kizengi*, the fool. This character frequently transgresses social norms of masculinity (Pype 2010), yet his gender-bending is never associated with homosexuality.

9. Similar idioms capturing the material prey of female sexual desire have emerged elsewhere in Africa: in Niger also Chic-Choc-Chèque (Masquelier 2009: 228); in Dakar, young women seek "the three Vs" (*villa, virement bancaire*—bank transfer—and *voiture*—car, Nyamnjoh 2005); and in South Africa "the three C's" refer to cash, cell phones, and cars (Hunter 2009).

10. Another expression used to denote the nature of young girls' sexuality is "to do the manjolina" (*kosala manjolina*). An older man explained to me that *manjolina* probably stems from the song "Manzoli-nzonzo," by the Thu-Zaïna orchestra. The song describes the "young, beautiful and fresh" girls who become the girlfriends of older, married men. These men have money and can show off with their cars by cruising the city. Financially they are better off than the young men who only have their words, their speech, to seduce young girls.

11. Daniel Van Groenweghe (1997: 234) speaks about "poverty polyandry," referring to sexual contacts with multiple men for the sake of survival.

12. These girls gave birth before entering the drama group, while "still in the world" and not yet involved in the evangelizing work.

13. Without alluding to historical analyses, I want to contrast the analysis of femininities and their representations in the serials with one of the few discussions that I found on Congo's media and their representations of gender. In 1972, in what was then Zaire, Bernard noted a discrepancy between the depiction of women in the mass media and the way they appeared in reality. He argued that women were represented as "modern women": air hostesses, nurses, professors, and soldiers, holding good jobs and partaking in economic, social, and political responsibilities. The "modern" Zairian woman of the mass media was literate, had a modern house and a well-equipped kitchen, and prepared Western dishes from recipes she found in magazines with ingredients that were not sold at the market. She was elegant, treated her skin, and cared for her children as an American housewife would. Bernard (1972: 268) argued that the quotidian life of women in Kinshasa was as far from the life of their grandmothers in the village as it was from the image on television. More than thirty years later, the image of women in Kinshasa's television was more complex and seemed to vary according to the array of visual genres that had originated since.

14. For material on masculinities in DR Congo see De Boeck (2000) and Cuvelier (2011).

15. Though I never met Bienvenu's mother, who was living in France at the time of my fieldwork, I am convinced that his memories are biased, since his maternal cousin Chapy, who was taken in by Bienvenu's mother, often described her as a "strong woman" (*maman ya makasi*).

16. I heard less frequently the concept of a "female man" (*mobali mwasi*). One occurrence was the TV actor Mbaliosombo, who in his teleserials invariably performs the role of a woman (his stage name is *la mama*). He was referred to as a *mobali mwasi*, in the same context the transvestite "Pamela" in Muyombe Gauche's troupe was also called a *mobali mwasi*. Whereas the concept in the

mwasi mobali is the gendered identity of the women, in the case of the *mobali mwasi* the line between gender and biological sex is blurred: in Mbaliosombo's context, his fictional identity was a female, although in regular life he behaved like any other man. "Pamela," however, was a man who dressed, spoke, and behaved like a woman both in and outside of his roles.

17. Other examples are female politicians.

18. Dorcaz has no fiancé, but marriage is one of those certitudes in the life of Congolese.

CHAPTER 10

Closure, Subplots, and Cliffhanger

As discussed throughout this book, in the last few years, Kinshasa's inhabitants have observed a gradual increase in the number of local television stations. Many of these channels are privately owned by Pentecostal pastors or by communities of born-again Christians. This dominance of Pentecostal Christianity in the city's media world contributes to the hegemony of this variety of Christianity in Kinshasa.

Although Pentecostal-charismatic Christianity has made a significant headway in Kinshasa's overall public sphere, there is some local disapproval of the workings and spread of the declared apocalyptic principles. Adversaries, who can be found among politicians, academics, and members of other Christian traditions, point to the manipulative and treacherous demeanor of prophets and pastors who abuse their followers' hopes for personal riches. I observed a similar condemnation of these Christian movements among certain academics I met at conferences in Europe. One encounter in particular stands out. At a conference in Sweden, I delivered the material of Chapter 5 (Mimesis in Motion), where I indicate how Pentecostal leaders categorize television programs as "good" and "bad" and thus attempt to mold the viewing habits of Kinois. After the presentation, a Swedish man in his fifties—who, I learned, was a specialist on African literature—came up to me and agitatedly demanded that my text stress that "We are responsible for this corruption" (his words). During the conversation, more a monologue than a dialogue, the man identified with a generation of Swedish missionaries who had spread Christianity in Congo. He understood Pentecostal Christianity as a major hindrance to the continent's growth and accused "the West" of having imported this ideology.

In my research, I have attempted to move away from any preconceived notions about this particular strand of Christianity. I do not accuse pastors and do not approach the believers as gullible audiences, but I try to understand the experiences and practices of people who actively contribute to the popularization of the beliefs and principles of Pentecostal Christianity. This book, then, provides an alternative perspective on the dissemination of the apocalyptic belief system by looking at the way Christian artists—local propagators who are not church leaders—deliberate on and negotiate the values of the Pentecostal standards and render these reflections in their artworks.

The concern in this book has not so much been to analyze how the discourses and images of the teleserials impact the city dwellers' life worlds but to document how these television programs come into being, and how Kinshasa's most popular narratives themselves derive from the fabric of social life in a postcolonial society. Therefore, the approach I have taken to the television serials leans on a social constructionist perspective that aims to disclose how people take part in the construction of their perceived social reality, and how this stands in a dialectical relationship with expressive culture. Television, religion, and society are understood as three intersecting systems whose confluence fosters new publics, alternative ways of acquiring and sustaining (religious) authority, and new arenas of culture making.

In concluding this book, I will focus on several key themes: the production of the apocalyptic imagination on and beyond the screen, the positioning of cultural producers within this apocalyptic horizon of experience, the significance of the *salon,* and, finally, the future of the genre of the Pentecostal melodrama.

The Melodrama on and beyond the Screen

This book shows how the *maboke,* defined as Pentecostal melodramas, are firmly ingrained in the apocalyptic framework propagated by pastors in Kinshasa. The strong moral overtone, the Manichaean ideology, the overbearing role of emotions in both the ideology and the transmission of the belief system, and the emphasis on quotidian urban life in all Pentecostal genres that articulate the apocalyptic scheme lead me to state that the Pentecostal ideology is itself quite melodramatic. The offered data therefore transcend this domain of popular culture, insofar as the analysis attempts to unravel how the apocalyptic ideology itself is constructed and transmitted.

In all chapters, I have examined major topics in the discourse of pastors and the strategies used to shape their principles and to transmit them. First of all, public and private urban spaces—rotaries, markets, bridges, neighborhoods where customary chiefs and healers reside, universities and high schools, bathrooms and toilets—are designated either "Christian," and thus safe, or "demonic," and thus dangerous. This symbolic matrix of the city offers city dwellers a schema by which to interpret the fellow citizens they meet in these spaces and the practices they observe there. Also, Christian leaders design a typology of "good" and "bad" experts, whom they either recommend to their followers as sources of social, medical, and spiritual assistance, or disapprove of. To the category of "bad experts" belong the healers, diviners, and magicians who wield great authority in non-Christian worlds. Pentecostal leaders label these specialists "occult practitioners" and put them on a par with society's rival, "the witch." The Christian pastors' and prophets' rejection of these experts undeniably pertains to Pentecostal leaders' larger plan to expand their influence over the lives of the Kinois. The chapter on the discourse on development illustrates the authority and confidence evangelizing artists find in the Bible and its propagators. Young Christians turn away from "customs" and "elders" who are unmasked as defending their own interests through occult means, and attach themselves to Christian leaders who promise to "unblock" and "liberate" them and the nation at large from the evil spell that the Devil, along with the elders and customary specialists aligned with him, have put on the city's young.

But the control the Christian leaders seek to exercise goes much deeper than the identification of "Christian" trustworthy authorities and seeps into the utmost private experiences of emotions and perceptions of the body. Love, sympathy, faith, and confidence are promoted as feelings becoming of a Christian. Sensations of anxiety, jealousy, envy, anger, and hatred are loaded with "unchristian" meaning. Pentecostal leaders signify these latter emotions as both outcomes of demonic agencies and entry gates for impure spirits to nest in the individual's life (see Pype forthcoming b). To counter the potential asocial effects of these rejected emotions, Pentecostal leaders exhort Christians to control their physical and emotional lives. These meanings also apply to the sensations Christians can feel when watching television. Being sexually aroused, agitated, or nervous might be the outcomes of watching "bad" television programs like pornographic films, action movies, wrestling shows, and thrillers. By contrast, "Christian" television programs are said to transmit a particular spiritual knowledge without triggering asocial effects.

A similar distinction is also made in the domain of songs, dances, and music videos. Christian dances that glorify God and Jesus and invoke the Holy Spirit are promoted as morally good, while urban popular dances that do not convey a Christian message or are performed in social spaces without an explicit Christian character are devalued as "demonic." Distress, as experienced on a personal and collective level, is translated into an apocalyptic causality: the Devil reigns, and the End of Time is coming closer. These apocalyptic explanations draw further on more long-standing local interpretations of the human body, emotions, sociality, and spaces, but these are transformed to fit into a meaningful narrative. In the rejection of "traditional" and "urban worldly" practices and meanings, these same forms and values are immediately recuperated. The circulation of familiar dance forms, concepts, and beliefs localizes the Pentecostal melodrama firmly within Kinshasa's society even as, paradoxically, it immediately proposes a new world as well. Old forms are recast and restored through practices that are sometimes subtle, other times more overt.

In addition, I show that the apocalyptic leaders ascribe a magical potency to modern consumer goods like the television set and the camera. Mass media are inserted in a magical universe and projected as potential technologies of enchantment. Both divine and occult forces can find their way in the living room through the television set and thus transform the spiritual quality of the viewing environment. This particular use of the medium demonstrates an appropriation of Western objects into religiously holistic experiences. Following the apocalyptic ideology, television becomes one of the many sites Christians occupy to combat the occult.

Cultural Producers in an Apocalyptic Society

The book spells out how heavily the apocalyptic scheme also impacts the dramatic work of the *maboke* artists themselves, social relations within the troupe, and relations with other drama groups and church leaders. Cultural producers such as TV actors are firmly embedded in local social and religious schemes. In particular, the apocalyptic understanding of "imitation" as dialogue with the spirit world can interfere with the private lives of the actors, as in the case of possessed artists. Actors' misbehavior (for instance, showing up drunk at prayer sessions or becoming pregnant) is interpreted as the outcome of occult forces triggered during the embodiment of particular roles (prostitutes, witches, "false Christians").

In the complex space of collegiality and competition between the many theater groups in the city, drama groups qualify themselves as "Christian" while labeling their adversaries as "demonic." Discord and rivalry between artists are also explained via the grid of divine and occult affiliations. This is how, for example, Clovis gave meaning to the conflict between the Cinarc head and the church leader. These kinds of interpretations were seen to lead to fissures between the drama group and its long-standing spiritual counselor, and eventually giving impetus to the formation of new subtroupes.

The small group of key informants comprised a mix of so-called "real Christians" and "Christians of the flesh." This offered me the opportunity to learn the fundamentals of the apocalyptic ideology from the most radical Christians. Meanwhile, my conversations with "Christians of the flesh" show that the evangelizing theater company harbored a spectrum ranging from "hard" believers to practitioners and people who took a more relative attitude toward the transmitted principles. The discussions with these actors furthermore demonstrate how so-called deviant behavior has to be suppressed and hidden, lest it damage the public Christian identity of the drama group.

The actors are thus mediators on various levels: they propose a diagnosis of the current situation, which they label as demonic, and they instantaneously offer an alternative: the immediate intervention of the divine. Their proposed solution to the unwanted situation demands the presence of the Holy Spirit, which they attempt to realize not only by convincing their audience of the beneficial outcomes of conversion to Pentecostal Christianity, but also by transferring divine spiritual powers onto the viewers. Here we see how, via an ingenious interplay of aesthetics, sensuous appeal, and rationality, "the imagined Christian community" comes into being. This is an illustration of the "aesthetic formation" recently formulated by Meyer (2009a).

The Recovery of the Salon

Although most of the data for this book was gathered from observations and participation in recording sessions and prayer gatherings, I also conducted a great deal of fieldwork in living rooms. Waiting for scenes to be shot, conducting formal interviews with key informants, and watching the telenarratives were activities that took place in the salon. The story I tell deals with the production of the story lines, and for that reason the social and political significance of this modern space—the most important place where television is watched—remains largely unexplored in the overall text. But here, in rounding up the loose ends of the vectors that shape the *maboke,* I want to point to two lines of analysis that have made the living room a topic, in and of itself, in my discussion of the making of Pentecostal melodramas.

The first line draws from the apocalyptic ideology that directs the city dwellers' gaze toward their personal and private experiences. Prophets and pastors warn people that hostile beings can even enter the domestic space; impurity may find its route through the invitation of Janus-faced beings. Furthermore, Christian leaders see the television set, which usually occupies a dominant position in this room, as a possible contributor to the spiritual quality of the salon. Through mass-mediated images and sounds, a living room can be transformed into a divine space or a locus of demonic beings. Kinshasa's Christians therefore place bills with biblical verses above the door, switch to channels playing Christian music videos, or participate in mass-mediated healing rituals to protect the living room from impurity or render the space safe again. Observations in the living room with the spectator in front of the television set, at times even touching the screen, watching narratives about healing and bewitchment indicate that a religious quality can be added to the domestic space.

The second line of analysis of the living room that I want to reconstruct briefly flows from the observations in Chapter 7, in which I demonstrate that spectators actively engage in the unfolding of the teleserials' plotlines and dialogue via phone calls and live encounters with the media stars. Furthermore, watching television in Kinshasa is a collective practice. Following story lines is sometimes rather difficult, as watchers comment constantly upon the shows. The television set, toward which all furniture is positioned and which is nearly always switched on, not only displays the financial capabilities of the inhabitants (sometimes the salon boasts two or more television sets) but also structures a public sphere. The salon is a prior locus where a cultural public sphere comes into being. These observations lead us to reconsider Jewsiewicki's argument that today, Kinshasa's salons are in crisis (2003: 148). Due to an increasing "culture of outside" (in particular the street), he writes, the salon has lost its identity. Drawing on his social history of the living room, Jewsiewicki defines the salon as a space of male authority. Adorned with modern paintings and portraits of the family heads, during the colonial period the living rooms became public spaces (like Habermas's literary salons) in which modern local politics were negotiated and found meaning in a group of adult men. They constructed themselves as modern citizens through the display of portraits and the discussions.

I agree with Jewsiewicki that the bourgeois ideal of a male family head surrounding the nuclear unit and inviting his friends in the living room has diminished. However, to describe it as a "crisis" neglects the participation of the young and of women in the public sphere and denies the political value of other modern items with which the inhabitants present themselves, construct their own identity, and even participate in public talk. The television set has replaced the centrality of the portraits and the paintings, which are still, although in altered form, present in the salon. Portraits of the married couple and their offspring adorn the walls, now accompanied by large posters of Western-style interiors and still lifes of fruits and vegetables or natural settings (water falls, jungle, etc.), as well as calendars and clocks—symbols and ma(r)kers of Western time consciousness. Yet these decorations rarely spark debates—it is television programs that now trigger conversations. Taking the historical-political role of paintings in mind, we can contend that whereas Kinshasa's public sphere has always been largely "cultural," the media governing the cultural public sphere have changed, as have the main speakers in the television public sphere: women and the young participate in a mass-mediated public sphere.

The Next Episode

Michael M. J. Fischer (2001: 476) writes that "it is not accidental that the most interesting filmic traditions for an exploration of contemporary religion should come from societies disrupted by social violence and Lyotardian differends of moral perspective." Experiences of trauma or crisis lead humans to craft symbolic material that constructs and articulates sense for their experiences. I understand the participation of many of Kinshasa's youth in the production of teleserials as a search for meaning. The close rapport between the serials and the lived reality creates a metonymic relationship between the real and the symbolic, helping producers and viewers alike to redefine their world.

The serials show again and again that the harmony achieved in the symbolic worlds is unstable. Precisely because this harmony, stability, or victory is quite precarious, repetition of the certainties is a main device to conquer the inchoate, the uncertainty, and the sense of alienation. As a result the serials have become a genre, continuously reproducing the same stories, using the same characters, and evolving along the same dramatic script. During fieldwork, some of the actors complained that older serials had already treated topics such as adultery, the workings of sirens, or "false pastors," thereby questioning the creativity of their troupe. Nevertheless, the recurrent representation of sinners in the teleserials falls neatly together with the focal themes in the Pentecostal ideology, thus controlling social worlds and transmitting firm social identities.

Kinois eagerly follow the serials, awaiting the unfolding of the plotlines in each new episode. I am curious to see the future of Kinshasa's television serials. Many Kinois are aware that the serials are a historical product of their sociocultural setting. Some of them even told me that they believed that as soon as the city/country became more stable on the social, economic, and political fronts, the fundamentalist churches would gradually disappear and Kinshasa's media world would transform profoundly. I can only guess, but if this analysis is correct, the genre of the Pentecostal melodrama will indeed vanish with the decline of the Pentecostal churches in a world where social instability is no longer translated in terms of spiritual conflicts and confusion. How will the new political era, which began the evening after I ended fieldwork, affect the Kinois' life worlds? And how will this be rendered in the media world, by those who hold power at the level of the channels and the lower level of the dramatic groups? How will the "new Congo" affect the cultural documents like the teleserials, the songs, and the dances?

Given the dominant position the television set has attained in the life worlds of Kinois, it is unlikely that Kinois will stop making their own teleserials. We can only expect that in other times, with another hegemonic ideology and with other social heroes, the teleserials will offer new key scenarios, introduce other fictive characters, and promote different closures. Popular cultures are never-ending affairs. Or, in the words of Misty Bastian: "They simply transmute into another form, maintaining traces of their pasts" (1998: 128). We can expect the post-post-Mobutu teleserials to add another layer to the dense palimpsests studied in this book.

Bibliography

Abu-Lughod, L. 1995. "Movie Stars and Islamic Moralism in Egypt." *Social Text* 42 (1): 53–67.

———. 1999[1997]. "The Interpretation of Culture(s) after Television." In S. Ortner, ed., *The Fate of "Culture": Geertz and Beyond*. Berkeley: University of California Press, pp. 110–135.

———. 2002. "Egyptian Melodrama: Technology of the Modern Subject?" in F. Ginsburg, L. Abu-Lughod and B. Larkin, eds., *Media Worlds: Anthropology on New Terrain*. Berkeley and Los Angeles: University of California Press, pp. 115–133.

Althusser, L. 1971. *Lenin and Philosophy and Other Essays*. Trans. Ben Brewster. New York: Monthly Review Press.

Anderson, A. 1991. *Moya: The Holy Spirit in an African Context*. Pretoria: University of South Africa Press.

Anderson, B. 1991. *Imagined Communities*. London: Verso.

Antze, P. 1996. "Telling Stories, Making Selves: Memory and Identity in Multiple Personality Disorder." In P. Antze and M. Lambek, eds., *Tense Past: Cultural Essays in Trauma and Memory*. New York: Routledge, pp. 3–24.

Askew, K. 2002. "Introduction." In K. Askew and R. Wilk, eds., *The Anthropology of Media: A Reader*, Blackwell Readers in Anthropology. London and Malden, MA: Blackwell Publishers, pp. 1–14.

Banégas, R., and J.P. Warnier. 2001. "Nouvelles figures de la réussite et du pouvoir." *Politique Africaine* 82: 5–21.

Barber, K. 1987. "Popular Arts in Africa." *African Studies Review* 30 (3): 1–78.

———. 1997a. "Views From The Field: Introduction." In K. Barber, ed., *Readings in African Popular Culture*. Bloomington: Indiana University Press and James Currey, pp. 1–10.

———. 1997b. "Preliminary Notes on Audiences in Africa." *Africa: Journal of the International Institute* 67 (3): 347–362.

Barthes, R. 1987[1957]. "The World of Wrestling." In R. Barthes, *Mythologies*. Trans. Annette Lavers. New York: Hill and Wang, pp. 15–25.

Bastian, M.L. 1998. "Fires, Tricksters and Poisoned Medicines: Popular Cultures of Rumor in Onitsha, Nigeria and Its Markets." *Etnofoor* 10 (2): 111–32.

———. 2001. "Vulture Men, Campus Cultists and Teenaged Witches." In H.L. Moore and T. Sanders, eds., *Magical Interpretations, Material Realities: Modernity, Witchcraft and the Occult in Postcolonial Africa*. London and New York: Routledge, pp. 71–96.

———. 2002. "Irregular Visitors: Narratives about Ogbaanje (Spirit Children) in Nigerian Popular Writing." In S. Newell, ed., *Readings in African Popular Fiction*. London: IAI and James Currey and Bloomington: Indiana University Press, pp. 59–66.

Bayart, J.-F. 2005[1996]. *L'Illusion Identitaire*. Paris: Fayard. Translated: *The Illusion of Cultural Identity*. London and Chicago: Hurst and University of Chicago Press.

———. 1998. "Fait missionaire et politique du ventre: une lecture foucauldienne." *Le Fait Missionaire* 6: 9–38.

Bayart, J.F., A. Mbembe, and C. Toulabor. 1992. *Le Politique par le Bas en Afrique Noire*. Paris: Karthala.

Beattie, J., and J. Middleton, eds. 1969. *Spirit Mediumship and Society in Africa*. London: Routledge and Kegan Paul.

Behrend, H. 2002. "'I Am Like a Movie Star in My Street': Photographic Self-Creation in Postcolonial Kenya." In R. Werbner, ed., *Postcolonial Subjectivities in Africa*. London: Zed Books, pp. 44–62.

———. 2003. "Photo-Magic: Photographs in Practices of Healing and Harming in East Africa." In "Media and Religion in Africa," ed. B. Meyer, special issue, *Journal of Religion in Africa* 33 (2): 129–145.

———. 2009. "'To Make Strange Things Possible': The Photomontages of the Bakor Photo Studio in Lamu Kenya." In K. Njogu and J. Middleton, eds., *Media and Identity in Africa*. Bloomington and Indianapolis: Indiana University Press, pp. 187–207.

Behrend, H., and U. Luig, eds. 1999. *Spirit Possession: Modernity and Africa*. Madison: University of Wisconsin Press.

Beidelman, T. 1997. *The Cool Knife: Imagery of Gender, Sexuality, and Moral Education in Kaguru Initiation Ritual*. Washington, DC: Smithsonian Institution Press.

Bekaert, S. 2000. *System and Repertoire in Sakata Medicine: Democratic Republic of Congo*. Uppsala Studies in Cultural Anthropology, 31. Uppsala: Acta Universitatis Upsaliensis.

Bellman, B., and B. Jules-Rosette. 1977. *A Paradigm for Looking: Cross-Cultural Research with Visual Media*. Norwood, NJ: Ablex.

Ben-Amos, P. 1980. "Patron-Artist Interactions in Africa." *African Arts* 13 (3): 56–57.

Benjamin, W. 1999[1935]. *The Work of Art in the Age of Mechanical Reproduction*. Trans. H. Zorn. London: Pimlico.

Bernard, G. 1971. "La contestation et les églises nationales au Congo." *Canadian Journal of African Studies* 5 (2): 145–156.

————. 1972. "Conjugalité et rôle de la femme à Kinshasa." *Canadian Journal of African Studies* 6 (2): 261–274.

Biaya, T.K. 1996. "La Culture urbaine dans les arts populaires d'Afrique: Analyse de l'ambiance Zaïroise." *Canadian Journal of African Studies* 30 (3): 345–370.

————. 2001. "Les Plaisirs de la Ville: Masculinité, Sexualité, et Femininité à Dakar (1997–2000)." *African Studies Review* 44 (2): 71–85.

Biebuyck, D. 1978. *Hero and Chief: Epic Literature from the Banyanga Zaire Republic.* Berkeley: University of California Press.

Boddy, J. 1989. *Wombs and Alien Apirits: Women, Men and the Zar Cult in Northern Sudan.* Madison: University of Wisconsin Press.

Botombele, B.E. 1975. *La Politique Culturelle en République du Zaire. Politiques Culturelles : Etudes et Documents.* Paris: Unesco.

Bourdieu, P. 1980. "Le Capital Social." *Actes de la Recherche en Sciences Sociales* 30: 2–3.

Brooks, P. 1976. *The Melodramatic Imagination.* New Haven, CT: Yale University Press.

Burke, K. 1962. *A Grammar of Motives and a Rhetoric of Motives.* Cleveland, OH, and New York: Meridian Books.

Cannell, F. 2006. *The Anthropology of Christianity.* Durham, NC: Duke University Press.

Capps, L., and E. Ochs. 1995. *Constructing Panic.* Cambridge, MA Harvard University Press.

Cohen, A.P. 1985. *The Symbolic Construction of Community.* London: Tavistock.

Cole, J. 2009. "Love, Money, and Economies of Intimacy in Tamatave, Madagascar." In J. Cole and L.M. Thomas, eds., *Love in Africa.* Chicago and London: University of Chicago Press, pp. 109–134.

Cole, J., and L.M. Thomas, eds. 2009. *Love in Africa.* Chicago and London: University of Chicago Press.

Coleman, S. 1996. "Words as Things: Language, Aesthetics and the Objectification of Protestant Evangelism." *Journal of Material Culture* 1: 107–128.

————. 2000. *The Globalisation of Charismatic Christianity: Spreading the Gospel of Prosperity.* Cambridge: Cambridge University Press.

Collier, J., and M.Z. Rosaldo. 1981. "Politics and Gender in Simple Societies." In S. Ortner and H. Whitehead, eds., *Sexual Meanings: The Cultural Construction of Gender and Sexuality.* Cambridge: Cambridge University Press, pp. 275–329.

Comaroff, J.L., and J. Comaroff. 1993. *Modernity and Its Malcontents: Ritual and Power in Postcolonial Africa.* Chicago: University of Chicago Press.

————. 2005. "Reflections on Youth: From the Past to the Postcolony." In A. Honwana and F. De Boeck, eds., *Makers and Breakers: Children and Youth in Postcolonial Africa.* Oxford, Dakar, and Trenton, NJ: James Currey, Codesria, and Africa World Press, pp. 19–30.

Comhaire-Sylvain, S. 1968. *Femmes de Kinshasa. Hier et Aujourd'hui.* Paris and The Hague: Mouton and Co.

Conteh-Morgan, J. 2004. "Francophone Africa South of the Sahara." In M. Banham, ed., *A History of Theatre in Africa.* Cambridge: Cambridge University Press, 85–137.

Corin, E. 1998. "Refiguring the Person: The Dynamics of Affects and Symbols in an African Spirit Possession Cult." In M. Lambek and A. Strathern, eds., *Bodies and Persons: Comparative Perspectives from Africa and Melanesia.* Cambridge: Cambridge University Press, pp. 80–102.

Couldry, N. 2002. *Media Rituals: A Critical Approach.* London: Routledge.

Corten, A., and R. Marshall-Fratani, eds. 2001. *Between Babel and Pentecost: Transnational Pentecostalism in Africa and Latin America.* London: Hurst.

Creten, P. 1996. "Gender en identiteit: een medisch-antropologisch onderzoek bij de Nkanu in Kinshasa en Zuidwest Zaïre." PhD dissertation, Leuven: Katholieke Universiteit Leuven.

Csordas, T. 1994. *The Sacred Self: A Cultural Phenomenology of Charismatic Healing.* Berkeley: University of California Press.

Cuvelier, J. 2011. "Men, Mines and Masculinities: The Lives and Practices of Artisanal Miners in Lwambo (Katanga province, DR Congo)." PhD dissertation, Leuven: Katholieke Universiteit Leuven.

Dasgupta, S. 2006. "Gods in the Sacred Marketplace: Hindu Nationalism and the Return of the Aura in the Public Sphere." In B. Meyer and A. Moors, eds., *Religion, Media and the Public Sphere.* Bloomington and Indianapolis: Indiana University Press, pp. 251–272.

D'Azevedo, W.I., ed. 1973. *The Traditional Artist in African Societies.* Bloomington: Indiana University Press.

De Boeck, F. 1991. "From Knots to Web: Fertility, Life-Transmission, Health and Well-Being among the Aluund of Southwest Zaire." PhD dissertation, Leuven: Katholieke Universiteit Leuven.

———. 1994. "When Hunger Goes Around the Land: Food and Hunger in Luunda Land." *Man (Journal of The Royal Anthropological Institute of Great Britain and Ireland)* 29 (2): 257–282.

———. 1995. "Het geheim als knoop. Een processuele en relationele benadering van geheimen en geheimhouding in Luunda initiatie- en genezingsrituelen in Zaïre." *Medische antropologie* 7 (1): 7–26.

———. 1998. "Beyond the Grave: History, Memory and Death in Postcolonial Congo/Zaire." In R. Werbner, ed., *Memory and the Postcolony: African Anthropology and the Critique of Power.* London: Zed Books, pp. 21–57.

———. 1999. "Domesticating Diamonds and Dollars: Identity, Expenditure and Sharing in SW Zaire." In P. Geschiere and B. Meyer, eds., *Globalization and Identity: Dialectics of Flow and Closure.* Oxford: Blackwell, pp. 177–209.

———. 2000. "Borderland Breccia: The Mutant Hero in the Historical Imagination of a Central-African Diamond Frontier." *Journal of Colonialism and Colonial History* 1 (2): 44p (electronic journal).

———. 2004. *Kinshasa: Tales of the Invisible City.* Photos by M.-F. Plissart. Ghent and Amsterdam: Ludion.

———. 2005a. "The Apocalyptic Interlude: Revealing Death in Kinshasa." *African Studies Review* 48 (2): 11–32.

———. 2005b. "The Divine Seed: Children, Gift and Witchcraft in the Democratic Republic of Congo." In A. Honwana and F. De Boeck, eds., *Makers and Breakers: Children and Youth in Postcolonial Africa.* Oxford, Dakar, and Trenton, NJ: James Currey, Codesria, and Africa World Press, pp. 188–214.

De Boeck, F., and R. Devisch. 1994. "Ndembu Divination Compared: From Representation and Social Engineering to Embodiment and Worldmaking." *Journal of Religion in Africa* 24 (2): 98–133.

Deger, J. 2006. *Shimmering Screens: Making Media in an Aboriginal Community.* Minneapolis: University of Minnesota Press.

de Lauretis, T. 1984. *Alice Doesn't: Feminism, Semiotics, Cinema.* Bloomington: Indiana University Press.

———. 1987. *Technologies of Gender: Essays on Theory, Film and Fiction.* London: Macmillan.

De Plaen, G. 1974. *Les structures d'autorité des Bayanzi.* Paris: Editions Universitaires.

Desjarlais, R. 1996. "Struggling Along." In M. Jackson, ed., *Things as They Are: New Directions in Phenomenological Anthropology.* Bloomington: Indiana University Press, pp. 70–92.

Devisch, R. 1985. "Perspectives on Divination in Contemporary Sub-Saharan Africa." In W. Van Binsbergen and M. Schoffeleers, eds., *Theoretical Explorations in African Religion.* London: Routledge and Kegan, pp. 50–83.

———. 1986. "Marge, marginalisation et liminalité: le sorcier et le devin chez les Yaka du Zaïre." In "Les dynamiques à la marge," ed. E. Corin, spécial issue, *Anthropologie et sociétés* 10 (2): 117–137.

———. 1991. "Symbol and Symptom among the Yaka of Zaire." In A. Jacobson-Widding, ed., *Body and Space: Symbolic Models of Unity and Division in African Cosmology and Experience.* Stockholm: Almqvist and Wiksell, pp. 283–302.

———. 1993. *Weaving the Threads of Life: The Khita Gyn-eco-logical Healing Cult among the Yaka.* Chicago: University of Chicago Press.

———. 1995. "Frenzy, Violence, and Ethical Renewal in Kinshasa." *Public Culture* 7 (3): 593–629.

———. 1996. "Pillaging Jesus: Healing Churches and the Villagisation of Kinshasa." *Africa* 65 (4): 555–586.

———. 1998. "Treating the Affect by Remodelling the Body in a Yaka Healing Cult." In M. Lambek and A. Strathern, eds., *Bodies and Persons: Comparative Perspectives from Africa and Melanesia.* Cambridge: Cambridge University Press, pp. 127–157.

———. 2004. "Yaka Divination: Acting out the Memory of Society's Life-Spring." In M. Winkelman and P. Peek, eds., *Divination and Healing: Potent Vision.* Tucson: University of Arizona Press, pp. 243–264.

De Vries, H., and S. Weber. 2001a. "In Media Res: Global Religion, Public Spheres, and the Task of Contemporary Comparative Religious Studies." In

H. de Vries and S. Weber, eds., *Religion and Media*. Stanford, CA: Stanford University Press, pp. 3–42.

———, eds. 2001b. *Religion and Media*. Stanford, CA: Stanford University Press.

DeWalt, K.M., B.R. DeWalt, and C.B. Wayland. 2000. "Participant Observation." In H. Russell Bernard, ed., *Handbook of Methods in Cultural Anthropology*. Walnut Creek, CA: AltaMira Press, pp. 259–300.

De Witte, M. 2005. "The Spectacular and the Spirits: Charismatics and Neo-Traditionalists on Ghanaian Television." *Material Religion* 1 (3): 314–335.

———. 2008. "Spirit Media: Charismatics, Traditionalists, and Mediation Practices in Ghana." PhD dissertation, Amsterdam: Universiteit van Amsterdam.

Diouf, M. 2005. "Afterword." In A. Honwana and F. De Boeck, eds., *Makers and Breakers: Children and Youth in Postcolonial Africa*. Oxford, Dakar, and Trenton, NJ: James Currey, Codesria, and Africa World Press, pp. 229–234.

Dorier-Apprill, E. 2001. "The New Pentecostal Networks of Brazzaville." In A. Corten and R. Fratani-Marshall, eds., *Between Babel and Pentecost: Transnational Pentecostalism in Africa and Latin America*. London and Bloomington: Hurst Publisher and Indiana University Press, pp. 293–308.

Douglas, M. 1977[1963]. *The Lele of the Kasai*. London: International African Institute.

———. 1969. *Purity and Danger: An Analysis of Concepts of Pollution and Taboo*. London: Routledge: London and Kegan Paul.

———. 1999. "Sorcery Accusations Unleashed: The Lele Revisited, 1987." *Africa* 69 (2): 177–193.

Drewal, H. 1996. "Mami Wata Shrines: Exotica and the Construction of Self." In M.J. Arnoldi, C.M. Geary, and K.L. Hardin, eds., *African Material Culture*. Bloomington: Indiana University Press, pp. 308–333.

Ellis, S., and G. Ter Haar. 2004. *Worlds of Power: Religious Thought and Political Practice in Africa*. London: C. Hurst and Company.

Edwards, J., and M. Strathern. 2000. "Including Our Own." In J. Carsten, ed., *Cultures of Relatedness: New Approaches to the Study of Kinship*. Cambridge: Cambridge University Press, pp. 149–166.

Evans-Pritchard, E.E. 1937. *Witchcraft, Oracles and Magic among the Azande*. Oxford: Clarendon Press.

Fabian, J. 1990. *Power and Performance: Ethnographic Explorations through Proverbial Wisdom and Theater in Shaba, Zaire*. Madison: University of Wisconsin Press.

———. 1996. *Remembering the Present: Painting and Popular History in Zaïre*. Illustrations by Tshibumba Kanda Matulu. Berkeley: University of California Press.

———. 1998. *Moments of Freedom: Anthropology and Popular Culture*. Charlottesville and London: University Press of Virginia.

Fair, L. 2009. "Making Love in the Indian Ocean: Hindi Films, Zanzibari Audiences, and the Construction of Romance in the 1950s and 1960s." In J. Cole and L.M. Thomas, eds., *Love in Africa*. Chicago and London: University of Chicago Press, pp. 58–82.

Ferguson, J. 1999. *Expectations of Modernity: Myths and Meanings of Urban Life on the Zambian Copperbelt*. Berkeley: University of California Press.

Fernandez, J.W. 1979. "On the Notion of Religious Movement." *Social Research* 46 (1): 36–62.

———. 1982. *Bwiti: An Ethnography of the Religious Imagination in Africa.* Princeton, NJ: Princeton University Press.

———. 1986. *Persuasions and Performances: The Play of Tropes in Culture.* Bloomington: Indiana University Press.

Fischer, M.M.J. 2001. "Filmic Judgement and Cultural Critique: The Work of Art, Ethics, and Religion in Iranian Cinema." In H. de Vries and S. Weber, eds., *Religion and Media.* Stanford, CA: Stanford University Press, pp. 456–486.

Fiske, J. 1989. *Understanding Popular Culture.* Boston: Unwin Hyman.

Foucault, M. 1988. *Technologies of the Self: A Seminar with Michel Foucault.* Ed. L.H. Martin, H. Gutman, and P.H. Hutton. Amherst: University of Massachussetts.

Frère, M.-S. 2007. *The Media and Conflicts in Central Africa.* London: Lynne Rienner.

Fuglesang, M. 1994. *Veils and Videos: Female Youth Culture on the Kenyan Coast,* Stockholm Studies in Social Anthropology, 32. Stockholm: Department of Social Anthropology, Stockholm University.

Garriott, W., and K.L. O'Neill. 2008. "Who Is a Christian? Toward a Dialogic Approach in the Anthropology of Christianity." *Anthropological Theory* 8 (4): 381–398.

Garro, L., and C. Mattingly, eds. 2000. *Narrative and the Cultural Construction of Illness and Healing.* Berkeley: University of California Press.

Gell, A. 1992. "The Technology of Enchantment and the Enchantment of Technology." In J. Coote and A. Shelton, eds., *Anthropology, Art and Aesthetics.* London: Clarendon Press, pp. 40–66.

Geschiere, P. 1997. *The Modernity of Witchcraft: Politics and the Occult in Postcolonial Africa.* Charlottesville and London: University of Virginia Press.

Gifford, P. 1994. "Some Recent Developments in African Christianity." *African Affairs* 93 (4): 513–534.

———. 1998. *African Christianity: Its Public Role.* London: Hurst and Company.

———. 2004. *Ghana's New Christianity: Pentecostalism in a Globalising African Economy.* London: Hurst and Company.

Ginsburg, F. 2006 "Rethinking the 'Voice of God' in Indigenous Australia: Secrecy, Exposure, and the Efficacy of Media." In B. Meyer and A. Moors, eds., *Religion, Media and the Public Sphere.* Bloomington and Indianapolis: Indiana University Press, pp. 188–204.

Ginsburg, F., L. Abu-Lughod, and B. Larkin, eds. 2002. *Media Worlds: Anthropology on New Terrain.* Berkeley: University of California Press.

Gobodo-Madikizela, P., and C. van der Merwe, eds. 2009. *Memory, Narrative, and Forgiveness: Perspectives on the Unfinished Journeys of the Past.* Newcastle upon Tyne: Cambridge Scholars Publishing.

Goethals, G.T. 1981. *The TV Ritual: Worship at the Video Altar.* Boston: Beacon Press.

Goffman, E. 1971[1959]. *The Presentation of Self in Everyday Life.* New York: Doubleday.

Gondola, C.D. 1997. "Popular Music, Urban Society, and Changing Gender Relations in Kinshasa, Zaire (1950–1990)." In M. Grosz-Ngate and O.H. Kokole, eds., *Gendered Encounters: Challenging Cultural Boundaries and Social Hierarchies in Africa*. New York and London: Routledge, pp. 65–84.

Graetz, T. 2010. "New Urban Radio Stations and the Success of Call-In Shows on Intimate Issues in Benin." Paper presented at the conference *Tuning into African Cities: Popular Culture and Urban Experience in sub-Saharan Africa*, Birmingham, 7 May 2010.

Hackett, R.I.J. 1994. "African Art and Religion: Some Observations and Reflections." *Journal of Religion in Africa* 24 (4): 294–308.

———. 1998. "Charismatic/Pentecostal Appropriation of Media Technologies in Nigeria and Ghana." *Journal of Religion in Africa* 28(3): 1–19.

Hall, S. 1997. *Representation: Cultural Representations and Signifying Practices*. London: Sage and Open University.

Harding, F. 1999. "Presenting and Re-Presenting the Self: From Not Acting to Acting in African Performance." *The Drama Review* 43 (2): 118–135.

———, ed. 2002. *The Performance Arts in Africa: A Reader*. London: Routledge.

Heidegger, M. 1977. *The Question Concerning Technology and Other Essays*. New York: Garland.

Helle-Valle, J. 2004. "Understanding Sexuality in Africa: Diversity and Contextualised Dividuality." In S. Arnfred, ed., *Re-Thinking Sexualities in Africa*. Uppsala: Nordiska Afrikainstitutet, pp. 195–210.

Hirschkind, C. 2001. "The Ethics of Listening: Cassette-Sermon Auditioning in Contemporary Egypt." *American Ethnologist* 28 (3): 623–649.

Hobart, M. 2002. "Live or Dead? Televising Theater in Bali." In F. Ginsburg, L. Abu-Lughod, and B. Larkin, eds., *Media Worlds: Anthropology on New Terrain*. Berkeley and Los Angeles: University of California Press, pp. 370–382.

Hollenweger, W.J. 1972. *The Pentecostals*. London: SCM.

Hughes-Freeland, F., and M.M. Crain. 1998. *Recasting Ritual: Performance, Media, Identity*. London: Routledge.

Hulstaert, G. 1971. "Sur quelques croyances magiques des Mongo." *Cahiers des religions africaines* 5 (9): 145–167.

Hunter, M. 2009. "Providing Love: Sex and Exchange in Twentieth-Century South Africa." In J. Cole and L.M. Thomas, eds., *Love in Africa*. Chicago: University of Chicago Press, pp. 135–156.

Institut National de la Statistique. 1991. *Zaïre: recensement scientifique de la population, juillet 1984. Totaux définitifs*. Kinshasa: Institut National de la Statistique.

Janzen, J.M. 1992. *Lemba, 1650–1930: A Drum of Affliction in Africa and the New World*. New York: Garland Publishing.

Jewsiewicki, B. 1991. "Painting in Zaire: From the Invention of the West to the Representation of Social Self." In S. Vogel, ed., *Africa Explores: 20ᵗʰ Century African Art*. New York and Munich: Center for African Art and Prestel, pp. 130–151.

———. 1995. *Cheri Samba: The Hybridity of Art*. Westmount, Quebec: Galerie Amrad African Art Publications.

———. 1996. "Zaïrian Popular Painting as Commodity and as Communication." In M.J. Arnoldi, C.M. Geary, and K.L. Hardin, eds., *African Material Culture*. Bloomington and Indianapolis: Indiana University Press, pp. 334–355.

———. 2003 "Une société urbaine 'moderne' et ses représentations : la peinture populaire à Kinshasa (Congo) (1960–2000)." *Mouvement social* 204: 131–148.

———. 2004. "Kinshasa: (auto)representation d'une société "moderne" en (dé)construction. De la modernisation coloniale à la globalisation." In P. Mabiala Mantuba-Ngoma, ed., *La Nouvelle Histoire du Congo. Mélanges eurafricains offerts à Frans Bontinck, C.I.C.M.* Paris and Tervuren: Musée Royal de l'Afrique Centrale and L'Harmattan, pp. 251–266.

Jules-Rosette, B. 1984. *The Messages of Tourist Art: An African Semiotic System in Comparative Perspective*. New York: Plenum.

———. 2002. "Afro-Pessimism's Many Guises." *Public Culture* 14 (3): 603–605.

Kalu, O. 2008. *African Pentecostalism: An Introduction*. Oxford: Oxford University Press.

Kamate, R. 2009. "Pentecostalism in Kinshasa: Maintaining Multiple Church Membership." *African Communication Research* 2 (1): 145–166.

Kapferer, B. 1997. *The Feast of the Sorcerer: Practices of Consciousness and Power*. Chicago: University of Chicago Press.

Kawata, A.T. 2003. *Bago – Dictionnaire Lingala/Falanse Français/Lingala*. Paris: Éditions Le laboratoire de langues congolaises.

Kerr, D. 1995. *African Popular Theatre: From Precolonial Times to the Present Day*. London and Portsmouth, NH: James Currey and Heinemann.

Kirby, M. 1972. "On Acting and Not-Acting." *The Drama Review* 1 (1): 3–15.

Kirsch, T.G. 2008. *Spirits and Letters: Reading, Writing and Charisma in African Christianity*. New York and Oxford: Berghahn Books.

Knappert, J. 1978. *Myths and Legends of the Congo*. London: Heinemann.

Kramer, F. 1993. *The Red Fez: Art and Spirit Possession in Africa*. Trans. M. R. Green. London: Verso.

Krings, M. 2009. "Karishika with Kiswahili Flavour: A Nigerian Video Film Retold by a Tanzanian Video Jokey." Paper read at the conference *Nollywood and Beyond*, Mainz, 13–16 May 2009.

La Fontaine, J. 1974. "The Free Women of Kinshasa: Prostitution in a City in Zaire." In J. Davis, ed., *Choice and Change: Essays in Honour of Lucy Mair*. New York: Humanities Press, pp. 19–113.

Lambek, M. 1981. *Human Spirits: A Cultural Account of Trance in Mayotte*. New York: Cambridge University Press.

Lambertz, P. 2011. "Congolese Ancestor Veneration from Japan? Perspectives on the Church of World Messianity/Eglise Messianique Mondiale/Sekai Kyuseikyo in Kinshasa (DR Congo)." Paper presented at the Graduiertenkolleg *Bruchzonen der Globaliserung*, Leipzig: Universität Leipzig/Institut fűr Afrikanistik.

Larkin, B. 1997. "Indian Films and Nigerian Lovers: Media and the Creation of Parallel Modernities." *Africa* 67 (3): 406–440.

————. 2008. *Signal and Noise: Media, Infrastructure, and Urban Culture in Nigeria.* Durham, NC: Duke University Press.

Levi, H. 1997. "Sport and Melodrama: The Case of Mexican Professional Wrestling." *Social Text* 15 (1): 57–68.

Lévi-Strauss, C., 1969. *The Elementary Structures of Kinship.* Trans. J. Bell, J. von Sturmer, and R. Needham. Boston: Beacon Press.

Liebes, T., and J. Curran. 1998. *Media, Ritual and Identity.* London: Routledge.

LiPuma, E. 1998. "Modernity and Forms of Personhood in Melanesia." In M. Lambek and A. Strathern, eds., *Bodies and Persons: Comparative Perspectives from Africa and Melanesia.* Cambridge: Cambridge University Press, pp. 53–79.

Lutz, C. 1992. "Culture and Consciousness: A Problem in the Anthropology of Knowledge." In F.S. Kessel, P.M. Cole, and D.L. Johnson, eds., *Self and Consciousness: Multiple Perspectives.* London: Lawrence Erlbaum, pp. 64–87.

Lyons, A.P. 1990. "The Television and the Shrine: Towards a Theoretical Model for the Study of Mass Communications in Nigeria." *Visual Anthropology* 3 (4): 429–456.

Lyons H.D., and A.P. Lyons. 1987. "Magical Medicine on Television: Benin City, Nigeria." *Journal of Ritual Studies* 1 (1): 103–135.

MacGaffey, W. 1983. *Modern Kongo Prophets: Religion in a Plural Society.* Bloomington: Indiana University Press.

————. 1986. *Religion and Society in Central Africa: The Bakongo of Lower Zaire.* Chicago: University of Chicago Press.

————. 1988. "Complexity, Astonishment and Power: The Visual Vocabulary of Kongo Minkisi." *Journal of Southern African Studies* 14 (2): 188–203.

Mair, L. 1969. *African Marriage and Social Change.* London: Cass.

Malaquais, D. 2001. *Anatomie d'une arnaque: feymen et feymania au Cameroun.* Les Etudes du CERI No 77. Paris: Centre d'etudes et recherches internationales.

Mankekar, P. 1999. *Screening Culture, Viewing Politics: An Ethnography of Television, Womanhood and Nation in Postcolonial India.* Durham, NC: Duke University Press.

Maran, T. 2003. "Mimesis as a Phenomenon of Semiotic Communication." *Sign Systems Studies* 31 (1): 191–215.

Marcus, G. 1997. "Introduction." In G. Marcus, ed., *Cultural Producers in Perilous States: Editing Events, Documenting Change.* Chicago and London: University of Chicago Press, pp. 1–17.

Marks, L. 2000. *The Skin of the Film: Intercultural Cinema, Embodiment, and the Senses.* Durham, NC: Duke University Press.

Marriott, M. 1976. "Hindu Transactions: Diversity without Dualism." In B. Kapferer, ed., *Transaction and Meaning: Directions in the Anthropology of Exchange and Symbolic Behavior.* Philadelphia: Institute for the Study of Human Issues, pp. 109–142.

Marshall, R. 2009. *Political Spiritualities: The Pentecostal Revolution in Nigeria.* Chicago and London: University of Chicago Press.

Marshall-Fratani, R., and D. Péclard. 2002. "Introduction au Thème La Religion du Sujet en Afrique." In "Les Sujets de Dieu," special issue, *Politique Africaine* 87: 5–19.

Masquelier, A. 2009. "Lessons from *Rubi*: Love, Poverty, and the Intellectual Value of Televised Drama in Niger." In J. Cole and L.M. Thomas, eds., *Love in Africa*. Chicago and London: University of Chicago Press, pp. 204–228.

Matangila, A. 2006. "Pour une analyse du discours des Eglises de réveil à Kinshasa: méthode et contexte." In "Expérience de recherche en République Démocratique du Congo: Méthodes et contexts", special issue, T. Trefon and P. Petit, eds., *Civilisations* 54 (1–2): 77–84.

Maxwell, D. 2000. Pentecostalism and Politics in Postcolonial Zimbabwe. *Africa* 70 (2): 249–277.

———. 2005. *African Gifts of the Spirit: Pentecostalism and the Rise of a Zimbabwean Transnational Religious Movement*. Oxford: James Currey.

Mbembe, A. 1985. *Les jeunes et l'ordre politique en Afrique Noire*. Paris: L'Harmattan.

———. 1997. "The Thing and Its Double in Camerounian Cartoons." In K. Barber, ed., *Readings in African Popular Culture*. London: James Currey, pp. 151–163.

McEachern, C. 2002. *Narratives of Nation: Media, Memory and Representation in the Making of the New South Africa*. New York: Nova Science Publishers.

Merriam, A.P. 1974. "Change in Religion and the Arts in a Zairian Village." *African Arts* 7 (4): 46–53, 95.

Meyer, B. 1995. "'Delivered from the Powers of Darkness': Confessions of Satanic Riches in Christian Ghana." *Africa* 65 (2): 236–255.

———. 1998. "'Make a Complete Break with the Past': Memory and Post-Colonial Modernity in Ghanaian Pentecostalist Discourse." *Journal of Religion in Africa* 28 (3): 316–349.

———. 1999. *Translating the Devil: Religion and Modernity Among the Ewe in Ghana*. Edinburgh: Edinburgh University Press.

———. 2003a. "Visions of Blood, Sex and Money: Fantasy Spaces in Popular Ghanaian Cinema." *Visual Anthropology* 16 (1): 15–41.

———. 2003b. "Ghanaian Popular Cinema and the Magic in and of Film." In B. Meyer and P. Pels, eds., *Magic and Modernity: Interfaces of Revelation and Concealment*. Stanford, CA: Stanford University Press, pp. 200–222.

———. 2004a. "Christianity in Africa: From African Independent to Pentecostal-Charismatic Churches." *Annual Review of Anthropology* 33: 447–474.

———. 2004b. "'Praise the Lord': Popular Cinema and Pentecostalite Style in Ghana's New Public Sphere." *American Ethnologist* 31 (1): 92–110.

———. 2006a. "Impossible Representations: Pentecostalism, Vision, and Video Technology in Ghana." In B. Meyer and A. Moors, eds., *Religion, Media and the Public Sphere*. Bloomington: Indiana University Press, pp. 290–312.

———. 2006b. "Religious Revelation, Secrecy and the Limits of Visual Representation." *Anthropological Theory* 6 (4): 431–453.

———, ed. 2009a. *Aesthetic Formations: Media, Religion, and the Senses.* New York: Palgrave MacMillan.

———. 2009b. "Pentecostalism and Modern Audiovisual Media." In K. Njogu and J. Middleton, eds., *Media and Identity in Africa.* Bloomington and Indianapolis: University of Indiana Press, pp. 114–123.

Meyer, B., and A. Moors, eds. 2006. *Religion, Media and the Public Sphere.* Bloomington and Indianapolis: Indiana University Press.

Meyer, B. and P. Pels, eds. 2003. *Magic and Modernity: Interfaces of Revelation and Concealment.* Stanford, CA: Stanford University Press.

Moore, H.L., and T. Sanders. 2001. "Magical Interpretations and Material Realities: An Introduction." In T. Sanders and H.L. Moore, eds., *Magical Interpretations, Material Realities: Modernity, Witchcraft, and the Occult in Postcolonial Africa.* London and New York: Routledge, pp. 1–27.

Morris, R.C. 2002. "A Room with a Voice: Mediation and Mediumship in Thailand's Information Age." In F. Ginsburg, L. Abu-Lughod, and B. Larkin, eds., *Media Worlds: Anthropology on New Terrain.* Berkeley and Los Angeles: University of California Press, pp. 383–397.

———, ed. 2009. *Photographies East: The Camera and its Histories in East and Southeast Asia.* Durham, NC: Duke University Press.

Munn, N. 1986. *The Fame of Gawa: A Symbolic Study of Value Transformation in a Massim (Papua New Guinea) Society.* Cambridge: Cambridge University Press.

———. 1996. "The Cultural Anthropology of Time: A Critical Essay." *Annual Review of Anthropology* 21: 93–123.

Murphy, W. 1981. "The Rhetorical Management of Dangerous Knowledge in Kpelle Brokerage." *American Ethnologist* 8: 667–685.

———. 1998. "The Sublime Dance of Mende Politics: An African Aesthetic of Charismatic Power." *American Ethnologist* 25 (4): 563–582.

Muteba, N.M. 1987. "Mukiya, Tshibau et Tshibindi: sanction sociale et morale chez les Luba du Kasaï." *Zaïre-Afrique* 215: 275–289.

Ndaya Tshiteku, J. 2008. "'*Prendre le bic.' Le Combat Spirituel congolais et les transformations sociales.*" PhD dissertation, Leiden: Centre d'Etudes Africaines.

Ndjio, B. 2008. "Feymen and Evolués: Old and New Figures of Modernity in Cameroon." In P. Geschiere, B. Meyer, and P. Pels, eds., *Readings in Modernity in Africa.* Edinburgh and London: IAI and James Currey, pp. 205-214.

Newell, S. 2002. "Introduction." In S. Newell, ed., *Readings in African Popular Fiction.* Bloomington: Indiana University Press, pp. 1–10.

———. 2008. "Corresponding with the City: Self-Help Literature in Urban West-Africa." *Journal of Postcolonial Writing* 44 (1): 15–27.

Nooter, M.H. 1993. "Secrecy: African Art that Conceals and Reveals." *African Arts* 26 (1): 55–69.

Ntambwe, K.T. 1983. "Le "likelemba" et le "muziki": nature et problèmes socio-juridiques en droit privé zaïrois." *Zaire-Afrique* 23 (177): 431–442.

Nyamnjoh, F. 2005. "Fishing in Troubled Waters: Disquettes and Thiofs in Dakar." *Africa* 27 (3): 295–324.

Nzeza Bilakela, A. 2004. "The Kinshasa Bargain." In T. Trefon, ed., *Reinventing Order in the Congo: How People Respond to State Failure in Kinshasa.* London, New York, and Kampala: Zed Books and Fountain Publishers, pp. 20–32.

Nzongola-Ntalaja, G. 1979. "The Continuing Struggle for National Liberation in Zaire." *Journal of Modern African Studies* 17 (4): 595–614.

Ochs, E., and L. Capps 2001. *Living Narrative: Creating Lives in Everyday Story-Telling.* Cambridge, MA: Harvard University Press.

Ortner, S. 2002[1973]. "On Key Symbols." In M. Lambek, ed., *A Reader in the Anthropology of Religion.* London: Blackwell Publishers Ltd., pp. 158–167

———. 1996. *Making Gender: The Politics and Erotics of Culture.* Boston: Beacon Press.

Parkin, D. 1985a. "Introduction." In D. Parkin, ed., *The Anthropology of Evil.* Oxford: Basil Blackwell, pp. 1–25.

———. 1985b. "Entitling Evil: Muslims and Non-Muslims in Coastal Kenya." In D. Parkin, ed., *The Anthropology of Evil.* Oxford: Basil Blackwell, pp. 224–243.

Parpart, J. 1994. "'Where Is Your Mother?' Gender, Urban Marriage and Colonial Discourse on the Zambian Copperbelt, 1924–1945." *International Journal of African Historical Studies* 27 (2): 241–271.

Payne, N. 2007. "La sculpture en bois, un métier en voie de disparition en Congo." *L'Avenir* 23 (April).

Peek, P.M., ed. 1991. *African Divination Systems: Ways of Knowing.* Bloomington: Indiana University Press.

Perani, J., and N.H. Wolff. 1999. *Cloth, Dress and Art Patronage in Africa.* Oxford and New York: Berg.

Peterson, Royce A. 2004. *Anthropology of the Performing Arts: Artistry, Virtuosity and Interpretation in Cross-Cultural Perspective.* Walnut Creek, CA: AltaMira Press.

Petit, P., and G.M. Mutambwa. 2005. "'La Crise': Lexicon and Ethos of the Second Economy in Lubumbashi." *Africa* 75 (4): 467–487.

Pinney, C. 2002. "The Indian Work of Art in the Age of Mechanical Reproduction: Or, What Happens When Peasants 'Get Hold' of Images." In F. Ginsburg, L. Abu-Lughod, and B. Larkin, eds., *Media Worlds: Anthropology on New Terrain.* Berkeley and Los Angeles: University of California Press, pp. 355–369.

Pitt-Rivers, J. 1968. "Kinship III: Pseudo Kinship." *International Encyclopedia of the Social Sciences.* New York: Macmillan, vol. 8, pp. 408–413.

Pollock, D. 2000. "Physician Autobiography: Narrative and the Social History of Medicine." In C. Mattingly and L.C. Garro, eds., *Narrative and the Cultural Construction of Illness and Healing.* Berkeley: University of California Press, pp. 108–127.

Price, L. 2007. "Narrative Mediation: A Transformative Approach to Conflict Resolution." *African Initiative for Mediation.* March, e-document, http://www.mediate.com//articles/priceL1.cfm, accessed 1 February 2011.

Probst, P. 2002. "Kalumba's Tänzer und Malandas Zorn. Polyzentrische Öffentlichkeit und die Kraft des Performativen in Zentralmalawi." *Paideuma* 48: 135–143.

Pype, K. 2006. "Dancing for God or for the Devil: Pentecostal Discourse on Popular Dance in Kinshasa." *Journal of Religion in Africa* 36 (3–4): 296–318.

———. 2007. "Fighting Boys, Strong Men and Gorillas: Notes on the Imagination of Masculinities in Kinshasa." *Africa* 77 (2): 250–271.

———. 2009a. "'We Need to Open Up the Country': Development and the Christian Key Scenario in the Social Space of Kinshasa's Teleserials." *Journal of African Media Studies* 1 (1): 101–116.

———. 2009b. "Historical Routes towards Religious Television Fiction in post-Mobutu Kinshasa." In "Faith and Film," ed. Jolyon Mitchell, special issue, *Studies in World Christianity* 15 (2): 131–148.

———. 2010. "Of Fools and False Pastors: Tricksters in Kinshasa's TV Fiction." *Visual Anthropology* 23 (2): 115–135.

———. 2011a. "Dreaming the Apocalypse: Mimesis and the Pentecostal Imagination in Kinshasa." *Paideuma* 57: 81–96.

———. 2011b. "Taboos and Rebels. Or, Transgression and Regulation in the Work and Lives of Kinshasa's Television Journalists". In "Media in Africa," ed. Sean Jacobs, special issue, *Popular Communication* 9 (2): 114–125.

———. Forthcoming a. "Religion, Migration and Media Aesthetics: Notes on the Circulation and Reception of Nigerian Films in Kinshasa." In M. Krings and O. Okome, eds., *Nollywood and Beyond*. Bloomington: University of Indiana Press.

———. Forthcoming b. "The Heart of Man: Mass Mediated Representations of Emotions, the Subject and Subjectivities"

Ramirez, F., and C. Rolot. 1985. *Histoire du cinéma colonial au Zaire, Rwanda et au Burundi*. Tervuren: Musée Royal de l'Afrique Centrale.

Rapport, N., and J. Overing. 2000. *Social and Cultural Anthropology: The Key Concepts (Key Guides)*. London and New York: Routledge.

Ricoeur, P. 1984. *Time and Narrative: Volume 1*. Trans. K. McLaughlin and D. Pellauer. Chicago: University of Chicago Press.

Robbins, J. 2004. *Becoming Sinners: Christianity and Moral Torment in a Papua New Guinea Society*, Ethnographic Studies in Subjectivity, 4. Berkeley: University of California Press.

———. 2007. "Continuity Thinking and the Problem of Christian Culture: Belief, Time and the Anthropology of Christianity." *Current Anthropology* 48 (1): 5–38.

———. N.d. *Keeping God's Distance: Sacrifice, Possession and the Problem of Religious Mediation*, unpublished manuscript, 29p.

Rofel, L. 1994. "'Yearnings': Televisual Love and Melodramatic Politics in Contemporary China." *American Ethnologist* 21 (4): 700–722.

Ruytinx, J. 1969. *La Morale bantoue et le Problème de l'éducation morale au Congo*. 2nd ed. Brussels: Editions de l'Institut de Sociologie (Collection Etudes Africaines).

Schatzberg, M. 2001. *Political Legitimacy in Middle Africa: Father, Family, Food*. Bloomington: University of Indiana Press.

Searle, J. 1969. *Speech Acts: An Essay in the Philosophy of Language.* Cambridge: Cambridge University Press.

Sharp, L.A. 1993. *The Possessed and the Dispossessed: Spirits, Identity, and Power in a Madagascar Migrant Town.* Berkeley: University of California Press.

Simmel, G. 1965[1908]. *Essays on Sociology, Philosophy and Aesthetics.* Ed. K.H. Wolff. New York: Harper and Row.

Smith, B.R., and R. Vokes. 2008. "Introduction: Haunting Images." *Visual Anthropology* 21 (4): 283–291.

Smith, D.J. 2009. "Managing Men, Marriage and Modern Love: Women's Perspectives on Intimacy and Male Infidelity in Southeastern Nigeria." In J. Cole and L.M. Thomas, eds., *Love in Africa.* Chicago and London: University of Chicago Press, pp. 157–180.

Sobschack, V. 2004. *Carnal Thoughts: Embodiment and Moving Image Culture.* Berkeley: University of California Press.

Spitulnik, D. 2002. "Mobile Machines and Fluid Audiences: Rethinking Reception through Zambian Radio Culture." In F. Ginsburg, L. Abu-Lughod, and B. Larkin, eds., *Media Worlds: Anthropology on New Terrain.* Berkeley: University of California Press, pp. 337–354.

Spronk, R. 2009. "Media and the Therapeutic Ethos of Romantic Love in Middle-Class Nairobi." In J. Cole and L.M. Thomas, *Love in Africa.* Chicago and London: University of Chicago Press, pp. 181–203.

Stoller, P. 1995. *Embodying Colonial Memories: Spirit Possession, Power, and the Hauka in West Africa.* New York: Routledge.

Stone, R.M. 1994. "Bringing the Extraordinary into the Ordinary: Music Performance among the Kpelle of Liberia." In T.D. Blakely, W.E.A. van Beek, and D.L. Thomson, eds., *Religion in Africa.* Portsmouth, NH, and London: Heinemann and James Currey, pp. 388–397.

Stout, D.A., and J.M. Buddenbaum. 1996. *Religion and Mass Media: Audiences and Adaptations.* Thousand Oaks, CA: Sage.

Strathern, M. 1988. *The Gender of the Gift: Problems with Women and Problems with Society in Melanesia.* Berkeley: University of California Press.

Stroeken, K. 2001. "Bringing Home the Heat: An Anthropological Study of Bewitchment and Mediumship in Sukumaland." PhD dissertation, Leuven: Katholieke Universiteit Leuven.

———. 2004. "In Search of the Real: The Healing Contingency of Sukuma Divination." In M. Winkelman and P. Peek, eds., *Divination and Healing: Potent Vision.* Tucson: University of Arizona Press, pp. 29–55.

Sundberg, M. 2000. *Conversion and Contextual Conceptions of Christ: A Missiological Study among Young Converts in Brazzaville, Republic of Congo.* Uppsala: Swedish Institute of Missionary Research.

Tansi, S.L. 2005–2006[1984]. "Le Sexe de Matonge." *Politique Africaine* 100: 118–124.

Taussig, M. 1993. *Mimesis and Alterity: A Particular History of the Senses.* New York: Routledge.

———. 2003. "Viscerality, Faith, and Skepticism. Another Theory of Magic." In B. Meyer and P. Pels, eds., *Magic and Modernity: Interfaces of Revelation and Concealment*. Stanford, CA: Stanford University Press, pp. 272–306.

Thomas, L.M. 2009. "Love, Sex, and the Modern Girl in the 1930s Southern Africa." In J. Cole and L.M. Thomas, eds., *Love in Africa*. Chicago and London: University of Chicago Press, pp. 31–57.

Thomas, L.M. and Cole, J. 2009. "Introduction: thinking through love in Africa". In J. Cole and L.M. Thomas, eds., *Love in Africa*. Chicago and London: University of Chicago Press, pp. 1–30.

Tomaselli, K.G. 1996. "The Scientifically Unexplainable: Magic and the Electronic Cosmos." *Media and Development* 4: 32–34.

Tonda, J. 2000. "Capital sorcier et travail de Dieu." *Politique africaine* 79 (October): 48–65.

———. 2002. "Economie des miracles et dynamiques de subjectivation/civilisation en Afrique centrale: Les sujets de Dieu." *Politique africaine* 87: 20–44.

Trefon, T. 2004. "Introduction: Reinventing Order." In T. Trefon, ed., *Reinventing Order in the Congo: How People Respond to State Failure in Kinshasa*. London, New York, and Kampala: Zed Books and Fountain Publishers, pp. 1–19.

Tsambu, L.B. 2004. "Musique et Violence à Kinshasa." In T. Trefon, ed., *Ordre et Désordre à Kinshasa. Réponses populaires à la faillite de l'Etat*. Tervuren and Paris: Africa Museum and L'Harmattan, pp. 193–212.

Tshimanga, C. 2001. *Jeunesse, Formation et Société au Congo-Kinshasa 1890–1960*. Paris: L'Harmattan.

Turner, V. 1975. *Revelation and Divination in Ndembu Ritual*. Ithaca, NY: Cornell University Press.

Van Caeneghem, R. 1955. *Hekserij bij de Baluba van Kasai*, classe des sciences morales et politiques. Mémoires in-8 N.S.; 3.1. Brussels: Académie royale des sciences coloniales.

Van de Port, M. 2006. "Visualizing the Sacred: Video Technology, "Televisual" Style, and the Religious Imagination in Bahian Candomblé." *American Ethnologist* 33 (3): 444–461.

Van der Geest, S. 2002. "From Wisdom to Witchcraft: Ambivalence towards Old Age in Rural Ghana." *Africa* 67 (4): 534–559.

Van Dijk, R. 1998. "Pentecostalism, Cultural Memory and the State: Contested Representations of Time in Postcolonial Malawi." In R. Werbner, ed., *Memory and the Postcolony: African Anthropology and the Critique of Power*. London: Zed Books, pp. 155–181.

———. 2000. "Christian Fundamentalism in Sub-Saharan Africa: The Case of Pentecostalism." Occasional paper, Copenhagen: Centre of African Studies.

———. 2001. "Witchcraft and Scepticism by Proxy: Pentecostalism and Laughter in Urban Malawi." In H. Moore and T. Sanders, eds., *Magical Interpretations, Material Realities: Modernity, Witchcraft and the Occult in Postcolonial Africa*. London: Routledge, pp. 97–117.

———. 2004. "Negotiating Marriage: Questions of Morality and Legitimacy in the Ghanaian Pentecostal Diaspora." *Journal of Religion in Africa* 34 (4): 438–467.

Van Groenweghe, D. 1997. *Aids in Afrika: oorsprong, verspreiding en seksuele netwerken in historisch en socio-cultureel perspectief.* Berchem: EPO.

Vansina, J. 1955. "Initiation Rituals of the Bushong." *Africa* 25 (2): 138–153.

———. 1984. *Art History in Africa.* London and New York: Longman.

Vasudevan, R., ed. 2000. "Shifting Codes, Dissolving Identities: The Hindi Social Film of the 1950s as Popular Culture." In R. Vasudevan, ed., *Making Meaning in Indian Cinema.* New Delhi: Oxford University Press, pp. 99–121.

Verbeek, L. 2006. *Contes de l'inceste, de la parenté et de l'alliance chez les Bemba.* Paris: Karthala.

Weber, M. 1947. *The Theory of Social and Economic Organization.* Trans. A.M. Henderson and T. Parsons. Ed. by T. Parsons. London: Hodge.

———. 1964. *The Sociology of Religion.* Trans. Ephraim Fischoff. Boston: Beacon Press.

———. 1978. *The Protestant Ethic and the Spirit of Capitalism.* Trans. T. Parsons. London: Allen and Unwin.

Weiner, J. 1997. "Televisualist Anthropology: Representation, Aesthetics, Politics." *Current Anthropology* 38 (2): 197–236.

Werbner, P. 1996. "Fun Spaces: On Identity and Social Empowerment among British Pakistanis." *Theory, Culture and Society* 13 (4): 53–80.

Werner, J.-F. 2006. "Comment les femmes utilisent la télévision pour domestiquer la modernité. Enquête ethnographique sur la diffusion et la réception des telenovelas à Dakar (Sénégal)." In J.F. Werner, ed., *Médias visuels et femmes en Afrique de l'Ouest.* Paris: L'Harmattan, pp. 145–194.

West, H., and G.T. Sanders. 2003. *Transparency and Conspiracy: Ethnographies of Suspicion in the New World Order.* Durham, NC, and London: Duke University.

White, B.W. 1998. "Modernity's Spiral: Popular Culture, Mastery and the Politics of Dance Music in Congo-Kinshasa." PhD dissertation, Montreal: McGill University.

———. 1999. "Modernity's Trickster: "Dipping" and "Throwing" in Congolese Popular Dance Music." *Research in African Literatures* 30 (4): 156–175.

———. 2004. "The Elusive Lupemba: Rumours about Fame and (Mis)Fortune in Kinshasa." In T. Trefon, ed., *Reinventing Order in the Congo: How People Respond to State Failure in Kinshasa.* London, New York, and Kamapala: Zed Books and Fountain Publishers, pp. 174–192.

———. 2005. "The Political Undead: Is It Possible to Mourn for Mobutu's Zaire?" *African Studies Review* 48 (2): 65–85.

———. 2008. *Rumba Rules: The Politics of Dance Music in Mobutu's Zaire.* Durham, NC: Duke University Press.

Winkelman, M., and P.M. Peek, eds. 2004. *Divination and Healing: Potent Vision.* Tucson: University of Arizona Press.

Wolfe, A.W. 1955. "Art and the Supernatural in the Ubangi District." *Man* 55: 65–67.

Zempléni, A. 1976. "La chaîne du secret." *Nouvelle Revue de Psychanalyse* 14 : 313–324.

Index

3C, 273. *See also kochina, chic-choc-chèque*
acting versus performing, 138–40
Adorons l'Eternel, 143, 161
adultery, 23, 54, 179, 184, 196n4, 233,
    248–54, 259, 268, 277, 297
aesthetic formation, 15, 295
aesthetics, 9, 138. *See also* dance, music
    Congolese art, 23, 102, 120, 211
    of the invisible, 61, 125. *See also*
        special effects
    in Kinshasa's media, 11, 15, 101,
        126, 165
    Nigerian films, aesthetics of, 9,
        160
agency, 24n1, 103, 127, 157, 165, 168,
    169, 173, 174–7, 180, 183, 189, 233
Althusser, Louis, 196n7
Aluund, 49, 60n12, 96, 114, 116,
    128n8, 223, 256n12, 257nn16–17
ambianceur, 48, 277
American catch. *See* wrestling
ancestors, 58
    artistic inspiration and, 103
    culture of, ancestrality, 33, 38,
        51, 147
    the life force and, 46, 227
    punishment and, 179, 220
    the Real and, 118
    resignification and, 47, 116, 180,
        209
    spirits of, 46, 103, 117, 250, 253
    spiritual confusion and, 58
    time and, 220

the village and, 251, 251
Anderson, Allan, 6, 14, 47, 61
Angola, 111
Animal, 176, 228n1, 256n8, 264
animism, 33
Apocalypse, 38–45, 57–60, 153, 162,
    182, 231n30
apocalyptic imagination, 39, 49, 52,
    61n18, 169, 189, 266, 292
Apostasy, 76, 95, 162, 279, 281
appearance
    attraction to others, 262
    cosmopolitan, 212
    reality as, 112, 118, 121, 139
    taking on the appearance of
        others, 131, 235
    youthful, 206
Askew, Kelly, 17, 128n6
audience
    as active producers of meaning,
        17
    Barber on, 164
    dialoguing with TV hosts,
        167n13
    during confessions, 190, 194
    evangelized, 12, 16, 151, 224,
        267–8, 295
    guiding the storylines of the TV
        serials, 24, 53, 94, 106, 145–6,
        218
    heterogeneous, 161, 269
    historical, 164
    praying along the TV set, 148

social interaction with
performers, 26n24, 69, 83,
137, 140
spiritual interaction with the
footage, 17, 155
aura, 23
art and, 103
Benjamin on, 158–9
Benjamin's thesis, revision of,
159–60
television serials and, 146
authority, 22
artists and, 107
the Bible and, 234, 293
concerning sexuality, 267, 270
conflict over, 82–5
drama groups, within, 65, 66,
69, 74
enhancing authority through TV
serials, 92
gendered dimensions of,
166n15, 212, 213, 281, 297
generations and, 203, 209
lineage, in the, 238
loss of, 42, 111, 153, 186, 212–3,
236
providing access to sacred
knowledge, 113
pastors and, 23, 34, 79, 101, 267
research and, 33, 91
of the state, 196n7
subversion of the elders'
authority, 210
transformations through
Christianity, 234, 254
witchcraft and, 51, 293
women having, 230n24, 283

Back to the Homestead, 21, 97n6
bad girl, 211–3, 229nn16–17, 230n17,
235, 244, 271
baKongo. *See* Kongo
baLuba. *See* Luba
Bana Bolafa, 72
Bana Mobutu, 203
baNkanu. *See* Nkanu
baptism, 77–8, 162, 168, 240
of the spirit and water baptism,
48

Barber, Karin, 17, 164
baSakata. *See* Sakata
Bastian, Misty, 212, 213, 298
baYaka. *See* Yaka
baYanzi. *See* Yanzi
Bayart, Jean–François, 64, 168, 227
beauty, 51, 88, 119, 152, 204, 205, 212,
214, 216, 240, 264, 270, 277
Behrend, Heike, 63, 122, 123, 128n10,
136, 148, 166n9
Bekaert, Stefaan, 40, 43, 46, 49, 115,
116, 117, 266
Bellman, Beryl, 123
Benjamin, Walter, 158–60
Bible
authority of, 32, 34, 36, 38, 45,
47, 48, 56, 59, 107, 141, 163,
194, 224, 228, 235, 268, 293
gender and, 234, 268, 278
Old versus New Testament, 201
as private object, 171, 200
in public places, 51, 56
reading, 21, 154, 271
on the screen, 16, 236
spiritual power of, 157, 16–2,
261
biography, 191, 216, 244
evangelizing actors, of, 65–7,
73–6, 87–90, 215–7
plotlines, influence of biography
on, 215–7
blindness, 53, 185, 186, 187
body
as a secret, 114
control of, 78. 168, 293
dance, 166n18, 262
life-force and, 46
feeling the Holy Spirit, 47,
61n14
female, 233, 241, 263, 272–3
inviting the Holy Spirit in, 123,
171–3
language of, 32, 186, 206
mediating invisible powers, 131,
164–5, 265–7
of the pastor, 117
of performers, 131, 137, 140,
163
of viewers, 131, 137

possession and, 110–1, 155, 158,
211, 214
purifying the, 36, 74, 174
seduction and, 212, 259, 261,
264
taken over by the Holy Spirit,
160
techniques of, 168
visible and invisible dimensions
of, 147–8
witchcraft and, 48, 50, 53, 182,
213, 277
Boeck, Filip De
and the apocalyptic imagination,
38, 41
on the crisis in Congo, 201, 202,
229nn1–2–4
on divination, 46, 48, 115, 117
on the entanglement of the
individual and the group, 223
on gender, 229n17, 256n12,
257n16, 289n14
on Kinshasa, 20, 97n1, 278
on mimetic excess, 61n19, 102
on Mobutu's regime, 34
on personhood, 96
on the secret, 114, 128n8
and witchcraft, 266
blood
"life" and, 46, 114
red and, 43
relatedness, 66, 246, 247
sacrifice, 51
spirits and, 265–6
witchcraft is in, 48
bomoyi. See life
bottle, 27, 119–20, 128n10, 157, 241
boys, 68, 72, 80, 110, 140, 202, 204,
206, 238, 240, 266, 270, 285, 299n2
bride price, 202, 226, 238, 243–4, 249,
273
Brazzaville, 26n13, 60n9, 111, 166n7,
184, 229n10
Brooks, Peter, v, 9, 54, 127, 194

camera, 15, 56, 70, 94, 100, 101, 104,
121, 126, 149, 153, 158, 179, 294
Carlito, 137
Caroline and Poupette, 215–8

Catholicism (Catholic groups), 6,
33–9, 52, 60n6, 171, 177, 196n3
cemetery, 44, 86
CFMC Maman Olangi, 35
charisma, 19, 22, 36, 108, 110, 119, 124
chic-choc-chèque, 270, 273, 275, 289n9
child of the night, 211
Christian community, 43, 51, 77, 190,
219, 223, 226, 227, 238, 255
boundaries, 77, 126
builders of, 51
emergence of, 6, 295
expansion of, 14, 126, 151, 249,
283
Christian pamphlets, 7
Christian of the flesh, 77–8, 90, 97,
176, 177, 270, 276, 295
Christian self, 173, 194
Church of the Holy Mountain, 62, 72,
79, 80, 82, 84, 112, 282
Cinarc
the church and, 12, 79–82, 83–4
history of, 65–73
splitting up, 82–85
cinematic space, 146
city
dangers in, 27–32
versus village, 31, 53, 242, 245
clientelism. *See* patronage
clothes
bad clothes, 182, 259, 263–4
buying as part of marriage
preparations, 243, 244, 273
causes of rivalry within *moziki*
groups, 279–82
pastors wearing designer clothes,
81
sexuality and, 90, 229n7, 241,
266, 273
urban culture and, 32, 78, 271
witchcraft and, 42–3, 49, 253,
268
Cole, Jennifer, 233, 243, 271, 273, 287
Coleman, Simon, 6, 136
Comaroff, Jean, 57, 229n6
Comaroff, John, 57, 229n6
Comhaire-Sylvain, Suzanne, 279
computer, 125, 181
concealment, 113

confession, 9, 23, 45, 57, 76, 132, 136, 168, 169, 173 183–92, 198, 223, 254
conflict mediation, 14, 197
conscience, 168, 189
contact
    form of social connection, 22, 65, 91–5, 216
    with the Holy Spirit, 110, 147
    sensuous contact with images, 151, 156–7
    through imitation, 138, 141
conversion
    baptism and, 245
    dramatic life change, 32, 78
    in the Pentecostal Melodrama, 10, 223, 254
    as solution for personal and collective crisis, 13–4, 225, 228, 295
    spiritual change, 195
    talking about one's, 74
copy
    becoming reality, 140
    Nigerian films, 19, 55
    reality versus, 124, 137–9
    the visible as copy of the visible, 41–2, 59
Corin, Ellen, 190–1
cosmopolitanism
    cosmopolitan lifestyle, 31
    Kinshasa as cosmopolitan city, 30, 33, 193, 233
    Pentecostal Christianity and, 6, 77
    postcolonial, 212
co-wife, 189, 191, 193, 205, 218
courtship, 233
creativity, 10, 11, 31, 57, 58, 102–3, 106, 132, 228, 297
Creten, Pascale, 46, 116, 117, 172, 246, 256nn11–13–15, 257n17, 259, 266
crisis, 116
    elders as cause of, 200–2
    experience of, 2, 199–200, 218, 223
    politics and, 6, 23, 29, 31, 35, 198–200, 227–8
    semiotic crisis, 43, 61n19, 297
Csordas, Thomas J., 128n4, 196n3

Cursed Neighborhood, The, 27–8, 57
customs. *See* tradition

dance, 103, 121, 131, 134, 137, 142–5, 152, 178, 187, 298
    ethnic or "traditional" dance, 16, 70, 190, 207, 209, 280
    politics, 208
    rumba, 16, 30
    the sacred and, 35, 132, 161, 194, 267, 293
    "worldly dance" or urban dance, 28, 33, 95, 105, 119, 132, 166nn7–17, 233, 244, 262–3, 294
Dasgupta, Sudeep, 160
death
    adultery leads to, 248–53
    in the apocalyptic imagination, 38, 110
    pagans as dead people, 77, 172, 184, 221, 227
    in the TV serials, 76, 86, 178–9, 181, 185–7, 191, 193, 214, 216, 218, 235–6, 248–53, 274, 280
    witchcraft and, 27, 48–9, 61n19, 131, 246, 267, 284
deliverance ritual, 11, 29
    agency and, 180
    confessions and, 192, 193
    discourse during, 174
    for the nation, 222
    for the person, 183, 186
    as purification, 168, 173
    in the TV serials, 169, 194, 223
demonic spirits, 39, 52, 104, 118, 155, 165, 242
Desjarlais, Robert, 200, 228n5
development
    drama and, 1, 2, 19, 25n7, 145, 194, 231n31, 233
    national, 7, 221, 226, 228
    spiritual, 166n2, 210, 223, 225–8, 293
Devil. *See also* elders, secrecy, witchcraft
    accepting his existence, 171
    ancestors and, 58
    the Apocalypse and, 38, 165, 175
    chaos and, 199, 202

children of, 40, 229n17
customs and, 210–1, 220, 253
doubt because of, 189
the origins of witchcraft and, 48
reign of, 202, 294
secrecy as the Devil's tool, 41–5,
134–5
sexuality and, 261, 264–5
strategies of, 164, 182, 268
takes advantage of bad words,
190
the white man's lore and, 39
women and, 270, 278, 288n2
working against, 245
Devisch, Renaat. *See also* Yaka
on the Congolese state, 203
on divination, 115–8
on healing (*mbwoolu*), 190–1
on the life force, 46–7
on personhood, 96, 204, 257n14
on religion, 34, 147
on symbolism, 43
on witchcraft, 49, 129n12, 266,
267
Devouring Fire, The, 26n15, 53–4,
196n10, 202, 241–5, 261
diaspora, 7, 9, 24, 63, 238
Dijk, Rijk Van, 6, 210, 220, 256n7
Dilemma, 23, 180–3, 241, 263–4
Diouf, Mamadou, 207
diploma, 73, 216, 240, 270, 271
discernment, spirit of, 121, 126, 127,
222
divination, 50, 115–8, 121, 191, 252
divorce, 252, 267, 277
Douglas, Mary, 48–9, 58, 118, 193,
257n17
dream
the American, 10
call from God, 66
erotic, 232, 266, 267
revealing the invisible, 101
technology of inspiration, 106
of travelling, 13, 198
Drewal, Henry, 212
dualistic worldview, 184

editing, 59, 119
ekobo. See incest

elders. *See also* gerontocracy
in the drama group, 68, 74, 106
La Kinoiserie and, 206, 210
marriage preferences and, 255,
287
obeying, 40, 60n10, 207, 209
the past and, 227
personhood and, 96
purification rituals and, 251
representation in the serials, 23,
178–9, 198, 210, 214, 237,
242, 245, 252
secrets and their knowledge, 113
versus youth, 201, 202–5
as witches, 47, 196n10, 209, 211,
229n10, 237, 247, 249, 293
embodiment, 105, 155, 184, 294
emotions, 9, 14, 46, 78, 81, 151, 153–8,
160, 164, 167n23, 189, 277, 278,
292–3
anger, 143, 163, 164, 167n23,
189, 192, 229n6, 253, 293
guilt, 184, 192
jealousy, 157, 164, 167n23, 188,
191, 193, 196n9, 212, 277–80,
291
joy, 29, 156, 163, 188, 226, 223,
275
love, 28, 53, 62, 74, 105, 123,
173, 188, 193, 212, 233–4,
243, 247, 255, 268–9, 271–5,
305, 306n6, 293
shame, 94, 189
emplotment, 219. *See also* audience
participation
conjunctive versus disjunctive
stories, 177–9
enchantment, 148, 158, 228n3, 294
Esobe, 3, 85
ethnicity, 69, 190, 237
Evangelists, The, 3, 70, 154
evangelization campaign, 159, 177,
214, 228
exorcism, 28, 36, 60n10, 132, 134, 193,
195
exposure, 115. *See also* revelation

Fabian, Johannes, 8, 16, 19, 25n2,
26nn18–22, 99n16, 208, 212

Fair, Laura, 26n19, 233
fake old men, 206
false, the, 42, 47. *See also* false pastor,
   false Christian
     criteria for marriage, 240
     knowledge, 49
     lovers, 283
     magic is false, 115
     promises, 270
     special effect, 123–4
     versus the true, 41–2, 127
false Christian, 77, 271, 294
fame, 63, 64, 92, 99n16. *See also*
   celebrity
father
     artistic father, 72, 73, 74, 76, 86,
       96, 230n25
     responsibilities, 222, 284
     spiritual father, 21, 73, 96, 225
     the state as father, 203
     witchcraft and, 241, 264
féticheur. See traditional healer
fétish
     arts and, 157
     demonization of, 58, 150, 152,
       184, 231n29
     healing through, 50
     magic and, 157
     prayer as, 107
     song, 137
     transformations in visual quality,
       121
     the TV set as, 157
fiançailles, 239, 241. *See also* marriage
fiction, 1, 7, 8, 9, 25n2, 177
     fictionalizing personal
       experiences, 76, 215–9,
       244–5, 280
     gender in, 26n19, 233
     media pedagogy in the churches
       and, 152–3
     veracity and, 101–2, 125,
       128nn1–2
fioti-fioti, 271
Fischer, Michael M.J., 23n26, 297
fool, 3, 10, 26n17, 46, 126, 135, 187,
   289n8
Fontaine, Jean La, 64, 88, 89, 98n15,
   262, 276

Foucault, Michel, 169, 188, 195n1, 258
freedom
     by accepting Jesus, 175
     from the Devil, 74
     of speech, 5
     to chose a marriage partner, 242,
       255
Freemasonry, 41, 51
fun space, 197, 208

Gell, Alfred, 158, 159
gender
     competing gender ideologies,
       233–4, 277
     confusion of gender and sexual
       identity, 289n8, 290
     defined by one's invisible
       double, 267
     differences in gaining prestige,
       285–6
     differences when watching
       wrestling shows, 167n18
     gender game, 233–4
     in the informal economy, 221n7,
       230n22
     kindumba and, 259
     mobility and, 283
     morality and, 14
     in patron–client relationships, 94
     playing different gender games,
       287
     politics in the churches, 269
     politics in Kinshasa, 277
     Pentecostal approaches to, 23
     of the researcher, 20
     sexuality and, 268–9
     technologies of, 258, 288
     witchcraft and, 196n5. *See also*
       witchcraft
gerontocracy, 210, 224. *See also* elders
Geschiere, Peter, 40, 45
Gifford, Paul, 6, 7, 35, 221, 231n28
Ginsburg, Faye, 13, 129n13
Gombe, 72
Gondola, Didier, 259
Graetz, Tilo, 268

Hackett, Rosalind, 7, 120, 129n15, 146
haptical visuality, 156

Harding, Frances, 131, 132, 139–40, 166n5
healing. *Also see* soul healing, narrative, traditional healer
    through confession, 168
    the country, 223, 296
    healing church, 37, 47
    indigenous healing cults, 47, 114–8, 128n7, 190–2
    mediated by the pastor, 111
    through *nkisi*, 121
    through pictures, 126, 148
    via television, 150–1, 159, 161
    through prayer, 133, 173–7
Heritage of Death, The, 23, 83, 185, 187, 189, 191, 193
Hobart, Mark, 26n24, 163
Hollywood. *See* American film
Holy Spirit
    acting and, 140
    as agent of transformation, 14, 78, 162, 169, 194
    as breath, wind, 172–3
    churches of, 147
    connecting with, 36, 210
    evoking, 125–6, 136, 138–9, 293
    as healer, 47
    impossible to store, 158
    as source of inspiration, 104–5, 107, 238
    in the living room, 149
    mediated by the pastor, 118, 166n11
    as the solution for the crisis, 295
    being touched by, 214
    viewers receiving, 164, 166n11
    walking with, 158
homosexuality, 267, 270, 289n8
household income, 207
humor, 65, 198, 208, 210
husband of the night, 150, 267, 288n5. *See also* wives of the night

identity, 29
    of the actor, 32, 63, 64, 65, 136, 275, 277, 284, 287, 295
    artistic father, 72
    as a Christian, 18, 56, 69, 78, 84, 86, 165, 168, 170, 176, 194, 225, 240, 284

cosmopolitan, 77
    criminal identity, 181
    ethnic identity, 70, 170
    female identity, 263, 278
    gendered identity, 290n16
    Kinois, 31
    occult identity, 213, 251
    as researcher, 21
    of the salon, 296, 297
    social identity, 172, 180, 207
    spiritual identity, 42, 50, 124, 157
    "traditional chiefs", 52
    as a youth, 205, 207
illness, 28, 53, 153, 179, 185, 186, 190, 191, 226
imaginaire, 46
imitation, 105, 131, 136
    danger of, 142–3, 294
    Taussig on, 137
    versus becoming the imitated, 138–9, 141
improvisation, 58, 102, 105–7, 181
incest, 23, 53, 105, 177, 180, 181, 184, 232, 241–7, 255, 256n8, 259
Indian
    concept of magic, 156
    Indian films, 123
    Indians in Kinshasa, 32, 198
    inspiration for *Mami Wata*, 212
infertility, 150, 245, 246, 268
initiation
    in occult worlds, 50
    rejecting traditional initiation cults, 220
    and secrets, 113, 114
instruction. *See also* teaching
    to act, 74, 133
    from informants, 171
    from the lineage, 237
    by pastors, 35, 169, 239
    sermons as, 123
    on sexuality, 268, 276
    through the TV serials, 102, 164, 269
Internet, 147, 205, 234, 268
intra-politics
    of a drama group, 13
    of a music band, 65
Islam, 32, 122

Jewsiewicki, Bogumil, 22n26, 56, 146, 296
Jules-Rosette, Benetta, 11, 123, 146

Kabila, Joseph, 5, 8, 25nn6–8–13
Kabila, Laurent, 5, 25nn6–8
Kafuta, Sony, 34, 35, 36, 101
Kalaonga, 119–20, 128n10, 211–3
kamoke sukali sukali, 271
Kapferer, Bruce, 196n11
Kasai, 48, 120, 123, 185, 248, 252, 257n18
key scenario, 9–11, 52–5, 201, 228
Kimbanguism, 6, 33, 34, 37–9, 215, 231n29
Kindoki. See witchcraft
kindumba, 135, 232, 258–9. *See also* sexuality
Kinoiserie, la, 29–32, 44, 143–4, 206, 233, 240, 259, 262
Kirsch, Thomas, 7, 107, 157, 161
Kitshuili, 243, 246, 256n9
kizengi, 3, 187, 196n8, 289n8. *See also* fool
knowledge. *See also* secret knowledge
    esoteric knowledge, 205
    experts of the occult, 49–52
    spiritual knowledge, 22, 43, 101, 114, 115, 124, 126, 152, 154, 161, 189, 293
    through modern means, 205
kochina, 270, 271–5
Kongo, 33, 49, 59, 61n13, 70, 79, 108, 121, 144, 157, 166n7, 177, 184, 196n2, 202, 203, 237, 253, 256n11, 259, 271
Krings, Matthias, 26n14, 128n10
Kutino, Ferdinand, 9, 25n13

Larkin, Brian, 55, 160, 233
Lauretis, Teresa de, 258, 278, 288
Lebanese, 32, 198
Léopoldville, 25n2, 199, 259
libanga, 92, 94. *See also mabanga*
life. *See also* death
    the extraction of, 45–52
living room, 24, 67, 104, 144, 167, 243, 264
    in crisis, 295–7

sacralization of the living room, 28, 148, 149, 152, 163, 294
    watching television, 9, 154
Living in Bondage, 128n10
love magic, 123
Luba, 8, 49, 52, 62, 69, 70, 113, 179, 180, 185, 201, 218, 234, 257n18, 283, 284
    culture and *tshibao*, 248–5
    stereotyping Luba culture, 237, 243
Lubumbashi, 8, 99n16, 177, 178, 208, 247n8

Mabanga, 92–4
MacGaffey, Wyatt, 49, 52, 59, 61nn13–18, 115, 116, 121, 157, 184, 196n9, 202
magic. *See* witchcraft
making a name, 63. *See also* fame, celebrity
Maman Pasteur, 79–100, 267, 282
Mami Wata, 192, 211–3. *See also* siren, bad girl
maquis, 85, 131–6, 270–1
Maquis Boys and Girls, The, 23, 59, 83, 84, 270–1, 272, 274
Marcus, George, 11, 12
mario, 266
Marks, Laura, 146, 155–7, 167n21
Mami Wata, 192, 211–3
marriage
    changes in courtship, 239–241
    customary marriage, 87, 272
    ethnic marriage preferences, 53, 243, 246, 256n11
    fiançailles, 239, 241
    godparents of the marriage, 241
    marriage politics, 237, 255, 256n15
Marriott, McKim, 176
Marshall-Fratani, Ruth, 6, 169
Marshall, Ruth. *See* Marshall–Fratani
mass mediation, 197
Matadi, 31, 255
Matonge, 29, 30, 60n4
Maxwell, David, 6, 25n11, 231n27
Mayimona, 145, 211–4, 234–7, 264
Mbembe, Achille, 120, 123, 203, 210
Mbuji-Mayi, 178, 250, 252, 277

mbwoolu, 190–1
media. *See* celebrity, religious media,
    mediation, photography, radio,
    television
mediation of the Real, 158
mediational complexity, 15
medium
    human medium, 15, 107, 158
    prayer as, 128
    television as, 124, 294
melodrama. *See also* Pentecostal
    melodrama
    emotions in, 164
    mediating between invisible
        worlds, 126–7
    the modern subject in, 195
    rituals and, 192, 194–5
    sexuality in, 258
    symbolic structure, 10, 54, 160
memory, 9, 58, 219, 281
men. *See also* patriarchy
    "Big Men", 92–6, 99n19, 272,
        274
    of God, 76, 81, 108, 111, 144,
        238, 242
Meyer, Birgit
    on aesthetic formations, 14–5,
        295
    break with the past, 220
    on exposing and revealing, 115,
        121
    on *Mami Wata*, 212, 230n19
    on melodrama, 127
    on religion, 6, 60n11, 121, 125,
        165n1, 196n13
    on religious media, 7, 25n12, 57,
        142, 126, 128n1
    on spiritual powers of media,
        146, 164
migration, 8, 29
mimesis, 23, 29, 57–8, 121, 139
    embodiment and, 138
    Taussig on, 137–8
mimetic faculty, 121
miracle, 128n6, 150, 163, 242
    pastor's charisma and, 7, 36, 51,
        53, 60n6, 108, 110–1
    pictures as proof of, 126

special effects as/and, 101, 119,
    124
Missamu, Marie, 235, 256n2
Mobutism, 121
Mobutu, Joseph Sese Seko, 2, 5, 7, 8,
    12, 25nn6–10, 34, 51, 121, 127, 133,
    203, 215, 216, 224
modernity, 230n18
    Afromodernity, 28, 212
    Benjamin on, 159
    the city and, 198, 214, 234
    Pentecostal, 195
    youth and, 205
    of witchcraft, 50
moments of freedom, 208–9
morality, 114
    agency and, 174–7
    conscience and, 188
    gender and, 14, 267, 277–8
    loss of, 32
    in media worlds, 87–90, 127,
        283–6
    pastors', 37
    restoring, 228
    serials as lessons in, 161, 208
moral movement, 171–2
Morris, Rosalind, 122, 124, 158
mother
    accused of witchcraft, 182, 187,
        213–4, 264
    end of role model, 82, 206,
        229n11
    the pastor's spouse as
        supermaman, 282–3
    stepmother, 62, 213
moziki, 279–82
Moziki Women, The, 193, 253–4, 266,
    277–81
Munn, Nancy, 63, 92, 219, 231n30
music. *See also mabanga*
    in the church, 111, 134, 162, 194
    demonic possession and, 143–4
    demonization, 76, 152, 262
    the expression of opinions via,
        208, 227
    informal economy and, 229n7
    Mobutu and, 7, 121
    religious music, 55
    rumors, 105, 248

seduction via, 233–4, 263, 275
transfer of spiritual powers to
    listeners/viewers, 152, 161,
    163
in the TV serials, 146, 161, 187,
    209
urban music, 29, 31, 32, 60n2,
    166n7
Muyombe Gauche, 3, 18, 70, 85–6, 105,
    139, 154–5, 223, 231n31, 289n16
mwasi mabe. See bad girl

nakedness, 32, 246, 251, 265
Nanas Benz, The, 20, 21, 132, 144–5,
    177–8, 266, 279, 280–1
narrative. *See also* emplotment, fiction,
    Pentecostal Melodrama
    broadcasting of, 151
    Bible as main, 56
    commercials interrupting, 70–2
    conjunctive and disjunctive,
        177–9
    dialogue between genres, 55–7,
        63
    dream narrative, 66
    emergent narrative, 59
    healing through the
        construction of, 190–2, 194,
        197–8, 200, 215–9
    life, 65, 77–8, 163. *See also*
        biography
    pastor appearing in, 80
    personal, 9, 188, 191
    as proof of charisma, 119, 292
    reality and, 102, 128n2, 198
    televised narratives, 33
    time and, 219
    viewers co–constructing, 13, 17,
        218
    of witchcraft, 7
nation, 220–4, 228, 293
ndoki, see witch
ndumba, 259
network
    female network, 280
    media network, 7
    social network, 7, 18, 22, 64, 65,
        68, 85, 91–5, 171, 184, 212,
        276

sexual network, 229n7, 274
    through the church, 35
    transnational network, 7
new person, 77–8
nganga. See traditional healer
ngatyul, 243–5
nguya, 46–7
Nigeria, 8, 9, 66, 111, 112, 127, 131,
    144, 213, 263, 279, 281. *See also*
    Nigerian film
Nigerian film, 9, 19, 55, 128n1, 160,
    219–20
Ninja film, 152
Nkanu, 116, 172, 196n2, 246,
    256nn13–15, 257n17
Nkisi. See fetish object
Nollywood. *See* Nigerian film
Nooter, Mary, 103, 113, 120
Nyamnjoh, Francis, 289n9
Nzita, José, 143
nzonzing, 85

occultism, 41. *See also* witchcraft
onction, 107, 265
Open Tomb, The, 130, 179, 189, 191,
    193, 218, 249–54, 277
optical visuality, 155
order and disorder, 40
orphan, 215, 217, 284
Ortner, Sherry, 10, 233

pagan
    as an animal, 264. *See also* animal
    audience as, 269
    before being reborn, 270, 275
    the Christian's Other, 45, 86
    cult, 184
    as demonic, 152, 209, 262, 280
    environment, 176–7
    lapse into a pagan life, 97
    marrying a, 240
paganism, 209
pastor, 51, 108, 116, 293. *See also*
    authority, charisma, miracle,
    knowledge
patriarchy, 20, 70, 212, 234, 252, 263,
    264, 277, 281, 288
patronage
    and clientelism, 22, 68, 93–4, 114

in media, 5
Peek, Phillip M., 115, 116, 117, 118, 136
Pentecostal-charismatic Christianity, 4, 7, 115, 116, 121, 194, 221
    definition, 24n1, 36–8
    history of, 32–6
Pentecostal imagination, 12, 28, 44. *See also* apocalyptic imagination
    emergence of, 58–9
Pentecostal melodrama. *See also* melodrama
    definition, 10, 26n18
    gender in, 282, 287–8
    as a genre of revelation, 126–7, 298
    the invisible and, 119, 121, 195
    music in, 163
    the past in, 220
    the promise of a new world and, 294
    ritual and, 162, 168
performance
    citing Big Men during, 93
    in the church, 12
    creating a performance, 103
    effects on viewers, 157–8
    evangelizing, 115
    feeding the soul, 173
    folkloric, 18, 119
    guest performances for other troupes, 85
    Harding on, 148–9, 166n5
    media, ritual and, 194, 199n13
    mediating role of, 163–5
    of miracles, 124
    preparing for, 106
    as propaganda for Mobutu, 7–8
    public performance, 97
    religious performance, 41, 136
    transformative aspects of, 107
    transgression through, 130–1, 137–2, 209
    versus TV drama, 26n24
    as zone of expression, 209
personhood, 23, 189. *See also* youth, elders, self
    in American films, 154
    customary approaches, 204, 206

dividuals and individuals, 176
    gendered, 272–3
    Pentecostal, 46–7
    sexuality and, 262
photography, 122, 123, 128n10, 147, 148, 166n10
Plaen, Guy De, 243, 246
politics, 29. *See also* intra–politics, marriage politics
    culture and, 8
    demons and, 44
    entanglement of the individual and national politics, 196n12
    Pentecostal–charismatic Christianity and, 222
    speaking about, 25n7, 208, 296
    tradition and, 287
politics of the body, 23
polygamy, 201, 232, 235, 237, 248
popular culture
    Barber on, 17
    Christian popular culture, 28, 43, 50, 101, 107, 158
    emotions in, 164
    fiction in, 128n2
    genres in Kinshasa, 55, 57
    as masks of the voice of youth, 207
    as mediation, 131
    morality and, 87, 283
    polémique, 57, 89n11
    as research object, 16, 19
    sexuality and, 248, 271, 288
    time and, 197–231
    versus high culture, 19
    and witchcraft, 51
pornography, 42, 152, 155, 259, 293
possession
    by the Holy Spirit, 174
    how it works, 135
    possibility of possession for artists, 135, 136–145
    possibility of possession for viewers, 145–161
    protecting viewers from, 160–3
    spirit possession cults, 190–2
    visualizing, 181
    and witchcraft, 15, 48, 166n4, 174

prayer
>to be inspired, 105–7, 132–5
>moral movement and, 168, 172
>performance of, 172
>to restore the nation, 220–5
>structure of, 172–4
>on television, 148–51, 162
>in the TV serials, 28, 76, 144–5, 162, 223
priest, 23, 49, 52, 81, 121, 126, 184
prison, 180–3
Probst, Peter, 208
prophet, 6, 39, 41, 42, 51, 57, 61n18, 66, 87, 116, 177, 188, 231n29, 291, 296
>false, 76, 112, 236
>Korean, 79
>Nigerian, 111, 281
>on television, 112
Protestantism, 6, 33, 37, 38, 60n6, 97n7, 121, 127, 129n15, 136, 168, 186
proverb, 56, 204, 207, 277, 278
purity, 172, 193, 196n1, 248

radio-trottoir. *See* rumor
radio, 6, 7, 15, 25n2, 34, 35, 60n6, 66, 112, 201, 233, 268, 269, 288nn1–6, 289n7
real Christian
>becoming a, 176, 192
>have more knowledge, 112
>opposed to Christians of the flesh and false Christians, 77–8, 85–9
>in the social environment, 239
>study and, 272
>urban culture and, 32
>viewing practices of, 115, 154, 161
>within the drama group, 90, 132, 140, 276, 295
religious mediation, 14–6, 23, 101, 124, 127, 164
>through *nkisi*, 157
>through photographs, 123
>through rituals, 168, 193
>through television, 121, 127, 147, 149

remediation, 14–6
reputation, 21, 37, 53, 85, 89, 105, 110, 111, 113, 120, 132, 237, 238, 282, 285
réseau, 91
respect, 100
>gender and, 286
>for elders, 204, 206, 227
>lack of, 179, 180, 206, 247, 252, 265, 271
>*Maman Pasteur*, 82
>for parents, 241
>performance of, 264, 274
>social rules of, 68, 69, 96
>for spiritual leaders, 108
>transformations in social rules concerning, 212, 227
restoration
>individual and social, 185, 192
>spiritual, 183, 197
>technologies of, 180, 182, 195
revelation, 22, 23
>in arts, 102
>Book of Revelation, 38
>and divination, 116
>and secrets, 114
>in sermons, 113
>via technology, 124, 126
>versus exposure, 115
>Western approach, 122
Ricoeur, Paul, 219, 228n5
ritual. *See also* prayer, baptism, confession, deliverance and marriage
>Pentecostal rituals, 132, 162, 194
>ritual and melodrama, 169, 194–5
>rituals of reparation, 248–52
Robbins, Joel, 15, 170, 201
role distribution, 68, 70, 163, 130
RTG@, 3, 5, 18, 82, 84, 100, 101, 119, 185, 251
rumor, 20, 21, 42, 45, 82, 83, 89, 99n20, 104, 105, 111, 132, 135, 137, 248, 276, 284, 286

sacrifice
>for the Devil, 27, 43, 51, 75, 105, 192, 214

for God, 84
melodrama and, 194
purification through, 193
Sakata, 49, 60n12, 116
Sans Soucis, 3, 18, 70, 97n5, 247
Sapeur, 81
salon, 292, 295–7. *See also* living room
Salongo
    drama group, 7, 8, 97n5, 127
    as work, 5
science, 14, 125, 128n1, 146, 152
secrecy
    in arts, 103, 113–8, 120
    versus exposure, revelation, 23
    as tool of the Devil, 134
    and initiation rituals, 128n8
    of *mabanga,* 93
    Pentecostal approaches to, 22,
      126
    and sexual relationships, 275
    and traditional religion, 121
    trope of, 41
secret, 112–8, 120, 205
    social boundaries and, 114, 126
    special effects and, 119–21
secret knowledge, 48, 107, 113,
    129n13. *See also* spiritual knowledge
secret powers, 41
secret religions, 41
secret societies, 50–1
secular modernity, 195
self
    Christian self, 173, 194
    technologies of the self, 169,
      188, 195n1, 258
senses, 14, 42, 49, 153–8
    hearing, 163
    sight, 42, 111, 178, 186, 191, 242
    smell, 205
    touch, 105, 119, 148, 150–1, 154,
      161, 167n21, 214, 265, 296
sexual freedom, 270
sexuality
    in the city, 9, 30, 32, 90, 258–63,
      286–7
    commoditization of love, 271–5
    controlling women's, 249
    and dance, 209
    danger of, 265–7

homosexuality, 267, 270, 289n8
    in initiation rituals, 114
    lesbianism, 83, 267, 270, 274
    and the *Mami Wata,* 212
    Pentecostals and, 232–4, 254,
      267–70
    young girls, 230n17, 289n10. *See*
      also bad clothes
shadow, 46, 47, 61n19, 122, 123, 147,
    149
sin, 13, 76, 154, 169–72, 173, 179, 184,
    253, 254, 256n8, 275
siren, 20, 21, 48, 119, 135, 137,
    144, 146, 177–8, 211–2, 297. *See*
    also Mami Wata, bad girl, 211–3,
    229nn16–17, 230n17, 235, 244, 271
sleeping, 78, 135, 266, 267, 273
social environment
    of Big Men, 68
    of Christians, 175–6, 195
    purifying, 176, 188, 190, 192
    of TV actors, 18
    urban, 29, 189
sorcery. *See* witchcraft
soul healing, 188–9
soul. *See also* soul healing
    artistry and, 103
    versus body and spirit, 46, 58
    healing the soul. *See* healing
    locking the soul, 119, 146n10
    and witchcraft, 48, 136, 261
space, 96, 101, 159, 234
    of conflict, 287
    cursed space, 58
    dangerous space, 283
    demonic and divine, 32–3, 44,
      148, 157, 183, 226, 238, 263,
      293
    domestic space, 148, 152, 154,
      264, 280–2, 295–6
    filth, 40
    of libertinage, 270
    liminal space, 198
    ludic space, 207–8
    masculine and female, 9, 88,
      167n18
    occupied by prostitutes, 51
    outskirts of the city, 51
    popular culture and, 214

public space, 6, 11, 56, 72, 81, 88, 137, 153, 215, 226, 273
    rehearsal space, 1, 74, 106
    revelatory space, 127
    social, 23, 24, 259
    symbolic, 200
    urban, 30, 32, 33, 72, 198, 259, 292
    of visual mutuality, 156
spaces of freedom, 22
special effects, 59, 61n20, 119, 128n10
spectatorship
    embodied, 146, 159
    Western, 156
spirits. *See also* deliverance ritual, the Holy Spirit, possession, prayer, witchcraft
    exchange of spirits, 266
    demonic spirits, 39, 52, 104, 118, 155, 165, 242
    interfering when acting, 139–145
    transferred when watching television, 145–53
spiritual confusion, 15, 59, 123, 131, 165
spiritual kinship, 22, 96. *See also* spiritual father
spiritual others, 168, 176, 195
spiritual warfare, 157
spiritual world, 48, 50, 80, 161, 164, 165, 183, 278
Spitulnik, Debra, 167n22
stagehand, 140
star
    as celebrity, 62–4, 86, 109, 264
    as manifestation of the soul, 59
    a spiritual entity, 266, 288n4
state
    authority of, 196n7
    controlling, 7, 25n13, 265
    in crisis, 6, 198–9, 203, 224, 228nn2–3
    critique on, 5
    promoting culture and arts, 8
steal the word, 207
Strathern, Marilyn, 65, 176
Street children, 42, 202
Stroeken, Koen, 30, 64, 115, 117, 118

subjectivity
    Christian, 23
    of evil, 186
    melodrama and new forms of, 195
    viewers', 156
    western, 122, 159

talk show, 1, 64
    Christian, 7
    conflict via, 86
    explaining TV serials on, 69, 132, 216–7
    foreign, 184
    Kimbanguist, 39
    Pentecostal leaders on, 5, 73
    on the radio, 12
    and reputation of the TV actor, 105, 140, 144
    about sexuality, 269
Taussig, Michael, 113, 115, 121, 137–8
teaching
    through the Bible, 59, 171
    about the Christian way of life, 18, 29, 37, 52, 141, 169, 179
    within the drama group, 72
    about gender, 173
    about sexuality, 242, 267
    through television, 151–2
    of World Messianity, 33
technology, 3, 99n17, 163, 173, 210, 218
    and witchcraft, 121–4, 146–7, 158–60, 166nn8–16
teenage mother, 204, 261
television
    as fetish, 157
    in the living room, 8, 148–9, 152, 154, 294, 295–6
    the senses and, 153–158
testimony
    of God's acts, 56
    uttered by witches, 45, 162, 194, 220
Thomas, Lynn, 230n21, 233, 243, 271, 273, 287
time
    breach between personal past and present, 77–8

imaginaire as interaction
between past, present and
future, 46
Pentecostals and, 219–220
present tense, 25n10
promise and, 224–7
reconfiguration of quality of
time, 210
touch. *See* senses
tradition, 5, 97, 122, 160
in the city, 57, 240
customary politics, 287
ethnicity and, 180, 247, 248
of marriage, 242–3, 246
in the TV serials, 237, 256
witchcraft and, 47, 50, 147, 237
traditional healer
categories, 49–50
compared with Christian
leaders, 115–118
and elders, 209
as life–takers, 52
and magic, 147, 220
opposed to Christian leaders,
115
and photographs, 148
responsible for the crisis, 15
in the TV serials, 130, 185, 250
visit to, 75–6, 87
tragedy, 73, 215
TropicanaTV, 3, 18, 53, 104
truth. *See also* the false
in the Bible, 56
localizing the truth, 102
told by elders, 205
truthfulness in films, 101, 125
trucage. See special effects
tshibao, 248–54. *See also* adultery
Turner, Victor, 115–8

United States, 24n1, 82

Vasudevan, Ravi, 195
vedette, 64, 87–8, 98n15, 277–86
Victoire, Rond Point, 44
village
authorial voice from, 207
intrusion in the city, 54, 106,
174, 242

and the lineage, 223, 252
as a space of witchcraft, 162, 184,
210, 245, 248, 251
versus city, 30, 31, 53
women in, 251, 278, 289n13
Vokes, Richard, 122
Vries, Henk de, 6, 101, 124

Weber, Max, 36, 66, 108, 110
Weber, Samuel, 6, 101, 124
Wemba, Papa, 81, 143, 183, 206, 262,
263
Werbner, Pnina, 198, 208
Werner, Jean-François, 26n16
White, Bob W., 60n3, 65, 92, 93, 94,
98nn11–13, 105, 228n2
witch type, 211, 229n16. *See also kizengi*
and bad girl
witchcraft
anti-witchcraft rituals, 36, 193
art and, 103
conscious and unconscious,
188–9, 196n9
defining, 45–9, 61n15
dialectical relationship with
emotions, 164, 167n24, 189
dreams and, 267
elders and, 47, 229n10
experts of, 49–52
and the fool, 196n8
and gender, 230n17
in Ghanaian films, 115
life and, 46
Luba concept of, 249
magic and, 49–50
mediational complexity and,
15, 17
money, sex, and, 261
and the nation, 222
versus the occult, 40, 41
origins of, 48
possession and, 136, 139,
166nn4–13
serials as witchcraft accusations,
211–4
as social critique, 209
versus sorcery, 40
special effects as manifestation
of, 119–21

technology and, 147
a tool of the Devil, 27
transformations in, 41, 49, 115, 118
in the TV serials, 3, 7, 22, 23, 179, 187, 242
in the village, 162
Witte, Marleen De, 6, 7, 146, 166n11
wives of the night, 266, 267, 288n5. *See also* husband of the night
women
accused of witchcraft, 230n24
age to marry, 204
associations of, 277–83
attracted by the appeal of youth, 206–7, 229n12
as believers, 151, 173
Big Women, 92–4
brides of Jesus, 82
as chaotic, 40
display of their fecundity, 263
the economic crisis and, 28, 205, 206, 212, 227, 230n24
evil and, 270
evil spirits and, 196n5, 202, 212–4, 259, 264, 268
female viewers, 150, 167n18, 287–8
gender crossing, 289–90n16
women of God, 51, 222
leading roles in the church, 81, 149
lesbian women, 267
of loose morals, 135
Luba, 248–9, 252, 257n18
as *Mami Wata*, 212–4
modern women, 289n13
as mistresses, 262, 272
older women, 266
within a patriarchal society, 70, 148, 207, 208
public women, 88, 259, 283–6
respectable clothing, 265
sexuality of, 99n15, 229n10, 234, 249, 262, 276, 289n9
strong, 23
unmarried women, 275
within urban culture, 31, 32, 144, 174, 259

women's group in church, 231n34, 267–8
in wrestling shows, 153, 167n18
young, 271–2
zebola – a women's cult, 190–2
word, power of the, 83, 92, 136, 151, 163, 190, 192
wrestling, 152, 154, 167nn18–19, 293

Yaka, 49, 60n12, 96, 116, 118, 129n12, 190, 257n17, 267
Yanzi, 209, 229n14, 242–6, 256nn10–11
youth
versus adulthood, 232
the Bible and, 200–1
camps, 270
chaos and, 40
against the elders, 202, 203, 209, 214
the emergence of, 207
female, 64, 238, 273
the future and, 210, 227
marriage and the end of youth, 232, 239
Pentecostal–charismatic Christianity and, 24, 77, 286
play/fun spaces and, 97n3, 208
sexuality and, 268–9
versus the state, 205, 224, 228
idiom of, 204
Luba, 251
male, 283–4
search for meaning, 297
mobility of, 199
transformations in approaches to, 205, 206, 278
youth group, 17

Zaire, 7, 228n2, 289n13. *See also* Mobutu
zebola, 19–1
Zempléni, Andreas, 114
zombie, 47